Believing

Exploring the Catholic Faith

Michele McCarty

BROWN-ROA

A Division of Harcourt Brace & Company

Dubuque, Iowa

Nihil Obstat
Very Reverend Jerome A. Carosella, Chancellor

Imprimatur
✠ John J. Nevins, D.D.
Bishop of Venice in Florida
August 17, 1994

Book Team
President—Matthew J. Thibeau
Executive Editor—Janie Gustafson
Developmental and Production Editor—Marilyn Bowers Gorun
Production Manager—Marilyn Rothenberger
Marketing Manager—Ginny Schumacher
Art Director—Cathy A. Frantz
Designer—Sue Maloney

Theological Consultant—Rev. Charles Angell S.A.
Fr. Charles Angell S.A. is director of interreligious affairs for the Diocese of Venice in Florida, and is the parochial vicar of St. Michael the Archangel Parish, Siesta Key, Sarasota, Florida. He is a Franciscan Friar of the Atonement (Graymoor, Garrison NY) and is a former professor of ecumenical theology at the Pontifical University of St. Thomas Aquinas, Rome. Born in 1929 in Brooklyn NY, he entered the Catholic Church in 1949, joined the Atonement Friars in 1952, and was ordained a priest in 1960. He attended Davis and Elkins College, Elkins WV (B.A. 1951), Catholic University of America and his community's affiliated seminaries (M.A. Sociology 1960) and the Pontifical University of St. Thomas Aquinas in Rome (Doctorate of Sacred Theology 1983). His previous assignments have included seminary teaching, editing his community's ecumenical publications, and ecumenical work. From 1978 to 1988, he represented his community in Rome as Procurator General to the Holy See, Rector of the Church of Sant' Onofrio al Gianicolo and Director of the Centro Pro Unione. His articles on ecumenical topics have appeared in the United States, Italy, England, and Israel.

Photo Credits are on page 259.

Print Credits
New Revised Standard Version Bible, Catholic Edition, copyright © 1993 and 1989, by the Division of Christian Education of the National Council of the Churches of Christ in the United States of America Used by permission.

Excerpt from *The Little Prince* by Antoine de Saint-Exupery, copyright 1943 and renewed 1971 by Harcourt Brace & Company, reprinted by permission of the publisher.

"A Meditation on the Lord's Prayer." Reprinted with the permission of Scribner, an imprint of Simon & Schuster from *Joy in Believing* by Henry Sloane Coffin, edited by Walter Russell Bowie. Copyright 1956 Dorothy Prentice Coffin; copyright renewed © 1984 Joan Bowie Evans, W. Russell Bowie.

ISBN: 0-697-17893-5
10 9

Contents

Dedication

To my husband, Phil—and all those who have believed in me . . .

Part One

"I Believe"—
The Meaning
of Faith

Our hearts are restless until they rest in God.

Chapter 1

The anchor is a sign of trust in God.

Believing in God

Now faith is the assurance of things hoped for, the conviction of things not seen.

Hebrews 11:1

God of all,
You give us spectacular skies and sunsets.
But we're still sometimes tempted to doubt that You exist.

You help us make telescopes that focus on distant galaxies.
But we say we can't find You.

You give us one another.
But we look elsewhere for You.

You give us a wonderful world.
But still we're not satisfied.

Guide us as we seek to discover and to love You.
Help us realize that only in You can our hearts be truly full.

Overview questions

1. Does everybody wonder about whether God exists?

2. Why does nothing in life ever seem to completely satisfy people?

4. Why is it sometimes hard for people to believe in God?

5. How can we know God exists?

6. What is the role of reasoning and questioning in faith?

7. Are there solid logical reasons to believe in God's existence?

8. Are there other good reasons for believing that there is a God?

The human longing for God

Is there really a God? What is God really like? Does God really care? If God loves us, why is there so much suffering in the world? What will happen to me when I die? Is there a heaven or a hell?

In college dorms, students from various religious backgrounds, and those from no religious background, often grapple with these questions late into the night. You and your friends no doubt wonder about these things too. This book is intended to help you as you search further for the answers.

You already know, though, that there is a desire in your heart to know complete love, happiness, and perfection. When rich and famous individuals who seemed to "have it all" take their own lives, people scratch their heads and ask: Why? But this earthly life as we know it is not our permanent home. Even the most deep and genuine loves in our life are but a glimpse of something—Someone—far more.

Our hearts are restless until they rest in Thee.

St. Augustine

Everyone sometimes feels lost in life. Such feelings are especially common among teenagers and young adults. You probably deal successfully with the inner pain this sometimes causes you by relying on the guidance and reassurance of wise and caring friends, relatives, or counselors. Hopefully you realize that turning to alcohol and other drugs instead soon dead-ends in despair. Embracing casual sexual relationships in the vain hope of discovering there the love that seems missing is ultimately disillusioning. Often enough today, it is also deadly. It is possible to find joy in life in a million other life-enriching ways.

There is an inner **void** in you, in all of us, that can never be completely filled by anything our earthly existence has to offer. There is in all of our hearts a desire to become closer to God. This spiritual dimension is the deepest, most important part of yourself. And it is this gradual discovery of God throughout your life—especially through the love which you give to and receive from others—which will multiply your joy. It is what will sustain you through the darkest times and the most painful and troubling hours.

Faith in God, though, like coming to believe in anyone, is a process—a journey of discovery. But it should be an intelligent journey! It should begin with honest, probing questions. And it is often accompanied by doubts. As St. Anselm once said, **even faith seeks to understand**. But the sincere search to discover the truth about and to truly know God leads to ever-deepening confidence, trust, and love. In the meantime, we can all take comfort in knowing that **whoever seeks God has already found God.**

No book can answer all your questions about God and religion. And you shouldn't just blindly accept what some-

one else says or believes. Your personal responses to life's religious questions must ultimately come from your own innermost convictions. This book, however, asks that you seriously think about the core beliefs of Catholic Christianity. It will also explore ideas which have helped others in making their personal faith decisions and commitments. Hopefully, they'll help you too as you search for the truth. ❧

Problems of belief

Why can it sometimes be hard to believe in God? Actually, today many people have trouble believing in much of anything or anyone at all! Institutions which used to represent security and meaning seem to have let them down. The high divorce rate and their own experience with divorce in their families often make teenagers skeptical about whether they will be able to create a lasting marriage in their future. Corrupt politicians and crooked merchants make people further skeptical about things in general. On top of that, technology is changing everything so fast that little in our society seems permanent.

TV commercials urge you to trust in material things. When you do, you discover that these things don't last—in fact, that they were planned to **not** last! Lightbulbs are scheduled to burn out. The thread in your clothes is meant to fray. Pantyhose are purposely designed to run. And cars are made to break down after a period of time. So if you attempt to put your belief in material, and therefore temporary, realities, you build your house on sand.

"And everyone who hears these words of mine and does not act on them will be like a foolish man who built his house on sand. The rain fell, and the floods came, and the winds blew and beat against that house, and it fell—and great was its fall!"

Matthew 7:26–27

Furthermore, even small children are given the impression today that it's such a brutal world that the only way to sur-

void

hole, space, opening

❧ Questions for discussion

1. When you and your friends have serious discussions about God and religion, what kinds of questions and topics come up?

2. What persons do you know of whose unhappiness led to their untimely death, even though they seemed to have "had it all"? Why do you think this happened?

3. Do you ever experience a kind of restlessness that nothing in your life seems able to satisfy? Explain.

4. Why do you think some teenagers who experience profound loneliness or other serious problems seek solutions in drugs or casual sex, while others don't? Where do you turn when your problems seem overwhelming?

5. What kind of void exists in everyone? Why can only God fill this void?

6. Why is your spiritual dimension the deepest, most important part of yourself? With whom do you share this part of yourself? Explain.

7. In what way is faith in God a process and a journey of discovery? What part can questions and doubts play in this process?

8. Why must your personal responses to life's religious questions ultimately come from your own innermost convictions?

vive is by letting others have it before they beat you up first. It has become harder and harder to trust people. Someone's word is no longer considered a sacred contract. Now it requires a mandatory credit check! But if people believe less in others today, they also find it even harder to believe in themselves.

Staggering numbers of individuals depend upon liquor, marijuana, or tranquilizers rather than on their own inner resources. Advertisers also appeal to this widespread lack of self-confidence. Ads promise that this or that product will make you feel better about yourself. You won't have to fear being thought less of by others if you buy this car or that deodorant or toothpaste. Or so you are told. And many people buy it. Interestingly enough, however, advertisers today find that one group in society is especially difficult for them to appeal to successfully: Marketing research finds that teenage boys tend as a group to be extremely skeptical!

Do you need proof of God? . . . Does one light a torch to see the sun?
—Oriental wisdom

It's no wonder, then, that people find it difficult to believe in God. It seems hard enough as it is to believe in the world, in life, in others, or in themselves. In self-defense, some just avoid all risk of belief. They try to live from day to day without heightened hopes or expectations, because they're afraid to be disappointed or frustrated. So they set aside belief in God, too.

On the other hand, some who feel rootless and disillusioned are willing to try anything in order to recapture their sense of belief in something. Trying to rediscover meaning and purpose in their lives, they end up believing in almost anything. Ads offer products or services that will replace lost beliefs, hopes, and even relationships. They promise assurance, guarantees, and "something you can trust in." Falling easy prey to such come-ons, people subconsciously buy belief in something, along with the products and services they purchase. These ads are used so widely because they work so well.

Other belief-seekers fall victim to the subtle and the not-so-subtle brainwashing techniques of harmful religious cults. They have little faith in themselves or anything else. They will do almost anything to belong—to be believed in and to believe. These are the people for whom religion or psychology, or health and physical fitness, or racial or religious intolerance becomes almost an obsession. Or, if their family life fails them, they join a local gang in order to belong. If the present social and legal "system" fails them, they turn to the illegal system of drug selling and other crimes.

The object of their belief does not enhance their life. It controls and represses it. Often this obsession leads them to become intolerant of all else. For some, life itself becomes a perpetual frantic and unfulfilling search. Wanting desperately to believe, they nevertheless find each cause or cult an empty disappointment, and they become even more dissatisfied and disillusioned than they were before. Seeing how fanatical and uncharitable these people become in their search for belief turns others off altogether to the idea. Instead, they come to view religion as just another passing, empty promise.

In order to believe in God, then, there are two temptations you may find that you, too, must honestly face and overcome in yourself:

1. Your lack of ability to believe in general

2. The tendency to compensate for this by abandoning yourself to one form of extremism or another ❧

Would you believe. . . ?

This activity will help you determine and compare with your classmates the things which tax your own credibility in today's world. Complete it as follows:

1. Read through the list of items given below.

2. In the blank spaces at the bottom, add three items not covered in the list which you also have trouble believing in.

3. Then rank all the items according to how believable they are to you. Do this by numbering them from 1 to 26 (1 being the hardest to believe in, and so on).

4. Be prepared to explain why you find it somewhat or very hard to believe in each item.

____ The current president of this country

____ Other drivers' judgment on the road

____ The safety of airplane travel

____ The world's future

____ That you'll be able to afford the kind of home you want in the future

____ Your parent(s) and/or stepparents or guardians

____ Politicians

____ Your teachers

____ Your classmates in general

____ Persons of the same gender

____ The news media

____ Those who sell illegal drugs

____ Persons of the other gender

____ Your future happiness

____ Used car salespersons

____ God

____ Law enforcement officers

____ Major corporations in this country

____ TV commercials

____ Your friends

____ This country's future

____ Church leaders

____ Yourself

____ _____

____ _____

____ _____

Questions for discussion

1. What material **things** do you find hardest to put your "belief" in? Why?

2. What people do you find hardest to believe? Why?

3. Do you feel more pressured today to believe, or to not believe, in things? In people? In God? Explain.

4. What most undermines your belief in people in general? In people you know?

5. To believe more in God, why must one also believe more in the positive possibilities of the world, people, and oneself? How can you do this in your own life?

By faith we understand that the worlds were prepared by the word of God, so that what is seen was made from things that are not visible. —Hebrews 11:3

1. Why can't God's existence be scientifically proved or disproved once and for all?

2. In what sense should faith be solid rather than blind or stupid? Why?

3. Why is it important to respect the fact that belief in God is an individual decision? How do people sometimes fail to do this?

4. Why is it foolish to not consider the reasons for God's existence which have convinced millions of people throughout history?

5. What do you think of the idea that God is just a mental device which people use to explain otherwise unexplainable things and to "satisfy their intellectual curiosity"?

6. Respond to the astronaut's comment that he hadn't seen God out in space. Explain.

7. Why is science not capable of proving God's existence conclusively?

How do we know God exists?

Can anyone prove God exists? In short, no one will ever be able to scientifically prove either that God exists or that God does not exist. That is precisely why we speak of religious **beliefs.** No human theory could be comprehensive enough in scope to prove or disprove God's existence scientifically. For our human knowledge is limited, and God, by definition, is Mystery far beyond our imaginings.

Reason and belief

Some people say God is just a mental device people use to satisfy intellectual curiosity or to account for the otherwise unexplainable. Others presume science can explain everything and see God as of little use. One of the early Soviet astronauts allegedly commented, on returning from outer space, that he had seen no God there. But should that surprise us any more than a brain surgeon's being unable to locate the human spirit in cerebral microsurgery?

Yet even though, as Catholic teaching acknowledges, there is no way to scientifically prove the belief that God exists, the Church does urge us to have good reasons for what we do believe about God. Solid faith shouldn't be blind or stupid! It must be based on sound reasons as well as on trust.

You also need to understand and respect the fact that someone else's reasons for believing that God exists might well be different from yours. And your reasons might not completely convince someone else. Likewise it's far better to be honest about which ideas do or don't make sense to you than to try to jam into the puzzle those pieces that, for you, just don't seem to fit right now. For faith is an individual matter of conviction and decision. And, as we will see further later on, faith is also a gift. ❧

Whodunit: The think tank murder

Read the following mystery story, paying close attention to the details.

When detectives . . . learned Lewis Sheffield had been murdered, they knew they had a top-priority case to solve. Sheffield was director of the Burling Institute, a think tank engaged in a secret project for the Pentagon.

The murder was reported to the police by Marilyn Atwood, Sheffield's beautiful fiancée, who discovered the body when she went to his town house. . . . The police arrived promptly, at 6:45 p.m. It was Wednesday, June 21.

Sheffield's body was in the study. He died from a stab wound in the chest with a steak knife, one of a set from the kitchen. Cash and credit cards were found in his pockets. The police took fingerprints and blood samples for DNA analysis; they also found a half-eaten open-faced turkey sandwich near the body, perhaps Sheffield's last meal.

A canvass of neighbors and a check into the victim's background turned up several possible suspects. These included Marilyn Atwood; Peter Langley, who had been engaged to Marilyn before she met Sheffield; Martin Elliot, who had been fired from the institute by Sheffield; and George Amos, whom Sheffield succeeded as director of the institute.

In addition, the police tracked down two men who were seen visiting the house on June 21. One was Frank Tanner, a television [repairperson], and the other was Jimmy Selwyn, a [delivery person] from a nearby dry-cleaning shop. Subsequently

Tanner produced company records that showed he had visited the house on June 20, not June 21. But because his prints were found, he was questioned. One witness reported a third visitor, but the description was vague and the person couldn't be located. There were no fingerprints on the murder weapon. Other prints recovered from the study matched those of five of the six possible suspects; no prints were found of Peter Langley.

The other five could [satisfactorily] account for their fingerprints. . . . While the investigation was in progress, a couple of curious twists occurred. Peter Langley disappeared, and at the same time the police discovered the body of the television repairman's estranged wife, Agnes Tanner. She had been found with a broken neck at the wheel of her car, which had plunged into the [river] on the night of June 23. Friends described the woman as being despondent after she was fired from her job as a typist; with no job, she had said, she would be unable to end her marriage. Later that week Langley reappeared, explaining he had left town because he was afraid he would be charged with Sheffield's murder. The police thought they had a lead when they found Sheffield had phoned an employment agency the day before the murder, seeking a private secretary. But later they learned the agency hadn't yet sent anyone to be interviewed.

Another curious twist occurred when the results of the DNA testing came back. Although some of the blood found at the scene matched the victim's, there was other blood recovered that was not Sheffield's. The police speculated that that blood had come from the attacker. At this point the blood of all six suspects was tested and compared with the unidentified sample. None matched the blood recovered from Sheffield's study. There the police investigation came to a dead end, the murder unsolved.

Because Sheffield had been engaged in secret work for the government, the Pentagon desperately wanted his murder solved. . . . The man given the assignment was Christian Alden, who, although unknown to the general public, often served behind the scenes in solving baffling mysteries. . . . In the course of his investigation, Alden uncovered only one more piece of evidence, obtained through a simple test. But that was all he needed to establish the identity and motive of the killer. [1]

Questions for discussion

1. Before Alden entered the case, what were the known facts about Sheffield's murder? What remained a mystery?

2. What further piece of evidence did Alden uncover?

3. Who was Sheffield's murderer? What was the motive?

4. What thought processes did you use in trying to deduce the killer's identity? What processes did Alden use in proceeding from the unknown to the known?

5. In what ways are the thought processes involved in solving this case similar to those of someone searching for what to believe about God's existence?

6. Is it still possible that Alden might be wrong about who Sheffield's real killer was?

7. Even in life-death cases, juries are held to the standard of establishing a conclusion beyond any "reasonable doubt." Do you think the same standard is a sensible one for a person seeking to discover the truth about whether God exists? Explain.

8. Why was too much at stake to simply dismiss the murder case or to arrive at a wrong solution? Why is too much similarly at stake regarding the matter of what to believe about God's existence?

Logical reasons to believe in God

In this section we will discuss some of the ideas which have led prominent philosophers and scientists alike to conclude that there is reason enough to believe God does exist. Remember that they're not intended to conclusively prove God's existence. So don't expect them to do so.

These five logic-based reasons for God's existence are based primarily on the thinking of the Greek philosopher Aristotle, and of the medieval Catholic theologian, Thomas Aquinas. Founded on logic alone, these reasons are still relevant and convincing today—even to some of the world's most respected scientific minds. Consider them.

lifeless**inanimate**

lifeless, not able to move by its own power

inert

still, motionless

❧ Questions for discussion

1. Which of the following explanations for motion in the world seems more logical and believable to you and why?
   - There has been an unending series of movers.
   - The first thing ever in motion was its own spontaneous source of motion.
   - There is a First Mover which is itself either unmoved or the eternal source of its own motion?
2. Can you think of another alternative to explain the original source of motion in the world? Explain.
3. Does this "reason from the need for a First Mover" make sense to you as a reason for believing that a God exists? Explain.

What started motion?

When you look around you and study the universe, you find that everywhere things are in motion. The stars and galaxies move. Even in the subatomic particles within each molecule of matter, there is motion. Yet, as you know from experience, it takes motion to cause motion. When an **inanimate** object is initially **inert,** it takes other energy or force in motion to put it into motion. When you see a ball flying past you in the air, you naturally wonder who has thrown it—what force started it in motion. When you see a watch working, you know that someone remembered to wind it or put in a battery. Indeed, motion almost **is** the physical universe!

> *The presence of a superior reasoning power . . . revealed in the incomprehensible universe forms my idea of God.*
> *—Albert Einstein*

In looking at all this motion, it's only natural to ask: How did it get that way? What is its source? What started all this motion? Inanimate things begin to move only by first of all being moved by something else. So what or who caused the very first moving thing to begin its motion? Only three logical alternatives can answer this question:

1. There is an infinite series of movers (one thing moved another thing, which moved another, and so on).
2. The first thing in motion supplied its own source of motion.
3. There was a first mover which is the source of all motion. It is itself either unmoved or the eternal source of its own motion.

Trying to imagine and understand any of these three alternatives is, at the very least, difficult! Many find it least difficult and more sensible to believe in the third possibility—that there initially must have been some first or "prime" mover which started the rest of the motion in the universe. This First Mover the Christian equates with God. But this reasoning also raises an additional question? Could the first mover have been a sort of "watchmaker" who once put the world in motion but has since just left it to run basically on its own, according to the manner in which it was made to function? ❧

Where does the universe come from?

The next logical reason for belief in God's existence has to do with the relationships between causes and their effects. If there is an effect, a result, then it seems only logical that there must be a cause of that effect or result. Your own existence and that of the world about you seem obvious results or effects of something. And, since every effect must have a cause of some kind, this no doubt leads you (and all the world's astronomers!) to ask, What caused the universe? What caused the first object or mass of energy to ever exist? Again, there are three logical alternatives:

1. There is a never-ending chain of causes (one thing causing another, which causes another, and so on).
2. The first thing to come into existence, whether matter or energy, caused itself to be.
3. There was ultimately a first cause which must therefore itself be uncaused (and, thus, eternal).

Once again, all three possibilities are impossible for us to comprehend fully. But many persons (including some of the world's most prominent scientists) find that the least difficult and most sensible of the choices is the third—that there must have been a first cause of some kind which itself caused something else to exist. Skeptical as he was in general about religious matters, even the evolution theory's author Charles Darwin concluded:

> *Another source of conviction in the existence of God, connected with the reason, and not with the feelings, impresses me as having much more weight . . . . I feel compelled to look for a First Cause . . . and I deserve to be called a Theist.*

Logically, not being part of an unending series of causes, this initial cause must itself be without a cause and, thus, eternal. This first cause the religious believer therefore recognizes as **God.**

The idea of **eternal**, of something which is unending, is also impossible to comprehend completely. Although it is challenging to believe in, the alternative is equally impossible to understand fully. For example, try to imagine space continuing on forever, never ending. . . . What do you picture? Very possibly, you envision running into a sort of "wall" or end of some kind. Now try to imagine space ending—coming into a place beyond which there is absolutely nothing, not matter or energy or even more space. . . . Isn't that, too, impossible to imagine? What people usually picture here is space continuing beyond the end of space!

So it is with the idea of an eternal reality. Yes, it is difficult to believe in a God who always was. But, as you can see, it is perhaps equally difficult to believe in a time when nothing was, not even space. The religious believer simply finds it more reasonable to suppose that there is a reality which always was, and names this First Cause **God.**

If we're good, what's perfect?

The fourth logical reason for belief in God is this: There are various degrees of things in this world, ranging from the minimum to the maximum. This is especially true of ideals or "per-

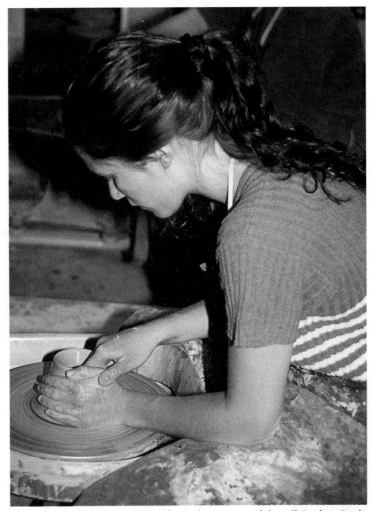

Our creativity reflects the Beauty of the All-Perfect Reality.

fections" such as truth, beauty, justice, goodness, love. We appraise ourselves and others based on how close to or how far away from the maximum degree of perfection we are.

If we can even conceive of a maximum degree of each perfection, if we can make such comparisons, then there must in fact **be** such a reality which possesses the maximum degree of each perfection. There must be a reality which is ultimate Truth, Beauty, Justice, Goodness, Love. Such an All-Perfect Reality describes what religious believers call **God.**

Questions for discussion

1. Does our ability to compare varying degrees of perfection with a "most perfect" seem a good reason to you to believe that there must be an "All-Perfect" source of all perfection? Explain.

2. Which of the following makes more sense to you about this "reasoning from the need for a Perfect Reality"? Why?

   • It seems a good reason for believing God exists.

   • It seems a good reason for believing in the perfection of the God who, for other reasons, you already believe exists.

Was the "Big Bang" just an accident?

The last of these logical reasons for belief in God asks you to observe the incredible order, organization, and complexity of the universe. Consider, for example, the following scientific information about just one microscopic part of your body:

In every cell, male and female, are chromosomes and genes. Chromosomes form the darkened nucleus which contains the genes. The genes are the main deciding factor as to what every living thing or human being shall be. They are so infinitesimal that if all of them which are responsible for the human beings on earth today, with their individuality, psychology, color, and race, could be collected and put in one place, there would be less than a thimbleful. A thimble is a small place in which to put all the individual characteristics of two billions of human beings. . . .

How a few million atoms locked up as an ultra-microscopic gene can absolutely rule all life on earth is still one of the greatest marvels of science. . . . They hold the design, ancestral record and characteristics of each living thing. They control in detail root, trunk, leaf, flower and fruit of every plant as exactly as they determine the shape, scales, hair, wings of every animal, including [humanity]. . . . Law governs the atomic arrangement in the genes, which absolutely determines every genus of life from beginning to extinction.[2]

Consider also the awesome complexity, yet the incredibly precise order which governs the whole universe. Study the structure and components of a plant, a human eye, a tiny insect, or venture farther out into the solar system. With all our intelligence, human beings do not create but only discover the laws operational in everything.

It often takes our geniuses many years or even centuries to uncover one such secret within the universe about us. We can piece together seven-story high replicas of a single microscopic DNA molecule. We can delve into nuclear physics and uncover its power and possibilities. But we did not put such laws of order there. We simply discover and attempt to understand them.

When you see a newly made bed, a clock telling perfect time, or an airplane soaring, you readily acknowledge that these things are products of intelligence. You recognize what degree of intelligence each required. The believer in God simply takes a long, hard look at the order and complexity of nature and the universe and reasons that all of this couldn't possibly result from mere blind chance. It could only be the product of an Infinite Intelligence. This, the believer calls **God.**

Belief in God as the origin of all intelligence and order within the universe doesn't at all rule out the theories of evolution as the way the universe developed thereafter. It simply means that such **evolutionary development must somehow have involved, in the planning stages at least, an infinite degree of intelligent thought.**

A battery-operated toy, for example, can go on working long after the toy is designed and built by its maker, and the batteries installed by one person or another. Still its continued functioning evidences the intelligence which first conceived of it. So it is with God's universe. It continues to operate under laws of incredible complexity and order which are all the more evidence of the intelligence of the God who first conceived of the universe and its possibilities.

Also, it demonstrates no more intelligence to create a working toy from nothing than it would to create its parts, and include within them the intelligent ability to come together in perfect running order on their own. Likewise, it would make no less of God that the universe, Earth, and people evolved from God's creating an initial mass of energy in a sudden "Big Bang," as scientists theorize, rather than suddenly creating this all within six days.

Stephen Hawking is widely recognized as one of the greatest scientific minds of our time. When readers of one of his books misunderstood his theorizing about the beginning of the universe as an effort to disprove God's existence, he responded in his next book:

You don't need to appeal to God to set the initial conditions for the universe, but that doesn't prove there is no God—only that [God] acts through the laws of physics.[3]

God does not die on the day when we cease to believe in a personal deity, but we die on the day when our lives cease to be illumined by the steady radiance, renewed daily, of a wonder, the source of which is beyond all reason.
—Dag Hammarskjold

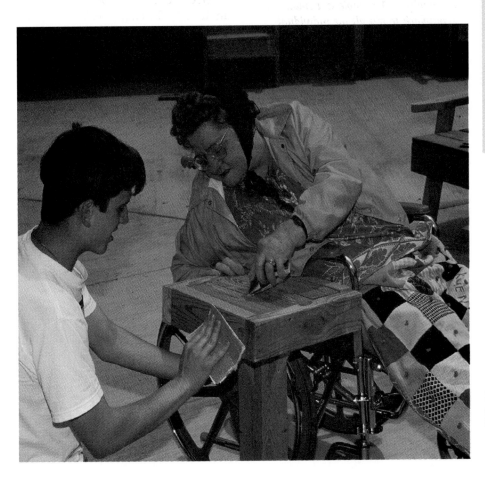

The believer sees the order and the complexity in the universe—and in the human hand.

❧ Questions for discussion

1. Which of the following do you think seems the more logical alternative to explain the universe's incredible order and complexity? Why?
   - An Intelligent Source of everything exists.
   - The universe was an accident, and we result from mere blind chance.

2. Can you think of another logical explanation for the incredible order and complexity of the universe?

3. Does this "reason from the need for an Ultimate Intelligence" make sense to you as a reason for believing God exists? Explain.

4. How is belief in such an Intelligence compatible with
   - Belief in evolution
   - Scientific theories of the physics principles according to which the universe first took shape

Could you prove that you exist?

Read the following true account, and then respond to the questions.

David Dickerson is alive and well and living in Kentucky.

That came as a surprise this week to . . . sheriff's investigators, who thought that Dickerson had been killed by an elephant while working for a . . . circus . . . . in fact, a . . . sheriff's detective made a call to Kentucky to report his death. Dickerson got on the phone to say he wasn't dead, but the detective didn't believe him. . . .

Somebody is [dead]. Somebody calling himself Dickerson—somebody using Dickerson's identity, and even his Social Security number—was leading three . . . elephants along the street . . . and while he was doing that, he was trampled to death by a 6,500-pound elephant . . . when the elephants were startled and inadvertently knocked him to the ground. . . .

That's why the detective was trying to notify the real Dickerson's family that he was dead, and wound up talking to the real Dickerson.

"It was very hard for me to prove I was actually who I was," Dickerson said. . . . Try to prove who you are sometimes. It's almost impossible."[4]

Questions for discussion

1. If you were in Dickerson's situation, how would you try to prove to the authorities that you really exist, that you're alive?

2. If you were the law-enforcement authorities, why would you be skeptical of Dickerson's claim to be who he is? Why would you be skeptical of the reasons you just gave on why you exist?

3. If you were God, how would you try to convince people that you exist? Why do you think some people would remain skeptical anyway?

4. How is the above account about Dickerson's situation similar to what people experience in seeking to discover whether God exists?

Personal reasons for believing

*Earth's crammed with heaven
And every common bush afire with
   God;
And only he who sees takes off his
   shoes—
The rest sit round it and pluck
   blackberries.*

Elizabeth Barrett Browning

In addition to logic-based reasons for belief in God, people also have more personal reasons. These are often arrived at when, after a human experience of great depth and meaning, you sit back and realize that you've just encountered that which is somehow holy. There is something which goes far beyond what you've just experienced. Something which makes that experience much more than a brief, relatively meaningless encounter in space and time—which makes it somehow sacred and eternal.

Perhaps that experience was what the person who wrote these words meant: "The only peace I find in parting is knowing—that all we have shared is alive and sacred somewhere." That is why belief in God gives even greater depth and meaning to all you see and touch and love. Things and people and achievements have even greater value. This is true because in them we confront the Infinite, Holy, and Eternal, of which they are an expression and reflection. Even more, it is true because God has redeemed this world and made all in it somehow holy and eternal too.

And so, sometimes you may feel that what you have encountered is far more powerful and precious than the experience itself. You may somehow sense that Life is bigger than we are—all of us put together—and that it is more personal than you had ever imagined. Have you ever had times, for instance, when you felt like thanking, begging, or blaming Something or Someone beyond yourself and others for what you could not seem to grasp or bear alone? Or when your joy and gratitude were too full and deep to contain? Or when your needs were more than your own resources seemed able to cope with? Or when your grief, anger, or despair seemed beyond your own solitary endurance?

Blessed are those who have not seen and yet have come to believe. —John 20:29

When the space shuttle Challenger exploded in the faces of people throughout the world watching the tragic event live on television, millions of people exclaimed aloud, "Oh, my God!" From the engineers watching in horror at the ground control center, to the president and his wife, to the high school students watching the event in their classrooms came the same audible gasp, "Oh, God."

At times like these, people often acknowledge with feeling the depth of what a part of life means. In doing so, they accurately address the only real Meaning or Hope we can find behind everything. Yet, until such dramatic moments lead them to turn to God (because there seems nowhere else to turn), sometimes people are reluctant to believe that God could be this real, this obvious, this close to us everyday. But if Jesus' words and life and death said anything, it was that God is always this relevant and real.

Reasoning and human experience can lead us only so far in our journey to believe. From there, we must take a risk of one sort or another, a "leap of faith." We must choose either to surrender ourselves to mystery or to forever teeter on the brink of doubt, unable to decide one way or the other.

You see, **God** actually names the Reality behind what you already experience in everything that means the most to you. When you come to understand this, you will be able to stop searching so hard intellectually for what you have really found and believed all along. You will recognize the One whom you have long since personally known. Then in awe and gratitude, you too, instead of plucking intellectual blackberries, will just respectfully "take off your shoes" ᴥ

Questions for discussion

1. What personal **experiences** of yours have brought you closest to believing that God exists? Why?

2. Which personal **experiences** of yours have made you feel farthest away from belief in God's existence? Why?

3. Do you think most people believe that God exists for "logical" reasons, for "personal" reasons, or a combination of both? Explain.

4. Aside from those in your text, can you think of other reasons for believing God exists? Explain.

Experiences of awe bring God's name to our mind and to our lips.

Of God and hamburgers

Read the following true account, and then respond to the questions.

Two pilots [Chris Bragman and Doug Miller] stranded in the Atlantic Ocean after ditching their plane stayed alive for 16 hours with talk of God and hamburgers—but also considered suicide to end their ordeal, they said.

After the crash, Bragman . . . had to push Miller out of a hatch. The plane sank within seconds.

The plane had no raft, but Bragman grabbed two life vests. He tied one around Miller and held his own with one hand. . . . Bragman said he grabbed Miller by the back of the pants and began kicking steadily, careful not to splash the water and attract sharks. Miller [who had been injured when his head slammed into the plane's windshield during the crash] kicked as much as he could.

They aimed at [a water tower they spotted on a nearby island]. . . . They saw planes and boats pass nearby, including a cruise ship.

They talked about their wives and religion. They prayed. "I don't particularly believe in God. But I did talk to [God]," Bragman said.

That was also when the two began to discuss the possibility of never making it, of dying a slow, painful death from exposure. . . . Then, night began to fall. . . .

"I told Doug that I had a knife, and that I could slit both our throats. And that would be it," Christ Bragman recalled. . . ."

[Finally,] they saw distant lights near the tower . . . . "And that was a motivator. . . ." In the end, [the two men] crawled ashore . . . early [in the] morning after drifting and swimming [an estimated] 30 to 50 miles. . . .

Miller . . . credited Bragman with saving his life.

"There's no question about it," Miller said. . . . "He was there every step of the way. He never left me."[5]

Questions for discussion

1. Why do you think Chris and Doug talked about God and hamburgers as they struggled to survive together? What do you think you would have talked about in their situation?

2. List the things you think probably motivated the men not to give up and just stop trying, or not to commit suicide. What would motivate you in such a situation?

3. Which of these things probably helped the men the most? Which do you think were most important to them? Which would have been the most important to you?

4. What contradiction do you find in Chris's statement that he doesn't particularly believe in, but nevertheless prayed to, God during the ordeal? Do you think he possibly believes in God more than he realizes?

5. What types of faith did the two men demonstrate and experience during their ordeal?

6. In what ways might this story be considered a parable which represents our journey of faith throughout life?

Chapter review

1. The human longing for God

- Explain what it means to say that people have a built-in human longing for God.
- Explain why Catholic teaching says that we can find our ultimate fulfillment only in God.
- List and explain some of the problems of belief about life and about people which can lead people to have more difficulty believing in God.
- Describe the two temptations which individuals may need to face and overcome in order to believe in God.

2. How do we know God exists?

- Explain the role of reasoning and questioning in faith in God.
- Explain whether or not it would ever be scientifically possible to prove or disprove God's existence.
- Describe why what convinces one person to believe God exists might not convince someone else.

3. Logical reasons to believe in God

- List and briefly explain each of the logical reasons proposed in this chapter for believing in God's existence.
- Explain the other types of personal reasons people often have for believing that there is a God.

Projects and assignments

1. Conduct one of the following interviews. Record or videotape the responses and play a five-minute segment of these for the class. Write a paragraph or videotape a segment adding your own responses in view of what was discussed in this chapter.

   Interview one of the following groups or individuals: five teenagers who are not taking this course, five adults, five young children (of any age), five senior citizens, a priest or nun or religious brother or a minister or rabbi. Ask your interviewees these questions:

   - Do you believe God exists? Why or why not?
   - (If the person answers, "no," also ask this question: Then how do you account for the universe's existence and incredible order and complexity?)
   - What do you find most difficult about believing in God's existence and why?
   - What is your biggest question, or what do you wonder most about God's existence?

2. Write at least a twenty-line song or poem about belief in God and/or about the human longing for God.

3. Read in John 20:26-29 the account of the apostle Thomas's disbelief. Write a prayer or an essay about your reflections on this passage and belief in God.

"If I go forward, he is not there; or backward, I cannot perceive him;
on the left he hides, and I cannot behold him;
I turn to the right, but I cannot see him." —Job 23:8–9

Chapter 2

Revelation—How We Know God

The secret things belong to the LORD our God, but the revealed things belong to us and to our children forever, to observe all the words of this law.

Deuteronomy 29:29

You've told us once and for all, God,
through Your word in the Bible
and Your Word-made-flesh—Jesus,
what You're like
and what we're to try to be like, too.

But You know how mixed up people still get about what the Bible means!

Anyway, thanks for taking the trouble to introduce Yourself to us
through Abram and Moses and all.

I know it wasn't easy,
since the Bible tells us that, just like today, people weren't always eager
to listen with an open heart to what You had to say.

Thanks especially for caring enough
to really want to help us get to know You personally,
especially through what Your Son, Jesus, said and did for us.

Help us realize more clearly what You have told us about Yourself.

And thanks for being patient with us
as we try to better understand.

Overview questions

1. How can we know more about what God is like?

2. What does God's own Revelation to us include?

3. How do Sacred Tradition and Scripture help us know God better?

4. What can we learn about God from Church Tradition, and what must it remain faithful to?

5. What is the purpose and role of Church doctrine, theology, and law?

6. What is meant by saying that the Bible is God's inspired word to us?

7. What is contained in the Sacred Scriptures? How should Catholics interpret the Bible?

Mt. Sinai

How do you let someone get to know you?

When you meet or date someone you think you might like to get closer to, how do you get to know each other better? What mistakes do you make that keep you from getting closer? This activity will help you assess some of these things.

Put the letter of your response to each item on the blank to the left of the item. For items indicated with "and/or," you may select more than one response letter.

____ **1.** In letting the other person get to know you, do you tend to

    a. talk too much about yourself,

    b. talk about yourself somewhat, but not too much, or

    c. be a bit too shy

____ **2.** Do you tend to

    a. express at first only your best qualities,

    b. let the person also see right away some of your worst qualities, or

    c. let the person see both your good and bad qualities a little at a time.

____ **3.** Do you tend to reveal deeply personal things about yourself, your family, and your life

    a. pretty soon in the relationship,

    b. only after you're positive the person won't misunderstand or think less of you for it, or

    c. hint at these things and wait until the other person seems interested in knowing more about these aspects of yourself

____ **4.** Do you freely express your honest ideas and opinions

    a. right away in the relationship,

    b. mainly when you sense the other person would accept and agree with them, or

    c. gradually, as you get to know each other better and whether or not you think the person will always accept or agree with them

____ **5.** When it seems at first that the other person isn't as interested in getting to know you as you are in becoming closer, do you usually respond by

    a. trying to prove your superiority,

    b. backing away from the relationship to protect yourself from getting hurt emotionally, or

    c. patiently continuing to make use of the opportunities you do have to let the person get to know you better

____ **6.** In order to gain the person's respect, do you tend to

    a. put on airs, acting macho or sophisticated,

    b. play hard to get, or

    c. treat the other person with kindness and respect

____ **7.** In trying to get to know the other person, do you usually

    a. bring up sensitive subjects before the other person seems willing to discuss them,

    b. stick to "safer," more superficial topics, or

    c. give the relationship more time to develop, while gradually and gently inviting the other person to reveal more about him or herself

____ **8.** When you want to meet someone you think you'd like to get to know, do you typically

    a. wait for the other person to introduce her or himself to you,

    b. rely on a third party to introduce you to each other, or

    c. take the initiative to introduce yourself

9. In finding out more about who the other person is, do you

a. rely on what the person tells you about him or herself,

b. listen to those who usually like to just criticize people, and/or

c. listen to what trusted friends who know you both well have to say about the other person

10. To find out more about what the other person is really like, do you most often

a. observe how the person relates with and treats others,

b. observe mainly the person's faults, or

c. give physical or other superficial characteristics top priority

What can we know about God?

self-revelation

making known personal aspects of oneself

Divine Revelation

the process of God's self-communication, and God's gift of making known to us truths about God which relate to us, our life's meaning, and our ultimate destiny

Our ability to think and reason helps us to know that God exists, as we discussed in the last chapter. But how do we know what God is like? How do we know that God really cares about us and about the world? How do we know that God isn't just the great "Toymaker in the Sky," who created the world and left it to function apart from God? How do we know God isn't a "Deadbeat Dad" who brought us into existence and then abandoned us to find our way through life all on our own? How do we get to know what God is really like?

You know how you feel when people have preconceived ideas about you that aren't true or completely accurate. You at least want the chance to tell people who you are yourself—even if afterward they don't accept who you are, or insist on continuing to mix in what you tell them with their own mistaken notions about you.

Likewise, others can get some idea of who you really are as a person from what they observe about your outward behavior. But that kind of knowledge is too subject to misinterpretation and mistaken conclusions. It's also limited—people can get to know only so much about you that way.

For someone to get to know you well, the opportunity must be there to communicate to the person personally and more deeply what you're really like. And if you're wise, you do this gradually, for **self-revelation** is a process and a gift one person shares with another. You introduce yourself. You tell the person more and more about yourself as the person seems interested in and capable of understanding and accepting you. You're patient (and perhaps persistent), but not pushy.

Let the word of Christ dwell in you richly; teach and admonish one another in all wisdom; and with gratitude in your hearts sing . . . songs to God.
—Colossians 3:16

It's the same with getting to know God. **Divine Revelation,** revelation with a capital *R,* is the process by which God has chosen to reveal to us who God really is, and what kind of relationship God wants to have with us. In the rest of this chapter, we'll look at God's process of self-revelation to us. In the next chapter, we will begin discussing more about just what God has revealed to us about God.

We humans can learn and conclude much about God on our own, through our ability to reason logically (as we saw in the last chapter).

Ever since the creation of the world his eternal power and divine nature, invisible though they are, have been understood and seen through the things he has made.

Romans 1:20

The Hebrew Scriptures describe God's self-revelation through the history of the Jewish people.

◆ Questions for discussion

1. Just how do you feel when people have preconceived, but inaccurate, ideas about you? How do you go about trying to correct these?

2. What true things about yourself can others probably learn from observing you and your behavior? What things couldn't someone learn about you this way? What might they misunderstand about you?

3. Why is it best to reveal the most important things about who you are to someone gradually, rather than doing so all at once?

4. What ideas about God did people have before humanity became aware of God's own self-revelation? Were these ideas accurate? Explain.

5. What does it mean to say that self-revelation is a gift? That God's Revelation is a divine gift?

But there are things about who God is that we would never know for sure—not unless God told us. And so, those unaware of God's special self-revelation have often enough made the mistake of confusing or replacing the Creator with the creatures:

> . . . for though they knew God, they did not honor him as God or give thanks to him, but they became futile in their thinking . . . and they exchanged the glory of the immortal God for images resembling a mortal human being or birds or four-footed animals or reptiles . . . and worshiped and served the creature rather than the Creator. . . .
>
> *Romans 1:21, 23, 25*

But as with self-revelation of all kinds, the Revelation God has shared with us is not something we're entitled to of our own merits. It's truly a divine gift. ◆

God's Revelation to us

To reveal your inner self to someone else, you must first know yourself. Divine Revelation began with God's own self-knowledge. The Hebrew Scriptures (Old Testament) of the Bible describe how God's revelation to humanity began gradually unfolding. They describe God as first making a **covenant** with Noah. Then God chose Abraham and his descendants with whom to continue this ongoing process of making Divine Revelation known to people of all nations and all times.

Through Moses and Israel's other leaders and prophets, God continued guiding the Israelites to form themselves into a holy nation. Through God's people of Israel, all others would eventually come to hear of what God is really like and of how this means that we

covenant

the agreement whereby God has promised humanity lasting support and faithfulness, and whereby we are to follow God's ways

🕊 Questions for discussion

1. Why must human self-revelation begin with self-knowledge? How is this true of God as well?

2. Describe the process by which Divine Revelation occurred, as recorded in the Hebrew Scriptures.

3. Why did God inspire individuals to record God's Revelation in the Hebrew Scriptures? What would probably have happened if none of this had been recorded? If those who recorded it were inspired only by their own whims and biases instead of by God?

4. What part of God's self-revelation is Jesus and his life and teaching? Explain.

should live and treat one another as God's children. And from the Jewish people, too, Jesus, the promised Messiah, would be born.

For you are a people holy to the LORD your God; the LORD your God has chosen you out of all the peoples on earth to be his people, his treasured possession . . . you are a people holy to the LORD your God. . . . The LORD will establish you as his holy people, as he has sworn to you, if you keep the commandments of the LORD your God and walk in his ways.

Deuteronomy 7:6, 14:21, 28:9

God also inspired individuals to write down the deeds and events which preserved the Israelites' growing understanding of who God is and what this means for people of all time to come. Finally, God gave us the ultimate Word of self-revelation in Jesus, the fullness of all God's Revelation.

Long ago God spoke to our ancestors in many and various ways by the prophets, but in these last days he has spoken to us by a Son, whom he appointed heir of all things, through whom he also created the worlds.

Hebrews 1:1–2 🕊

Sacred Tradition—divinely inspired to bring us God's Revelation by means of

- **Sacred Scriptures,** which contains
  - —*The Hebrew Scriptures*, handed down to us by means of
    - – oral tradition, and finally
    - – written tradition
  - —*The Christian Scriptures,* handed down to us by means of
    - – oral tradition, and then
    - – written tradition
- **Apostolic Church Tradition**

Sacred Tradition

the process by which God inspired certain individuals and groups to pass on basic truths of Revelation from generation to generation

tradition

the handing down of beliefs, customs, and so on, from generation to generation

oral tradition

the passing on of beliefs, laws, customs, and ideas through the spoken word

Tradition and Scripture

How we know what God has revealed

Sacred Tradition

The process through which God's Revelation was handed down to us is called **Sacred Tradition.** *Tradition* means "to deliver," but there were certainly no telephones, televisions, or other electronic delivery systems in the days of our ancient ancestors!

Sacred Scripture

In early times, before forms of paper were invented, peoples passed on their most important beliefs to succeeding generations by **oral tradition,** word of mouth. This is probably how some of your school traditions have been passed down from year to year—with the present group of students explaining them verbally to the new students every year. Before parts of the Hebrew Scriptures began to be written down, the truths God was beginning to reveal to the ancient Hebrews through Abraham and his successors were passed on orally.

Gradually—not all at once—somewhere between 1300 and 900 B.C.E., this oral tradition began to be written down. This was the beginning of the **written tradition** of God's Revelation which continued through the following centuries. Probably some of your older, traditional school cheers have been put in writing by now. Newer ones, however, aren't always written down right away—until there is a need for it, such as to quickly teach them to the whole student body at a rally.

God's Revelation in the Bible reached its fullness in God's ultimate Word to us, Jesus. **Judeo-Christian Tradition** refers to that part of God's Revelation in the Hebrew Scriptures which Jews and Christians have shared

from ancient times to today. The apostles, as Jesus had commissioned them to do, continued his teaching. At first they did this orally, too. Only somewhat later were parts (but not all) of this oral tradition written down in what we call the **Christian Scriptures.**

With the last apostle's death, God's Revelation to us in Sacred Tradition was complete. Most of God's Revelation in Sacred Tradition is contained in the writings we call **Sacred Scripture.** This is why Scripture is such an vitally important part of the Christian religion, and of Catholics' faith.

B.C.E. ("Before the Common Era") and C.E. ("Common Era")

use of these abbreviations respects the fact that much of today's world does not believe in Jesus as their Messiah, Savior, or as God's Son.

written tradition

the passing on in writing of beliefs, laws, customs, and ideas

Christian Scriptures

God's Revelation in Jesus, as taught by his apostles and written down under divine inspiration

Sacred Scripture

the writings God inspired which contain the fundamental truths of God's Revelation for all peoples and all time

Sacred Scripture and Church Tradition

complementary ways God's truth is channeled to us, with Scripture being the touchstone by which Church Tradition develops

"Thus the Lord has said, 'I revealed myself to the family of your ancestor in Egypt when they were slaves to the house of Pharaoh.' "
—1 Samuel 2:27

Hebrew and Christian Scriptures together form our ***Sacred Scripture.***

Christ

the anointed one

❧ Questions for discussion

1. Describe the process by which God's Revelation in Sacred Tradition was handed down to us.

2. What portion of this tradition do Jews and Christians of today share?

3. Why does the Catholic Church rely on both Scripture and Apostolic Tradition?

4. Why does the Church consider it so important that there have been successors to the apostles in the Church? Who are they today, and what are their main responsibilities in the Church?

5. What is the relationship between Sacred Scripture and Church Tradition?

6. List as many similarities as you can between the process by which Sacred Tradition was transmitted and the way your school traditions have been passed on to new students over the years.

Apostolic Tradition

The apostles were especially chosen by God to witness and hand on God's Revelation in Jesus. God's Spirit inspired individuals to record the apostles' teaching and understanding about what they had witnessed, so that God's Revelation in Jesus' message of salvation would be handed on to all future generations whole and intact in the Scriptures.

God's Spirit also inspired Jesus' early followers to form themselves into a Church community who would continue to faithfully live Jesus' message and share it with others. Thus, God's presence through Jesus would remain actively with us in the Church.

Finally, the apostles appointed leaders in the Church to succeed them in faithfully handing on Jesus' teaching and guiding the Church to live it. Thus the Church's leaders as the apostles' successors are responsible for doing three things:

1. Continuing to see that God's entire Revelation is preserved faithfully

2. Explaining it so people of different times and cultures can understand and live it

3. Helping to make God's Revelation known to people everywhere

Scripture and Church Tradition

Sacred Scripture and the Tradition of the Church handed down from the apostles complement each other. They are each ways God's truth is passed on to us. Both have God as their source and make present the living mystery of Jesus, the **Christ.** Through this Apostolic Tradition which continues in the Church, the Church grows to understand better God's word as handed down in the Scriptures and especially through Jesus. **Christian tradition** refers to the message of Jesus faithfully handed down from one generation of the Christian community to another through the apostles' successors, under the guidance of God's Spirit.

Scripture, however, always remains the touchstone by which Church Tradition must develop. Church Tradition must always remain faithful to and not contradict or stray from God's Revelation as contained in the Scriptures. ❧

. . . these things God has revealed to us through the Spirit; for the Spirit searches everything, even the depths of God.
—1 Corinthians 2:10

How well do you know the Catholic faith?

This activity will help you determine how accurately you understand the Catholic faith. Complete it by responding to each of these items as your teacher directs you.

1. List those beliefs you are positive are essential to the Catholic faith and are therefore unchangeable.

2. List those beliefs you're sure are a way to **understand** or **interpret** the Church's main beliefs, but which could change in the future.

3. List those things that you're sure are **laws** of the Church intended to uphold its basic beliefs, but which could also be changed in the future.

4. List those things you know are closely connected with the Catholic faith, but aren't sure which of the above categories to put them in.

Understanding the faith

In the past, many changes have taken place in the Catholic Church. In future years, many more will undoubtedly occur. For example, throughout past centuries only males were allowed to be altar servers. Now bishops may allow women and girls to fulfill this role as well.

Some people readily accept such changes, while others may find them hard to adjust to. When sweeping changes occurred in the Catholic liturgy after the Second Vatican Council in the 1960s, some Catholics said they felt like their whole religion was disappearing. By now, however, Catholics have become accustomed to the changes and wouldn't want to undo them.

What will happen, though, when the Church finds it necessary in the future to adapt its liturgy of the Eucharist, for instance, to accommodate the special atmospheric requirements of space colonies? Will you wonder whether or not your religion itself is being "lost" as you have known and grown up with it? (If you had trouble properly categorizing things in this last activity, then it's much more likely that you just might feel this way!)

You might well find future changes frustrating and confusing unless you learn how to make this important distinction about the elements of your religion: **Some things are essential, and therefore unchangeable in the faith, and others are nonessential and therefore may be changed.** In this next section we will discuss this distinction and why it is such an important one.

Doctrine—essential beliefs

At the heart of any religion, including the Catholic faith, are doctrines, or dogmas. **Doctrines** are the religion's basic beliefs, the essentials. Without them there would be no such religion. Were these to be changed in any way, the religion, too, would fundamentally change. The number of doctrines can be added to, as a religion expands its understanding and awareness of God and of itself. But they can't be deleted or basically altered without changing the religion's very nature.

If religion has failed, it is because it has confused the essential with the non-essential. —A Hindu philosopher

We might compare a religion's doctrines to the liberties, rights, and form our government guarantees us in the Constitution. These are the basic beliefs on which the government is founded. Were any of these fundamental rights and liberties to be deleted, or were the structure of government it provides for to be substantially changed, the whole nature of our country would change as well.

The Constitution has, at times, been added to as our understanding of what our government should be and do has grown. Even this has been done only with the consent of the proper authorities, including the people of the entire country. It's somewhat similar with the doctrines, the basic beliefs, of any given religion. But as we will see, there can also be important differences here.

In other words, doctrines are those things which one must believe in, adhere to, in order to call oneself a true and good-standing member of the religion. One who does not wish to accept the religion's doctrines as true says, in effect, that she or he does not really believe in or wish to belong to this religion. If one were to believe in most, but not all, of the doctrines, it would be more accurate to say that the person believes in something similar to, but not in this particular religion.

In the Catholic faith, there is an order of truths which recognizes that some truths of faith are more fundamental to

ᵃ Questions for discussion

1. Why is it important to distinguish between what is essential and unchangeable, and what is nonessential and changeable in a religion?

2. How important are a religion's doctrines? Why?

3. Why can't a religion's basic doctrines be changed or deleted without changing the nature of the religion itself?

4. Why is it important that you know which aspects of your religion are basic and unchangeable? Know which are not essential and subject to change?

In former generations this mystery was not made known to humankind, as it has now been revealed to his holy apostles and prophets by the Spirit. . . . —Ephesians 3:5

---

reconcile

bring together; resolve differences

religious sect

organized religious group or denomination

---

the Christian faith than others are. Those which the Church considers most essential for Christian life are defined and proclaimed as doctrines which represent what all Catholics are to believe. Such formal declarations of doctrine are rarely made any longer, probably because most, or perhaps all, of the essentials of Catholic belief have already been specifically identified. They express the fullest authority and teaching of the Catholic faith. ᵃ

Theology—understanding better

Faith in anyone grows through intelligent understanding. So does faith in God. **Theology**, the study of religion and of religious beliefs and ideas, is the intellectual effort to understand better what faith in God means. The word *theology* comes from the Greek words for "god" (*theos*) and "word" (*logos*).

Each religion has men and women called "theologians" who have been especially educated in the study of their faith. These theologians seek to interpret the meaning of the religion's basic beliefs (doctrines) in the context of contemporary life. Theology, then, studies what the faith means and should mean for people today.

Theology is based on careful, prayerful examination of the faith. Theologians often provide a clearer, better way to look at what the faith means. But a theologian's views about what a particular doctrine of faith means aren't always completely accurate or the best interpretations. In fact, theologians can and often do disagree among themselves about which viewpoint of several best interprets the faith.

It's something like the debate years ago over whether or not the Constitution's guarantee of equal rights also applied to women, and whether women should therefore be allowed to vote. Various interpretations were debated about what the basic belief in equal rights means and how it should be understood and lived. Eventually, the interpretation which was adopted led to reversing previous law and practice. This didn't mean that a basic constitutional guarantee was changed. It was merely clarified, and more fully and accurately understood and put into practice.

So it is with theology. Theologies can and do change with the times and with the theologians. For example, what some Catholic theologians of several centuries ago thought was a good and relevant way to explain the Sacrament of Anointing the Sick is understood today by the Catholic Church to have been incomplete in some respects. Now there is a better approach to the theology—the explanation and understanding—of this sacrament, and how and when to celebrate the sacrament.

Adopting a different theological way to interpret a dogma sometimes leads to changes—even major changes—in certain rituals, practices, or ways of thinking about one's faith. But it needn't change the basic beliefs or the religion itself. Sometimes, though, a particular theological approach, or way of trying to understand it, may, in essence, actually contradict a religion's basic belief.

For instance, theologians in some Christian denominations tried for centuries to justify the practice of human slavery with Jesus' teaching. As Christians now see more clearly, there is no way to **reconcile** the two! Any theology that supports human slavery fundamentally contradicts Jesus' life and message. Popular preachers of radical theologies still spring up from time to time in every major **religious sect**—whether Christian, Jewish, Muslim, Buddhist, or Hindu.

Even today in each of the world's major religions, there are some individuals who preach hateful ideas. For example, they may try to promote racism or **anti-semitism** in the name of the religion—ideas which oppose basic things every one of the world's major religions actually stands for! Through their slick words and dynamic personal appeal, such individuals twist religious ideals to suit their own purposes (not God's) until they convince some people that the distortions are believable. Their "charisma" and the lively controversy they spark may help them draw an audience on television or on college campuses. But they stir up controversy in ways which are not positive but only anguishing, confusing, divisive, and harmful.

This doesn't mean that new ways of truly understanding their faith better will never arouse heated debates among believers, including among Catholics. There were plenty back in the 1950s and 1960s when prominent Catholic theologians proposed that the sacraments should henceforth be celebrated in peoples' own languages instead of in the traditional Latin! At first these courageous individuals took a lot of heat for a position that seemed so different from then-current practice, but later their ideas became part of what is standard practice in the Catholic Church today.

The guidance of Church leaders

Beginning with the Second Vatican Council, Church officials were able to instruct and guide Catholics to see that, controversial or not, some of the theologians' ideas about needed change in the Church were right—and actually more in accord with how the apostles understood and celebrated Jesus' teaching. Now the vast majority of Catholics would never want to return to regularly celebrating the Eucharist in a language they couldn't understand or a manner in which they couldn't actively participate!

Now perhaps you can better see why the Church believes that God's Spirit inspired the apostles to appoint successors who, under God's guidance, can continue the job of seeing that the whole Church never strays from what Jesus really taught. This is why Catholic officials oversee theologians' work to help ensure that ideas are in accord with its basic beliefs before they are officially taught as representing the faith of Catholics. This is why it's also important for Catholics to clearly know the basic beliefs of their faith—and to understand the difference between basic doctrine and theological interpretation.

Unlike doctrine, then, theology can change without altering anything essential to the faith. To remain true to your own religious beliefs, remember: Don't confuse theology, or ways of **interpreting** doctrines, with the basic beliefs themselves. ❧

The Church's teaching authority

Catholic doctrines are founded on Scripture, and on Church Tradition as a basis for interpreting the Scriptures. Some people, however, seem to think that the list of Catholic dogmas is practically endless. They confuse Church laws and Church teaching (which largely consists of theological interpretations intended to support and explain dogma) with basic Church doctrine. Actually, the Church's basic beliefs are summed up rather succinctly in the Apostles' and the Nicene Creeds.

One dogma, which is itself the source of much confusion, is that of infallibility. Many non-Catholics mistakenly think the pope intends to be speaking infallibly whenever he holds a press conference! Jesus promised that the Holy Spirit would always be with and guide his followers in living his teaching. From this, the Church concludes that God will not let the entire Catholic Church community be mistaken in the beliefs

anti-semitism

prejudice or discrimination against Jews

❧ Questions for discussion

1. What is the meaning and importance of theology for a religion? Of theologians?

2. What differences are there between theology and basic doctrine within a religion? Why is it important to understand this?

3. In what ways has your understanding of some of your religious beliefs changed since you were a small child? What areas of your own faith would you like to understand better?

4. In what ways do you think your religious faith could be better explained to make it more meaningful for children? For teenagers? For adults? For you personally? Explain.

1. On what are Catholic doctrines founded?

2. What do people sometimes misunderstand about the Church's doctrine of infallibility? How would you explain it to someone who feared that electing a Catholic leader of this country would result in having the pope run the country?

3. What obligation do all Catholics have regarding Jesus' teaching?

4. What is the difference between the Church's official *magisterium* and what is called the *ordinary magisterium* of the Church? Why is it important to understand this difference?

magisterium

the Catholic Church's highest teaching authorities

law

rule of behavior or conduct established by a group's authorities

Catholics share in common about what is essential for salvation. Guided by God's Spirit, the whole community of faithful Catholics has a sense of the faith which cannot be wrong in matters of their faith.

The Church also understands that Jesus gave his apostles, and the pope and other bishops as their successors in the Church, the authority to guard and authentically interpret the gospel and the moral law. Catholic belief in the ability of Church authorities to teach without error (infallibly) under certain conditions is, in fact, based on belief in the infallibility of the whole Church.

This doctrine of infallibility, however, is limited in its nature, scope, and implications. It applies mainly to matters of faith (beliefs) or morals (how Catholics ritually celebrate and live the Christian faith) which have been revealed by God as necessary for salvation. Thus the Church's official **magisterium** may exercise the infallible authority to defend, authentically explain, or preserve beliefs or practices necessary for salvation.[1]

. . . in due time he revealed his word through the proclamation with which I have been entrusted by the command of God our Savior. . . .
—Titus 1:3

It should be stressed that the Church's infallible teaching can pertain only to matters of faith and morals—and not to strictly secular matters. When John Kennedy was elected the first Catholic president, many non-Catholics sincerely feared that the pope might try to run the U.S. government from the Vatican in Rome! They didn't understand the nature and limitations of the authority God has vested in the Church.

In fact, all Catholics are seriously obliged to understand, proclaim, and strongly defend (although not infallibly) the truth of Jesus' teaching.[2] A teaching's infallibility, however, refers only to what the teaching **means,** and not to how it is **expressed.** The Church may change the way an infallible teaching is phrased or communicated to reflect a fuller understanding of it or to make it clearer or more meaningful for a future generation.

The pope and the bishops can also teach with truth and authority as Christ's representatives without doing so infallibly. This is known as exercising the Church's *ordinary magisterium* and is the usual way Church authorities teach. The pope and the other bishops of the Church teach this way, for example, when, as Christ's representatives, they teach as individual bishops about faith and Christian living. ☙

Law—living the faith

Almost any group has certain guidelines, however informal, which the members are expected to follow. This enables the group to establish an identity. It helps insure the cooperation of its members in realizing the group's purpose. Athletic teams, businesses, and children's clubs have such rules and regulations, and so do religions. When the rules become more formalized as a way to define what is expected of the group's members, then such regulations begin to take on the nature of a **law.**

Ideally, the purpose of any law, whether civil, religious or otherwise, should be to foster in practice the living out of the group's basic beliefs which promote the common good. To the extent that it does promote this, a law is a good one for that group. If a law runs contrary to this, such a law is a bad one for the group and should rightfully be questioned by the members.

Ultimately, it should be changed. Laws are based on particular interpretations of basic beliefs, and, like such interpretations, laws too can change without altering the fundamental beliefs themselves.

Jesus demonstrated this by responding on several occasions to questions about obeying the law. He obeyed and encouraged obeying just and legitimately authorized civil and religious laws. He also showed that there are times when a law should be disobeyed in order to meet a human need which claims greater priority—for example, to feed the hungry or minister to the sick. The Catholic Church, in fact, has always recognized this principle. For example, when the obligation of Catholics to participate in the weekly Eucharist would impose a significant hardship on a person or would conflict with a greater obligation of charity, the Church holds its members excused from obeying this law in such instances.

A group member who disagrees with a certain law should first of all try to have it changed, as Jesus constantly challenged those religious leaders who placed blind obedience to law above the demands of charity. One can still remain a faithful member of a group while working within the group's laws and structure to change a law or laws. But one's purpose in doing so should be to further correspond the laws to the group's basic beliefs.

If change is not forthcoming and if abiding by the law in the meantime would force one to act contrary to a basic belief of the group, then it can sometimes be necessary to respectfully disobey the law. Such civil disobedience, however, should take place not out of disrespect for what the law is trying to accomplish, but precisely for the opposite reason—out of respect for and belief in what the law should be helping to promote but is not.

For example, the Constitution guarantees citizens the right to life. Our traffic laws attempt to insure that we are given that right in practice by helping to keep us from mowing each other down on the highway! If, however, obeying a particular traffic signal would endanger rather than protect life in a certain situation, then we might well have cause to break or disobey that law in that particular situation. In doing so, we would be intending no disregard or disrespect for law itself, for the government's right to make, to impose, and to enforce laws in general, or for the basic belief behind the law—namely, belief in the right to life. And we would still remain good and loyal citizens.

On the other hand, arbitrarily, carelessly, or recklessly disobeying traffic laws shows a disregard for both human life and the structure necessary to protect this right. Thus, it violates in practice one or more of society's basic beliefs. The violator is rightfully subject to censure or punishment by the courts in order to insure that other citizens' right to life won't be further jeopardized. Similarly, disobeying religious laws in the same fashion violates the very beliefs one claims to hold and stand for.

The distinctions we have made in this chapter concerning doctrine, theology, and law should help you better understand three distinctions regarding your own religious convictions:

1. That you know what your most fundamental, unchanging beliefs are, so that you might never unwittingly compromise them

2. That you know the ways you should remain open to change and to understanding your faith better

3. That you know the real purpose of the laws you live by, so that you don't jeopardize your basic beliefs by disregarding the laws which promote and protect them, or contradict your beliefs by blindly obeying laws which undermine them.

In other words, try to know as fully as possible what you believe, why you believe it, and how you can and should live your religious convictions faithfully. ❧

❧ Questions for discussion

1. What should be the purpose of law? Why are laws important?

2. What purpose and function do the laws within a religion fulfill?

3. When is a law a good one? Why should religious and civil laws generally be obeyed?

4. What did Jesus demonstrate about obedience to religious and civil laws?

5. What happens when civil or religious laws are arbitrarily, carelessly, or recklessly disobeyed?

6. Using Jesus' teaching and example as a guide, when should a law be changed? When and for what reasons should it be disobeyed?

7. How should a person go about trying to change a law which needs changing?

8. Why is it important to your own faith that you understand the distinctions among doctrine, theology, and law in regard to your religion?

Building a school community

This activity will help further demonstrate the purpose, meaning, and differences among fundamental beliefs or doctrines, theologies which interpret them, and laws. Complete it by following the directions given below for Part 1. (Use your own notebook paper to do this.) Then follow the further directions your instructor gives you.

You are a member of the faculty of a new high school. Before the new school opens, the principal askes the faculty to draw up the school's basic philosophical beliefs—what it is to stand for and try to achieve. You are also to list those behavioral rules and expectations that all students will be expected to abide by at the school. They must be ones which all faculty members will be willing to help enforce. You are to give the reasons why you would include these rules, regulations, outcomes, and expectations. You must also identify those which are of major importance and those which are of minor importance. Students who violate the major expectations will be subject to expulsion from your school.

Part I

1. Briefly describe the basic philosophy you think the school should have—its purpose, goals or outcomes, and principles.
2. List the **major** rules or expectations for students you think your new school should have. Next to each, tell why you think this expectation is essential to being a member of this school community.
3. List the **minor** rules or expectations for students you think your new school should have. Next to each, tell why you think this expectation is necessary to help promote the school community's basic beliefs and goals or outcomes.

Part II

At a faculty meeting you and the other faculty members must decide on the final philosophy statement and lists of major and minor behavioral expectations. List below those your faculty group agrees upon. Do this by a process of consensus—list only those expectations as major or minor which **everyone** in your group agrees to:

1. School philosophy (purpose, goals or outcomes, and principles).
2. Major rules or expectations, and reasons why essential to belonging to this school community.
3. Minor rules or expectations, and reasons why important to support the school's basic purpose, goals or outcomes, and principles.

A school community works out of a basic philosophy.

SIBLING REVELRY

by Man Martin

What is faith?

What is a believer?

People often refer to those who practice a religion as *believers* and to those who don't as *nonbelievers*. But when it comes to God and to religion, everyone who takes a definite stand one way or the other is, strictly speaking, a believer.

> *[People] may believe what they cannot prove. They may not be put to the proof of their religious doctrines or beliefs. Religious experiences which are as real as life to some may be incomprehensible to others.*
> —*William O. Douglas,*
> *U.S. v. Ballard*

To say "I do not believe in God" actually means "I **believe**—that there is no God." Likewise, to say "I don't believe in" a certain religion or in certain religious beliefs actually means "I believe—that this religion or that these religious beliefs are not true." The person does not **know**—indeed, cannot know—with scientific certainty that there is no God or that certain religious beliefs are false.

Only a total skeptic can be called a true *non-believer*. Such a person actually suspends rather than denies belief in God or religious realities. All others, though, are believers, religiously speaking.

Realizing this, belief in God shouldn't feel like an oddity. In fact, according to recent polls, over 90 percent of the people in our society believe in God. Yet believers in God sometimes feel put on the defensive, as if only they must prove that what they believe is true, whereas those who believe there is no God seem relieved of this burden of proof. In reality, both **believe.**

Faith is a way of knowing

To understand how we can know God better through faith, it's important to understand the relationship between belief and knowledge.

In this world, we can **know** by means of logic or experience. You can demonstrate for yourself that 1 + 1 = 2. If you have one apple and someone gives you another apple, you can see for yourself that you now have two apples. You then **know** that 1 + 1 = 2 because concrete evidence has demonstrated it to you.

Your ability to reason logically also tells you, for instance, that if it's true that you're alive, and if it's also true that

Questions for discussion

1. Respond to this statement: Except for skeptics who suspend belief, everyone is a believer regarding God and religion. Explain.
2. Why do you think people sometimes feel too defensive about, or try to put others on the defensive about, their religious beliefs? Do you ever experience this among teenagers? Explain.
3. Do you think it's more difficult to believe that there is a God or to believe that there is not? Why?

✿ Questions for discussion

1. Explain the relationship between knowing and believing.

2. Describe the difference between knowledge based on concrete evidence, and that based on logical deduction. Give an example of how you might rely on each when buying a car.

3. If we can reason to God's existence by means of logic, why did we need the revelations about God contained in Scripture and Tradition?

4. In what sense is faith a way of knowing? Why is it a gift?

5. What two things does friendship with God require? Why?

what is alive can't at the same time be dead, then you can conclude that if you're alive you therefore aren't dead. You can **know** this through logical deduction. (In this particular case, you can also know it by experience!)

Through our natural ability to reason, we are able to conclude with logical certainty from created reality at least that God exists as the origin and end of all things, though we may never be able to prove this scientifically. For us to know more **about** what God is like required that God help explain God to us—by means of the Revelation we have received in Scripture and Tradition. But to come to know God more personally, as a Friend, also requires God's offering us this gift, or grace, of friendship—and our response in belief and trust. ✿

I believe because I understand, and I understand because I believe. —St. Augustine

---

Through our human friendships, we understand better that God is a Friend.

Intelligent faith

Belief should be intelligent, not absolutely blind. Remember that, as St. Anselm pointed out, "Faith seeks to understand." Even though what you believe must necessarily go beyond what you can prove, it's only sensible to desire and require good reasons before putting your trust in someone or something. That includes God and religion.

One major difference, obviously, between believing in human beings and believing in God is that you can readily experience that other human persons exist by seeing and hearing and touching them. Even so, everybody usually requires some amount of knowledge based on experience or reason before being willing to believe in someone or something.

If people have consistently been honest with you and everyone else, you tend to believe what they tell you. You may **believe** them even though you have no concrete evidence that they're telling you the truth. Your frequent experience that the sun "rises" and "sets" supports your belief that the same will again be true tomorrow and the next day—and that it also happens even on days so cloudy you can't see the sun at all! So, you make plans for the weekend. You're fairly confident that the sun's going off course won't make the world end between now and then, even though you can only **believe** that.

On the other hand, if you know someone has a habit of lying, you might well doubt the person's word. If you're planning a picnic, but the weather has been rainy and the forecast is "showers," you might change your mind about the outing. In each case, you use both your head and your previous experience to shift the weight of conviction in your mind from **believe in favor of** to **believe against** someone or something. Or, you're left in doubt—unable to believe either way.

In each instance, experience and intelligent reasoning provide a basis for your belief, but they don't guarantee concrete scientific proof of it. That usually honest person just might be lying to you this time. The world could end this afternoon. The sun might shine after all. You operate on the basis of probability according to what your experience has told you in the past and what you can logically conclude. From there you make a decision to believe one way or another.

So it is with God and religious ideas. It's only intelligent to ask good questions and to try to draw reasonable conclusions to help you make your decisions. But at some point you'll still be left with two choices: To remain altogether skeptical, or to decide—whether for or against—to believe. You'll be left in the same position as the mathematical physicist who, after years of questing to understand the universe scientifically, concludes:

> . . . "ultimate" questions "will always lie beyond the scope of empirical science as it is usually defined"; there will probably always be some mystery at the end of the universe. At the same time . . . the fact that human beings "carry the spark of rationality that provides the key to the universe," indicates that [humanity's] existence is not a mere quirk of fate. . . .
>
> ". . . the existence of mind in some organism on some planet in the universe is surely a fact of fundamental significance. . . . This can be no trivial detail, no minor byproduct of mindless, purposeless forces. We are truly meant to be here. . . .
>
> "Through my scientific work I have come to believe more and more strongly that the physical universe is put together with an ingenuity so astonishing that I cannot accept it merely as a brute fact. There must, it seems to me, be a deeper level of explanation."[2]

Believing in God does go beyond just believing that God exists. Like this scientist, to really begin believing in God you'll eventually need to abandon your desire for concrete scientific proof and be willing to accept uncertainty. Faith will forever remain somewhat of a mystery to us in this life. Yet, that's the very reason it's far more meaningful and valuable than scientific proof which is only a type of knowledge. For genuine faith in God is most of all a relationship.

Faith is an experience

There is another type of very real knowledge which is also based on experience, yet isn't subject to concrete scientific proof. This is the knowledge of belief—of faith. It's really the most important way of knowing people and of knowing God.

Would it mean more to you, for example, that a friend **knows** you're telling the truth because you've presented concrete evidence of that, or because your friend **believes** in and trusts you as a person? In which case would you feel that the person really does **know** you better?

Only one is possible here—the knowledge of concrete evidence, or that of trust based on good reasons. As St. Thomas Aquinas once pointed out, you can't both know about and believe in exactly the same thing in the same way at the same time. In that sense, the knowledge of belief and the knowledge of concrete evidence may at times be mutually exclusive. You can choose only one—to know **about** or to believe **in**.

We generally believe unless we have reason to doubt. Yet, living in a scientifically oriented world, people sometimes dismiss belief as unimportant. Especially when it comes to religion, some people still react as if believing is ridiculously unintelligent. In fact, they themselves rely on belief most of the time in their daily lives.

Questions for discussion

1. What does it mean to say that belief in God should be intelligent? Why should it be?

2. What reasons do you usually need before you can trust someone? What reasons lead you to mistrust someone?

3. What reasons did the scientist quoted in this section have for concluding that

   • Always beyond the scope of science there will be "ultimate questions" and mystery.

   • There must be "a deeper level of explanation" for the physical universe than science can provide.

4. Does this scientist's reasoning make sense to you? Does it prompt more questions in your mind? Explain.

5. Why does believing in God ultimately require a willingness to accept uncertainty and mystery?

As you've already seen, most of what you think, say, and do every day is based not on concretely demonstrated knowledge, but on belief. It's based not on things you've proven scientifically, but on what you believe about things, ideas, and people. Without even being aware of it, we all rely far more every day on what we believe than on what we know.

> *It is [God] alone who has immortality and dwells in unapproachable light, whom no one has ever seen or can see. . . .*
> —1 Timothy 6:16

We are all believers most of the time. We believe in certain people, and trust that they won't lie to us. So we accept something as true because they tell us it's so, without always checking it out for ourselves. In fact, many types of human experiences are far more meaningful than concrete, scientific ones.

Whether you're feeling wowed by the music at a concert or very touched by someone's gentle kindness, you don't stop to pick apart the experience analytically. You appreciate it for the somewhat mysterious gift it is. You suspend your search for scientific knowledge and savor the experience. When you look into a loved one's eyes, you don't think about pupils, irises, and corneas. You let yourself experience the love.

In these ways, you encounter to some extent the very real kind of knowledge and experience which belief involves. It is especially believing in someone which leads to more understanding, which leads to deeper belief, which leads to greater understanding, which leads to love. The belief, the trust, involved in loving someone is the deepest kind of knowing.

This is also why so many people find that it's through their loving relationships with other people that they feel closest to knowing and experiencing God. Faith in a human person is different from, but a path which often leads to, growth of faith in God. 🙢

The need for faith

All persons are called to have a relationship with God. But what does it mean to say that "The one who believes and is baptized will be saved; but the one who does not believe will be condemned" (Mark 16:1)?

One television preacher not long ago interpreted this passage literally to mean that those who are not Christians—and members of his particular flock at that!—would not be saved. That is **not,** repeat **not,** what the Catholic Church believes and teaches! The meaning of such a passage must be understood within the entire context of Jesus' teaching and actions.

God, who is as near to all of us as life and breath, "desires everyone to be saved and to come to the knowledge of the truth" (1 Timothy 2:4). Catholic teaching also points out that people who don't even know about God, Christ, or the Church can achieve eternal salvation by sincerely seeking God, and trying to follow their conscience and live a good life. In fact, the goodness or truth found in such persons is itself a gift from God.

Crisis faith

The religious beliefs and practices of earliest peoples were directed toward fulfilling certain basic needs: for food, protection, and a stable population. They concluded that superhuman or divine powers controlled those things. They felt compelled to acknowledge and appeal to these forces because, practically speaking, to them it was a matter of believe and worship—or perish.

Believing in God as a way to ensure everyday survival might seem far-fetched in this age of technology. Yet even the most sophisticated persons sometimes display remnants of this type of "crisis faith." Do you remember when, caught in the middle of some childhood trouble, you prayed to God for protection or survival: "Oh, please, God, don't let anyone find out! I'll be good. I promise, I'll never do anything bad again!"

A movie entitled *The End* once **satirized** this contradictory tendency in many people—an indifferent or casual attitude toward the divine as long as all goes well, but an immediate begging for God's help the minute one is in trouble. Told by doctors that he has only a short time to live, the movie's main character decides to commit suicide by swimming too far out into the ocean. On almost reaching the point of no return, however, he changes his mind and tries to swim back.

All the while, the man tries to make a series of deals with God. In each instance, he promises God some sacrifice—if God helps him safely reach the shore. While furthest away, he generously vows to give up everything and dedicate his whole life to God! Swimming still nearer to shore, he promises only to give up his dishonest practices and donate some of his wealth to charity. The closer he comes to safety, the less he's willing to give up. By the time he finally lands exhausted on the beach, the man has taken back all of his promises.

This type of need-based, crisis-oriented religious faith is all too common. As in ancient times, many people today often think about God only when they need something. A teenager who otherwise doesn't bother about God and religion might bless himself or herself with the sign of the cross before the crucial free throw in a basketball tournament. A teenager who otherwise has little time for God might pray earnestly for a date to the prom or help on a test. This kind of faith is rather superficial and short-lived.

A former soldier tells how, when he was in the military during wartime, chaplains of various faiths would hold services which some of the soldiers would not bother to attend. But those same men, he recalls, sure pleaded and cried for God's help when the going got rough. "Battlefield conversions"

sometimes abruptly introduce someone to God as the source of life, goodness, and blessings. Or they can be merely temporary manifestations of human fear, dependence, and the need for survival.

This type of attitude acknowledges God in a burst of belief at the moment of crisis, promptly forgets God, and consults God again only in the next crisis. But if disaster befalls anyway, God is blamed or rejected as useless. Shallow belief, though, doesn't pay God much of a compliment. "Believing" every time one is in need and **only** in time of need can be just a form of trying to use God to get one's own way. Most people wouldn't tolerate so-called friends who tried to use them like that. Fortunately, God has more patience!

This approach to faith is child**ish**—not child**like.**

He called a child, whom he put among them, and said, "Truly I tell you, unless you change and become like children, you will never enter the kingdom of heaven. Whoever becomes humble like this child is the greatest in the kingdom of heaven."

Matthew 18:2–4

The childlike faith Jesus speaks of in the Gospels involves having a relationship of genuine trust in God as a child trusts in a loving parent, not merely using God as an emergency liferaft.

Mature faith

Mature faith in God should enhance human love—not attempt to replace it.

We all need to be loved. Lacking love elsewhere in their lives, some people turn to God to provide a cure for loneliness. Some even become "religious recluses," feeling that God alone will ever care about them. Jilted in love, they may seek the love of God instead of trying to love people at all!

Religion can indeed provide support during lonely times. Believing God cares, understands, and accepts us even when no one else seems to can be very

satirize

to use sarcasm or ridicule to attack faults, failings, and so on

Questions for discussion

1. If faith is "necessary for salvation," can people who don't even know about God, Christ, or the Church be saved? Explain what Catholic teaching says about this.

2. How do people sometimes exhibit a "crisis-oriented faith" in God? On what occasions have you been a "battlefield believer"? Explain.

3. Why do you think people who aren't otherwise very religious turn to God in their hours of need?

4. What **should** religious faith provide for the religious believer during times of difficulty?

5. How would you describe the difference between a faith that is childish and one that is childlike, as Jesus spoke about in the Gospels?

Questions for discussion

1. What is the difference between relying on God during lonely times and trying to love God instead of people?

2. What does the Bible say about those who claim to love God but who don't love others?

3. What role do you think belief in God **does** play in fulfilling the human need for love? What role do you think it **should** and **shouldn't** play?

4. What should belief in God be based on?

5. What do people risk by separating God and religion from the rest of their life?

6. How would you describe what a mature religious faith means to you? Explain.

Our love of God is shown in how we relate to other people.

comforting. But there's a difference between finding in God's love the strength to help us get through times of loneliness, and using love of God as a means to escape our responsibilities to reach out in love to others.

Those who say, "I love God," and hate their brothers or sisters, are liars; for those who do not love a brother or sister whom they have seen, cannot love God whom they have not seen.

1 John 4:20

Ideally, belief in God shouldn't be based on an unfulfilled need for human love, but on a desire to be more closely united with, and to acknowledge with praise and gratitude, the Source of all our human loving.

Certainly, there's a place in our hearts and lives that only God can fill. But we shouldn't separate God and religion from the rest of life so that **only** "religion" becomes meaningful or important. To do this is to risk not finding real fulfillment in both life and in our religious faith. It's to miss the whole point of Christianity.

Adult Christian faith, on the other hand, never stops finding and helping to create meaning in life. For faith should give meaning not to just one hour a week, or only rescue us from despair when all else fails. It should consistently enhance all facets of our life. It should become the richest part of life's beauty and meaning—not an alternative for really living it!

"In God's hand"

Read the following true account. Then respond to the questions.

A couple trapped in a snowbound car kept a diary leading up to their deaths, calmly saying of their ordeal: "Here we are, completely and utterly in God's hand!! What better place to be!!"

Jean and Ken . . . ate tummy mints and drank melted frost while waiting for someone to rescue them. No one did. . . .

[While on a sixty-mile auto trip] their car skidded into a snowbank [in the forest. Two months later] their bodies were found by a forest ranger during the spring thaw.

The couple's diary, [was] written by the light of their glove compartment. . . .

After their first 12 hours trapped in the car, [Jean] wrote:

"So many things I want to say. I want you all to enjoy your life and remember what is so dreadful today will be forgotten next year. Please be a family!! And let my grandchildren know that I love them."

The diary goes on to explain how the couple occupied themselves by singing hymns, taking catnaps and quoting Bible verses. She also wrote how they ate [stomach mints], a stick of gum and two teaspoon-sized packets of jelly, and would scrape frost off the windows to drink.

"We began to realize that we were on a road that isn't maintained during the winter. Truly a miracle if anyone comes by. . . . We have no idea what lies ahead . . . so here we are, completely and utterly in God's hand!! What better place to be!!"

. . . [After they met and married] the couple began years of charitable work. . . . [After four days in the snowbank] the diary said: "We're wondering if anybody has missed us yet. We thought maybe there would be helicopters or snowmobiles out looking."

A week later [Jean] wrote: "A drink of water for me will never go unappreciated again. And a bite of food— any kind. . . . Today is the first day that I have noticed any weakness. I love you all. . . ."

By [the 18th] day, her husband had died:

"Dad went to the Lord at 7:30 this evening. . . . It was so peaceful I didn't even know he left. The last thing I heard him say was 'Thank the Lord.' I think I'll be with him soon. . . . So much to say and so little time. I can't see. Bye. I love you.[3]

Questions for discussion

1. From their diary, what did you learn about this couple? About their relationship with God?

2. How did they respond to their ordeal? To the realization that they would die?

3. How do you imagine you would respond in the same situation? Why? Why do you think this couple responded the way they did?

4. How would you describe the faith this couple seemed to have—crisis-oriented or a more mature kind of faith? Explain.

1. When you were a small child, whom did you believe in most? Why?

2. What are some of the things you were told as a child that you have now begun to question seriously? Why?

3. Why is the transfer of belief from others' judgment to your own both desirable and necessary in developing real faith?

4. Why do you think some persons seem afraid to critically examine and question their childhood beliefs?

5. What can happen if wrong and harmful childhood beliefs go unchallenged? Give examples.

6. Have you come to feel more, or less, disillusioned with the adult world than you felt as a child? Explain.

7. On what should mature religious faith be based? Why?

8. What does believing "from the outside in and from the inside out" mean to you? Why?

9. How do you think that a person can best learn to believe for himself or herself rather than simply because that is what one was taught?

fallibility

ability to make mistakes or to be wrong

Why believe

As a very small child, you probably began your faith life by believing more in your parents and teachers than in God. You believed what they said about God and about religion because you trusted and loved them. At that early age, if you were taught certain ideals and ideas by your parents, then by your teachers, you may have initially accepted them without question. You probably did so because you believed in those who taught them to you.

As a teenager, however, you've probably begun questioning much of what you have been taught. You want to believe in important things because **you** think them right, and not just because someone else tells you to. This is actually one of the stages in developing real faith. You've begun to believe certain ideas and values for their own merits. This transfer of belief from your parents or others to your own judgment is both desirable and necessary if you're to fully grasp and live your convictions.

Unfortunately, some individuals remain too afraid to critically examine and question their childhood beliefs. Once told, perhaps, by parents, teachers, or others not to question, they're now afraid to do so. Consequently, they remain at a childhood level of growth in faith. They continue to believe in others not in addition to, but instead of in themselves.

These persons never really learn how to examine matters of faith and conscience for themselves with God's help. They simply accept what they've been taught from childhood, not because they're now convinced of it, too, but just because it's what they were taught. (Unfortunately, this also includes the wrong and harmful beliefs many learned in childhood, which also go unchallenged!)

By now you've begun to see more clearly the faults and flaws, the **fallibility,** of certain childhood role models whom you once thought could hardly say, do, and believe any wrong. Maybe you've become disillusioned enough with their imperfections to feel like automatically rejecting everything they taught you. This childish reaction, though, bypasses the opportunity to weigh on their own merits the truly good ideals and beliefs you may have learned in childhood. By responding that way, you rob yourself of the chance to believe personally in many things which could increase your life's happiness.

> *". . . by hearing the message of salvation the whole world may believe; by believing, it may hope; and by hoping, it may love."*
> —*"Dogmatic Constitution on Divine Revelation,"* 1.

Mature religious faith isn't based mainly on need or unthinking acceptance of one's upbringing. But what is the best reason for believing in God? First, you should understand what the belief means and involves. To do this, listen to what you have been taught, listen to your heart and your own experiences, and ask God's help. Then, perhaps after weighing other alternatives, freely choose to believe in God because you find it's the most life-enhancing possibility of all.

In other words, believe because you find from the outside in, and from the inside out, that this makes sense to you intellectually, personally, and spiritually. Believe because you're convinced it's true. Believe because you're willing to rely on God's promise that it will give you the opportunity to live the most meaningful, happy life possible, and allow you to help others do the same. Believe in God because, more than anyone, God is worthy of your trust. 🦋

Belief in God is a choice and a gift.

Firmly believing

The LORD your God you shall follow, him alone you shall fear, his commandments you shall keep, his voice you shall obey, him you shall serve, and to him you shall hold fast.

Deuteronomy 13:4

Belief in God won't cancel all doubt and uncertainty. (Even those who believe there is no God at times question their unbeliefs!) To choose belief in God is to say that you're willing to live with the questions and confront the doubts, because the risk of believing will make your life far more meaningful and worth living:

. . . these are the ones who, when they hear the word, hold it fast in an honest and good heart, and bear fruit with patient endurance.

Luke 8:15

What about when problems seem to overwhelm you and you're tempted to give up on believing in yourself, in life, or in God? Belief in God certainly won't promise you a life free of troubles. At such times, though, you can look to the example of Jesus' mother, Mary, who believed that "nothing will be impossible with God" (Luke 1:37). And by "looking to Jesus the pioneer and perfecter of our faith, who for the sake of the joy that was set before him endured the cross, disregarding its shame" (Hebrews 12:2).

At such times,

. . . hold fast to the LORD your God, as you have done to this day.

Joshua 23:8

. . . hold fast to the mystery of the faith with a clear conscience.

1 Timothy 3:9

Let us hold fast to the confession of our hope without wavering, for he who has promised is faithful.

Hebrews 10:23

Finally, as with loving, there are various degrees of believing. It is a lifelong process of striving to proceed from the childish to the adult, from crisis faith to real commitment in a relationship with God. But remember that, ultimately, it's what and who you choose to believe in, and how deeply, that will determine what your life really means. 🍂

🍂 Questions for discussion

1. Why doesn't belief in God cancel all doubt and uncertainty? Why doesn't it guarantee a trouble-free life?

2. At what times are you most tempted to give up on believing in yourself? In the brighter possibilities of life? In God?

3. How do you usually respond when these beliefs of yours are challenged? What helps you most to overcome your doubts and hold fast to your beliefs?

4. How were the faith of Mary and of Jesus challenged? How did each respond?

5. Of the people you know or have heard about, whose example most inspires you to hold on to and to live what you believe in? Why?

Why do you believe in God?

A newspaper surveyed three teenagers and four adults about belief in God. The question they were asked was, "Do you believe in God? Why?"[4] Read each answer, and then respond to the questions below.

1. **Teenager (age 18)**

   "I believe in God. I guess because I'm here, and if God didn't exist, we wouldn't be here."

2. **Adult (age 20)**

   "I believe in God. If there wasn't a God, how would everything have gotten here? If you read the Bible, it really does relate to everyday life."

3. **Adult (age 74)**

   "I believe in God. Who else would have put us here on this Earth?"

4. **Adult (age 51)**

   "I don't believe in God. I feel that there's an order to our universe. Some people may call it God. I feel that it's just an evolution, and we are just an evolution."

5. **Teenager (age 16)**

   "Yes. I was brought up that way. I believe from going to church and being taught that way."

6. **Teenager (age 15)**

   "Yes. You just know [God's] there because you're here."

7. **Adult (age 38)**

   "Yes, because we all need something to believe in, and what better greatness than God?"

Questions for discussion

1. What types of reasons did these individuals have for believing in God? On what did each person seem to base his or her belief?

2. What similarities and differences were there between the adults' and the teenagers' responses? What reasons do you think most people really have for believing in God? Should ideally have?

3. How did those interviewed seem to interpret "believe in God"? How did their responses compare with what this chapter has said belief **in** God should mean?

4. How would you have answered the interviewer's questions? Why?

Every time I hear a newborn baby cry, or touch a leaf, or see the sky, then I know why I believe.
— From the song "I Believe."

Chapter review

1. I believe

- In what sense is faith in people or in God risky? What risks are involved?
- What two things are necessary to believe?
- Why is Abraham called "the ancestor of all who believe"?
- Why does the surrendering of trust make belief so special and meaningful? Why is the ability to believe a gift from God?

2. Having a relationship with God

- Why is believing that God exists only the beginning of faith? What is even more important? Why?
- Why should belief in God be a relationship? What should this relationship involve?

3. What is faith?

- Regarding God and religion, what is a "believer"? Who is truly a non-believer? Why?
- What is the relationship between faith and knowledge? What can we know about God from our ability to reason logically? What else is necessary for us to know God more?

4. Intelligent faith

- Why and how should religious faith be intelligent?
- Why is faith more meaningful and valuable when it ultimately involves mystery?
- In what sense is faith in God an experience? How can human experience be valuable to faith in God?

5. The need for faith

- What does it mean—and not mean—to say that faith is necessary for salvation?
- What is crisis-oriented faith? Why does it tend to be superficial?
- What is mature faith, what should it be based on, and what part should it play in one's life?

6. Why believe

- How does a person's religious faith usually develop from early childhood on? Are there degrees of faith?
- Why is it necessary to examine one's faith?
- What are the better reasons to have for believing in God?
- Why doesn't belief in God cancel doubt or lead to a problem-free life? What is the best response to challenges to one's faith in God?

Projects and assignments

Write a one-page paper, or at least a twenty-line song or poem about one of the following topics (and, if you want, you may use humor and/or satire to convey a serious point):

- The risk of believing in people and in God
- The experience of believing in people and in God
- My relationship with God
- Intelligent and unintelligent faith
- Faith as a way of knowing

- How you experience God
- "Battlefield belief"
- Mature faith
- Reasons for belief
- Facing things that challenge belief

Chapter 4

Religion— *"We Believe"*

May the God of hope fill you with all joy and peace in believing, so that you may abound in hope by the power of the Holy Spirit.

Romans 15:13

Be with us always, loving God.
Light our darkness,
and help the bonds of faith we share with others to grow.

Strengthen our weakness,
and help us not to give up on ourselves or on You,
especially when people try to give either of us a bad name.

Comfort us and give us strength to meet life's challenges.
Safeguard our freedoms—especially the freedom
to practice what our belief in You means.
Help us stay close to You,
and help us grow closer to each other.

Overview questions

1. What is the purpose of religion? Of organized religion?

2. What does it mean for Catholics to say, "we believe"?

3. What did Jesus say about religious hypocrisy and about what real religion should involve?

4. What does the Catholic Church teach about religious freedom?

5. Why must religious faith be a free, personal choice? What factors can inhibit people from making this choice?

6. What is the difference between relying on and expressing one's faith in positive, healthy ways, and doing so in unhealthy ways?

7. What are religious cults? Why are they harmful and dangerous?

What is the purpose of religion?

The word *religion* comes from Latin words meaning to "re-link." Humanity has always understood that religion is supposed to help re-link people with God. But Jesus taught us that genuine religion is also supposed to help us reconcile and reunite with one another.

It's supposed to help us build a better world where, as God's children, we live in harmony together.

But does this second goal seem impractical and unreachable to you? Do you think religion is probably irrelevant to resolving some of the world's toughest problems?

That's not the way former U.S. President Jimmy Carter described it from his experience. He told how the religious beliefs shared by the leaders of three countries were a key element in successfully negotiating the peace treaty that was the high point of his presidency—even though each of the three leaders belonged to a different religion! He has also said that "even atheist leaders he dealt with" from other countries "regularly drew him aside to talk privately about religion."[1]

Although it rarely gets the publicity it deserves, the positive role religion plays throughout the world as a source of hope and goodness shouldn't be overlooked or underestimated!

Real religion

Jesus taught that religion isn't meant to be just lip-service to beliefs that are rarely or never put into practice. It's meant to be lived—every day. Rather than being empty rituals, your religious observances should express what you find truest and most meaningful about God, yourself, other people, and the world. The command to love God and others as ourselves is at the heart of Jesus' teaching:

> ". . . 'you shall love the Lord your God with all your heart, and with all your soul, and with all your mind, and with all your strength. . . . You shall love your neighbor as yourself.' There is no other commandment greater than these."
>
> *Mark 12:30, 31*

Jesus, in fact, agreed that

> ". . . 'to love him with all the heart, and with all the understanding, and with all the strength,' and 'to love one's neighbor as oneself,'—this is much more important than all whole burnt offerings and sacrifices."
>
> *Mark 12:33*

People are sometimes afraid, though, that being religious means they will have to become a type of person they don't want to be. They think being truly religious is probably too demanding and too difficult—that it means they'll be less happy and have to give up all the things that make life enjoyable and worth living.

On the contrary, genuine religion makes life happier. In fact, studies at major universities have consistently shown that older persons who are active in their religious faith rate relatively high in life satisfaction. When they near the end of their lives, people seem to realize the positive difference religion has made in them. Many researchers are now puzzling over why it is that people actively involved in their religion are also likely to be healthier overall. Some connect this with the more positive attitude they find among practicing believers.

In any event, God doesn't want us to be grudging, miserable believers, and it seems that most religious believers are actually more, not less, happy because of their religious beliefs. Jesus said the point of his teaching was to bring us real happiness:

> "I have said these things to you so that my joy may be in you, and that your joy may be complete."
>
> *John 15:11*

As Jesus also taught, and showed us by example, the one who is truly religious in God's eyes is to actively care for other people and help those in need:

> Then he said to them, "Is it lawful to do good or to do harm on the sabbath, to save life or to kill?" But they were silent. He looked around at them with anger; he was grieved at their hardness of heart and said to the man, "Stretch out your hand." He stretched it out, and his hand was restored.
>
> *Mark 3:4–5*

If you can't find your ultimate happiness in truly loving, where on earth do you expect you'll ever find it? Religion shouldn't provide an escape from having to be an alive, involved human being who is concerned about this world. Christianity is meant to make one more, not less, committed to people and to the world's goodness.

Questions for discussion

1. How does the meaning of the word *religion* explain the purpose of religion? What positive role does religion play in the world?

2. What kind of hardness of heart made Jesus angry?

3. What did Jesus say real religion involves? How did he show this by his example?

4. Why shouldn't religion be viewed as a way to escape the concerns of this world so long as one cares about "heavenly" things?

5. When people shy away from religious commitment because they think it will make unreasonable demands of them, what might they really fear? Do you think any of their fears are justified? Explain.

6. How would you hope that persons' religious beliefs would change their lives? How has religion affected your life? Explain.

7. Why belong to an organized religion rather than just praying, believing, and practicing one's faith individually?

8. What does "we believe" mean for a Catholic? Explain.

The prophet Micah summed up the requirements of religion this way:

> . . . and what does the LORD require of you
>
> but to do justice, and to love kindness,
>
> and to walk humbly with your God. . . .
>
> *Micah 6:8*

And in case anyone hadn't gotten the point, the apostle James put it quite bluntly:

> Do you want to be shown, you senseless person, that faith apart from works is barren?
>
> *James 2:20*

Religion can help you change your life in many good ways. This doesn't mean that you have to become somebody you don't want to be. It means that who you are gets even better, that you realize more possibilities than ever for being a happier, better person.

"We believe"

Why belong to an organized religion? Why not just pray and believe privately, and practice your faith only as an individual?

Religion isn't meant to just be a private matter "between me and God." We don't live alone, nor are we meant to believe alone. You have some of your most treasured beliefs because others have cared enough to transmit them to you by word and example. What you believe just as surely affects others.

One of the most important purposes of the Christian religion is to ultimately draw all humanity together as Jesus prayed:

> ". . . that they may all be one. As you, Father, are in me and I am in you. . . ."
>
> *John 17:21*

To set the example for and help bring this unity about, Christians must first of all come together as a Church to share, celebrate, and live their faith. In fact, national polls show that the majority of people seem to recognize religion's value in bringing about peace and building community. Religion is consistently the institution in which people say they have most confidence. Both the average citizen and political and social experts now say they view religion as the most effective instrument for helping to solve major community problems such as crime, violence, poverty, and homelessness. Some historians and sociologists think religion might be the only "social glue" strong enough to hold together the diversity in our society.

Religion should be our steering wheel, not our spare tire.
—Charles L. Wheeler

Organized religion gives individuals an opportunity to share and help one another grow in, live, and celebrate their most important beliefs. When people unite to share and live common religious ideals, together they really do change the world.

Despite all the differences of language, politics, and culture, Catholics throughout the world believe together in one faith. The Catholic in the United States or Canada holds the same religious beliefs as the Catholic in South Africa or India or Europe. This faith involves a personal commitment to all God has revealed, as contained in the Scriptures and passed down to us by the Church throughout the centuries.

We believe that these convictions are true primarily because we believe in God who has revealed them to us. We are grateful for our faith, recognizing that it's a special gift from God, to which, with the help of God's Spirit, we're asked to freely respond. Through the faith of the whole Church, of Catholics together everywhere, our own individual faith is kept alive and nourished. But we also believe that our faith only reflects the fuller and more wonderful way we will one day know and experience God forever.

Hypocrisy and lack of charity are failings of teenagers, as well as of adults.

Religious hypocrisy

Teenagers are often most bothered by the **hypocrisy** and lack of charity sometimes seen in so-called "religious" individuals. Well, that should bother you! It's one of the things that bothered Jesus the most, too. He condemned the behavior of those who deliberately acted superior to or deceived others, or behaved selfishly or unkindly in the name of religion. But it's not fair to judge religion's merits by those who fail to live its ideals, instead of by those who succeed!

It's especially maddening to see various groups of religious believers being intolerant and violent toward one another throughout the world—for what they claim are religious reasons. Most of the world's armed conflicts now are being waged in the name of religion—something which leaders from all the world's major religions jointly condemn. Most of the time, it's actually the long-standing, deep-seated political differences between groups which are the real root of the problem. Religious affiliation is just a convenient way to identify cultural and political groups. Religion is the excuse and tool used to promote a one-sided political viewpoint, instead of the bridge it is meant to be linking all people together.

You also need to realize that people aren't perfect. We all make mistakes and do wrong at times. But it's foolish to give up on Christianity, for instance, just because some Christians fail quite miserably at practicing what Jesus preached. Instead of focusing on others' bad examples, it's much better to set a good one ourselves.

"Crime in the name of religion is the greatest crime against religion."
—*A joint declaration of Orthodox, Roman Catholic, and Muslim religious leaders in a war-torn area.*

So learn from others' errors. Don't let them disillusion you about the true meaning and role of religion. Take heart from the examples of dedicated religious believers like Mohandas (Mahatma) Gandhi, Martin Luther King, Jr., and Mother Teresa, who have inspired and changed the world for the better by genuinely living their religious beliefs. ⁊

hypocrisy

knowingly acting the opposite of what one says one believes or represents

⁊ Questions for discussion

1. How would you describe what religious hypocrisy is?

2. What's the difference between not always practicing what you believe in, and not "practicing what you preach"? When does the latter amount to religious hypocrisy?

3. Why isn't it fair to judge religion's merits by those who fail to live its ideals?

4. What was Jesus' response to religious hypocrisy?

5. What examples of religious hypocrisy bother you the most? Why?

6. How does the bad example of religious believers affect others? How does it affect you? Explain.

7. What do you think is the best way to respond to religious hypocrisy?

How does religion influence your life?

A major life insurance company conducted a nationwide survey about people's basic beliefs and values in our society. Part of the survey dealt directly with how religion actually influences people's lives. This self-test is based on the survey's questions. Complete it by answering each question as your instructor directs you. Your responses will remain anonymous, unless you volunteer to discuss them. When you have finished, you will have the opportunity to compare your responses with the national poll results.[2]

1. Would you consider yourself to be
   a. a very religious person
   b. a somewhat religious person
   c. not religious at all
2. Are you interested in learning more about your religious faith and encouraging others to turn to religion?
3. Do you pray fairly often?
4. Have your religious beliefs changed your life in any way?
5. Do you voluntarily participate in religious services regularly?
6. Do you try to live your religious faith in your daily life?
7. Do you plan, by whatever job or career you choose in the future, to help people in some way?
8. Do you find your present life interesting?
9. Are you generally satisfied with your family, social, and other relationships?
10. Do you strongly believe in reconciling with others when you have disagreements or difficulties with them?
11. Do you frequently volunteer to give of your time and energies to help others?
12. Do you usually vote in school elections?
13. Do you feel as if you are able to have a significant influence on
    a. your school community
    b. your community of close friends
    c. your family life
14. Despite the difficulties and disappointments which occur in your life, are you happy?
15. Do you think people who try to develop a closer relationship with God are
    a. more likely to live by the values contained in the Bible
    b. less likely to live by the values contained in the Bible
16. Do you think people who are deeply and sincerely religious tend to be
    a. happier than people who are less religious
    b. less happy than people who are less religious
17. Do you think living your religious beliefs makes you
    a. less successful in life
    b. more successful in life
18. Do you personally believe becoming more religious would
    a. bring you greater personal happiness
    b. bring you less happiness

Faith is a free act.

Free to believe

The following statements adapted from the "Declaration on Religious Freedom" represent the Catholic Church's position about religious freedom.[3] Read them and respond to the questions.

1. It is one of the major beliefs of Catholic doctrine that humanity's response to God in faith must be free.

2. Therefore no one is to be forced to embrace the Christian faith against the person's own will.

3. This doctrine is contained in the Word of God and it was constantly proclaimed by the Fathers of the Church.

4. The act of faith is of its very nature a free act.

5. Humanity, redeemed by Christ the Savior and through Christ Jesus called to be God's adopted child, cannot agree with and support God's self-revelation unless God draw the person to offer to God the reasonable and free submission of faith.

6. It is therefore completely in accord with the nature of faith that in religious matters every manner of forcing people should be excluded.

7. As a result, the principle of religious freedom significantly contributes to creating an environment in which people can without obstacles be invited to Christian faith, and embrace it of their own free will, and profess it effectively in their whole way of living.

Questions for discussion

1. How important for Catholics is belief in religious freedom?

2. What does this belief in religious freedom mean and include? On what is it based?

3. What is first necessary before a person can believe in God?

4. What does the Church say should be excluded in religious matters? Give examples of what you think this might mean.

5. What kind of environment does the principle of religious freedom help create for Christians?

Religious freedom

Religious freedom and personal choice

Guilt, fear, and religious freedom

There are many reasons why people believe religious convictions. Some do so because that's what they were taught. Others believe because to them it makes sense, and because they experience the truths of these convictions in their life. Some believe out of a sense of obligation—because they'd feel guilty if they didn't. Others are afraid to hurt their families by disagreeing with the beliefs they were brought up with. Let's look further at some of these reasons, and see which are the soundest ones for believing in God.

We all notice how commonly advertising appeals to people's guilt, fears, and insecurity. Ads try to convince us to become "believers" in a product by making us feel guilty or fearful in some way if we don't buy it. You won't smell good if you don't use Doozy Deodorant, or be as popular if you don't drink Sipsy Soda, or as attractive if you don't wear Snappy Sneakers or Jazzy Jeans. You'll let a major phone company down if you don't remain its "loyal" customer (no matter that its prices are higher than the competition's).

Advertisers know very well that most people don't try a new product because they've carefully examined their need for it, the alternatives available, and the product's actual effectiveness. Rather, they're often motivated to buy it because they've subconsciously been made to feel guilty, insecure, or fearful without it.

To be fair, research indicates that it's not religion that causes the underlying guilt for most persons with depression and anxiety disorders. In fact, more psychiatrists are discovering that, contrary to what they've expected, those who suffer from major anxiety and depression disorders are among the least likely of their patients to be religious.

As do the ads, however, some religious preachers appeal to the underlying guilt people experience for other reasons. These preachers urge people to be afraid of God and to fear what will happen to them if they're not. Guilt and fear are used to motivate people to jump on the "believers" bandwagon. Contradictory as it seems, some people are scared into believing, whether they believe or not!

Some televangelists boldly appeal to their listeners' fear, guilt, and vulnerability in order to increase their number of "converts"—not to mention, of course, their own financial profits! One preacher, for instance, claimed Jesus had been talking to him for weeks, telling him to ask each viewer for a few hundred dollars—in exchange for which Jesus would show them "spectacular" exhibits of his miraculous power. Another preacher recently told his TV audience that "it's when you don't have any money to give that God wants you to give it the most." Then, while the preacher continues to live his well-known luxurious lifestyle, the poor contributor is to live and feed a family on faith alone?

Jesus did not preach a religion based on guilt or fear (and certainly not on one's ability to donate money!), but on forgiveness and love. He even forgave those who put him to death in the name of what they thought was right. As the Scriptures point out, fear and appeals to fear are signs of a lack of Christian love.

Faith—a free, personal choice

Sometimes people mistakenly think that being a Catholic Christian means being expected to give up one's **conscience** and only obey the dictates of a religious leader or a code of religious

---

You can force someone to enter a church . . .but you cannot force someone to believe.
—*St. Augustine*

conscience

the ability of persons to determine right from wrong

conduct. In fact, the Church strongly teaches that individuals should **never** be asked to violate their conscience—but to see that it's properly informed and guided so that it's not in error.

Ultimately, your religious beliefs must be your free, personal choice. (Isn't it impossible anyway to believe what you don't believe?) But faith develops in stages, not all at once. At this point in your life, you're hopefully moving from believing things because that's what you were taught to believing them because you're convinced for yourself that they're the truth. You must make your own eventual choices about religious belief.

Even though you might be a pretty independent thinker by now, it's still difficult for people to arrive at personal life convictions of any kind until they've lived on their own for a period of time. So you might not be ready to make a fully adult commitment to your religious beliefs until you're no longer so closely guided or influenced by others at home or at school.

In time you might come to realize that your deepest religious convictions are different from what you were raised to believe. Not long after the old Soviet Union collapsed, its former foreign minister was baptized a Christian. He explained that he had long ago begun to question his previous belief that God did not exist. He said deciding to become a Christian came after "a long process of reflection" about the world and about himself.

Or (as so often happens) you might find yourself deeply convinced of everything you were taught—even though for a time you might have thought you disagreed. But eventually your religious beliefs must become your own. You must honestly believe and freely choose them.

Whatever you ultimately choose to believe about God and religion—about the ultimate meaning and destiny of your whole life—believe it and act accordingly with all your heart and soul. For in these beliefs will lie the way you live and shape your life, and the happiness you find.

> *There is no fear in love, but perfect love casts out fear; for fear has to do with punishment, and whoever fears has not reached perfection in love.*
> *—1 John 4:18*

Questions for discussion

1. What are some of the reasons people have for their religious beliefs?

2. Give examples of three current advertisements that appeal to guilt or fear to get people to buy a product.

3. Have you heard any type of religious preaching that appeals mainly to guilt or fear? Explain.

4. Have any of your attitudes about religious belief been affected by some kind of guilt or fear? Explain.

5. Why must religious belief ultimately be a free, personal choice?

6. Do you think most people freely choose and are convinced of their religious beliefs, or hold them for some other reason? Explain.

7. What reasons should people have for their religious beliefs? Why?

8. Why is it hard to arrive at personal life convictions until one is living on one's own? At what point do you think you'll be ready to make a fully adult commitment to your religious beliefs? Explain.

A "long process of reflection" should precede any decision concerning religion.

Exploring your faith

As we've seen, pressures to believe all sorts of things out of guilt and fear are quite pronounced in our culture. Due to such influences, some people never do reach the point where their religious faith is truly their own free, personal choice. They let themselves remain at a childhood stage of faith development. So growing from childhood to adult faith requires some honest soul-searching. To help yourself successfully make this important transition, here are some questions and tips you need to think about:

1. What are your religious beliefs, and your attitudes about religion?

   You should, after all, know what you believe, instead of just taking it for granted.

2. How do your religious beliefs affect your life right now, and the ways you act and relate with others?

   You should be aware of how your religious beliefs affect you, and your attitudes, relationships, and behavior.

3. **Why** do you believe what you believe?

   Start with where your religious beliefs came from. Think about what they really mean to you and why they're worth believing now.

4. Is the wrong kind of religious guilt, fear, or other pressure influencing your religious beliefs?

   To some extent, this may be true. If so, don't automatically become the religious rebel, dumping all your beliefs overboard. That's not being sensible. Instead, examine them intelligently, on their own merits and for the real meaning they can have for your life.

5. Do you have any questions or major problems with your religious beliefs?

   If so, seek the advice of someone you trust who is knowledgeable in your religious faith. Also ask God's help to see the truth more clearly and to believe in it more firmly.

6. Being honest with yourself, what "hardness" is there in your attitude that keeps you from opening your heart more to faith in God—and in other people?

   Try to understand how belief in God can make your life more meaningful and joyful. Seek the truth sincerely, and then know that God will accept your honest response.

Questions for discussion

1. Why is each of these questions and tips important? Which ones seem most important to you? Why?
2. Do you think some teenagers are inclined to be "religious rebels" as described above? Explain.
3. Do you ever feel resentful about the ways you were raised regarding religious belief? Why isn't religious rebellion a sensible response? What is?
4. Do you know anyone who has given up a religion because of how he or she was once treated by a member of that religion? Have you ever had an experience that made you feel negatively about religion? Explain.
5. In what ways do you think religion should make life more meaningful? Has it made your life more meaningful in these ways? Explain.
6. What kind of "hardness" of attitude do you think often keeps people from opening their heart more to belief in God? In other people?

Religious extremes

Comfort, challenge, or "crutch"?

When hurting and helpless, whether emotionally or physically, we naturally rely on something or someone other than ourselves for support until we can make it on our own again. But if we continued depending upon a "crutch" long after we were well, and so failed to develop our own strength, we'd gradually weaken and lose our ability to support ourselves. So it is with religion.

Religion does not relieve us from the duty of thought; it makes it possible for [us] to begin thinking.
—G.A. Studdert-Kennedy

People certainly do find that their religious beliefs help relieve some of the pain and pointlessness of life's miseries. Belief in God often gives us the strength to make it through some of life's most difficult times. Without their faith convictions, many people say they wouldn't have had the strength or courage to cope. Relying on God this way isn't unhealthy at all. It's normal and reasonable.

But religion can be an unhealthy "crutch" if individuals use it to keep from developing healthy personalities and relationships. Or if they rely on God for help while doing nothing to help themselves (or others). Indeed, we insult God as well as ourselves if our religion inhibits our imagination, creativity, sense of wonder and exploration, or the development of our inner strengths and abilities.

Those who let that happen use religion like a drug. They let it make them **complacent** about life, so that they never explore life's possibilities. They accept everything with a **fatalistic** attitude. Instead of actively trying to solve problems, they just put up with whatever happens as "the **inevitable**" or "God's will."

It has been said that true Christian faith, on the other hand, should "comfort the afflicted, and afflict the comfortable," the "comfortable" being the smugly self-satisfied and lazily complacent. Genuine religious faith should give us support when our inner resources are challenged. But it should also challenge us to use our own energies in striving for a better life and a better world.

The danger of religious cults

Many young persons today are attracted to religious **cults** whose codes of conduct are generally strict and confining. Those who join must surrender their will and freedom to the cult leader, who dictates and guides their lives. Cult members are not to question the leader's intentions and directions, but to view following them as obeying God's will.

Why do these individuals join a cult, while most other teenagers and young adults experience instead a need for more independence and freedom and less control?

Many psychologists conclude that people commit themselves to religious cults out of need. Some have emotionally turbulent backgrounds. They seek inner peace and stability, which they mistakenly believe the cult's rigidly structured religious environment offers them. Amidst life's chaos and confusion, they crave order and security. Some are just very confused about what they want to do with their lives. They find it much easier to let someone else make this decision for them.

---

complacent

content, often in a smug or self-satisfied way

fatalistic

viewing all as predetermined and so unavoidable and unchangeable

inevitable

definite, bound to happen

Questions for discussion

1. What is the difference between relying on God or religion in a healthy way and as an unhealthy kind of crutch? Give examples of each.
2. Have you met people who you think depend upon God or religion in wrong or unhealthy ways? Without mentioning names, explain.
3. In what ways do you rely on God? On your religious beliefs? Explain.
4. What is meant by using religion as a kind of drug?
5. In what sense should true Christian faith "comfort the afflicted and afflict the comfortable"?

cult

an exclusive, extremist religious group which seeks to control or exploit members' thoughts and behavior

---

instability

state of being insecure, not steady, unpredictable

compulsion

feeling of being inwardly forced to act a certain way

holocaust

sacrificial offering among the ancient Hebrews in which the victim offered to God was completely destroyed

Holocaust

the Nazi attempt to exterminate all Jews during World War II

fanaticism

highly unreasonable passion or enthusiasm for something

Many are also attracted to cults out of loneliness. In fact, very often they don't even realize they're becoming involved with a cult. They don't feel loved by family and friends, or they're away from home and lonely at college. And they're easy targets for cult recruiters who dress just like they do, hang out at the same places, and lavish attention on them. Gradually, subtly, the new recruits are pulled into the cult environment. Then, by using psychological pressure, threats, and lies, the cult attempts to isolate them from their families and friends outside the cult.

Surrendering their will to the cult in complete obedience seems to relieve these young persons from the pressures of coping with their problems. At the same time, it appears to provide the "blessing" of religion and of "following God's will." So it doesn't seem like the escape from assuming personal responsibility for one's life which it really is. On the other hand, God's will is for us to "have life, and have it abundantly" (John 10:10)—to be fully alive, not fully programmed or robbed of our freedom.

The tragic consequences of twisting and distorting the idea of "God's will" have been seen clearly in the twentieth century. Unquestioningly, many Nazi soldiers rationalized that they were acting in the name of "God's will" as they obeyed the commands of Adolph Hitler (who also claimed to be following God's will). Their systematic attempt to exterminate the Jewish people in the **Holocaust** and their killing of millions were absolutely opposed to God's will! In the name of religious obedience, hundreds of unquestioning followers of a cult leader committed mass suicide in Guyana. More recently, many members of the Branch Davidian cult armed themselves in a belief that they stood with God against an evil and unfriendly world.

In the broadest sense, the word *cult* may be used to refer to any system of religious worship. But the term is more commonly used today, as it has been used here, to refer to those which are dangerous and harmful. ❧

Religious fanaticism and addiction

Feelings, emotions, are an important part of being human—and a good part. Without emotion we'd be lifeless robots without sparkle, drive, and enthusiasm. We wouldn't feel compassion or affection. But there are people who repress all emotion, and others who let their emotions control their lives.

It isn't always easy to keep an emotional balance, as you know! But it's much harder for individuals who tend to have serious psychological problems and personalities which tend toward extremes. Extreme forms of religious expression attract these individuals who seek either a greater release or a more controlling structure for their emotions. They become as fanatical about religion as they would otherwise have been about something else. Their religious commitment, however, is not due to intelligent conviction, but to inner **instability** or even **compulsion**.

We all have basic needs which must be satisfied—physical needs (for food, basic comfort, health), and emotional and intellectual needs (for security, love, and a purposeful existence). There's nothing wrong with trying to satisfy these needs—we must do so if we're to develop fully as a person and be more able to give to others. But how do you tell religious **fanaticism** from the authentically radical way of witnessing to the gospel that has characterized some of the saints' lives?

Fanaticism remains stuck only at the need level. It doesn't move beyond that to making well-reasoned, mature choices about love relationships, life decisions, and religious beliefs. Religious fanaticism is need-centered in unhealthy ways which stifle human growth. It replaces Christ with oneself as the one who "saves" everybody—but by promoting fear and shame, rather than the love, gentleness, and real justice Jesus preached. It actually uses religion to justify one's own contempt for and abuse of others.

A great many people, however, find that turning to God and to religion is the key which enables them to kick an alcohol **addiction,** another drug addiction, or another type of addictive behavior. The rest of us should understand why these courageous individuals may need, for a time, to be rigid about relying on religion while they try to achieve greater independence and self-control in their lives. In fact, a standard step in the most successful recovery programs involves recognizing the role of a "higher power" in one's life, rather than relying only on oneself.

Some individuals, however, become psychologically addicted to religion in an unhealthy, compulsive way. They expect that religion will control every aspect of their life. Religion itself becomes a drug-like substitute on which they become so totally dependent that they can't make truly free choices of their own.

On the other hand, an emotionally healthy person believes religious convictions out of personal **choice** and not primarily in order to satisfy basic psychological needs. This person can truly say, "I believe because I freely choose to believe." Current research in psychology recognizes that this type of religious belief is good for people's mental health. It helps people to resist doing wrong and to order their priorities so that they focus more on what really matters in life. In fact, the noted authority C.G. Jung once said this:

During the past thirty years, people from all civilized countries on the earth have consulted me. Among all my patients in the second half of life—that is to say, over thirty-five—there has not been one whose problem in the last resort was not that of finding a religious outlook on life. It is safe to say that every one of them fell ill because he [or she] had lost that which the living religions of every age have given to their followers, and none of them has been really healed who did not regain [his or her] religious outlook.

Genuine religious **conversion** leads people to become kinder and easier for others to relate to. They do more good for others. False "conversions," however, lead people to become more intolerant of other people and religions, less kind and just. It's often harder for good and loving friends and relatives to live with and relate to them. Although such persons may be quite sincere about their convictions, the real nature of their faith is shown by its results. For, as Jesus said:

You will know them by their fruits. Are grapes gathered from thorns, or figs from thistles?

Matthew 7:16

Remember this: The sign of genuine Christian faith is that, in genuine ways, it helps us grow closer in love to God—and to others. 🙠

addiction

a habit which is very difficult to overcome

conversion

change of heart and mind; in the Christian sense, an inner change of attitude leading to a total change of one's life to love of God and neighbor

🙠 Questions for discussion

1. What is meant by repressing emotions? Keeping a healthy emotional balance? Letting emotions control one's life?

2. Why are some types of individuals more attracted to extreme forms of religious expression? What is a fanatical religious commitment really based on?

3. What needs does everybody have? Why must these needs be met? What role does religion play in helping to fulfill these needs? What role **should** it play?

4. How can you tell religious fanaticism from authentically radical ways of witnessing to the gospel? Have you ever encountered religious fanaticism? Explain.

5. How has turning to God and religion helped persons overcome an addiction? Why? Do you know anyone for whom this is true?

6. Why may some individuals in recovery at first be rigid about religion? How can our understanding this help them?

7. What is an emotionally healthy approach to religious belief? Why is it good for one's mental as well as spiritual health?

8. What, according to Jesus, is the sign of genuine religious faith? Of genuine and false conversions?

Letter from jail

Going to extremes because of one's religious convictions is not always unhealthy or harmful. Sometimes the Christian understands that it is necessary. Jesus' own views and behavior were considered radical and revolutionary at the time. But this is certainly different from an ignorant, intolerant religious fanaticism!

In 1963, the Reverend Martin Luther King Jr. was jailed for leading and encouraging nonviolent protests against racial discrimination. From his jail cell in Birmingham, Alabama, Dr. King wrote a letter to a group of religious leaders who had called for an end to these nonviolent protests. In the letter, he explained his reasons for having disobeyed the civil laws in order to peacefully pursue the cause of civil rights. The following views are based on the reasons he gave for his nonviolent actions against injustice. Read them and respond to the questions.

- The biblical prophets spread God's word against injustice far and wide. Paul traveled through large parts of the Greco-Roman world preaching the radical message of Jesus. At times we too must be willing to leave our comfortable little world to respond to calls for help. Dr. King referred to this as "the gospel of freedom."

- All persons are connected. We can't uncaringly sit back and do nothing when injustice is happening somewhere else. Injustice in one place threatens justice everywhere. Our mutual bond is "a single garment of destiny." What happens to one person influences and affects everyone.

- Rather than being satisfied with a superficial view of social problems, we must address the causes that underlie the problems.

- Dr. King suggested that people actively and nonviolently oppose injustice in a systematic way:

  1. Gather the facts to clarify the injustice.

  2. Try to arrive at a peaceful, mutually agreeable solution to the problem(s).

  3. Weed out the faults in ourselves that we oppose in others. This will give people the moral strength to determine the right way to eliminate injustices.

  4. Actively do what we can to oppose the injustices and to help eliminate the causes. The chosen course of action should be wise, appropriate, and nonviolent.

- Those who take part in nonviolent protest for the sake of justice will be considered extremists. Jesus was also thought of by many in these terms, but, according to Dr. King, Jesus was "an extremist for love," which he practiced and preached. The prophet Amos and the apostle Paul are other important examples from Scripture. King also mentioned Abraham Lincoln and Thomas Jefferson from U.S. history as persons who helped to shape and preserve the ideals of democracy, while appearing to many to have extreme views.

In one sense, whenever we take a strong stand on a controversial issue, we can't avoid being seen by others as extremist. The important thing is to be the right kind of extremists: people whose intentions and actions promote justice and love rather than injustice and hate.

Questions for discussion

1. Why was Rev. King in jail? Why had he come to Birmingham?

2. What does it mean to say that all people are connected, bonded "in a single garment of destiny"?

3. What do you think some of the religious leaders were ignoring in the Christian message when they called for an end to the nonviolent demonstrations?

4. What famous "extremists" did Dr. King mention? How were the views and/or behavior of each one extreme?

5. How would you describe the difference between going to extremes for religious reasons, and being fanatical about it?

6. What four steps are part of a nonviolent campaign? Why is each necessary?

7. What examples can you give today of religious extremism for a worthy cause? Of religious fanaticism?

8. How were Dr. King's position and actions based on his religious beliefs? How are they an example of a healthy approach to religion?

9. Are there any causes today that you'd support an extreme position or action for because of your religious beliefs? Explain.

Chapter review

1. What is the purpose of religion?
- What did Jesus teach about what genuine religion is and should do? How did he show this by example?
- Why isn't religion meant to be just a private matter between the person and God?
- What should the role of organized religion be? Of Christian Churches in particular?
- Explain what saying "we believe" together means for Catholics.
- What positive and practical role does religion appear to play in the world? In individuals' lives?
- What is religious hypocrisy, and how did Jesus respond to it? What is the best way for us to respond to it?

2. Religious freedom
- What does the Catholic Church teach about religious freedom? How important to the Catholic faith is this teaching?
- How are appeals to guilt and fear part of our culture? How can they harm religious freedom?
- What do the Scriptures say fear is a sign of? What do they say Jesus' teaching is based on?
- Why must an individual's religious faith be a free, personal choice?
- Explain the childhood, the transition, and the adult stages of faith development.
- Why is what you believe about God and religion so important for your life?

3. Religious extremes
- Explain the differences between the comfort and challenge of an emotionally healthy faith and an emotionally unhealthy approach to religious belief.
- What does genuine Christian faith involve, and how does it differ from false experiences of religious "conversion"?
- What are religious cults? Why are they harmful, dangerous, and in opposition to what Scripture says God's will is?
- What good role should religion play in helping to meet human needs, and what unhealthy role should it not play in trying to do this?
- What is the difference between religious fanaticism, and authentically radical ways of witnessing to the gospel?

Projects and assignments

1. Write a one-page paper explaining how you would respond if someone said to you, "People just believe in God and religion because they **need** to, not because they **want** to."
2. Jonathan Swift once wrote the "Tale of a Tub" as a satire on what he thought were religious excesses. Write a one-page satirical essay, song, or poem of your own about religious hypocrisy, religious excesses, or false religious "conversion."
3. Watch a television show about a religious topic. Write a one-page paper analysis of its content based on what was discussed in this chapter about genuine and healthy approaches to Christian faith, and about religious hypocrisy and excesses and unhealthy approaches to religion.
4. Bring to class examples of advertisements which appeal to guilt or fear to sell products that teenagers buy. Write a one-page paper describing how the ads do this. Prepare an oral report.
5. Write a one-page essay on the positive role religion plays in today's world.
6. Conduct one of the following interviews. Record or videotape the responses and play a five-minute segment of these for the class. Write a paragraph, or videotape a segment, adding your own responses in view of the concepts discussed in this chapter:
   - A college chaplain about the methods cults use to lure college students to join them
   - Someone who has successfully kicked a drug habit about the role God or religion has played in recovery
   - Someone in your local faith community who has taken an active role in helping the sick or needy about the role their religious beliefs play in what they do
   - Two clergypersons of different faiths about the purpose of organized religion, and the role their religion plays—especially in cooperation with other faiths—in your civic community
7. Write a one-page paper describing your idea of what religion should be in light of what James 1:27 says in the Bible.

Part Two

Professing the Christian Faith

Religious art speaks to the depth of belief.

Chapter 5   God

Belief in God illumines life.

Overview questions

1. What does it mean to believe that God is One, that God is Truth, and that God is personal?

2. What does belief in God as Trinity mean?

3. In what sense is God near to us?

4. What does it mean to say that God is almighty and all-knowing?

5. Does God's omnipotence and omniscience contradict human freedom?

6. What does belief in God as Creator mean?

. . . God is love.

1 John 4:8b

God, by what name should I call You?
How should I think of You?
It's frustrating when people misunderstand what I say or who I am.
Do You ever feel this way?
It wouldn't be surprising—
people have had some pretty strange notions about who You are!

You desire truth in the inward being;
*   therefore teach me wisdom in my secret heart. . . .*
Teach me your way, O LORD,
*   that I may walk in your truth;*
give me an undivided heart to revere your name.

Psalms 51:6 and 86:11

Who is God?

I believe in God. . . .

The Christian creeds start this way, but what do we really mean when we say these words? We've already talked about what belief is, but who or what is God?

We've seen that **believing in** someone involves far more than believing that the person exists. It means trusting and having some kind of relationship with the person. We've also seen that we know about what God is like from Revelation, and that we experience God's reality in other people and in the created universe. But what do these things tell us about **God**?

Many people have ideas about God which they wouldn't consider at all flattering to themselves! Some people think God is the "Stern Judge" who waits for the chance to pounce on and punish us for the slightest mistake. Others see God as the "Almighty Bookkeeper" who keeps meticulous account of all our faults and who will cancel our account forever if our failings exceed our good deeds. Many still imagine God as an "Old Man," with white hair and a long white beard. Others envision God as a vague Entity or Being somewhere "up there" or "out there." Here's the way one teenager describes how he views God:

As a child I was afraid of God and didn't want to do anything wrong to anger God. As I grew older, I sometimes doubted that there is a God. Sometimes I still wonder if God really cares about me. And sometimes I feel like God cares a lot. But now at least I'm not afraid of God.

I don't really talk to God very much, though, except when I'm in a jam. But as I grow older, I hope to be more serious about God and try to think about God as more important in my life. And I hope to pray to God more to help me understand, so I'll believe in God just a little bit better than I do now.

Like this teenager, you've probably wondered about God, prayed to God, doubted God, trusted God, and somehow loved God since you were small. But who or what exactly is this God of yours? What is God like? Does God really care? Is God really all-powerful? Does God really know everything and, if so, then can we really have a free will or does God then control us? Where is God?

In this chapter we'll talk about these and other questions people often ask about God. Hopefully, the beliefs and insights you discuss here will help you clarify and deepen your own convictions about and relationship with God.

God "quiz"

Complete this activity by following the directions your instructor gives you.

	Column A	Column B	Column C
1	◯	(face with hat)	(face with curly hair)
2	•	?	!
3	△	◯	(spiral with arrow)
4	(smiling face)	(frowning face)	◯

Questions for discussion

1. As a small child, how did you picture God? Where did those ideas come from?

2. Are there any ideas about God that you believed as a child but later found difficult to accept? Explain.

3. What is your idea now of what God is like, and why?

stereotype

categorize without allowing for change, variation, or individuality

vengeful

filled with the desire to seek revenge

Images of God

You know how you hate it when people **stereotype** you or get a false impression of you. Is it important what others think of you? Up to a point, sure it is. Because how they view you affects how they relate to and treat you. You also know that it can be hard to get through to people, to convince them what you're really like. And there are always people who, despite your best efforts to explain and show them, will forever insist on seeing you the way they want to see you.

It's similar with how you view God. What you think God is like is vitally important. It's important first of all to you as you decide what kind of person you want to be. Created in God's image, we're supposed to reflect God's presence in the world. So we must know what God is like. The way you view God is bound to affect what you think of yourself and how you perceive and relate with other people.

... they exchanged the truth about God for a lie. —Romans 1:25

Your personal image of God is also important to society and to the world. The wars influenced by religion which have bloodied history from ancient times until today haven't really been fought over whether or not God exists. People continue the killing because of what they believe God is like and therefore requires of them.

A **vengeful** image of God tends to produce ruthless followers who seek revenge instead of justice. A fearful image of God inspires social climates of unquestioning obedience to cruel leaders. But belief in a forgiving God inspires people to negotiate rather than to annihilate. Belief in a liberating, loving image of God inspires people to seek real justice and freedom based on human dignity and community. These are just some of the implications of the way you view God:

- Is God male or female, and does God have a certain ethnic identity?

  How are you therefore to treat persons of the other gender or of another ethnic background?

- Is God a cold, aloof tyrant or friendly and personal?

  How should you relate to a person—as just another factor in the national economy, or as a human being with valuable gifts to contribute, rights that are to be respected, and needs that must be met?

- Is God spiteful and full of revenge, or merciful and forgiving?

  How should you respond to those who wrong you or society? Should you try to get even and show the same cruelty they dished out, or should you try to understand and improve instead of seeking to destroy?

- Is God strong or weak, and does God really care about you and how you act?

  So how should you respond in life—by standing firmly for certain ideals, or by caving in to pressure or hate-filled feelings?

You see, we tend to treat each other according to the image we have of, and the relationship we have (or don't have) with God. And, yes, the reverse is also true. Unless people have a chance to learn otherwise, they tend to view God according to the way they and/or their cultures view human beings.

≈ Questions for discussion

1. When others stereotype you, how do you feel about it? How do you try to convince them what you're really like? Why do you think some still insist on stereotyping you anyway?

2. Why do you think your personal images and ideas about God are important
   - To your image of yourself
   - To how you perceive and relate with other people
   - To how you respond to social issues and world problems

3. How have your own images of God actually affected each of those three areas?

4. Do you think it's really God some teenagers find it hard to believe in, or some of the ideas and images they have about God? Explain.

5. What images of God have bothered you personally? Why?

When you love you should not say,
"God is in my heart,"
but rather,
"I am in the heart of God." —Kahlil Gibran

Do you believe in a wooden God?

Read the following statement by the famous Russian author, Leo Tolstoy. Then respond to the questions.

If the thought comes to you that everything that you have thought about God is mistaken and that there is no God, do not be dismayed.

It happens to many people.

But do not think that the source of your unbelief is that there is no God.

If you no longer believe in the God in whom you believed before,

this comes from the fact that there was something wrong with your belief,

and you must strive to grasp better that which you call God.

When someone ceases to believe in a wooden God,

this does not mean that there is no God,

but only that the true God is not made of wood.

Questions for discussion

1. What point is Tolstoy making here? Do you think he's right? Explain.
2. What is your idea of a "wooden" concept of God? Explain.
3. What "wooden" concepts of God do you think most often prompt believers in God to doubt? Why?
4. What advice does Tolstoy give for coping with doubts about God? What do you think of his advice and why? What advice would you add?
5. How do you think you can best prevent your own idea of God from becoming "wooden"?

God is One

I believe in one God. . . .
      Nicene Creed

Humans have always believed in divine beings which they worshiped as goddesses or gods and described in human terms. Our earliest ancestors were **polytheists** who worshiped many goddesses or gods. They identified these divine beings as male or female and understood each one to have certain limited roles and powers. Greek, Roman, and Norse mythology, for example, is filled with fascinating tales about the deeds, romances, rivalries, and revenge of these gods and goddesses—and about how they helped people on earth, but also caused them lots of problems!

Some peoples were pantheists who believed that God was nothing more than the sum total of the universe itself:

God is everything, and everything is a piece of God. Many people in the world today still believe in and worship many gods. Others have the more pantheistic view that everything is God to some extent.

But if we're to know who God really is, then who is more qualified to explain God to us than God? Jews and Christians believe that God began revealing this to us gradually through the ancient Hebrews.

At first the Hebrews and their Israelite ancestors were practical monotheists: They believed other gods existed but followed and worshiped only one god. Only much later in Old Testament history did their people become absolute **monotheists,** understanding clearly that, by definition, there can be only one God. The practical monotheism of Israel, which worshiped Yahweh above all other gods, became the absolute monotheism of Judaism:

polytheists

those who believe more than one god exists

monotheism

the belief that only one God exists

❧ Questions for discussion

1. What have you read or heard about the ancient Greek gods and goddesses? About other ancient peoples' beliefs about a god or gods?

2. How did Christians come to believe there is only one God—how did God tell us about who God is?

3. What is the difference between practical monotheism and absolute monotheism? Between pantheism and polytheism?

4. When Moses sought to know God's name, what was God's response? What did this mean?

5. Have you ever had a nickname you didn't like? If so, how do you feel it stereotyped or limited you unfairly?

6. Why is it important not to try to pin God down to only one name? Image? Role? Gender?

I am the LORD, and there is no other;
besides me there is no god.

Isaiah 45:5

Furthermore, God, as the Hebrews came to know, is unique—present to, but not a part of the created universe. Moses is credited with being the historical figure most responsible for bringing God's Revelation about this to the world:

God said to Moses, "I AM WHO I AM." He said further, "Thus you shall say to the Israelites, 'I AM has sent me to you.'"

Exodus 3:14

When Moses asked for God's name, that was God's response. In effect, people shouldn't—can't, in fact—pin God down by identifying God with just one name, image, role, or gender.

Jesus confirmed (see Mark 12:29) the strong belief which today's Christians, Jews, and Muslims share: Only one God exists. Hindus today often believe that all of their other gods are really a part or manifestation of the one God whom they call *Brahman*. Many others have concluded that it makes much more sense to them to believe in one God than in many gods. ❧

". . . the Lord our God, the Lord is one. . . ."
—Deuteronomy 6:4 and Mark 12:29

A burning bush attracted Moses to an encounter with God. Who or what are the burning bushes in your life?

God is Truth

Our ability to reason can tell us that, if God has created us to value truth, and if God is the fullness of perfection, then God must be Truth itself. Furthermore, God's Revelation in Scripture assures us over and over that God is Truth. But why is this important? Because "no lie comes from the truth" (1 John 2:21). So we can believe what God's Revelation in the Scriptures tell us.

I the LORD speak the truth,
I declare what is right.

Isaiah 45:19

God's truth to us is contained particularly in the revelation of God's Son, Jesus:

And we know that the Son of God has come and has given us understanding so that we may know him who is true; and we are in him who is true, in his Son Jesus Christ. He is the true God and eternal life.

1 John 5:20

To follow Jesus, we, too, must be faithful to and "walk in the truth" (see 3 John 1:3):

Jesus answered ". . . For this I was born, and for this I came into the world, to testify to the truth. Everyone who belongs to the truth listens to my voice."

John 18:37

The one thing we need to be able to count on before we can trust people enough to love them, and to believe they'll be faithful and loyal to us, is that they won't lie to us. People probably lie and cheat and steal over money more than anything else. Yet, ironically, even on the back of all U.S. currency are engraved the words "In God we trust"!

Trust is basic to all human relationships. And trust in God is the basis of all other trust. It also give us the confidence that God's promises to us will be kept. We can count on God.

And now, O LORD GOD, you are God, and your words are true, and you have promised this good thing to your servant. . . .

2 Samuel 7:28

Sometimes, it may feel, as it did for the psalmists in the Bible, as if God is the **only** one who can be completely counted on! But when we feel lost, hurt, or afraid, at least we always know that we **can** count on God:

And those who know your name put their trust in you,
for you, O LORD, have not forsaken those who seek you.
. . . when I am afraid,
I put my trust in you.

Psalms 9:10 and 56:3

. . . for I know the one in whom I have put my trust. . . .

2 Timothy 1:12

God is personal

I believe in one God, the Father. . . .

Nicene Creed

Christians believe in a personal God. Not all religions hold this belief. What difference does it make to believe that God is personal, rather than just an impersonal force?

First of all, *impersonal* means "not possessing those qualities essential to the nature of being a person." Such qualities as goodness, fairness, forgiveness, compassion, love, and the ability to reason are essential possibilities for personhood.

To believe God is impersonal would be to say that God lacks the abilities to reason and love. It would be to claim that we're better than God! It would lower God to being mindless and loveless. Certainly no compliment! It would rule out all possibility of a relationship between God and ourselves. For one can relate in a "personal" way only to another who is likewise "personal" in nature.

To say God is personal is quite different from saying God is only or merely **a person,** like a sort of magnified human being. To say God is "person**al**" is

. . . God . . . never lies. . . .
—Titus 1:2

ᵈ✦ **Questions for discussion**

1. Why must God, by definition, be at least better than we are? Why must God therefore be personal?

2. What is the difference between thinking of God as personal and viewing God as just a sort of magnified person?

3. Besides those mentioned in your text, how else did Jesus point out and demonstrate the personal nature of God?

4. Why is it so important that, in addition to being infinite and ultimate, God is also intimate to us?

5. At what moments did you feel the closest to God as a child? At what times do you most feel God's presence in your life now? In what areas of your life do you feel that you fail to appreciate, or perhaps take for granted God's presence in your life?

6. What images in the Bible tell us what God is like?

7. What image would you use to describe your relationship with God at this point in your life? What would you like to improve about your relationship with God? Why?

to say that God possesses—that God indeed **is**—the fullness of the best qualities which can be found in human persons. At the same time, it also lets God be far more.

The Scriptures use images of God as a mother who lovingly cares for her young (see Deuteronomy 32:11, Isaiah 49:15, and Matthew 23:37). God is the loving father who loves and cares for us despite our faults and ingratitude:

> When Israel was a child, I loved him,
>   and out of Egypt I called my son.
> The more I called them,
>   the more they went from me. . . .
> Yet it was I who taught Ephraim to walk,
> I took them up in my arms;
> but they did not know that I healed them.
> I led them with cords of human kindness,
> with bands of love.
> I was to them like those
>   who lift infants to their cheeks.
> I bent down to them and fed them.
>   Hosea 11:1–4

God is certainly no abusive or uncaring parent! So personal is God, that Jesus encouraged us to call God "Father." In fact, the word *abba* which he used for God may actually have been closer in meaning to our word *Daddy*.

Every child has biological parents. But it's a very special gift to have a Mommy or a Daddy in whose lap the child can snuggle and be safe and loved no matter what, without condition. Jesus invited us to a relationship with God that is this close and loving. God, he said, is good, compassionate, merciful, and unconditionally forgiving beyond all measure. God is the loving parent who runs to joyfully embrace the ungrateful son who had run away.

> But while he was still far off, his father saw him and was filled with compassion; he ran and put his arms around him and kissed him.
>
> Luke 15:20 ᵈ✦

Faith is not belief without proof, but trust without reservations. —Elton Trueblood

God is Fullness of Love

It's hard to express in human terms what God is like, and impossible for us to comprehend God fully. But people often have trouble believing not so much in God as in some of the ideas they've heard or learned about God. People commonly rebel against the idea of God as a harsh, authoritarian judge or ruler who's ready and willing to punish ferociously. This God of fear is out to scare us to death so we will behave. Obviously, this completely misunderstands who God really is.

But what about the Old Testament's statements that we should "fear the Lord"? Primarily this didn't mean being afraid of God (that certainly wasn't the prophet Hosea's idea of God as our loving parent!). Rather, it meant that we should be in awe of God—that we should respect the Mystery of the One who is intimately involved in every aspect of our daily lives and destinies.

We should respect God's word and follow God's laws, yes, but not because we're afraid of God. We should do so because it's a way to grow closer to God and others, and because we don't want to damage or sever our relationship with the One who loves us always and most of all.

We must also remember that the Old Testament describes humanity's growth in faith and understanding. So as with all early peoples, fear as we know it did play some part in what the ancient Hebrews believed at first about God and how they felt they were to respond. They gradually had to learn that God wasn't a bloodthirsty tyrant who sought human sacrifice (as many other ancient peoples believed and as some people still do). They eventually came to learn that God is love and mercy.

Some Christians, though, remain stuck at the fear level of the earliest type of Old Testament faith. They, too, think of God as vengeful and are scared of God. Their religion is about how to respond with fear. But this misunderstands the very message which makes one *Christian*. Yet, in the name of Christianity, people have been scared to death of God countless times. No wonder others have a problem believing in such a scary God.

God is essentially a God of love, not a God of fear and revenge—this was Jesus' message. This was why he came. As St. John tells us, "There is no fear in love . . . for fear has to do with punishment, and whoever fears has not reached perfection in love" (see 1 John 4:18). Love only fears hurting, offending, or losing someone one loves. So what we should fear, therefore, is not God, but becoming callous and unloving persons. For, as St. John assures us, "Whoever does not love does not know God, for God is love . . . if we love one another, God lives in us" (see 1 John 4:8 and 12).

God's Son assumed the human nature and condition and, as a man, died for love of us. Such things only a personal God would do. Such is the God of Christian belief. What does it really mean, then, to trust in God? It means having a relationship with God whose care for us is without limit and whose real name and essence is "Love."

Trinity

Is God lonely? Was God lonely before people were created who could love God? No. God is and always was fullness of love. Scripture has revealed to us that God is a Trinity of persons— Father, Son, and Holy Spirit.

Belief in God as Trinity is the key mystery of the Christian faith. Admittedly, however, it's one of the more difficult concepts for people to understand. Theologians throughout the centuries have tried to explain better for people what this means.

Belief in God as Trinity doesn't mean that there are three distinct gods, or "three people in God" the way we think of three human beings! The nature of God is Mystery beyond our imagining. Being limited in intelligence, we can understand only to a certain extent. So we must take God's word for it.

The Scriptures contain many references, in fact, to God as Creator (Father), Redeemer (Son), and as Sustainer of the world (Spirit). Jesus, God's Son, is the invisible God made visible for us. In Jesus' name, God sends the Spirit to guide, comfort, encourage, and empower us to love God and others more.

Our language also limits our ability to describe who God is and how God relates to us. We understand that one solitary person is lonely, that two love each other, but that when their love produces a third person, then the community of their love is complete. To say that God is *three persons in one* is the best we can do in describing God's reality. So we use the word *Trinity* to name God as fullness of love from all eternity. But Father, Son, and Spirit are one and the same God.

In a practical sense, belief in God as Trinity helps us to not limit God's reality. When Christians make the *Sign of the Cross* "In the name of the Father and of the Son and of the Holy Spirit," we are really expressing belief that God is and has always been fullness of love, and that God loves and always has loved fully.

God as Father is the personal and life-giving Creator of the world. To believe that God is Father is to believe that God is love. God's Son has become one of us for our sakes, as humanity's Redeemer. To believe that God is Son is to believe that God loves. And God as Spirit remains ever-present to us as all-embracing, unconditional, empowering Love whom we encounter in all beauty, truth, goodness, and love. To believe that God is Spirit is to believe that God's love always brings and calls forth further life and love. ❧

Questions for discussion

1. Have you come across ideas about God that seem designed to "scare people to death"? That have been somewhat frightening to you, perhaps as a small child? Explain.

2. If someone said each of the following to you because "it's what the Bible says," explain how you would respond, and why:
   - You should "**fear** the Lord's wrath."
   - God will "take vengeance on sinners."

3. Is God or has God ever been lonely? Explain.

4. What does it mean to believe that God is Trinity? Why do Christians sign ourselves in the name of the Trinity?

5. What is the most important belief you have about who God is to you personally? Explain why it's so important to you.

God is found in the middle of our lives.

God is very near

*The LORD is near to all who call on him,
to all who call on him in truth.*
                        Psalm 145:18

We've already seen how the concept of One God was gradually revealed to the Hebrews and their Israelite ancestors. But they also advanced from thinking God was localized in just one place, to understanding that God is always with us everywhere. They began to understand that God is just, compassionate, and desires a mutual, loving relationship with people.

One teenager says, "When I talk to God, I hardly ever refer to God as *God.* I usually call God 'the man upstairs,' or nothing at all." While this teenager may have a close relationship with God, the name he gives to God does seem distant. For some people God is a being who exists "out there" somewhere, not the Reality we experience in everything that is good. Others think God and re-

ligion are irrelevant. Religion, they imagine, consists in observances designed to honor Someone who is out of sight and out of touch.

On the other hand, God is to be found precisely in the middle of what is already most meaningful to our lives. Our religion is the way we live our lives acknowledging and fostering this Meaning—this Goodness and Love whom God is in all fullness. Religious observances should be celebrations of everything our lives mean.

Scripture tells us to "draw near to God" and God "will draw near to you" (see James 4:8). To grow closer to God in a personal way, try to open yourself to discovering God's loving presence. Let it delight and surprise you in a million beautiful, unexpected ways! Learn to let God be God for you. Don't confine your experience of God just to church, or religious celebrations, or praying in a formal way. Try not to limit but to expand your experiences of God's love, presence, and meaning in your life.

*From one ancestor [God] made all nations . . . so that they would search for God and perhaps grope for him and find him—though indeed he is not far from each one of us.
—Acts 17:26–27*

Recognize more clearly, more often, and more gratefully the infinite Beauty that is in, yet goes beyond, the flowers, the sunsets, and the faces of your loved ones. Acknowledge that aspect of ultimate Truth which you perceive when you think and reason. Believe in the everlasting Love which you experience in, and which encompasses, all of your human loving. Let yourself live more in the joy and the wonderful mystery of being loved by Love.

Questions for discussion

1. How did the ancient Hebrews' ideas about where God is change and grow? Do you ever hear people talk of God today in ways that give the impression God is distant from us?

2. According to the Scriptures, where is God to be found?

3. The Hebrews called God *YHWH (Yahweh)*—a sacred name describing God's creative presence among people. What is your personal name for God?

4. What does it mean to "let God be God"? In what ways do you think people commonly fail to do this? In what ways do you not do this?

5. On what occasions have you felt that God seemed especially close to you? At what times did you feel like God was most distant? Explain.

6. What discovery would you say you've made about God this year? Explain.

We do not stand alone

Read the following account of a true incident. Then respond to the questions.

The athletes stand atop podiums, holding medals around their necks and bouquets in their hands. Anthems play and flags rise. They receive the applause of the world.

They do not, however, stand alone. Platform plywood is not the only thing that elevates them. The competitors are literally the tip of an iceberg of human hope and effort. . . .

Underneath the Olympic rings, we've been introduced to some remarkable family circles. . . . Fathers and sons. Mothers and daughters. Husbands and wives. Sisters and brothers. . . . They provide inspiration for this marathon called life.

One of the nicest moments . . . didn't involve a medal. It didn't even involve a final.

On the backstretch of a 400-meter semifinal . . . [one of the athletes] injured his hamstring. His medal hopes were finished; the pack sped away.

[He] grimaced in pain—and struggled on around the oval, though hopelessly far behind. His father . . . climbed out of the stands and joined [his son] on the track.

The son limped along and leaned on the father. The crowd cheered as the two came down the homestretch. Together, they crossed the finish line.[1]

Questions for discussion

1. In what sense is life like the Olympic marathon?
2. What does the author say elevates the Olympic athletes? How does this provide inspiration to others?
3. Why did the author describe as one of the Olympics' "nicest moments" this one which didn't involve a medal?
4. Why do you think the father climbed out of the stands to join his son?
5. How was the athlete finally able to make it across the finish line? Why do you think the crowd cheered, even though the athlete didn't have a chance of winning the race?
6. In what ways is this incident a kind of parable of God's presence to us? Why?

The Almighty

Catholic Christians believe that God is **infinite,** while our **finite** minds are very limited (as you well know if you've ever done poorly on a test!) Yet, we do possess some degree of intelligence and intellectual curiosity. It's therefore natural for us to want to know as much as we can about God. It's "only human" for us to express what little we do know in human words and images.

Scientists tell us that there's not only a good chance that other beings exist in outer space, but that they probably don't look anything like we do. Yet, our more creative science fiction can picture or portray them only by using categories of reality familiar to us. As we conceive them, they almost always have some type of appendages that function as arms or legs (though these might be retractable, or protrude from the creatures' heads). They invariably have some way of "seeing," "hearing," or "knowing." They become "angry." Other categories of being than those familiar to us might exist, but our minds can imagine only combinations of those we've experienced. This is also true of our perceptions of God.

infinite

without end or limitation

finite

having definite limits or boundaries

Questions for discussion

1. What does the belief that God is infinite mean to you? Explain.

2. Why can't our minds ever fully understand God?

3. What dangers are there in too narrowly limiting our human understanding of God? Explain and give examples.

4. How can people let their ideas about God contradict their other religious beliefs? Do any of the ideas you've ever had about God seem to contradict your present religious beliefs? Explain.

5. If God is infinite and ultimate, why does it seem only logical that God must also be intimately present to us?

6. If you were an intelligent inhabitant of outer space, what ideas about God do you think you might have if you were completely ignorant of what we've learned about God through God's Revelation? Do you think we earthlings sometimes take for granted what has been revealed to us about God? Explain.

---

logical contradiction

a statement containing two ideas, each of which cancels the other out, contradicts the other

---

omnipotent

unlimited in power

One danger in doing this, however, is that we too narrowly limit our understanding of God, even in human terms. For example, thinking of God **only** as "out there" limits the scope of God's presence. It prevents us from experiencing God right here, right now. Limited ideas of God can even distort belief so that it contradicts what God has revealed to us in the Scriptures. As we've seen, God as "Angry and Unrelenting Judge" seems to contradict the ever-merciful, forgiving God about whom Jesus spoke.

On the other hand, if God **is** infinite, why shouldn't we feel free to envision and relate to God in whatever way we find most meaningful? In fact, you should feel free to do so as long as you keep these things in mind:

1. Don't let your concept of God become so narrow that it rules out our knowing and experiencing God with greater fullness and in different ways.

2. Don't unwittingly let your ideas of God contradict your basic religious beliefs—which also include what you believe about life and people.

3. Remember that if God is **infinite** and **ultimate,** then God must also be **intimate**—personal and very near to you.

God's power and knowledge, and human freedom

I believe in one God, the Father Almighty. . . .
Nicene Creed

God's omnipotence

The Scriptures call God **Almighty,** or **omnipotent:**

". . . and I will be your father,
and you shall be my sons and daughters,
says the Lord Almighty."
2 Corinthians 6:18

Potent means "power"; *impotent* means "without power"; and *omnipotent* means "all-powerful." But the concept of God's omnipotence commonly raises a few questions. For instance, somewhere along the line students always ask, "If God is all-powerful, can God make a rock so big that even God can't lift it?"

To be omnipotent is to be capable of doing anything which is, in itself, possible. What might be impossible for a human being to do, God, being omnipotent, could accomplish—provided that the task be a real one which is capable of being done. A "rock so big that God couldn't lift it," however, is, like a "square circle," not a real possibility. It's a contradiction in terms.

Such **logical contradictions** are not realities, but are in themselves impossibilities. Strictly speaking, logical contradictions like "square circles" aren't even real "concepts," since it would be impossible even for an infinite mind to picture or conceive of them. A "square circle" is thus just a combination of words, not a real concept. Therefore, God, being almighty, or omnipotent, can do anything which is possible and create anything which is capable of being made real. Logical contradictions are neither realities nor possibilities.

Another question students often ask about God's omnipotence is whether believing that God is all-powerful means that God directly determines or controls human destiny, denying human freedom. Catholic teaching has always held that human beings are created by God free—that we possess free will, that we, and no one else, is ultimately responsible for determining our individual eternal destiny.

Omnipotence would enable God to directly run the world and our lives. Instead, God chose to exercise this power by creating a world based on certain principles of evolution and human freedom, rather than by constant, direct divine intervention. God chooses to respect our human freedom. (After all, it is God who has given us this gift!)

> *Every generous act of giving,*
> *with every perfect gift, is from*
> *. . . the Father of lights, with*
> *whom there is no variation or*
> *shadow due to change.*
> —James 1:17

God enables us to make decisions which are of our own choosing, rather than preprogramming us to merely carry out ones God has already made. (Observing how we often bungle things by abusing this gift of freedom, some have jested that God's power must also be involved in exercising restraint from taking over and doing a better job!)

God's omnipotence, then, doesn't rule out human freedom. On the other hand, it evidences God's own greatness and freedom in giving us this most precious gift—despite the misuses to which we sometimes put it. God does intervene to sustain and guide us—giving us strength, wisdom, personal peace, and love.

God's omniscience

> *And by this we will know that we are*
> *from the truth and will reassure our*
> *hearts before him whenever our hearts*
> *condemn us; for God is greater than*
> *our hearts, and he knows everything.*
>
> *1 John 3:19–20*

To be almighty is also to be **omniscient.** Here students commonly ask: "If God knows everything and therefore knows in advance the choices and the fates which will befall us, are we therefore destined beforehand to behave that way? Do we really have no free choice?"

Catholic teaching has always held strongly to belief in both God's omniscience and in human freedom. To say that we are "predestined" in a way that would make human freedom impossible would deny what is fundamental to us as human beings. It would rob us of the possibility of loving (for which free

The dome unites heaven and earth, symbolically bringing God into the world, into the lives of people.

choice is a requirement) and turn us into robots. (There are, however, ways to understand the idea of predestination which do not contradict human freedom.)

"Omniscience" means, then, that God knows in advance what we will freely choose and, therefore, also knows what the consequences of our choices will be. That is very different from saying God makes these choices for us! For example, if someone were able to "read your mind," that wouldn't mean that the person was determining or controlling your thoughts. To know what you will do tomorrow isn't the same as controlling your will to determine what you will do. For God to know our future doesn't mean God completely controls it. God chooses, instead, to respect our freedom.

omniscient

all-knowing

Questions for discussion

1. What does it mean to say that God is almighty, omnipotent?

2. How would you explain to someone why God can't make a "square circle" or "a rock so big even God can't lift it"?

3. Why doesn't God's omnipotence cancel out human freedom? What does it mean for us instead?

4. Does God's "inability" to accomplish logical contradictions cause you to question or doubt your faith in God? Explain.

5. What would you say to someone who thinks that to believe God is all-knowing is to deny us free choice? Explain.

6. Why does belief in God as all-knowing mean believing more fully in God's complete concern for and fidelity to us?

7. Explain why our inability to comprehend God fully doesn't mean that we can't know or experience God at all.

Jesus speaks instead of God's omniscience in ways which tell us how important we are to God individually: "And even the hairs of your head are all counted" (Matthew 10:30). We need never be afraid that God will discover our true weaknesses and turn from us, for God knows them all already. In fact, Scripture tells us that it's our obvious need to rely on God's strength which makes God's power all the more evident: "My grace is sufficient for you, for power is made perfect in weakness" (2 Corinthians 12:9a).

Are not two sparrows sold for a penny? Yet not one of them will fall to the ground apart from your Father. . . . So do not be afraid; you are of more value than many sparrows.

Matthew 10:29 and 31

Thus, belief in God's omniscience assures us that we are watched over with care by a loving God—not in order to be controlled or condemned. We're known completely and accepted just as we are. When our own hearts condemn us, it is God who reassures and helps renew us. Omniscience gives us greater reason for believing in God's promise of unwavering love for us.

Faith does not consist in the belief that we are saved; it consists in the belief that we are loved. —Alexandre Vinet

---

It's true, then, that we can never know or experience all of God. That shouldn't surprise or dismay us. It shouldn't cause us to doubt that we can know God in any way at all. We can't even completely comprehend the mystery that is ourselves, or is another human person! But we can know something of the essential nature and qualities of ourselves and someone else. We can and do experience others in their laughter and compassion, in their generosity and their loving touch. Knowing them in these ways, we come to believe in, to trust them. Trusting them, we come to love them. And, in loving them, we find great meaning and joy.

So it is with God. Once we let ourselves experience God's presence in all we encounter in this world, we, too, can come more deeply to believe in, to love, and to find our life's delight and purpose in the God who is Love.

And if you would know God be not therefore a solver of riddles.

Rather look about you and you shall see [God] playing with your children.

And look into space; you shall see [God] walking in the cloud, outstretching . . . arms in the lightning and descending in rain.

You shall see [God] smiling in flowers, then rising and waving . . . hands in [the] trees.[2]

God's will

Some people look upon God as the great "Problem-Solver." They expect God and religion to automatically solve or eliminate all their problems in life. They depend on God in such a way that they also neglect to develop their own inner strengths. Then they become disillusioned when they feel that God has somehow failed them. They blame God for their own failures or the failures of others. Eventually, they may even reject the idea of God altogether.

What is at fault here is a misconception of what God and religion are all about. God helps us, giving us strength and wisdom. But God requires our co-operation! To avoid having to wrestle with this problem, remember the old maxim: "God helps those who help themselves."

Similarly, some people understand the idea of following God's will as sort of magically trying to read God's mind about what they're "supposed" to do or think, or what decisions they are "supposed" to make. They pray that "God's will be done," then act as if they expect a voice to boom from the heavens declaring what that will is. Or they look for "signs" of God's will in magical ways.

If your Bible opens to a certain verse when you have an important decision to make, that doesn't automatically mean God is telling you that you should literally do as the verse says! It could be a way God is guiding you, but it might also not be! "Following God's will" doesn't relieve us of the responsibility to use our God-given intelligence and common sense!

"Following God's will" doesn't mean mystically trying to read God's mind. In fact, Jesus spelled out very clearly what God wants of us. He said it's that we try to love God, and to love others as much as possible in a truly life-giving way. For above all else it is God's will for each of us, that we should "have life, and have it abundantly" (John 10:10). ❧

❧ Questions for discussion

1. In general, what is God's will for us? How would you describe what this means?

2. How can a person best determine what God's will is in a given situation? How should a person not do this?

Faith is to believe, on the word of God, what we do not see, and its reward is to see and enjoy what we believe. —St. Augustine

Awesome!

Our incredible universe dazzles even the scientists who research its components and how it functions. To give you some idea of the wonders of God's creation, consider for a moment each of the following facts. Then respond to the questions.

Researchers say they appear to have shaved off parts of individual molecules. . . . The remaining bits were so tiny that a row of a quarter-million of them would extend only the width of a human hair.[3]

By the time you finish reading this sentence, trillions and trillions of subatomic particles from space, called neutrinos, will have zipped through your body.[4]

Adults with normal color vision can distinguish from 120 to 150 color differences across the visible spectrum. . . . If saturation and brightness are added, the number reaches into the millions.[5]

A Chinese researcher "discovered what she calls 'the phenomenon of the microvessels,' a force that shoves blood through veins thinner than human hairs."[6]

Every bird knows how to build a particular kind of nest. A turtle that ranges far at sea can find, when it's time to reproduce, the very beach where it was itself hatched. A honeybee "dances" to show other bees where the nectar is.[7]

A Ruby-throated Hummingbird that weighs only ounces can beat its wings nonstop across the Gulf of Mexico. . . .[8]

A human heart is about as big as a clenched fist and weighs half a pound or less. This little organ has the power to contract forcibly more than 100,000 times in the minutes that pile up to a 24-hour day. Multiply 100,000 by 365 days and then by . . . the 75 years or so . . . [of] life expectancy. . . . We have to respect the design and durability of a heart. . . . Also consider the complex ramifications of the route [that the blood which the heart pumps must travel]. Blood vessels . . . crisscross, intersect, empty into one another or may be shunted elsewhere. If all these little tubes could be dissected and placed end to end, they would form a pathway 60,000 miles long . . . [that] reach every cell in the body. . . .[9]

"Every time you see something, a photon has come into your eye and struck [a protein]. That bond twists and makes basically a new molecule, which starts a series of chemical reactions. . . ." If the first stage of the twisting reaction were slower, humans would see much more poorly. . . . Researchers observed the first stage of the twisting, in which the bond between two carbon atoms twisted 90 degrees in 100 millionths of a billionth of a second. The twisting continues for another 400 millionths of a billionth of a second. . . . "The initial twisting is so bloody rapid, so no other competing processes can keep it from happening."[10]

Scientists have discovered that, yes, every single snowflake has a delicate pattern of its own which is different from that of every other snowflake.

. . . stars congregate in galaxies, galaxies in clusters and clusters of galaxies in superclusters that stretch across hundreds of millions of light-years of space. . . .[11]

Have you ever asked yourself: Which is the most complex—the 100 billion nerve cells in your brain, or the 100 billion stars in the sky? Whatever your choice, only the 100 billion nerve cells in the brain can determine the answer.[12]

Questions for discussion

1. Which of the above facts about you or the universe amazes you the most? Why?
2. Which of these leads you to think most about God's existence? God's omnipotence or omniscience? God's love?

The universe is centered on neither the earth nor the sun.
It is centered on God.
—Alfred Noyes

God, our Creator

I believe in God . . . Creator of heaven and earth,

and of all that is seen and unseen.

Nicene Creed

Scripture tells us that God is the source, the sustainer, and the end of all that exists. All things are from God, through God, and to God (see Romans 11:36). The child who prayed, "God, please take good care of Yourself, because if anything happens to You, we're all sunk" definitely spoke a profound truth. ". . . nor is [God] served by human hands, as though he needed anything, since he himself gives to all mortals life and breath and all things" (Acts 17:25). God preserves our very being in existence. God doesn't need us, but we sure do need God!

The Bible's creation accounts

The Scripture account of creation was never intended to be an historically accurate account of exactly how everything, from aardvarks to zebras, quasars to quarks, came to be. Scientific research about how people and other things originated can help increase our knowledge of God's creation and our appreciation of its Creator. In fact, there's more than one version of the creation story in the Bible—a combination of various early writings. But these creation accounts do tell us the most important truths about creation.

They tell us that God, the ultimate Source of all creation, created the initial stuff of matter, energy, spirit, and life out of nothingness. God created deliberately and with wisdom and love—the universe's intelligent design tells us it wasn't just a random accident. God reigns over creation in a good and caring way and is beyond yet present in all creation to preserve it in existence.

The covenant stories of the Hebrew Scriptures and Jesus' teaching in the Christian Scriptures also tell us why we are created—for ultimate union with God, and in God, with one another and with all of creation.

Created with care

There is a progression of creatures, as we can see from the one-celled amoeba and the complex dolphin. Yet all creatures are interdependent and are to be valued and not abused. Human persons, however, are the highest of earthly creatures in importance and dignity. Body and spirit, we are created in God's own image. We share, though to a limited extent, in God's own qualities and goodness—a reason why we should especially reverence "the gracious gift of life" (see 1 Peter 3:7) in every human being.

God has chosen to share the capacity for freedom with certain creatures. The Bible seems to assume that, in addition to human beings, God also created pure spirits who are endowed with the ability to reason and with freedom. The Bible simply speaks of these as being *angels,* which means "messengers," who seem somehow able to influence us. **God created all creatures for good, but God also gave all rational creatures the freedom to accept or reject the good.** This ability to make free choices is necessary in order to be able to love.

God is the infinite, initial Creator and final destiny of everything, and the perfect Source of all perfection. The loving care with which God created and sustains the universe, and the purpose God has designed for it, is referred to as **Divine Providence.**

Our abilities to reason and love are the highest qualities we possess as human beings. To believe, then, that God is infinite is surely to believe that, at the very least, God is better than we are! Therefore, God must also possess these same essential personal qualities we do, but to an infinite degree. God, our caring Creator, encompasses the qualities of, yet reaches beyond, all human or finite categories of reality.

Created to care

Male and female, **we are created equal in dignity.** Human persons are to respect one another and to live in harmony with one another and with all of creation. **We are to enjoy and care responsibly for the gifts of creation God has given us.** All God created is good, but, as we will discuss in a later chapter, God deliberately didn't program the world and people to be entirely perfect. Nevertheless, we should appreciate the way in which every creature reflects something of God's beauty.

From all eternity, God has planned a wonderful destiny for human persons and for all creation. The act of creation was just the beginning of God's plan, and Christ is its highest point. Our role is to cooperate with God in helping to bring about the new creation which Christ's redeeming death and resurrection initiated:

> *So if anyone is in Christ, there is a new creation: everything old has passed away; see, everything has become new!*
>
> *2 Corinthians 5:17*

So when you feel like you're all alone in life and that no one else cares, don't forget how lovingly God has prepared the universe for you to enjoy. Remember that second by second, breath by breath, thought by thought, your very being depends on God's active loving care to keep you in existence (see Acts 17:25). **In God, "you live and move and have your being"** (see Acts 17:28). With each heartbeat you should know how very much you are loved and valued:

> *See, I have inscribed you on the palms of my hands;*
> *[you] are continually before me.*
>
> *Isaiah 49:16* ❧

❧ Questions for discussion

1. What truths do the Scripture accounts of creation communicate to us? What kind of truths were they not meant to accurately describe?

2. How are we to view and treat all God's creatures? In what practical ways do you think this is and is not being done today?

3. Why is it important to society today to understand that
   - There is a progression of earthly creatures in which human persons are the highest.
   - Every human person is created in God's image.

4. What do the best of our human qualities tell us about God?

5. How are people to view and treat one another? What are the practical implications today of the belief that male and female persons are created equal?

6. What destiny has God designed for human persons, and for all creation? Explain.

Divine Providence

the loving care with which God created and sustains the universe, and the purpose God has designed for it

"The day I played God"

Read the following account of one man's experience at "playing God" for a day. Then respond to the questions.

Creating a new world is complicated—and risky.

In the beginning I created the heavens and the earth—well, almost. I actually started with a lump of molten rock, gave it a hundred million years or so to cool off and then began to form the clear blue oceans and the landmasses that would eventually become continents. After a few billion years had gone by (it seemed like minutes to me), I created the first lifeforms and triggered the start of their long evolution. Before I knew it, my world was filled with thousands of self-replicating molecules, millions of one-celled organisms, whole armies of invertebrates, crustaceans and primitive mollusks. What on earth had I done? . . . this computer exercise . . . let me do the one thing I've always wanted to do: play God.

And what a feeling it was! By pointing and clicking . . . I could pick up a square of green from one corner of the screen, drop it on a barren stretch of land and watch it blossom into a prairie. I could sprinkle the forest primeval with dinosaurs, insects and birds. I could fill the seas with starfish, lobsters and whales. I could rattle my little planet with computer-generated earthquakes and hurricanes.

. . . as in the real world, the great natural processes that shape the environment—volcanoes, erosion, continental drift—interact with one another. Climate, vegetation and geology are represented as interrelated systems, each with controls that can be adjusted. Animals multiplying too fast? Just crank down the reproduction dial. Tired of waiting for evolution to work its wonders? Just speed up the mutation rate. Earth getting too hot for its own good? Just turn off the greenhouse effect.

Things really get interesting when the creatures on my pet planet develop intelligence. The program is set up so that the beings that become smart are not necessarily human. They can as easily be dolphins or spiders. In one game I played, it was a lizard that discovered fire. Africa was soon littered with Stone Age reptile cities.

Whatever animals get the gift of intelligence, it is the player's job to nurture and protect them, guiding their technological development by directing investments in science, medicine, agriculture and the arts. But playing the Almighty, I discover, is complicated—and dangerous. Skimp on medical research, and your SimEarthlings are pestered by plagues. Cut back in the philosophy department, and wars break out. Let the master race linger too long in the industrial age, and the planet is choked with pollution. . . .

Suddenly, rather than "playing" God, I found myself working overtime to keep my oceans from boiling away, my jungles from bursting into flame and my populations from suffering yet another mass extinction. . . . If God had to adjust all these systems by hand, he'd (sic) never get a day of rest.[13]

Questions for discussion

1. How might this simulation creation game reflect what was and is actually involved in God's creation and guidance of the universe?

2. In what ways has God chosen to act differently than did the player in this game?

3. Have you ever played a simulation creation game? From this man's experience (and perhaps your own), what did you learn about God and God's creation?

4. If God really did let you take absolute control of the whole earth for one day, how would you try to influence its development and inhabitants? Explain why.

sic

as written in the original

Chapter review

1. Who is God?

- In what ways do people sometimes stereotype God unfavorably?
- Why is one's concept of God important?
- What does it mean to believe that God is One? Where did Jews, Christians, and Muslims get this belief about God?
- What reason do we have to believe God's Revelation in the Scriptures?
- Why is it important to believe that God is Truth?
- What does it mean to believe that God is personal? Why is this belief so important?
- What does it mean to say that God is Love? In what sense should and shouldn't people "fear the Lord"?
- What does belief in God as Trinity mean? Why do Christians have this belief about God?
- How near is God to us, and what should this mean for our lives?

2. The Almighty

- What does it mean to say that God is infinite, the Almighty? To say that God is omnipotent and omniscient?
- Does belief in God's omnipotence and omniscience contradict God's gift to us of human freedom?
- What is God's will for us? What does it really mean to follow God's will?

3. God, our Creator

- What truths did the Bible's creation account intend to convey? What type of truths did it not intend to tell about?
- What does belief in the "progression of creatures" mean? Where do human persons fit into this progression?
- What role are we to play in God's creation? What is our destiny?
- What does our ability to love and reason tell us about our Creator?

Projects and assignments

1. Interview five adults, five teenagers, or five young children about their concept of God. (You may include individuals who believe there is no God, since they will also have some idea of the kind of Being they believe does not exist!) Record or videotape the responses and play a five-minute segment of these for the class. Write a paragraph or videotape a segment adding your own responses in view of what was discussed in this chapter of Catholic teaching about God.

2. Write a one-page paper explaining what you think one author meant by saying that "We were created in God's image, but unfortunately people keep trying to repay the compliment by creating God in their image!"

3. Paraphrase a psalm that speaks about the wonders and beauties of God's creation, or write your own prayer or song of praise about this (at least twenty lines).

4. Write a one-page paper about the wonders of God's creation which impress you as most reflecting their Creator's power and wisdom, and those for which you're personally most grateful.

5. Write an "uncreation" song or poem of at least twenty lines, describing humanity's lack of gratitude for and abuse of God's gift of creation.

6. Write a one-page paper about how and why concern for our natural environment is a responsibility of Christians.

Chapter 6

The Person and Message of Jesus

God's love was revealed among us in this way: God sent his only Son into the world so that we might live through him.

1 John 4:9

Lord, make me an instrument of your peace—
Where there is hatred, let me bring love;
Where there is injury, forgiveness;
Where there is disunity, harmony;
Where there is error, truth;
Where there is doubt, faith;
Where there is darkness, light;
Where there is despair, hope;
Where there is sadness, joy.

Lord, let me seek—
To comfort more than to be comforted;
To understand more than to be understood;
To love more than to be loved;
For it is by giving that we receive;
It is by forgiving that we are forgiven;
It is by dying that we are born to eternal life.

St. Francis of Assisi

Overview questions

1. Who is Jesus of Nazareth? What do the titles used of him mean?

2. Is Jesus both human and divine?

3. What do we know about Jesus and his life?

4. What did Jesus' death accomplish?

5. Why is the resurrection of Jesus so important for Christians?

6. What hope do Jesus' ascension and resurrection give us?

7. What impact did Jesus have on human history?

8. What main values did Jesus teach and live?

Who is Jesus?

I believe in Jesus Christ, God's only Son. . . .

Jesus is God spelled out in language that people can understand.
—Adapted from S.D. Gordon

The life of Jesus

. . . when the fullness of time had come, God sent his Son, born of a woman, born under the law, in order to redeem those who were under the law, so that we might receive adoption as children.

Galatians 4:4–5

Jesus of Nazareth was born a Jew in about 4 B.C.E. and died about 29 C.E. (Jesus wasn't born in our year 1 B.C.E. —the monk who centuries later started calculating our calendar from Jesus' birth date actually miscalculated it by about four years!) Is there historical evidence that Jesus really lived? Yes, both from the testimonies of eyewitnesses which are recorded in the Christian Scriptures, and also from the writings of Roman historians.

The Scriptures tell us that Jesus was conceived by the power of the Holy Spirit and born of the Virgin Mary, who has been acknowledged since early Christian times as Mother of God, Mother of the Church, and Mother of us all. Thus, God's Word "became flesh and lived among us" (see John 1:14) in order that we might be forgiven and united with God in love, even sharing in God's own divine nature.

United in one person, Jesus is truly divine and truly human. The Scriptures refer to Jesus by the divine titles "Lord" and "the only Son of God," which recognize his divinity. But human like us, Jesus also had a human consciousness and will. He was subject to the same temptations we are in life, except that he was without sin. So Jesus can understand and "sympathize with our weaknesses" (see Hebrews 4:15).

The name *Jesus* comes from the Hebrew word for Joshua, which means "God saves." **Christ** is not Jesus' last name, but a title which comes from the Greek word for **messiah,** which means "anointed one." Ancient royalty were often installed by a ritual anointing with oil. Ancient Israel's priests, kings, and prophets were God's anointed ones— those responsible for helping to lead others to live by faith, integrity, and justice. Thus, Jesus' followers used this title to express their belief that Jesus was the messiah longed for in the Old Testament, and also much more.

There isn't enough information available today for anyone to write an historical biography of Jesus. There are no accurate records of what Jesus looked like or detailed descriptions of his personality. The Christian Scriptures which we do have contain a combination of information about Jesus' life and teaching as used by the early Christians to understand and teach their faith.

The **Gospels** were not intended to be detailed biographies, but proclamations of "the good news of Jesus Christ, the Son of God" (see Mark 1:1). The purpose of Christian **catechesis** is to help connect people more closely with Jesus and what he taught.

The Christian Scriptures are the only sources we have today of Jesus' life and teaching, but more recent discoveries of ancient manuscripts from Jesus' day are helping to give us more information about the cultural and religious environment in the time and area Jesus lived. From the Gospels we know that Jesus' whole life was intended to reveal to us who God is and wants to be for us.

We don't know much about Jesus' birth and early life. The accounts of his birth were written after Jesus' death. And they are told in a literary style of writing which mostly intended to convey the main message about who Jesus

---

Christ

title for Jesus; from the Greek word for *Messiah,* meaning "anointed one"

messiah

Savior and spiritual guide who Christians believe is Jesus

Gospels

the "good news" of Jesus' teachings as received from the early Christians and written in the Christian Scripture books of Matthew, Mark, Luke, and John

catechesis

sharing instruction in the beliefs of faith

☙ Questions for discussion

1. What is Jesus' background as an historical person? When did he live? How do we know he really lived?

2. Which do you find more challenging—that Jesus was really human like we are, or that he was also divine? Explain.

3. What is Jesus' actual name, and what does it mean? What does *Christ* mean and why was Jesus called "the Christ"?

4. Are the Gospels biographies of Jesus? Explain.

5. Whom did Jesus especially help during his public life? What was the real gift he was offering them and us?

compassion

literally, "feeling strongly with"; expressing sensitivity to and understanding of others' thoughts, feelings, and difficulties

was and why he had come. The Gospels tell us that Jesus' family was poor and that he spent most of his life as a manual laborer, working as a carpenter. Throughout his life, he devoutly practiced and upheld the commandments of his Jewish religion and participated in its religious rituals, but he openly criticized those who demeaned or distorted its real meaning.

> *That a few simple [individuals] should in one generation have invented so powerful and appealing a personality, so lofty an ethic and so inspiring a vision of human [unity], would be a miracle far more incredible than any recorded in the Gospel.* —*Will Durant*

Jesus' public life began with his baptism by John the Baptizer and included his teaching and ministry in service of others. During his public life, Jesus taught and showed special **compassion** for and ministered to those in need,

especially those considered hopeless and avoided by others. The Scriptures record that, to help them, Jesus sometimes accompanied his words of hope and healing "with deeds of power, wonders, and signs that God did through him" (Acts 2:22) which indicated that his power and teaching authority were of God.

> *Now Jesus did many other signs in the presence of his disciples, which are not written in this book. But these are written so that you may come to believe that Jesus is the Messiah, the Son of God, and that through believing you may have life in his name.*
>
> *John 20:30–31*

But Jesus didn't look for fame; he avoided the publicity which accompanied the help he gave others. The real gift Jesus was offering was the true meaning and purpose for life, including its pain and suffering. His public life was short, lasting just a few years until his death by crucifixion. Yet today even objective historians maintain that Jesus of Nazareth has been the most influential person who has ever lived. ☙

Jesus' saving death

Throughout his life, Jesus gave of himself freely to save others from suffering and from sin. Jesus' offering of himself for the sake of all humanity was accomplished most fully in his freely accepted suffering and death on the cross—which is the central Christian **sacrifice**. As a man, Jesus really died—he wasn't just faking it!

Jesus' death was brought about by very specific persons, among whom were some of the Roman and Jewish leaders of Jesus' day. But **it's ignorant and it's wrong to blame all Jews of Jesus' time, or of all time, for Jesus' death,** as many Christians have done in the past. The anti-semitism which led to the Holocaust began by falsely blaming all Jews as being "Christ-killers." After all, Jesus himself was a devout Jew, and so were his most loyal followers and active supporters!

In fact, it's our own sinfulness we should examine. For, most importantly, Jesus died that we might be united with God and one another, that we might be saved from the results of our sins which separate us from God and from one another. Thus, Jesus' death is the once-and-for-all-time effective act through which we're all made holy and redeemed. It's the ultimate act which shows how much God loves us.

> *He himself bore our sins in his body on the cross, so that, free from sins, we might live for **righteousness**; by his wounds you have been healed.*
>
> *1 Peter 2:24*

Jesus' sacrifice on the cross opened up for all humanity new possibilities for closeness with God. 🔔

---

sacrifice

literally, "act of making sacred or holy"

righteous

standing right with God

▶ Questions for discussion

1. Why is Jesus' suffering and death on the cross called the "central Christian sacrifice"?

2. Who was responsible for Jesus' death? Why is it wrong to blame the Jewish people for Jesus' death?

3. Why did Jesus freely accept his suffering and death? What did it accomplish?

Here and now

Read the following and respond to the questions.

Once, in addressing a group, Peter found it necessary to compress into short compass what Jesus did during his lifetime. His summary? "He went about doing good" (Acts 10:38). A simple epitaph, but a moving one. Circulating easily and without affectation among ordinary people and social misfits, healing them, counseling them, helping them out of chasms of despair, Jesus went about doing good. He did so with such single-mindedness and effectiveness that those who were with him constantly found their estimate of him [increasing] . . . . They found themselves thinking that if divine goodness were to manifest itself in human form, this is how it would behave.[1]

Questions for discussion

1. If God's Word had become enfleshed in a human being today, what type of good do you think Christ would be doing? Be specific.

2. In what manner do you think Christ would be doing these things?

3. How do you think people would respond? How do you think you would respond? Explain.

4. Who do you think are the most Christ-like models in recent world history? Why?

5. Describe the most Christ-like person you have ever known personally.

paschal

passing over, as from death to life

➤ Questions for discussion

1. What are Jesus' resurrection and ascension, and what do they confirm and mean for Christians?

2. Which is the main Christian celebration of the year for Christians? Why?

3. Who experienced the risen Christ? Did this experience eliminate the need for faith, to believe? Explain.

4. What did Jesus' followers understand more clearly after Jesus' resurrection?

5. What was to be the role of Jesus' followers after he parted from them? To whom did Jesus assign special responsibilities, and what were they?

6. What does Jesus' ascension express? How was Jesus to remain with his followers afterward?

7. What is meant by the Mystery of Redemption and what does it include?

redemption

act of buying back, as from slavery or sin

The risen Christ

The central belief of Christian faith is that God raised Jesus from suffering and death to live in eternal glory. Easter, not Christmas, is the main Christian celebration! For it celebrates the **Paschal Mystery**, by which, united with Jesus and by God's power, we too are enabled to pass over from despair and death to hope and new life.

> *. . . and if Christ has not been raised, then our proclamation has been in vain and your faith has been in vain.*
>
> *1 Corinthians 15:14*

It is Jesus' resurrection and ascension—his triumph over suffering and death on behalf of all humanity—which confirm the central Christian belief and hope.

According to the Gospels, it was Mary Magdalene and other women followers of Jesus who first met the risen Jesus and brought this news to the other apostles. They, too, experienced the risen Christ, although, even then, it took faith for them to believe it was really true (as the account of "doubting Thomas" shows in John 20:27). But it was that experience which led them to more fully understand (and then record in the Gospels) who Jesus really was and what his life and teaching were really all about.

What the apostles also experienced was that, after Jesus' resurrection, his physical presence was no longer limited by space and time. Jesus would, as he had promised, remain with them always. Once they understood this, Jesus entered once and for all into God's glory to reign over all creation.

Before his death, Jesus had especially chosen men and women among his followers. They were to continue his mission to teach and minister to others (especially to the poor and suffering) as he had done—lovingly, forgivingly. For this task, Jesus had especially commissioned the twelve apostles, and entrusted the apostle Peter with the primary leadership role. Now Jesus' disciples also became witnesses of his risen presence and his ascension.

> *While he was blessing them, he withdrew from them and was carried up into heaven.*
>
> *Luke 24:51*

> *And they went out and proclaimed the good news everywhere, while the Lord worked with them and confirmed the message by the signs that accompanied it.*
>
> *Mark 16:20*

God became what we are that God might make us what God is. —St. Athanasius

---

To say that Jesus "ascended," however, doesn't mean that Jesus went "up" to sit forever in the sky someplace. It expresses that the person of Jesus—body and spirit—somehow entered into God's glory. And **in Jesus' resurrection and ascension is the source and hope of our own glorious future:**

> *But in fact Christ has been raised from the dead, the first fruits of those who have died. For since death came through a human being, the resurrection of the dead has also come through a human being; for as all die in Adam, so all will be made alive in Christ.*
>
> *1 Corinthians 15:20–22*

> *Therefore it is said,*
> *"When he ascended on high he made captivity itself a captive;*
> *he gave gifts to his people."*
>
> *Ephesians 4:8*

Jesus' life, death, resurrection, and ascension encompass the entire Mystery of **Redemption** whereby God has desired to save us. In particular, Jesus' resurrection and ascension are the foundation of our belief as Christians that God's Spirit remains actively present to us now as we try to live Jesus' teaching, and of our hope that one day we too will then be resurrected in glory forever.

> *"And remember, I am with you always, to the end of the age."*
>
> *Matthew 28:20* ➤

Jesus' impact on humanity

Read the following and respond to the questions.

Jesus of Nazareth,

without money and arms
conquered more millions than Alexander, Caesar, . . . and Napoleon;

without science and learning,
he shed more light on things human and divine
than all the philosophers and scholars combined;

without the eloquence of the school,
he spoke words of life such as were never spoken before, nor since,
and produced effects which lie beyond the reach of orator or poet;

without writing a single line,
he set more pens in motion and furnished themes
for more sermons, orations, discussions, works of art, learned volumes, and sweet songs of praise
than the whole army of great [people] of ancient and modern times.

Born in a manger
and crucified as a malefactor,
he now [influences] the destinies of the civilized world. . . .
Philip Schaff

Here is a man who was born in an obscure village, the child of a peasant woman.

He grew up in an obscure village.

He worked in a carpenter shop until he was thirty, and then for three years he was [a traveling] teacher.

He never wrote a book. He never held an office.

He never owned a home. He never had a family. He never went to college.

He never traveled, except in his infancy, more than two hundred miles from the place where he was born.

He never did one of the things that usually accompany greatness.

He had no credentials but himself.

While he was still a young man, the tide of popular opinion turned against him.

His friends ran away. One of them denied him.

He was turned over to his enemies. He went through the mockery of a trial.

His executioners gambled for the only piece of property he had on earth, his seamless robe.

When he was dead, he was taken down from the cross and laid in a borrowed grave through the courtesy of a friend.

. . . centuries have come and gone, and today he is the center-piece of the human race and the leader of all human progress.

I am well within the mark when I say that
all the armies that ever marched,
all the navies that ever were built,
and all the parliaments that ever sat, and all the [rulers] that ever reigned,
put together,
have not affected the life of [humanity] upon this earth as powerfully
as has this one solitary [personality].
James A. Francis

Questions for discussion

1. How did Jesus conquer more than history's great military leaders did?
2. How did he shed more light on things than have all the well-learned experts?
3. How were his words more life-giving than those of any other person?
4. How did Jesus inspire more writing, art, and music than did any other person in history?
5. According to purely worldly criteria, why should Jesus have been among the last to ever make a major impact on humanity and humanity's future?
6. Why do you think Jesus has had such an important impact on human history?

"Alexander, Caesar, Charlemagne and I founded empires; but upon what did we rest the creations of our genius? Upon force. Jesus Christ alone founded his empire upon love; and at this hour millions . . . would die for him." —**Napoleon Bonaparte**

What Jesus taught

The essence of Jesus' message is that we should, above all, love God—with our whole heart and soul and mind—and that we do this only insofar as we love others as we love ourselves. In telling us what this means in practice, Jesus taught certain principles and values to guide us. These are to be our **touchstones**—the way to measure how truly loving we are. In his own life, Jesus lived each one and showed us what it means.

Consider seriously these teachings of Jesus. What you believe about them will color and shape your life. What you believe and value will determine how you live and act. Your choices and decisions will, in turn, determine what your life means and the happiness you find.

Have mercy

In the societies of Jesus' time, people were used to exacting strict revenge for wrongs committed against them:

Show no pity: life for life, eye for eye, tooth for tooth, hand for hand, foot for foot.

> *Deuteronomy 19:21*

. . . the injury inflicted is the injury to be suffered.

> *Leviticus 24:20*

Jesus, however, told those who followed him to be merciful instead. In showing others **mercy,** we're told we too will be shown mercy.

"Be merciful, just as your Father is merciful."

> *Luke 6:36*

"Blessed are the merciful, for they will receive mercy."

> *Matthew 5:7*

Forgive

Understanding that we're all good but weak, Jesus said we are to forgive—without counting how many times.

*"If another disciple sins, you must **rebuke** the offender, and if there is repentance, you must forgive. And if the same person sins against you seven*

touchstone

a test of authenticity or genuineness, a rock once used to test the purity of precious metals

mercy

forgiveness or kindness—especially as shown to one's enemies or to the guilty

rebuke

sternly correct

times a day, and turns back to you seven times and says, 'I repent,' you must forgive.''

Luke 17:3–4

We're to accept other's sincere **repentance,** just as God is willing to accept ours.

Just so, I tell you, there will be more joy in heaven over one sinner who repents than over ninety-nine righteous persons who need no repentance.

Luke 15:7

In showing others forgiveness, we're told we too will be forgiven.

"Forgive, and you will be forgiven. . . ."

Luke 6:37

By his example, Jesus showed us what this means. He didn't just forgive others their sins against somebody else. He forgave those who took his life.

Reconcile

Union with God is empty unless we're willing to be reunited with one another. So we're not just to seek God's forgiveness in prayer for the harm our wrongdoing causes others, we're to make a positive effort to reconcile with those whom we've wronged.

So when you are offering your gift at the altar, if you remember that your brother or sister has something against you, leave your gift there before the altar and go; first be reconciled to your brother or sister, and then come and offer your gift.

Matthew 5:23–24 🍃

repentance

true sorrow for wrongdoing, verified by trying not to do wrong again and by trying to undo the damage one has caused

🍃 Questions for discussion

1. In Jesus' time, how did many people respond when they were wronged by others? Give examples of how people still act this way today.

2. How did Jesus say we should respond to those who wrong us? How do you usually respond? Explain.

3. How many times did Jesus say we should forgive someone, and under what conditions?

4. Are we to reconcile with someone whose repentance is phony? How can you tell when someone is truly sorry?

5. If you wrong someone, what do you think is the best way you can show you're really sorry and get back together with the person?

6. How did Jesus show mercy and repentance in his own life? What reward did he say there is for being forgiving and merciful?

Long ago God spoke to our ancestors in many and various ways by the prophets, but in these last days he has spoken to us by a Son, whom he appointed heir of all things, through whom he also created the worlds.—Hebrews 1:1–2

Reconciliation is an important part of Jesus' message.

Seek goodness

Jesus told us to have an attitude that looks for goodness, not evil. In this way, we can experience more of God who is Goodness. The goodness or evil in our hearts also affects both ourselves and others. The kind of attitude we have becomes obvious to others in what we say as well as in what we do.

The good person out of the good treasure of the heart produces good, and the evil person out of evil treasure produces evil; for it is out of the abundance of the heart that the mouth speaks.

Luke 6:45

Seek peace and unity

Jesus taught us to be peacemakers, rather than creating tension and stirring up trouble (see Matthew 5:9). For, God's nature is unity. To be united with God, we must seek unity with one another. In fact, Jesus' whole mission is expressed in his prayer:

The glory that you have given me I have given them, so that they may be one, as we are one, I in them and you in me, that they may become completely one, so that the world may know that you have sent me and have loved them even as you have loved me.

John 17:22–23

We must be seekers of goodness and peace, and try to bring about greater unity—among our friends and acquaintances, in our community and nation, among all peoples of the world.

Be honest and fair

Jesus told us to be honest and to say what we mean and mean what we say.

"Let your word be 'Yes, Yes' or 'No, No'. . . ."

Matthew 5:37

Jesus pointed out the value and implications of being trustworthy.

"Whoever is faithful in a very little is faithful also in much; and whoever is dishonest in a very little is dishonest also in much."

Luke 16:10

Jesus' own honesty in preaching and living what he thought was true cost him his life.

Finally, Jesus gave many examples illustrating how we're to be **just,** to treat others fairly. He said,

". . . justice and the love of God; it is these you ought to have practiced. . . ."

Luke 11:42

> **Many teachers of the world have tried to explain everything—they have changed little or nothing. Jesus explained little and changed everything. —E. Stanley Jones**

Respect others

Jesus also taught us, by his example as well as by his words, that every human being is equal in worth, and that we shouldn't consider ourselves better than anyone else:

"For all who exalt themselves will be humbled, and those who humble themselves will be exalted."

Luke 14:11

We should respect and treat others with dignity:

"So if I, your Lord and Teacher, have washed your feet, you also ought to wash one another's feet. For I have set you an example, that you also should do as I have done to you."

John 13:14–15

Instead of causing humiliation, genuine kindness and respect for others increase both our dignity and theirs—a dignity which flows from our having been created in God's image.

But Jesus called them to him and said, "You know that the rulers of the Gentiles lord it over them, and their great ones are tyrants over them. It will not be so among you; but whoever wishes to be great among you must be your servant, and whoever wishes to be first among you must be your slave; just as the Son of Man came not to be served but to serve, and to give his life a ransom for many."

Matthew 20:25–28 ❧

Be gentle and compassionate

Jesus also taught us to be **gentle,** for it's the gentle who win people's hearts from the inside out.

". . . learn from me; for I am gentle and humble in heart. . . ."

Matthew 11:29

Jesus taught us to have compassion—to feel with others and to share their grief, loss, suffering, misfortune, and pain. On many occasions the Scriptures tell how he felt and showed compassion for others (see, for instance, Matthew 9:36, 14:14, and 20:34).

Compassion is attitude and action.

gentle

tender, responsive, kind, gracious, not rough or pushy

❧ Questions for discussion

1. If you caught someone telling you a small lie, would you still find it as easy as before to trust the person in an important matter? Explain.

2. What evidence is there that Jesus' teaching about human equality is being more and more widely accepted in the world? That humanity still has quite a way to go in accepting this teaching?

3. Describe what traits you admire about someone who is truly a humble person.

4. What do you think is the best way to help and be of service to others while at the same time respecting their dignity, so that your charity does not appear to demean them?

5. Without mentioning names, in what ways do teenagers you know sometimes try to "lord it over others"? How would you tell these persons to act instead?

6. In what ways do teenagers treat each other unfairly? How could you be a fairer person?

7. What does justice mean to you? How do you usually try to bring justice to your dealings with others, and to theirs with you?

generosity

willingness to share or give of oneself or one's goods to others

Golden Rule

Jesus' command to always treat others as we would want them to treat us

judgment

criticism, condemnation, ruling on the worth of

Questions for discussion

1. Describe the characteristics of a gentle person. A compassionate person. A kind person.
2. How and why do people win hearts "from the inside out" by being gentle?
3. What examples of selfless generosity have you witnessed on the part of other teenagers?
4. In what areas are teenagers most often judgmental of each other? How is this harmful? How has it hurt you?
5. What is the difference between not treating others as you wouldn't want them to treat you, and treating others as you'd like them to treat you?
6. Which of those two attitudes do you think more teenagers have and show?

Be generous and unselfish

Believing in God's **generosity** to us, we in turn are to give generously to others. Be generous, Jesus said, and not only in your heart:

Give to everyone who begs from you, and do not refuse anyone who wants to borrow from you.

Matthew 5:42

In the end, what you give is what you'll get in return—and so much more:

". . . give, and it will be given to you. A good measure, pressed down, shaken together, running over, will be put into your lap; for the measure you give will be the measure you get back."

Luke 6:38

Don't judge people

Jesus told us not to pass **judgment** on other persons' goodness or evil.

"Do not judge, and you will not be judged; do not condemn, and you will not be condemned."

Luke 6:37

In fact, Jesus said we should examine our own conduct and intentions!

"Why do you see the speck in your neighbor's eye, but do not notice the log in your own eye? Or how can you say to your neighbor, 'Friend, let me take out the speck in your eye,' when you yourself do not see the log in your own eye? You hypocrite, first take the log out of your own eye, and then you will see clearly to take the speck out of your neighbor's eye."

Luke 6:41–42

Be kind

Above all, Jesus taught the **Golden Rule**—that we should love one another unselfishly. He didn't merely say that we shouldn't do to others what we wouldn't want them to do to us. That was a standard code of conduct among many peoples before his time. (Unfortunately, it still is among too many people!) Jesus went one step further:

"Do to others as you would have them do to you."

Luke 6:31

Jesus said to him, "Have I been with you all this time . . . and you still do not know me? (John 14:9)

After twenty centuries
is there one of us He couldn't say the same thing to?. . . .
  "You haven't yet understood
  that I'm hungry
    and thirsty
    and poor;
  that I was where you found
    nothing to honor or admire,
    nothing to fear or reverence;
  that I was precisely where you felt so sure
    I couldn't be."

—Louis Evely, That Man Is You.

Love without condition

Jesus taught us to love unconditionally—as God loves us. Not just our friends. Not just our relatives. We must love **all** persons, yes, even our enemies.

"But I say to you that listen,
Love your enemies,
do good to those who hate you. . . ."

Luke 6:27

We're to love with no strings attached, because conditions cancel out love. There are different types of love, and different ways of showing love, but all real love is unconditional. It has the other person's welfare, not our own, at heart. But Jesus didn't ask us to do anything he himself didn't do:

"This is my commandment, that you love one another as I have loved you."

John 15:12

In so loving God and our neighbor, Jesus promised that we would live fully:

". . . do this, and you will live."

Luke 10:28

Living all these values of Jesus, not just displaying bumper stickers and T-shirt slogans, should be how people can really identify us as Christian!

Questions for discussion

1. Why is all real love unconditional? What does loving unconditionally mean? Give examples.
2. What kind of conditions do you think teenagers most often impose about loving somebody? To the extent that these conditions exist, how do they cancel out the love?
3. Speaking of T-shirts and bumper stickers, what are examples of some which you think do promote a real Christian attitude and value? What are examples of some that you think express an unchristian attitude or value?

Love is a way of life.

Which would you rather . . . ?

This activity will help you evaluate for yourself what meaning Jesus' values have for your life. To complete it, put the letter of your answer on the blank next to each question.

Answer each question as honestly as you can, but put down only answers you're convinced of! If you don't know what you believe, leave the space blank. Imagine actual situations you might be faced with and ways you would really like to respond.

Would you rather . . .

____ **1.** that your love for others be

   a. unselfish—for their own sake

   b. only for what you want to get in return

____ **2.** that others love you

   a. unselfishly

   b. only for what they want of you in return

____ **3.** always treat others

   a. justly and fairly

   b. unfairly at times if you would profit materially

____ **4.** others treated you

   a. justly and fairly

   b. unfairly at times if it would allow them to profit materially

____ **5.** live by the belief that

   a. all persons are equal in value and dignity

   b. some persons are superior in value and dignity to others

____ **6.** others live by the belief that

   a. all persons are equal in value and dignity

   b. certain others are superior in value and dignity to you

____ **7.** believe

   a. in human unity

   b. that life is a matter of "everyone for himself or herself"

____ **8.** be the kind of person who

   a. is forgiving and able to show mercy

   b. bears grudges and cannot forgive

____ **9.** others be the kind of persons who

   a. are forgiving and able to show you mercy

   b. bear grudges against and can't forgive you

____ **10.** try to be

   a. a good person

   b. someone who doesn't care at all about being a good person

____ **11.** others try to be

   a. good to you

   b. not care at all about being good to you

____ **12.** be someone who is

   a. at peace within yourself and with others

   b. not at peace within yourself and with others

____ **13.** others be people who

     a. try to be at peace with you and other people

     b. don't care about living peaceably with you or others

____ **14.** be someone who

     a. is honest and trustworthy

     b. is dishonest and untrustworthy when it suits your selfish purposes

____ **15.** others be people who

     a. are honest and trustworthy with you

     b. may lie or betray your trust when it suits their selfish purposes

____ **16.** be the kind of person who

     a. is humble and honest about your capabilities, but doesn't put yourself above others

     b. boasts and brags about your abilities with a superior attitude

____ **17.** others be the kind of people who ,

     a. are humble and honest about their capabilities, but don't put themselves above you or others

     b. boast and brag about their abilities with a superior attitude

____ **18.** be the kind of person who is

     a. gentle and kind

     b. pushy and inconsiderate

____ **19.** believe that all you suffer

     a. has meaning and purpose

     b. is senseless and merely to be endured

____ **20.** be someone who

     a. is generous and enjoys giving

     b. is preoccupied mainly with what you can get

____ **21.** others be people who

     a. are generous and enjoy giving

     b. are preoccupied mainly with what they can get

____ **22.** be the kind of person who is

     a. compassionate and capable of feeling with and for others

     b. insensitive to and not bothered by the feelings or problems of others

____ **23.** other people be

     a. compassionate and capable of feeling with and for you and others

     b. insensitive to and not bothered by your feelings or problems, or those of others

____ **24.** be the kind of person who is

     a. judgmental of others

     b. leaves judgment of others up to God

____ **25.** others be the kind of people who are

     a. judgmental of you and others

     b. leave judgment of you and others up to God

The day the teenagers took over the town

Read the following account of a true incident and respond to the questions.

When they heard that a few hundred thousand teenagers would be descending upon their city from all over the world for a week or two, city officials were deeply concerned. What would happen? Would the violence that has become so common among teenagers in gangs and at schools make it a bloody, tragic event?

Law enforcement officials beefed up security. But, they said, they didn't have enough personnel to guarantee everybody's safety. They just couldn't protect the people of the city completely from muggings, burglary, rape, or shootings if the kids got out of control.

The countries some of these kids were coming from were involved in brutal, bitter wars. Would the hostility of these international conflicts become personal when kids from these different areas encountered one another? Might an international incident ensue?

When these tens of thousands of teenagers gathered together for the occasion's main event, the summer sun would be hot and stomachs empty. After spending hours in line waiting to get in, attitudes would certainly be irritable. Would tempers flare? Would fights break out? Would groups of the teenagers confront other groups? Would the use of alcohol or other drugs lead to violence?

City officials hoped for the best, but prepared for the worst as best they could. In just the week before the kids arrived, there had been a tragic incident at a local high school in which one student killed another.

But to skeptics' pleasant surprise, the whole happening turned out to be a pleasant, positive experience. Police found that their job consisted mainly of giving directions about how to get from here to there, and exchanging jokes and amiable conversation. Residents experienced the teenagers as "friendly" and "delightful" to meet on the street. The main event went off as scheduled. There were some major problems—thousands of people sought medical attention due to lack of water and dehydration in the hot sun. But there were no drugs, no guns, and there was no violence of any kind.

Eyewitnesses reported that, instead, the kids' attitude seemed to be one of trying to help each other and get to know one another. They exchanged buttons, pins, and T-shirts. They had long discussions at night that lasted until dawn. They shared information about their hometowns and home countries, and gained new friends and penpals.

The day after the kids left town, the city's major newspapers reported, with something of a sense of relief and disbelief, that there hadn't been one incident of crime or violence when the kids visited the town. Not one.

Questions for discussion

1. When you read the title for this activity, did you first think it was going to present something negative, or something positive about teenagers? Why?

2. Would you say the fears the town had before all the teenagers arrived were well-founded?

3. If you were a city official in your town faced with hosting a few hundred thousand teenagers, what problems would you prepare for? Why?

4. Have you been at a small or large gathering of teenagers where there were some serious problems? Explain.

5. What are the main serious problems among teenagers who live in your community? Have there been violent incidents in your school or neighborhood?

6. How does teenage violence in our society affect you and your life?

7. What seemed unusual about the behavior of this gathering of teenagers? What impression did they make on others?

8. What do you think probably accounted for the fact that there were no incidents of crime or violence among these teenagers?

Chapter review

1. Who is Jesus?

- What do we know and not know about the historical Jesus?
- What do the Christian Scriptures tell us about Jesus and his early life? Why isn't an historical biography of Jesus possible?
- What are the names and titles used for Jesus, and what beliefs of faith about him does each signify?
- What are the Gospels meant to be?
- What did Jesus do during his public life?
- How and why did Jesus die? Why aren't the Jews collectively responsible for his death? What does Jesus' death mean for humanity?
- Why is belief in Jesus' resurrection the central belief of Christian faith?
- What did Jesus' followers experience about him after his resurrection?
- What special mission did Jesus give to his followers, and to the apostles in particular?
- What does belief in Jesus' ascension express?
- What is the Mystery of Redemption, and what hope does it give us?

2. What Jesus taught

- What did Jesus teach about each of the following, and what does his teaching mean for your life?
    - mercy, forgiveness, and reconciliation
    - seeking goodness, peace, and unity
    - being gentle and compassionate
    - being generous and unselfish
    - not judging people, and being kind
    - loving unconditionally

Projects and assignments

1. Write a one-page "personal profile" of Jesus, using clues from what the Gospels tell about him, his habitual activities, his relationships with people, and so on.
2. Write a one-page paper giving reasons why you are nominating Jesus for a major magazine's "person of the year" award or for a Nobel All-Time Peace Prize.
3. Research the art books in your library for representations of how Jesus has been depicted through the centuries. Based on his teaching and subsequent influence on humanity, write a one-page paper or report to the class explaining which representations you found to be the worst, and which you found to be the best.
4. Interview five adults or five teenagers, asking them what three main guidelines they would recommend that Christians follow in living as Jesus taught. Record or videotape the responses and play a five-minute segment of these for the class. Write a paragraph, or videotape a segment, adding your own responses in view of what was discussed in this chapter about what Jesus taught.
5. Read the account of the apostle Thomas's encounter with the risen Jesus in John 20:24–29. Then write a one-page paper explaining why it takes faith even to believe in miracles.
6. Jesus asked the apostle Peter ". . . who do you say that I am?" (Mark 8:29). Write a one-page paper giving your own response to this question.

Chapter 7

Church—Living in God's Spirit

Then afterward
I will pour out my spirit on all flesh;
your sons and your daughters shall prophesy,
your old . . . shall dream dreams,
and your young . . . shall see visions.

                                        Joel 2:28

O Great Spirit,
Whose breath gives life to the world
* and whose voice is heard in the soft breeze*
We need your strength and wisdom
May we walk in beauty.
May our eyes
* ever behold the red and purple sunset*
Make us wise so that we may understand
* what you have taught us*
Help us learn the lessons you have hidden
* in every leaf and rock*
Make us always ready to come to you
* with clean hands and straight eyes*
So when life fades, as the fading sunset
* our spirits may come to you without shame.*[1]

                                  Native American prayer

Overview questions

1. What is the role of God's Spirit in the Church?

2. What does it mean to say that the Church is the People of God, Body of Christ, and Temple of the Holy Spirit?

3. What are the hallmarks of the Catholic Church? How should individual Catholics live these?

4. How can the Catholic Church best prepare for the future?

Spirit—Giver of Life

I believe in the Holy Spirit, the Lord and Giver of Life. . . .

Nicene Creed

Spirit is one of the lively words in our language! There's "school spirit," "team spirit," and "getting in the spirit of things." Sometimes you try to "keep up your spirits," or you help someone else whose "spirits" are sagging. We talk about having a "spirit of friendship," "spirit of cooperation," or "the human spirit." When somebody joins in and contributes in a positive fashion, people say "that's the spirit!" *Spirit* is part of our everyday life experiences and our ordinary ups and downs.

It's also a word used to describe the **spiritual** realities which are the deepest, most important parts of our lives and ourselves as human beings—love, truth, goodness, beauty, courage, thought, and other nonphysical realities and abilities. The word *spirit* comes from the Latin word for "breath" or "breathe." The Hebrew Scriptures' word for *spirit* also meant "wind." It was used of God's creative, saving, dynamic power.

Spirit is energy, life, and power. It's what gives **life** to life. As the biblical author did, we can use our ordinary understanding of what *spirit* means to help us understand more about who God's Spirit is:

For what human being knows what is truly human except the human spirit that is within? So also no one comprehends what is truly God's except the Spirit of God.

1 Corinthians 2:11

Native Americans have had many names for God, but have often called God the *Great Spirit* whose guidance gives wisdom, and whose help brings hope, strength, and peace. The Bible and Christian tradition likewise have many traditional names and symbols for the Holy Spirit which represent similar characteristics. For instance, God's Spirit has been called the **Paraclete** or *Helper,* the *Consoler,* the *Spirit of Truth, Giver of Life, Spirit of God, Spirit of Christ,* and *Spirit of the Lord.*

Here are some traditional symbols for the Holy Spirit's actions in helping and guiding us—and what each one represents:

- The **water** of baptism: new life in God's Spirit
- **Holy oil:** God's strength and power
- **Fire:** energy bringing about new life in God
- **Clouds** and **sunlight:** biblical symbols of God's active, saving presence
- The **"seal"** of certain sacraments: their transforming permanence
- A **hand, finger,** or **touch:** God's saving, life-changing touch
- A **dove bearing an olive branch:** hope of God's peace and new life

The Hebrew Scriptures tell how God's Spirit has been present from the very beginning—at creation, in the covenants with God's people in the Old Testament and the Commandments given through Moses, in the Kingdom of Israel and, after its destruction, with the Jewish people in exile. In the Bible, feminine as well as masculine terms refer to God's Spirit. This parallels the feminine and the masculine qualities we need in our total spiritual dimension as a complete human person.

God's Spirit also witnesses to the truth of Jesus' teaching. The Christian Scriptures tell how Jesus promises, in place of his bodily presence among his followers, to send God's Spirit to remain with them:

But the [Helper], the Holy Spirit, whom the Father will send in my name, will teach you everything, and remind you of all that I have said to you.

John 14:26

". . . you will receive power when the Holy Spirit has come upon you; and you will be my witnesses . . . to the ends of the earth."

Acts 1:8 ❧

---

paraclete

one who is at your side to help

Guard the good treasure entrusted to you, with the help of the Holy Spirit living in us.
—2 Timothy 1:14

---

spiritual

of the spirit or soul, a non-material reality

❧ **Questions for discussion**

1. What parts of your experience does "spirit" affect and describe?

2. Explain how spirit is what gives life to life.

3. Which of the titles used for God's Spirit do you find most meaningful? Why?

4. What parallels or connections are there between

   - How the traditional symbols are used for the Holy Spirit's actions, and how these symbols are used today in our society

   - The actions of God's Spirit, and how people experience "spirit" in everyday life

I don't know Who—or what—put the question, I don't know when it was put, I don't even remember answering. But at some moment I did answer Yes to Someone—or Something—and from that hour I was certain that existence is meaningful and that, therefore, my life . . . had a goal.
—Dag Hammarskjold

The Spirit among us
Pentecost

Pentecost

commemorates God's Sinai covenant with the Jewish people, and the apostles' experience of the Holy Spirit which marks the birth of the Christian Church

Questions for discussion

1. What do you think Jesus' disciples felt like after he physically (in his bodily presence) left them for the last time? How might you have felt in their situation?

2. How does the Pentecost account describe the change which occurred in Jesus' followers? Why did this change occur?

3. What mission had Jesus given them? Why do you think their efforts in carrying out this mission were ultimately so successful?

4. Ideally, how would you like to set the world on fire with goodness? Where would you begin? When can you start?

Some fifty days after Jesus had celebrated his Last Supper with them, his followers gathered to observe the Jewish feast of **Pentecost** (which means "fiftieth" in Greek). This feast commemorates God's covenant with the Jews at Mount Sinai and their commitment as a free people to holiness, justice, and compassion. For Christians, Pentecost celebrates God's New Covenant with humanity and the birth of the Christian Church.

After the risen Jesus' bodily presence left his disciples for the final time, his disciples remained together and prayed about what to do next. At first, they were probably disheartened and confused—until they experienced the enlivening power of God's Spirit. The Bible's account of Pentecost (see Acts 2:1ff) vividly describes this:

When the day of Pentecost had come, they were all together in one place. And suddenly from heaven there came a sound like the rush of a violent wind, and it filled the entire house where they were sitting. Divided tongues, as of fire, appeared among them, and a tongue rested on each of them. All of them were filled with the Holy Spirit. . . .

Acts 2:1–4

As in the Hebrew Scriptures, it seems likely that the wind and fire were used symbolically here in a special, qualified way to describe how the Spirit's active presence affected these disciples. The Pentecost account reflects that they were aware they had a universal mission to all peoples. The Christian Scriptures, though, tell us Jesus' disciples actually arrived at this awareness only later, after much prayer, reflection, and debate among themselves.

So the Pentecost account may have been written much later than the time it describes. By the time it actually was written, it may have been intended to summarize the ways God's Spirit had been inspiring the early Christian Church to continue Jesus' mission.

However suddenly or gradually it really happened, the attitudes and lives of Jesus' followers changed completely. They began to understand more fully the real purpose of Jesus' mission of life-giving love and unity. They realized more and more what Jesus had meant by telling them that, with the help of God's Spirit, they were to continue his mission:

"Go therefore and make disciples of all nations, baptizing them in the name of the Father and of the Son and of the Holy Spirit, and teaching them to obey everything that I have commanded you. And remember, I am with you always, to the end of the age."

Matthew 28:19–20

There's no doubt that this small group of individuals, empowered with God's Spirit, became enthusiastically confirmed in faith and hope. The community of Jesus' followers became the Christian Church. They dedicated themselves to living the life of divinely inspired loving service to everyone which Jesus had lived and taught. And they set out to share Jesus' teaching about this with everybody in the whole world.

How successful were they at this? Successful enough that Jesus' teaching has now reached every part of the globe. Successful enough that the world's nations and legal codes now recognize his values and principles as fundamental to democracy, freedom, peace, and human rights and dignity. With the help of God's Spirit, these first Christians certainly did begin setting the world on fire. But as we look around us, it's obvious that there's still a lot of work to be done! So with God's help, now it's up to us to carry the flame.

Church

I believe in the Holy Catholic Church. . . .
Nicene Creed

Why belong?

If one can believe in God and be a Christian without belonging to a particular Church, then why belong to one? First, we human beings are social creatures. We like having people around us. We need to belong to a group. We want to share things which mean a great deal to us. (We'd much rather celebrate Christmas with loved ones than by ourselves!) When we're feeling weak or discouraged, we rely on others' support and encouragement. It's often much more enjoyable—and we get more done faster—when we team up with others.

For similar reasons, **it's more meaningful to belong to a Church community than to simply live our faith convictions alone.** At the beginning of Jesus' ministry, he gathered a group of followers. Through them, he told us to continue sharing, mutually supporting, and celebrating and working **together** to live the way of life he preached.

The ultimate purpose and meaning of most religions is to unify all persons with God and with one another. It only makes sense that those who share the same faith join together while we look and work toward this ultimate goal of unity.

Belonging to a faith community who share, express, and celebrate with us our most important life convictions and commitment

- is more meaningful and gives life more joy

- is more supportive, fulfilling, and effective than trying to love and help others only on our own

- encourages us when we feel weak, and strengthens us to face problems and overcome obstacles

- is the best way to begin building a harmonious world community

We belong to a community of faith.

So think about the opportunities which belonging to a faith community provide. Being part of a faith community can magnify the help and support you receive and give. Your life can have much greater impact and joy if you link up with others, than if you try going it alone. Aren't your deepest beliefs and commitments too meaningful to go unshared? 🐚

The believing community

When you look at the hunger, poverty, and downright meanness all over the globe, and maybe your own neighborhood, do you dream of a better world? Do you envision a day when everybody will get along, will be safe and secure, will be loved and well cared for, will be trustworthy and kind? Do you dream of a time when you'll be together again with everyone you've ever loved but lost in death?

Are you ever afraid you're just deluding yourself with such thoughts—that it's only wishful thinking? God's revelation in Scripture says no, you're

🔖 Questions for discussion

1. Why do people feel the need to belong to a group? What evidence is there of this need among teenagers?

2. What groups do you belong to? Why do you choose to belong to each of these groups?

3. Ideally, what reason do you think a person should have for belonging to a Church? What opportunities can belonging to a faith community provide?

4. What reasons do you think most people have for belonging or not belonging to a certain Church? What are your reasons? Explain.

☙ Questions for discussion

1. What are your dreams and visions for people and for the world? For yourself?

2. Do you ever feel like your hopes and dreams amount to only useless, wishful thinking? Why do you think people give up on their dreams? Do you ever feel this way? Explain.

3. What does God's Revelation in Scripture tell you about holding onto your dreams for a better life and world?

4. Of what is the Church meant to be a sign? How can the Christian community best do this?

5. What does *God's reign* mean? What does it include?

6. How can you go about realizing your dreams for the future? How is realizing your personal dreams also a way to help bring about a better future for humanity?

Church

originally from the Greek word *ekklesia,* meaning a gathering together of those who have full rights as citizens

God's reign

the final, everlasting unity of persons with God and, in God, with one another

not! It proclaims that the idea of all people one day being united with God and with one another originated in God's heart, not just in your brain. You're not aimlessly treading water through life until you die. Humanity isn't on a dead-end course in the universe, just waiting until some giant wayward meteor zooms out of deep space and vaporizes everybody into nonexistence. There's a purpose and destiny for our being here that come from, lead to, and can find fulfillment only in God.

Only, live your life in a manner worthy of the gospel of Christ . . . standing firm in one spirit, striving side by side with one mind for the faith of the gospel. . . .
—*Philippians 1:27*

The relationship Christians share as the **Church** Christ instituted is the living mystery of the unity between humanity and God. The Christian community is meant to be a sign, or kind of sacrament. **Together, we're supposed to show people that it really is possible for everybody to get along and to live harmoniously with each other. We're supposed to be a sign of the kind of unity all humanity can have with God and with one another.**

But as Church, the Christian community is both spiritual and visible. It's divine because its source, center, and sustainer is God. But it includes people, so it's also very human! Therefore, it's subject to human imperfection.

Using the language of his day, Jesus called the complete, lasting unity of all humanity in God **God's reign.** While the process of achieving this unity has already begun, it is the Church's mission to proclaim and help realize this more fully among all people, a task which won't be complete until the end of time.

We will see this ideal finally realized—although probably not in our earthly lifetime. In the meantime, Christians are to live in faith, hope, and love. We're to believe in God and hope in this ideal future God has promised. And we're to lovingly serve as God's instruments, leading all humanity to realize our glorious final future. ☙

Discovering the Church

Teenagers often ask, "How does one decide which is the right religion or Church to belong to?" Some people choose a Church or religion because it's the largest, or its laws and rules are the easiest or the strictest. But these are certainly superficial reasons on which to base such an important life decision!

Instead, one's choice about this should depend upon one's innermost convictions about God, and about what is the best way of living and of loving others. The faith community one belongs to should be one whose basic religious convictions one shares.

You shouldn't feel pressured to belong to a Church or religion only because it's the way you were raised, or because others expect it of you. It is false and hypocritical (and not at all what Jesus preached) to try to live beliefs one doesn't think are true.

At the same time, **you have an obligation to God and to yourself to earnestly seek the objective truth about God and religion.** This important decision shouldn't be based on superficial things like which Church or religion has the easiest or strictest rules, the biggest or the smallest congregation, or the best music and sermons at religious services. Catholics believe that for us the Catholic Church represents the most complete truth about the Christian faith.

Try to reach a point, though, where you're firm in your religious beliefs. Those who are unsure about their own beliefs often feel the need to assume a rigid defensiveness and an intolerance of what others believe. Those who are sure of what they believe can be more flexible. They can recognize what they share in common with others despite the differences and can learn from others' beliefs without compromising their own.

In belonging to a certain community of believers, please also realize this: **Every group of people needs some sort of leadership and structure, and some leeway for personal initiative**—which always involves the making of some mistakes! So whenever you join up with others—whether as a family, on a team, in a club, working on a project, at a job, or in the Church, expect that you will have to operate within some type of structure. Also expect not to always agree in every way with your companions in the group.

People aren't perfect! Since people are the Church, expect that, to the extent that it is human, the Church won't be perfect either. But, as Church, we do have Jesus' assurance that God's Spirit will remain always with us to guide us. Believing in God's guidance and in the convictions you share with others, find ways to resolve major disagreements and keep minor differences in perspective. Understand and be willing to forgive. **Don't let others' human frailty cause you to abandon your fundamental beliefs and your hopes for what, together, you can become and accomplish.**

Questions for discussion

1. Which reasons for deciding which Church or religion to belong to are superficial ones? What should this important decision be based on? Why?

2. If a friend asked you how someone can know which is the right Church to belong to, how would you respond? Why?

3. In what sense can those who are firm in their religious beliefs be more flexible than those who are unsure about what they really believe? Why do you think this is true?

4. What realistic attitude should individuals have about belonging to a group? About being part of a Church community?

Bandwagon believers

Read the following and respond to the questions.

We all have a natural desire to belong. Our instincts tell us we're social beings not meant to be isolated. But, when followed blindly, the instinct to belong can lead to attitudes that can have disastrous consequences: "My country right or wrong." "My political party right or wrong." "My friends right or wrong."

People can belong to a group, not because they agree with its goals and how it proposes to accomplish them, but because it's been a family tradition, or because of the leader's appealing personality.

*It's always tempting to want to rally around something or someone that makes us feel good, included, and important. But, if history should teach us anything, it should tell us never to give blind allegiance to any group, cause, or **charismatic** personality. Hitler and Attila the Hun evidently had lots of **charisma**, but those who blindly followed them committed horrible human atrocities.*

Yet today many people are still blindly drawn to jump on the religious bandwagon merely because of the powerful, showy appeal of a preacher's personality. Jesus must have been a charismatic person, too, but he made it clear that he wanted committed followers, not bandwagon believers!

Questions for discussion

1. What evidence do you see in our society of the tendency to become blind followers of a cause or a group?

2. Give examples of how teenagers also have a tendency sometimes to blindly follow the crowd.

charisma

personal magnetism, an appealing personality or style that others are drawn to follow

charismatic

having an especially appealing gift of leadership

3. Being honest, what groups have you joined because "everybody else" was? Have you ever rethought your participation or membership in a group? Explain.

4. To what extent do you think people vote for political leaders based mostly on the candidates' charisma? Do you think people realize how much their decision is based on or influenced by this? Do you think you always realize this?

5. In student elections at your school, who is more likely to be elected— someone who is popular, or someone who has more solid leadership skills?

6. What is the danger of blindly appointing or following a charismatic leader in general? With regard to religion?

7. Describe the difference between a committed Christian and a bandwagon believer.

8. Draw up a checklist of things that would help prevent you and other teenagers from becoming too influenced by others in making your decisions.

---

community

a group of people who share certain things in common

prophet

one who sees and tells the truth about the good and evil influences of certain human behaviors and their consequences

☙ Questions for discussion

1. What different views or images do people have of what "Church" is and means? What image of "Church" have you had until now? Explain.

2. What was the early Christians' ideas of Church? How did they live this in practical ways? What were they noted for?

3. Describe what the Catholic Church means by "Church."

4. List five ways in which you've made a positive difference in the world. In what five ways would you like to make more of a positive difference in the future?

People of God

Many people mistakenly think "the Catholic Church" is mainly an organization headed by certain leaders, kind of like an international spiritual corporation. When they speak about "the Church," they refer mainly to Church leaders, or the church building.

The earliest Christians, however, worshiped in homes. (A few centuries later their communities grew too large for this, and worship in special buildings became the standard Christian practice.) The apostles whom Jesus had selected were official leaders in the early Christian communities. But everyone's main concern was how to grow in relationship with God and one another by living in the kind, loving, and morally good way Jesus had.

These early Christians became known by others not for their buildings, or how they were organized, but for how they treated each another. They shared everything they owned—no one ever was without a home, or food, or other life necessities. These Christians cared for the sick among them with the same loving concern Jesus had shown for those in special need. They gathered together to worship in Jesus' name as he had instructed them to do. And they realized that **they**—all Christians together—**were Church, the gathering of God's People.**

Today Catholic teaching clearly emphasizes that *Church* is and means **community.** Together as Christians, we are the People of God. Together, we participate by our faith and our baptism in the role of Christ as priest, **prophet,** and leader. Together **we are Church.**

. . . you are a chosen race, a royal priesthood, a holy nation, God's own people, in order that you may proclaim the mighty acts of him who called you out of darkness into his marvelous light.

1 Peter 2:9

Through our rebirth in water and in God's Spirit, God has chosen us as the Christian community, to help raise the world's standards and turn its darkness into light. With Christ as our leader and model, we're to live with the dignity and freedom of God's children according to the new law of love in God's Spirit. Our goal is to help extend the reign of God until God brings all things to perfection at the end of time. With God's help, we're supposed to make a positive difference in the world! ☙

*"You are the salt of the earth.
. . .You are the light of the
world."*
—Matthew 5:13–14

One Body in Christ

As Church, Christians are also called the **Body of Christ.** The earliest Christians understood this to mean that they each had a vital role to play in the Christian community. Nobody was to feel or be left out. Everybody's contribution was valuable.

Like these early Christians, today's Catholics understand more clearly that everybody in the Church is important, not just priests or the pope. Everyone has something important to contribute:

The gifts he gave were that some would be apostles, some prophets, some evangelists, some pastors and teachers, to equip the saints for the work of ministry, for building up the body of Christ. . . .

Ephesians 4:11–12

Lay Catholics are no longer expecting priests and nuns to "run the Church," but are participating in an increasing variety of Church ministries. Catholic **laity** are realizing the gifts God has given us as **laypersons.** But this means we mustn't be swayed from what we know is true. We must work together as a unit, rather than pulling apart. For, it's all of us united together as one body in Christ who are the Church.

. . . speaking the truth in love, we must grow up in every way into him who is the head, into Christ, from whom the whole body, joined and knit together by every ligament with which it is equipped, as each part is working properly, promotes the body's growth in building itself up in love.

Ephesians 4:15–16

There is one body and one Spirit, just as you were called to the one hope of your calling.
—Ephesians 4:4

lay

persons who are not members of a certain profession, or who are not ordained clergy

laity, laypersons

Church members who are not ordained ministers

Lay Catholics have gifts to share within the Church.

Rooted. . .

Read the following and respond to the questions.

Some seeds sprout with just a little rain and sunshine. Others germinate only under the intense heat of a raging forest fire.

To become tall, a tree's roots must delve deep into healthy soil as its upper branches push toward the sky.

A healthy tree continues sprouting new leaves and limbs, so that the tree's shape is constantly changing.

Each year leaves die, fall off, and new growth replaces them.

Throughout these changes, trunk and roots must remain solid and healthy, carrying nourishment to old and new limbs.

Trees stop growing when they become too diseased, dry, or damaged and their branches fail to receive this vital nourishment through their roots and trunks.

If their trunks or branches remain too rigid and don't bend enough with the wind, or if they bend too far, trees break.

Thus, roots and trunk, old and new limbs form a single, living unit.

Always, it takes time for a tree to grow.

Trees can teach us a lot.

Questions for discussion

1. How does this description of a tree parallel how you grow inwardly as a person?
2. How does this description parallel the Church as God's People and the Body of Christ?
3. What lessons can we learn from trees? What lessons have trees taught you?

Questions for discussion

1. Compare Christians as the Church to a human body. What does it mean to call the Church the *Body of Christ*?
2. How must each part of your body work together to enable it to function properly? How is this the same with the Church?
3. What difference does a singular rather than a plural concept about team make in the team's success? How does this same principle apply to the Church as Christ's Body?
4. What happens when a hotshot team member lacks genuine team spirit? **Why** is every member of a team important?
5. What do the Christian Scriptures say about different gifts? What are the five main gifts you have to offer others?

. . . remember that it is not you that support the root, but the root that supports you. —Romans 11:18

Temple of God's Spirit

Have you ever thought about why we especially emphasize *spirit* in cooperative efforts? *Spirit* implies positive action and teamwork in achieving a shared goal. **Spirit is what binds a group of very different individuals together to work in sync as one.** To foster this team spirit, some athletic teams adopt a singular rather than plural team name or mascot—for instance, "the Cardinal" instead of "the Cardinals." This deliberately spotlights the whole team, rather than isolated players. For, however good any one player is, no player is effective without the team!

In a similar way, as Church, Christians are to work together as one in the Spirit of God. To help us do this, in Jesus' name, God sends the Spirit to guide, comfort, encourage, and empower us as Church to love God and others more. God's Spirit gives each of us different gifts with which we must work together toward a common goal. As individuals, but especially together as Church, we are the living Temple of God's Spirit.

There is a variety of gifts but always the same Spirit; there are all sorts of service to be done, but always to the same Lord; working in all sorts of different ways in different people . . . .

1 Corinthians 12:4–6

The hallmarks of the Church

I believe in the one, holy, catholic, and apostolic Church. . . .

Nicene Creed

This line from the Creed expresses the four **hallmarks** of the Catholic Church. These characteristics should also distinguish every Catholic.

One and holy

Jesus prayed for the unity of all humanity in God, and that is the primary goal of Christians. Every one of us should desire and seek this unity. As Church, Catholics are to be a sign of how and why such unity is possible. Catholics should be known by others for being the ones who settle disputes rather than fuel arguments, who negotiate peace rather than pick fights.

Although they come from every different culture and country, Catholics are one in the most important respects. We share common beliefs about God and what life means. We worship together, and we share common roots in the tradition which has come from the apostles.

You can't have so many people in one community, though, without having some differences and disagreements now and then! Even close-knit families sometimes quarrel. Sadly, though, there have been some serious separations in the Christian community since our beginning. The fact that there are different Christian Churches today reflects this fracture in the Body of Christ.

As with family members who grew apart or became estranged over the years, today the various Christian Churches are deliberately trying to bridge the gaps which historically came to divide us. We seek greater religious unity among all Christians that we might be credible and effective in our ministry to the world. This effort is called **ecumenism.** It is one of the most important tasks for the Catholic Church today. The **interreligious dialogue** which attempts to seek greater understanding and cooperation between Catholics and those of other religions is also considered extremely important. Sad examples of interreligious strife in our world today underline this.

This doesn't mean that Catholics ignore honest differences. It does mean that we emphasize what we share in common with others and build from there. Part of this ecumenical effort also includes reaching out in mutual understanding, respect, and cooperation to religious people who are not Christian and even to atheists, so that we can all work in harmony to build a better world together.

But is it hypocritical to call the Catholic Church a "community" when Catholics sometimes strongly disagree among ourselves? *Community* means "union together with." It doesn't mean having a robot-like conformity or putting on a phony front of surface-only friendliness! Although he was a devout Jew, Jesus tangled at times with others in his own Jewish community. Even he and his apostles didn't always see eye to eye at times.

The first Christian communities often had heated debates. Christians strongly disagreed with each other, and sometimes even with their leaders, about how Jesus' teaching was to be understood and lived (a key example of this: Paul confronted Peter about whether Gentile converts should have to observe Judaism's ritual laws). Sometimes there were hurt feelings and unkind remarks and behavior. In fact, some parts of our Christian Scriptures resulted directly from the controversies which led the early Christians to more strongly, clearly understand their faith and common commitment.

The shared belief in Jesus and his teachings, and the apostles' sometimes gentle and sometimes firm guidance, bonded these early Christians together far more solidly than their differences divided them. Their unity became real and solid because they were so honest

---

interreligious dialogue

effort to achieve greater understanding and cooperation between, for example, Catholics and those of nonchristian religions

---

hallmarks

signs of genuineness, authenticity, and quality

I therefore . . . beg you to lead a life worthy of the calling to which you have been called, with all humility and gentleness, with patience, bearing with one another in love, making every effort to maintain the unity of the Spirit in the bond of peace.
—Ephesians 4:1–3

---

ecumenism

effort to achieve inter-Church understanding, reconciliation, and cooperation between Christian Churches

1. What are the four hallmarks of the Catholic Church?

2. What is ecumenism? What is interreligious dialog? Why is fostering these an important task for Catholics?

3. How can Catholics participate in and promote these efforts?

4. What is a community? What did the early Christians learn about being a community, and how did they learn this? In particular, how did the apostles counsel the early Christians to handle their disagreements?

5. What do you mean by "community"? What should the Church as a community be like? How might the Church become a better community? Be specific.

6. Do you ever have a tendency to dismiss as "stupid" those who disagree with you? List three ways you could improve how you deal with the differences you have with others.

7. Explain what it means to say that the Church is holy. How should the characteristics of being one and holy distinguish every Catholic?

diocese

territory over which a bishop has jurisdiction (an archbishop is a bishop who usually oversees a larger territory called an *archdiocese*)

with each other. Their commitment to each other as Church wasn't based just on external observances. The apostles constantly challenged them to be fair and kind about how they handled their disagreements. As a result, **these Christians learned from and grew as a community—not despite, but precisely as a result of their differences!**

Human nature hasn't changed since then. Why should we expect it to be any easier or different for us now? Would we really want it to be? Whether world, family, or religious—all communities, like those of us who compose them, are and will always be imperfect. Expecting absolute agreement always about the **non**essentials of the faith—or of anything else—is unrealistic. On the other hand, if we lose the essentials we share, or let go of our ideals about building a better community, we'll never get anywhere!

Rather than shut out or dismiss as stupid those who disagree with us, we all need to learn how to listen more fairly, kindly, and intelligently to one another's concerns and criticisms. **Remember, the Church isn't a building or an organizational structure. It's the People of God.** Since people are imperfect, as God's Church on earth, we'll never be a perfectly harmonious group. Like families and groups of friends, we'll have our disagreements and differing viewpoints.

United with Christ and guided by God's Spirit, however, the Church is also **holy.** When human imperfection overwhelms us, this is what we need to hang onto. We do share common beliefs in the ideals which matter most. We have at heart a common concern for one another. As people in search of holiness, we must challenge ourselves as individuals and as Church to improve, just as we must challenge our society to do so. But with God's help, we **can** build a better Church, better personal relationships, and a better world community—not just despite our differences, but because of how we learn, grow, and improve as a result of them. 📖

. . . you are God's people. . . .
—1 Peter 2:10

Catholic

Catholic means "universal." The Catholic Church is *catholic* because it brings Jesus' presence and carries his mission to all humanity.

Who is Catholic? Individuals, local parishes and congregations, and **dioceses** who try to follow Jesus' commandment to love others, and who are in complete communion with the Church of Rome and its essential teachings, fully belong to the Catholic Church. Baptized non-Catholic Christians are also linked with the Catholic Church, though in a less complete way. Who may become a Catholic? Anyone who wishes to enter into full communion with the Catholic Church may become a Catholic.

Jesus himself preached and lived a universal message which excluded absolutely no one from God's loving concern. In fact, Jesus constantly went out of his way to help society's rejects—those with mental and physical illnesses, the social outcasts, the objects of ridicule, scorn, discrimination, and segregation. Among his last acts, Jesus forgave those who carried out the governing politician's order to crucify him. He also promised eternal life to the thief who, in the end, showed compassion for the innocent Jesus rather than bitterness about his own brutal punishment.

In these final acts of forgiveness, Jesus showed us he wasn't exaggerating when he said we too must learn to love everybody—including our enemies. He told his followers to spread this message to all peoples, baptizing them in the name of the Father and of the Son and of the Holy Spirit.

At first, Jesus' earliest followers, who were Jews, continued the religious practices of their Jewish religious tradition. In addition, they studied, talked about, and tried to live Jesus' teachings. Gradually, they began understanding that some of their important beliefs set them apart from other members of their Jewish religion. Finally they recognized that they were a distinct community.

Realizing this was painful for these early Christians and for their Jewish relatives, friends, and neighbors. Unfortunately, it sometimes led to prejudice and hostility between the Christians and other Jews of the time, as some parts of the Christian Scriptures reflect. Ironically, at first, these early Christians also didn't allow non-Jews (**gentiles**) to be part of their Christian community! Likewise, the early Christians' attitudes and behavior regarding women and slaves were not always fully in keeping with Jesus' teaching and example.

Mainly because of the apostle Paul's efforts, the early Christians began to change some of their thinking. They started to realize that they too were to be apostles sent forth to share Jesus' saving message with all others. They had known that Jesus' teaching was based upon the Old Testament. But as they started to see more clearly that Jesus had broadened the idea of God's "Chosen People" to include everyone, they encouraged gentiles to join their community. They began to realize that their identity as the "New People of God" was *catholic,* universal. They were to be the community of believers through whom God's love and Jesus' message should be brought to everybody in the world.

This mission of being **universal** has been the very name of the *Catholic* Church for many centuries. Unfortunately, Catholics haven't always been totally faithful to what this means. There were times in Church history when this universal viewpoint became overshadowed through cultural pressures and events.

For instance, when the Fourth Lateran Church Council declared that "outside the Church there is no salvation," many Catholics misunderstood this teaching. Rather than realizing that the salvation which comes through Christ and the Church is available to all persons who seek God with a sincere conscience, they interpreted "Church" in the narrowest, most rigid sense. So they presumed that every non-Catholic was an eternally damned enemy. At times Catholics discriminated against Jews and Muslims. (And non-Catholics sometimes adopted similarly biased and discriminatory attitudes against Catholics.) There have been sexism and racism in the Church, and gender and racially segregated roles and pews.

Today the Catholic community more clearly sees how wrong—how un*catholic*—these attitudes and behaviors are! Many Catholic officials have made it a point to apologize for, and are trying to correct such wrongs. Catholic teaching now makes it crystal clear that Catholics are, in fact, linked by a special bond with those of the Jewish faith. We share a common spiritual tradition and covenant relationship with God.

"[Whoever] shall introduce into public affairs the principles of primitive Christianity will change the face of the world." —Benjamin Franklin

Catholics are also urged to respect and to help protect and support what is good, true, and holy in the Muslim, Hindu, Buddhist, and other religions. Catholic officials are making a deliberate effort to understand and include more the various gifts each unique culture has to offer. Women are participating more actively in formal roles of parish ministry and Church leadership.

Jesus' universal message and the Church's universal mission haven't changed in two thousand years. But there's no use pretending that everything is perfect in the Catholic community. As in the rest of our society and world, there are still biases and wrongful behaviors within the Catholic Church which must be challenged and changed. God's Spirit will give us the courage, and will show us how. 🍂

"And remember, I am with you always. . . ." —Matthew 28:20

gentiles

persons who are not Jews

🍂 **Questions for discussion**

1. What does *catholic* mean? How did Jesus demonstrate what it should mean for the Church to be *catholic?*

2. Who is Catholic? Who may become a Catholic?

3. How did the earliest Christians have to grow in their understanding of their "catholic" mission? How have Catholics at times in the Church's history misunderstood this mission?

4. How are Catholics today to view and relate to those of other religions? In what ways do you think Catholics can do this?

5. What biases and wrongful behaviors have you noted or experienced on the part of religious believers?

6. What hasn't and can't change about the Catholic Church's mission? From your perspective as a teenager, what things do you think need challenging and perhaps changing in the Catholic community in order for it to better fulfill its mission? Explain.

The Church of my dreams

Read the following, which is one person's idea of the ideal Church. Then respond to the questions.

This is the church of my dreams:
The church of the warm heart,
Of the open mind,
Of the adventurous spirit;

The church that cares,
That heals hurt lives,
That comforts old people,
That challenges youth;
That knows no divisions of culture or
*   class,*
No frontiers, geographical or social;

The church that inquires as well as
*   [proclaims its own beliefs],*
That looks forward as well as backward;
The church of [Christ],
The church of the people,

High as the ideals of Jesus,
Low as the humblest human;
A working church,
A worshipping church,
A winsome church,

A church that interprets the truth
*   in terms of truth,*
That inspires courage for this life and hope
*   for the life to come;*
A church of courage
A church of all good [people],
A church of the living God.

*   John Milton Moore*

Questions for discussion

1. Summarize this author's idea of the ideal Church. Which of these ideals best represent your own? Are there any you would add?

2. How does this person's "dream Church" compare with
   • The earliest Christians' view of Church
   • The Catholic Church's view today of what it should be

3. How do you think Catholics could do a better job of realizing their ideal mission as Church?

". . . let your light shine before others, so that they may see your good works and give glory to your Father in heaven."
—Matthew 5:16

The Church is the People of God.

Apostolic

The Catholic Church is **apostolic.** It is founded on the apostles whom Jesus personally chose to carry on his mission. They, in turn, entrusted this work to the Christian communities they founded in Jesus' name. There is a **hierarchy** or progression of leadership and authority in the Catholic Church. The pope, as bishop of Rome, is the successor of the apostle Peter, whom Jesus appointed to lead the other apostles. The pope is the highest visible authority in the Catholic Church.

As the apostles' successors, the **college of bishops** today continues the mission of faithfully preaching and preserving Jesus' teaching. The worldwide college of bishops share the pope's primary authority when united with the pope, especially when taking part in an **ecumenical council** which is called or later confirmed by the pope. The college of cardinals is the group of bishops specially delegated to choose the pope.

The group of bishops within a country are called an **episcopal conference.** The individual bishop is the highest visible spiritual authority within each diocese. With the help of priests, the bishop oversees the **pastoral ministry** to teach the authentic gospel message, and tend to the spiritual needs and concerns of the local Catholic communities. Today Catholic teaching makes it clear that all leadership roles in the Catholic community should be thought of as ways of serving God's people—first of all in the Church community, and also in the world.

Laity and clergy are equal in dignity in the Catholic Church. Laity and clergy need each other, and we need to cooperate with each other. Our ministries are both important, and, as part of the Church, the laity have rights as well as responsibilities. All baptized Christians are to play an active role until everybody finally "gets the message" Jesus taught. The laity do this in the ordinary secular affairs of the world, as well as by contributing our services in Church ministries.

Laypersons such as nuns, monks, and religious brothers are members of the consecrated life. They live **vows** of **poverty, consecrated chastity, and obedience** within an established way of life that is formally recognized by the Church community. All laypersons and clergy are to live lives of loving service to others while seeking a closer relationship with God. ❧

❧ Questions for discussion

1. What does it mean to say that the Catholic Church is apostolic?
2. How would you describe the way the Catholic Church is structured, and the relationship between the laity and the clergy in the Church?
3. Why does the Church need some type of structure or leadership?
4. How does Catholic teaching view the purpose and role of the leaders in the Catholic community?

---

hierarchy

a progression of leadership or authority

collegiality, college of bishops

all Catholic bishops united in teaching and leading the Catholic Church

ecumenical

worldwide, including representatives of peoples throughout the world

Church council

formal gathering of bishops to address issues of faith, and of Church teaching and practice; an ecumenical council is one to which all bishops are invited

episcopal

pertaining to a bishop

episcopal conference

a nation's group of bishops

pastoral

like a shepherd, looking out for the welfare of those in one's care; as Jesus was the Good Shepherd

ministry

the ways one regularly reaches out to help and serve others

vows

sacred promises

vow of poverty

sacred promise to live simply, unattached to material things

vow of chastity

sacred promise taken by religious to not marry

vow of obedience

sacred promise to do God's will in service to others

A communion of saints

I believe in the communion of saints. . . .
Nicene Creed

Catholics believe that all good persons—those living and those who have died—make up one family, the **communion of saints.** Those of us who are still pilgrims on earth remain closely linked as a community with all good persons who have died, and we can pray for and help one another.

Jesus' mother, Mary, is called *Mother of Christ* and *Mother of the Church.* The Catholic *Feast of the Annunciation* celebrates how Mary was chosen by God, and especially blessed because she believed in and followed God's word:

> *Then Mary said, "Here am I, the servant of the Lord; let it be with me according to your word."*
> *Luke 1:38*

> *"Blessed are you among women. . . . And blessed is she who believed that there would be a fulfillment of what was spoken to her by the Lord."*
> *Luke 1:42 and 45*

The Bible also tells us how Mary saw her role in relationship to God—as an instrument through whom God's goodness shines through in a greater way:

> *And Mary said,*
> *"My soul magnifies the Lord. . ."*
> *Luke 1:46*

As someone who listened to and followed God's word, as the woman who first brought Christ's body to the world, Mary is especially the model for Christians. Catholics celebrate Mary's goodness in the *Feast of the Immaculate Conception,* which acknowledges that, by a special gift of God, Mary had no trace of sinfulness from the very beginning of her life. This belief prompted the poet William Wordsworth to refer to Mary as "our tainted nature's solitary boast."

. . .for the Mighty One has done great things for me. . . .
—Luke 1:49

The Scriptures mention examples of Mary's concern for others when she went to help her pregnant cousin Elizabeth, and when she asked her son Jesus to address the embarrassing problem which arose because a couple's wedding celebration had run out of wine. And she faithfully and lovingly supported her son throughout his life, and stood by him through the agony of his death on the cross. In the *Feast of the Assumption,* Catholics celebrate belief that, when she died, God immediately welcomed Mary's complete person to eternal life.

That is why Mary inspires this hope and confidence among us—that our average life is not just ordinary. It's precisely in our everyday joys, problems, tasks, and tears that we do meet God, and through which we, too, will one day experience final glory. This is one

---

communion of saints

the spiritual union in God which links together all good persons, living and dead

---

THE FAMILY CIRCUS®   By Bil Keane

8-7
©1993 Bil Keane, Inc.
Dist. by Cowles Synd., Inc.

"I wish Granddad could've been at the reunion, too."

reason why Christian tradition has always honored Mary as the Christian ideal.

Instead of emphasizing how to imitate her example in following God's word, unfortunately there has been at times—and still is today—a tendency for some Christians to become miracle seekers with regard to Mary. This tendency is often encouraged by emotionalism and sensational media hype. There is a great possibility of fraud and of misguiding the faithful. There is danger here that searching for "Marian miracles" may distort and cheapen Mary's true role and meaning for Christians. Sometimes there are other dangers as well—as for all the sincere pilgrims who recently, at several sites of supposed Marian "apparitions," suffered eye damage while looking at the sun!

This is why Catholic officials are extremely cautious about and, where warranted, rigorously investigate alleged "apparitions," "miracles," and "messages" from Mary. In fact, Vatican officials have strongly discouraged publicity about and public pilgrimages to places where "miraculous appearances" are supposed to have taken place, as long as there is an open question about how valid these alleged private "revelations" really are.

The Church's official process of investigating and approving these claims involves, among other very strict criteria, making sure that they're not frauds which intentionally or unintentionally deceive people. They mustn't just be products of pious imagination, or manifestations of psychological problems. They mustn't exploit people in order to gain money or attention, or result from other evil intentions.

Not since the apparition of our Lady at Fatima, Portugal, in 1917, which has received worldwide attention through the efforts of Catholics, have so-called subsequent apparitions been given equal status. We are not obliged to believe in these apparitions, nor are they on a par with Divine Revelation. When the Church does approve an apparition, it is simply saying that there is nothing contrary to Catholic faith in it. In fact, Catholics should generally view new claims of apparitions as do Church officials—with extreme caution.

. . . thanks to the communion of saints, no good can be done, no virtue practiced by individual members, without its contributing something also to the salvation of all.
—*Pope Pius XII*

Some people get scared about the "dire warnings" such revelations are often supposed to contain. But it's important to realize that no miracle or apparition, however authentic, will ever contain anything new about what we must do to achieve eternal salvation. That message has already been given to us fully and finally in Divine Revelation.

It's also worth remembering this wise guideline which Church officials themselves apply when investigating the authenticity of "miraculous" claims: **Never presume a supernatural explanation for an unusual phenomenon where a natural explanation is just as possible.** Jesus' own response to those who fail to keep a proper perspective about his mother was definite and direct:

> *"My mother and my brothers are those who hear the word of God and do it!"*
>
> *Luke 8:21*

For Mary, too, was a believer. Contrary to what others have sometimes thought, Catholics do not worship Mary! Catholics honor her for her **faith** in and **faithfulness** to God. That is why all generations have come to call her blessed. 🙢

🙢 Questions for discussion

1. How would you explain what the Catholic belief in the communion of saints means?

2. What role does Jesus' mother Mary play in the Church? How would you explain to a non-Catholic what each of the titles and feasts related to Mary means?

3. How did Mary view her role in relationship to God? Why is she considered a model for Christians?

4. Why do Catholic officials, and why should all Christians, take an extremely cautious approach to claims of Marian "miracles" and "messages"?

5. Why is it a good guideline not to presume a supernatural explanation for an unusual phenomenon where a natural explanation will suffice?

6. If someone asked you, "Why do Catholics worship Mary?" how would you respond? How would you explain why she is honored in the Church?

Getting the message

Read the following and respond to the questions.

If you look at the world around you, you can see that helping people to "get the message" of Jesus is no small task. We watch the horrors of war abroad and witness the wounds of senseless violence in our schools, neighborhoods, and communities. We watch acquaintances die from drugs, and friends die from AIDS. But when we make up our minds to make a difference, and pool our efforts, together we can accomplish what the priest in the pulpit can't do alone.

In our society, teenagers have notably demonstrated how highly successful this team effort can be. During the past several years, the number of deaths caused by teenagers who drink and drive has decreased dramatically.

This is not due just to stiffer criminal penalties or greater media publicity. It's because, among yourselves, friend-to-friend and classmate-to-classmate, you have "gotten the message" across.

You and your friends have made it much clearer that, because you care for one another, you won't let each other die—or cause others to die—needlessly. You've made it socially unacceptable to act with such reckless stupidity.

Your common sense and concern have caught on.

Questions for discussion

1. How do you and your friends try to get across the message that it's not acceptable to drink and drive?

2. What can you and your friends do to help bring about just as dramatic a decrease in the following widespread problems that hurt so many teenagers?
   • Teenage pregnancy
   • The use of illegal drugs
   • Date rape
   • AIDS and other sexually transmitted diseases
   • Violence among teenagers
   • Teenage suicide

3. Why is it important to team up with others in helping to "get the message across" about important concerns like these?

4. When you're tempted to do something that might be hurtful, what is the most effective way your friends can get the message across to you that you shouldn't do it?

5. How do you think the Catholic Church might do a better job of getting across Jesus' message of love and unity? What role can individual Catholics play in this?

I pray that . . . Christ may dwell in your hearts through faith, as you are being rooted and grounded in love.
—Ephesians 3:16–17

Looking to the future

To understand the Church at present and its possible future directions, it helps to recall the Church's simple beginnings without large membership or magnificent buildings. The Church started with only a small band of committed believers. But what people noted about these earliest followers of Jesus was how they loved one another.

The emphasis on love was primary and obvious. Both inviting and sensible, it was why Christianity seemed so appealing and spread so rapidly. Love is contagious. It offers irresistible hope for meaning and happiness.

The earliest Christians realized very well that they were the Church. They banded together not because they felt pressured into it or were raised to do so, but because they were committed to who Jesus was and what he had stood for. They became Church in order to help each other live out their shared beliefs in God and in humanity.

At a time when many others were motivated by greed, power, or selfishness, these individuals stood strongly instead for love, gentleness, and generosity. Together they committed themselves to promoting these ideals. Together they worked, prayed, and risked their lives to make human kindness and unity the standard reality.

When a small group grows large very quickly, there are always growing pains. There is need to provide greater organizational structure to accommodate the expanded size and needs. There's also a need to be sure that the group's essential focus isn't diluted or distorted as new members with different backgrounds and perspectives come on board.

The growing Church, too, needed to focus on similar concerns. In the process, however, it sometimes became so influenced by secular concerns that it assumed political, economic, and even military power. In protecting their community against false teachings, Christians sometimes became too defensive, and even intolerant. At times religious externals were emphasized so much that the Church's central mission of expressing God's loving presence in the world became somewhat overshadowed.

This is why the Christian community has always found it necessary to periodically reevaluate how well we're carrying out our mission as Jesus' followers. In more recent history, the Catholic community did this at the Second Vatican Council in the 1960s. Catholics looked back again to our origin as Church and renewed and refocused on the basic commitment to love, unity, and service as the People of God.

At that time, the Church sought to simplify its structure and practices. Becoming less encumbered with externals prepared the Christian community to adapt more flexibly to a rapidly changing world while remaining true to the essence of the Christian message.

Today the Church must continue finding ways to communicate and adapt Jesus' unchanging message about divine and human love to a highly complex, contradictory world: a world of high-tech advances where so many still lack life's bare necessities, and a world where the global communications linking us together make everybody more aware of the divisiveness and violence which still pull us apart. ❧

. . . the Church in no way desires to inject herself into the government of the earthly city. She claims no other authority than that of ministering to [humanity] with the help of God, in a spirit of charity and faithful service. . . .
—*"Decree on the Missionary Activity of the Church," number 12.*

Questions for discussion

1. In the beginning, why did Christianity seem so inviting and appealing, and begin spreading so rapidly?
2. What growing pains do groups experience when their size increases quickly? Have you ever experienced this in a group you've belonged to? Explain.
3. What "growing pains" did the Church experience as it grew in size and geographical scope?
4. Why has the Church found it necessary to periodically reevaluate its understanding of its mission?
5. How did the Church do this at the Second Vatican Council? How did this better prepare the Church for the future?
6. What complexities and contradictions in the world challenge the Church most today? Why?

1. How do you think you can best prepare now for the changes you will encounter in your life after leaving high school? How can the Church prepare for the changes it must make to adapt to the future?

2. What is the value of experimentation in the process of changing? Why must there be some limits on this, and what can happen if there are none?

3. Why must positive change in the Church come from both the laity and the clergy?

4. What main challenges do you think the Catholic Church faces today and for the future? Explain.

5. In the future, what do you think the Church will need to emphasize? How do you think it will need to adapt? Which types of changes do you think will be required for the Church to adapt to the needs of the future? Why?

6. Besides the essentials, which will not change, which other things about the Church would you like to see remain the same in the future? Why?

Preparing wisely for change

It's foolish to think that the Church community should never change at all. The technological advances alone demand that all religious believers understand and apply our beliefs in new ways. People change. The Church is people, and so must change, too. But it's also unreasonable to expect the Church community to change completely, or that everyone will always immediately like the changes that occur.

Instead of childishly resisting all change, Catholics should address these questions:

- What changes are necessary and good?
- Which ones are unwise or impossible?
- How can we help bring about good changes in the best possible ways?
- How can we best help everyone adapt to the changes?

One way to prepare for change is to begin with smaller experiments. Have you ever talked your parent into agreeing to let you try something out, to just give you a chance to prove it could work? In finally agreeing to this, your parent might have said, "Okay, just this once, and then we'll see. . . ." Maybe the experiment succeeded and you convinced your fearful, reluctant parent to let the change become permanent. Or maybe it was a disaster and showed that you weren't yet ready for the change, or that it was a bad idea entirely.

Some of the aspects familiar in today's Catholic liturgies were once frowned upon while they were being tried experimentally on a limited basis—for instance, the use of guitars at Eucharistic celebrations. As more and more people became acquainted with them, it became clear that a guitar could be as appropriate as an organ for accompanying the singing at Mass. The idea became more popular, and is now a common practice at some liturgies.

Innovations have often occurred this way throughout Church history. Sometimes the results have eventually been recognized as wise and appropriate. At other times, new practices were rejected—as when some of the popular practices of the Middle Ages led to harmful superstition. To prevent all innovations, even if that were possible, would be to close one of the important avenues through which God's Spirit has renewed the Christian community since the apostles' time. But to put no limits on this process ignores the action of God's Spirit in preserving the gospel's essential message. Positive change must come from both the laity and the clergy.

As Church laws and practices change in the future, the basic beliefs and needs will remain unchanged. The world will still need instruments of God's healing forgiveness. More than ever, people will feel the need to find a meaning for life which goes beyond superficial pleasures and achievements to lasting peace and happiness. And more than ever before there will be a need for people to join together as a community of those convinced in the overriding, overwhelming power and presence of Love. 📌

Let all things be done for building up.
—1 Corinthians 14:26

Music at liturgy changes from one era to another.

Expedition

Read the following and respond to the questions.

According to national surveys, most teenagers believe that a hundred years from now people will be living and working out in space. If you're such a believer, according to space engineers you may be right.

But first we have to get from here to there.

The U.S. government has projected that astronauts could land on Mars within the next twenty years. The first space sojourners to Mars would be confined and isolated together in a small space for 18 months to 2 years. But in planning this first human expedition to Mars, scientists and politicians have some important concerns.

- *Would the hundreds of billions of dollars required for the mission be worth the price, given the present problems on Earth?*
- *What kind of people should be picked to make the journey together? (The fear is that, after a time in such close confinement, they might kill each other.)*

Questions for discussion

1. What inward changes would you have to make to adapt to the changes of living in space?
2. What kind of people would you pick to make the first journey to Mars? Would you be a good type of person for the journey? Explain.
3. What values and beliefs will those chosen to be on this first expedition to Mars need? Why?
4. How can the same means the Church uses to help people prepare for changes be useful in preparing society for the changes of living in space?
5. What positive role can the Church play in humanity's future in space? What adaptations do you think the Church will have to make to do this?
6. What aspects of the Church will always be the same—even in life in space?
7. Given the values Jesus taught, do you think humanity should spend the hundreds of billions of dollars it will cost to venture into space soon, or put the money into addressing Earth's pressing problems first? Explain.

Chapter review

1. Spirit—Giver of Life

- What does the Bible tell us about God's Spirit?
- What titles and symbols have been used to represent the Holy Spirit's actions?

2. God's Spirit among us

- What does the Feast of Pentecost celebrate in the Catholic Church today?
- How does the Bible describe the apostles' special Pentecost experience? What new awareness and attitude did it reflect on their part?
- How successful were Jesus' first followers in carrying out the mission he gave them?

3. Church

- What positive opportunities does belonging to a faith community offer that practicing one's religious beliefs by oneself alone does not?
- What does God's revelation in Scripture proclaim about the dreams people have for humanity's future?
- How is the Church meant to be a sign, or a kind of sacrament?
- What does it mean to say that the Church is both spiritual and visible, divine and human?
- What is meant by *God's reign,* and when and how will it be fully realized?
- What are good and poor reasons for choosing a religion or Church? On what should people base this decision?
- What is the best way to cope with the imperfections one finds in one's faith community?
- What does it mean to say that the Church is a community? That it is the People of God? That Christians are one Body in Christ, and the Temple of God's Spirit?

4. The hallmarks of the Church

- What are the four hallmarks of the Catholic Church? What does each one mean?
- How did Jesus live the meaning of each hallmark? How can and should individual Catholics live each one of these?
- What are ecumenism and interreligious dialog? Why are these important efforts for Catholics ?
- What can we learn from the early Christians about what being a Church community means and what it involves?
- Who is Catholic? Who may become a Catholic?
- Explain what each of the following terms means in the Catholic Church: hierarchy, the college of bishops, an ecumenical council, the college of cardinals, an episcopal conference, a bishop or archbishop, a diocese or archdiocese, pastoral ministry.
- What is the role of the laity in the Catholic Church? What is the relationship between Catholic laity and the clergy?
- What is the consecrated life? What does it involve?
- What is the communion of saints?
- What is the place and role of Jesus' mother, Mary, in the Catholic Church? What are some of her main titles? What do the feasts honoring her celebrate?

5. Looking to the future

- What can Catholics learn from the Church's beginnings and past history about how to best prepare for the future?
- Why is it necessary for the Christian community to periodically reevaluate how it's carrying out Jesus' mission?
- What questions need to be addressed as the Church prepares to adapt wisely to the future?
- How can the process of experimentation help change happen more smoothly and with greater support in the Church? Why must there be safeguards on this process?
- What will remain unchanged in the Church of the future?

Projects and assignments

1. Read the account of the new covenant promised in Joel 2:28 and Ezekiel 36:26. Write a one-page paper about the kind of "stone hearts" you would like to see replaced with "new hearts" in our society, and the kind of "dreams" and "visions" you would like to see your generation work to make real in the world.

2. Read the account of the Tower of Babel in Genesis 11:1–9 and of the apostles' experience of being filled with God's Spirit in Acts 2:1–12. Write a one-page paper about the connections you see between these two accounts, and how the apostles' experience is the reverse of what happened in the Babel story.

3. Read Acts 4:32–35 about how the early Christians lived. Write a one-page paper about the difference you think it would make in society if all Christians lived that way today.

4. Conduct one of the following interviews. Write a one-page paper recording the responses (or videotape and play a five-minute segment of them for the class). Add a paragraph (or video segment) giving your own responses in view of what Catholic teaching says about the topic as presented in this chapter.

   • Five adults or five teenagers who belong to your Church or religious community about what the idea of "Church"/"faith community" means to them

   • The pastors of at least two congregations about how they view their role in relation to the rest of their congregation

   • Five members of a Church or religious community which is different from your own about what the idea of "Church"/"faith community" means to them

   • Five teenagers or adults who belong to your Church/religious community about what possible changes they would like to see made in their Church/religious community and why

   • Five members of a Church/religious community different from your own about what possible changes they would like to see made in their Church/religious community and why

Chapter 8   Eternal Life

"... everyone who lives and believes in me will never die. Do you believe this?"

John 11:26

O Lord,
support us all the day long
throughout the troubles of life,
until the shadows lengthen,
and the evening comes,
and the busy world is hushed,
and the fever of life is over,
and our work is done.
Then in your mercy grant us a safe home,
and a holy rest,
and peace at the last
forever.

John Henry Newman, adapted

Overview questions

1. What does belief in God's forgiveness of sin mean?

2. What is the Christian belief about everlasting life based on? What hope does it give us?

3. Who determines one's eternal destiny?

4. Where did the traditional images about heaven and hell come from?

5. What does the Catholic belief in the resurrection of the body mean?

6. What should Catholics believe about heaven, purgatory, hell, and judgment after death?

7. What does it mean to believe that all things are being renewed in Christ?

We will live forever

- Is there life after death? What happens to us when we die?
- Is there a heaven and a hell? If so, what are they really like?
- If you've been a bad person but really do change, is there hope for you after you die?
- Does God send people to hell? How can God be good and send people to a place of everlasting torture?
- What about reincarnation—is believing in it against the Catholic faith?

This chapter will explore these and other often-asked questions about life after death.

Believe in God's forgiveness

I believe in the forgiveness of sins. . . .
Apostles' Creed

Facing death often prompts the most profound thoughts and questions about what life means. Yet death and what lies beyond the grave remain a mystery. People often admit that they're at least somewhat afraid of death, but what are they really scared of?

Sometimes people are afraid that they've been too bad in this life to ever be rewarded in the next. But one of the things Jesus emphasized most is that **God is always willing to forgive.** To show how forgiving God is, Jesus often forgave sinners. He also linked forgiveness of sins to faith and to baptism, as does one of the Christian creeds:

I believe in one baptism for the forgiveness of sins. . . .
Nicene Creed

For Christians, baptism is the first and main sacrament by which sins are forgiven. Baptism celebrates our union with Christ who died and was raised from the dead so that we might rise from our sins.

God's forgiveness, however, isn't limited to "Christians only." Jesus told his followers to tell this to everybody: If you're truly sorry for your sins, God will forgive you. Because of the total message of Scripture and ongoing Church Tradition, **the Catholic Church teaches that those who are not baptized Christians can also experience God's forgiveness and salvation** if they sincerely try to do God's will by following their conscience and are truly sorry for the wrongs they do.

Furthermore, God's forgiveness isn't just a once-only proposition or a distant decree. Even for the wrongs we've done after baptism—no matter how horrible these may be—God is willing to forgive us up through the very last second of our lives. Through Jesus, God has entrusted to the Church this special ministry of reconciling sinners with God. (We will see later how this ministry is exercised in particular in the Sacrament of Reconciliation.)

As Jesus illustrated in the moving parable of the runaway son, this forgiveness always includes being reunited with God. God welcomes us back with the joyful love of a parent affectionately embracing the lost child who has returned. Remember, with God, it's never too late. So never be afraid that God won't forgive you.

The final heartbeat for the Christian is not the mysterious conclusion to a meaningless existence. It is, rather, the grand beginning to a life that will never end.
—James Dobson

But the souls of the righteous are in the hand of God, and no torment will ever touch them.
In the eyes of the foolish they seemed to have died, and their departure was thought to be a disaster, and their going from us to be their destruction; but they are at peace.
For though in the sight of others they were punished, their hope is full of immortality.
—Wisdom 3:1–4

suicide

the taking of one's own life

🐚 **Questions for discussion**

1. What questions do you have about life after death?

2. Why are people afraid of dying? Are you? Explain.

3. Have you ever felt like you'd done something so bad that somebody wouldn't forgive you for it? Explain in general, without naming any specifics related to sinfulness.

4. Which of the things Jesus said about God's forgiveness means the most to you? Why?

5. What does having a "pie in the sky when you die" attitude about belief in resurrection mean? Why shouldn't heaven be thought of as an escape?

6. Why do you think so many teenagers (almost one-fourth) contemplate suicide at one time or another?

7. What would you do if you found yourself thinking seriously about taking your own life? How would you try to help a friend who seems suicidal?

8. If the Church opposes suicide, why are Catholics who commit suicide allowed to be buried in a Catholic cemetery?

Live in hope

The question of whether there is a life after this one appears to be as old as humanity. Archaeologists tell us that belief in some kind of a life after death is extremely ancient. Humanity has long desired to believe that life doesn't end with death, and hoped for an existence beyond this life. In the Scriptures, we see how the Christian belief in being resurrected from the dead was revealed to humanity only gradually.

Christian hope in an eternal life of everlasting happiness after death is based on an **experience,** a **promise,** and a **belief:**

The experience—Jesus' disciples experienced him alive after his death and resurrection.

The promise—Jesus' assured us that, if we love each other and love God, we will also live in happiness forever.

The belief—Jesus is risen from the dead to live in glory forever, and he will keep his promise to us: If we follow him in living God's word, we too will live forever with God in happiness.

Our lives as Christians should reflect this belief in resurrection. We should share this hope with others who, when facing their own doubts and death, ask us the reason for our hopefulness.

But belief in resurrection doesn't mean having a "pie in the sky when you die" attitude that doesn't try to make the present life better. It doesn't mean just passively putting up with or trying to escape from present problems in order to experience heavenly bliss. Jesus didn't talk about heaven as a way to escape life's problems, but as the reward for doing something about them.

"If any want to become my followers, let them deny themselves and take up their cross daily and follow me. For those who want to save their life will lose it, and those who lose their life for my sake will save it."

Luke 9:23–24

Never lose hope

Belief in resurrection should give us the kind of hope we need to face and overcome our present problems right here, in this life. Many teenagers especially need the kind of hope that will let them see beyond their present problems. In fact, **suicide,** which most often results from lack of hope, is one of the leading causes of death among teenagers in our society today.

It's extremely important that anyone who seriously thinks of committing suicide obtain **at once** the help needed to overcome this crisis and renew hope in creating a better future. If you're ever afraid that someone you know might be suicidal, take an active role immediately to encourage and assist the person to get this help. In general, try to be more understanding of—and not to add to!—the personal problems others face. Also try to be more positive and sensible about how you handle your own personal problems.

Realize, too, that you can't solve others' deep-seated personal problems for them. There's only so much you can do. Letting someone become too dependent on you can actually keep the person from getting the real help they need. Trying to act as someone's liferaft when you feel like you're sinking too can be more dangerous than helpful for both of you.

Catholic teaching opposes the act of suicide as morally wrong, but passes no moral judgment on persons who take their own lives. The Church celebrates Catholic funeral services on behalf of such persons, and they may be buried in a Catholic cemetery. The Church realizes that the great despair which leads individuals to take their own lives may lessen or remove their ability to understand the moral implications of their action. Catholics are encouraged to help console the surviving loved ones and to pray for those who have committed suicide, while entrusting them to our merciful, loving God. 🐚

> *. . . he will swallow up death forever.*
> *Then the Lord GOD will wipe away the tears from all faces. . . .*
> —Isaiah 25:7–8

Life scenes

The first "life scene" below is from the play "Secrets" which Stacy, a teenager wrote not long before she committed suicide. The second is from a letter written by a young adult with cancer. Read them and respond to the questions.

Scene 1—A life

(In the guidance counselor's office)

Mr. Mullen *(to Amber)*: I called you down here because I've been getting a lot of memos from worried teachers. *(Amber looks down.)* Mr. Simmins says you don't do your homework anymore, Mrs. Buckley says you sometimes burst into tears in the middle of class, Ms. Santos says you look depressed every time she sees you, and the comments go on and on. *(He pauses.)* Do you want to tell me what's going on?

Amber *(shakes her head)*: Not really.

Mr. Mullen: Well, something's wrong, right? These teachers aren't just imagining this. *(Amber shrugs.)*

Mr. Mullen: Please talk to me, Amber. I want to help you.

Amber: I can't tell you.

Mr. Mullen: Why not?

Amber: You'll tell my mom.

Mr. Mullen: No, I won't.

Amber *(looks up at him)*: Do you promise?

(Mr. Mullen nods slowly; Amber pauses.) Um, have you ever felt like you were totally alone and nothing mattered anymore?

Mr. Mullen: No, I don't think so. Have you?

Amber *(looks down)*: All the time. It's like I don't care about anything. Not even whether I live or die.

Mr. Mullen: Have you ever thought of killing yourself?

Amber: Yeh. I imagine how peaceful and beautiful it would be to be dead. Away from all the problems and stresses of living. *(She smiles sadly.)*

Mr. Mullen: Is that how you've been feeling lately?

Amber *(pauses, looks up, gets up)*: I really should go now. I don't want to miss my algebra test. I studied really hard.

Mr. Mullen: Okay. Well, thanks for talking to me. I'll talk to you some more tomorrow.

Amber *(under her breath)*: I doubt it.

Mr. Mullen: Huh?

Amber: Never mind. See ya. *(She walks offstage.)*[1]

Scene 2—Another life

I . . . want desperately to live. I am fighting like a tiger to do just that. I didn't wish for cancer, but I have it. I would be the happiest person alive [if I could have many more years to live.] I am doing everything in my power to cooperate with the doctors who are trying to help me beat this cruel and ruthless disease.[2]

Questions for discussion

1. What indications were there before Amber saw her counselor that she might be contemplating suicide?

2. Do you think Amber's counselor could or should have done more to help her than he did? Explain.

3. Do you think Amber got the help she needed?

4. What do you think Stacey, the play's author, was trying to communicate in this scene from her play? How did she do this by what her characters didn't say, as well as by what they did say to each other?

5. Why do you think the person in Scene 2 wanted so much to live, while Stacey lacked that same will to live? Had Stacey not committed suicide, do you think she would later have found a will to live? Explain.

6. Do you think Stacey would still have wanted to die if she had been the one told she had cancer? Explain.

7. How would you respond to a friend who told you the same things Amber told her counselor? Explain.

Don't be afraid

. . . there is this most startling fact. . . that [whoever] has put on the faith of the cross. . . is not afraid of death.
—St. Athanasius

Ironically, healthy persons tend to fear death far more than do those who are actually dying. Some people are so afraid to die that they structure a good part of their life around this fear. Instead of just taking sensible precautions, they constantly worry that this or that might kill them or those they love. Their fear of dying keeps them from fully living. Even truly good persons are often afraid they'll be "sent to hell."

According to what Jesus taught, we're actually the ones who choose our eternal destiny. God gives us this freedom. Throughout our lives, we continually make choices either to keep close to God by loving others, or to reject God by ignoring or harming others. **It's our own choices, according to Jesus, that determine our real relationship with God and our eternal destiny.**

"Those who love me will keep my word, and my Father will love them,
and we will come to them and make our home with them."

John 14:23

Just as God can never force us to love, so God will never "send" us to hell. When we die, our final destiny won't be a big surprise. We already know how loving or unloving we are—and how much room we have to improve!

Sometimes people fear death because they're afraid of what lies beyond this life, or that there might be nothing there—that death might be annihilation, complete loss of one's self, no longer existing at all. But Jesus said that it's "death" that no longer exists! He told his followers that they already possessed eternal life:

Jesus said. . . "I am the resurrection and the life. Those who believe in me, even though they die, will live, and everyone who lives and believes in me will never die."

John 11:25–26

What does that really mean? It means that we were born never to die. What we call "death," then, is not the end of us. It's a transition. It's an experience of change in the way we exist. **Death is not the end of life, but its transformation.**

To the extent that we love, we already experience on earth part of that happiness we call *heaven* and generally think of as being somewhere else. In fact, research confirms that those who face death most peacefully are those whose lives were mainly oriented toward loving service for others. At the end of life, people seem to understand clearly that fame and fortune really aren't important.

What does it profit them if they gain the whole world, but lose or forfeit themselves?

Luke 9:25

It's natural that we rebel against the idea of completely disappearing from existence. Our body is **mortal,** but God has also given us a spiritual dimension which is **immortal**—we can never become just dust and ashes. If we try to be good persons in this life, we should look at death the way Jesus told us to— as a wonderful new beginning of life. We shouldn't fear death as a non-future, or as a future of possibly horrible surprises.

In fact, many of the persons who have been pronounced clinically dead and then revived say they have had similar "near-death" experiences. They speak of being bathed in light and of being welcomed by God or by loved ones who have died. Some of these persons also say they have had an out-of-body experience—a sensation of being above or separated from their body, and of watching all the medical procedures that were used to resuscitate them. They describe these as peaceful experiences and ones which give many of them a new outlook on living and leave them no longer afraid of death.

Researchers studying various aspects of the dying process from a scientific viewpoint also report that a person's last conscious sensation seems to be a feeling of peace. They are even finding this to be true in many near-death, almost-fatal incidents that happen suddenly— like falling from a height, being shot, or being in a car crash.

When a person begins to die, an explosion of electrical impulses is released in the brain—especially in an area responsible for our visual perceptions. Researchers theorize that the magnificent visions of light, and so on, which people report seeing in near-death experiences may be due to these electrical impulses rather than to a supernatural experience of the afterlife.

Researchers are also looking into the nature of the "out-of-body experiences." To determine whether these are actually what they seem to be or a type of hallucination, researchers have put special signs in operating rooms in a place where the patient couldn't possibly see them from the operating table, but could hardly miss them if they actually did have an out-of-body experience. So far, no patient has reported seeing the signs.

Researchers likewise theorize that, when the body's systems shut down prior to death, a built-in response may automatically flood the body with chemicals called endorphins which produce a sense of contentment and well-being at the very end of life. Even if they are only natural phenomena, all of these near-death sensations may be our Creator's final earthly gift to us. And Jesus' own message to us about death— the night before he himself died—was also one of peace:

"Do not let your hearts be troubled, and do not let them be afraid."

John 14:27

"In my Father's house there are many dwelling places. If it were not so, would I have told you that I go to prepare a place for you? And if I go and prepare a place for you, I will come again and will take you to myself, so that where I am, there you may be also. And you know the way to the place where I am going."

John 14:2–4

mortal

capable of dying

immortal

living or lasting forever, never dying

Questions for discussion

1. Why do you think healthy persons tend to fear death far more than dying persons do?

2. Why won't our eternal destiny surprise us?

3. Based on what was discussed in this section, what is your idea of what death is?

4. Are you really convinced that you're already living a forever existence—that you will never really die? What difference should realizing this make in a person's life? Explain.

5. Do you know someone who has had a near-death experience? What do many such experiences have in common? What do they perhaps tell us about death?

6. What do dying persons seem to understand about what is and what isn't important in life? Why do you think more people don't realize this throughout life?

the state of final self-exclusion from communion with God and those united with God

I believe in the immortality of the soul because I have within me immortal longings.
—*Helen Keller*

Images of the afterlife

Where do people get some of the images they have about what heaven and hell are like? How did people come to picture the afterlife in these ways?

Ancient images

Ancient ideas of the afterlife usually included a place of happiness and reward, and a place of unhappiness or punishment. Natural curiosity, dreams, hallucinations, and other human experiences probably gave rise to the more graphic details people have imagined about what the world beyond is like.

Abundant evidence shows that early peoples believed a spirit world exists. They prepared their dead for burial in such a way that those who had died would be accepted into the life beyond. The Egyptian pyramids were filled with material provisions people thought the departed would need or continue to find pleasure in after death. Nor were the Egyptians the only ones. Evidently having a similarly still-undeveloped concept of the afterlife, one man recently insisted on having his treasured sports car buried alongside him!

Until about five hundred years ago, people believed that the earth was flat. There were logically only two places beyond it for people to go—up or down. Most of the forces people perceived as good and depended on for survival were located up, in the sky—sun, rain, wind to move sailboats, stars to travel by. So the ancient Greeks, for instance, thought of their gods as living toward the sky on Mount Olympus. Many people still think of heaven as a place located "up there" somewhere, or refer to heaven in ways which imply that "up" is where it's located.

To ancient peoples, the more mysterious destructive forces seemed to come from the earth's depths—earthquakes, volcanic eruptions, the flooding of lakes and rivers, and so on. So they often thought of the *netherworld*—a shadowy place of mystery—as located underneath the ground, and sometimes as the home of evil gods. Some of the ancient Greeks simply thought of **hell** as being bogged down forever in a muddy swamp! The famous Greek philosopher Plato also talked about a place of temporary purification in the afterlife for those who weren't irreversibly bad when they died, and a place of everlasting punishment for those who were.

A few centuries later, shortly before Jesus' time, some of the Jews began to develop the idea of hell as a place where the wicked would be punished. They evidently became frustrated with the injustice they experienced in the world: It just didn't seem fair that some people could appear to "get away with murder" in this life without having to pay any consequences.

Christian images

It's only natural to wonder what heaven is like. It's also understandable that Christians began to imagine heaven in terms of the material pleasures (wealth, luxury, ease) which for most of them in this life were only a distant dream. So people began to envision heaven as the ideal version of elaborate earthly kingdoms and trappings of royalty. They viewed heaven's entrance as having "pearly gates," and its streets as lined with gold. Their images of heaven were idyllic.

In contrast, hell eventually came to be envisioned as a place of punishment and horrible tortures below the earth. Among Christians, the more specific image of hell as a place of eternal "fire and brimstone" is usually based on the Bible passages where Jesus refers to the "hell of fire." What these verses in the Christian Scriptures actually said, however (according to the earliest manuscripts we have of them in their original Greek language), was that those who didn't keep God's word about loving others would be thrown into the *"Gehenna* of fire." It's this word *Gehenna* which is translated as *hell* in most modern Bibles.

Gehenna was actually a ravine outside the city of Jerusalem. Because of the Hebrew Scripture references to children's bodies having been burned there in earlier times, it was later thought that human sacrifices had once been offered there to the pagan god Molech. Recent archaeological findings, however, indicate that Gehenna may instead have been a **crematorium,** where the bodies of all who had died were routinely burned—perhaps in the context of religious rituals.

Jews have always considered human sacrifice abominable. For religious reasons, they have also rejected the practice of cremation. So whether it was human sacrifice or cremation which had once been practiced there, the Jews of Jesus' time would have considered Gehenna an absolutely horrible place. In addition, by Jesus' time, Gehenna was also a pretty awful place for other reasons, too. It had become a smelly, smoky garbage dump where rubbish, including animal carcasses, was constantly being burned. The fires of Gehenna probably never did go out.

Thus Jesus wouldn't literally have meant that all wicked persons would one day wind up being burned forever in a garbage dump, much less this particular one outside of Jerusalem! He seems to have used the "fire of Gehenna" as a figure of speech to graphically make his point about how wrong certain things are. Without concocting visions of a place full of fire beneath the earth, Jesus' listeners would have understood very well what he was saying: **Doing evil will ultimately lead to permanent unhappiness unless one changes one's ways.**

Within a few centuries after Jesus lived, Christians began imagining how those who had lived evil lives would suffer the most painful fate anybody could experience. Being burned by fire naturally came to mind as one image of the ultimate endless punishment. That, plus the Scripture references to "the hell of fire," gave rise to the popular image of unrepentant evildoers' final fate as endlessly burning in fire.

In subsequent centuries, Christians dreamed up even more ingenious tortures which suited each person's sins—gossips, for example, would be hung by their tongues. Much later, in the fourteenth century, the poet Dante provided vivid examples of such punishments in "The Inferno," the first part of his famous work *The Divine Comedy.* The late fifteenth century painter Hieronymous Bosch depicted hell in a variety of imaginatively gruesome ways—even using musical instruments as tools of torture. (It's not hard to imagine what he must have thought about the kind of music the young people of his day enjoyed!)

The biggest surprise about heaven'll be that there's nothing new there. . . . we'll find ourselves clasped in the same arms that've always held us.
—Louis Evely

The eighteenth-century preacher, Jonathan Edwards, scared his congregation to death with his sermon, "Sinners in the Hands of an Angry God," saying that God dangles sinners like spiders over the fiery mouth of hell. Twentieth-century imaginations have been more inclined to envision hell in terms of psychological torments. Author Jean-Paul Sartre's play, "No Exit," for example, portrayed hell as being isolated forever with people who get on your nerves.

So people came to think of heaven and hell as being places which were "up" or "down," and their images about what these places were like arose from the tendency to picture spiritual realities in concrete human terms. These images were often exaggerations of the physical pleasures or cruelties human beings might experience in this life. Later in this chapter, we will discuss what the Catholic Church believes today about the afterlife and what happens to us after we die. 🙠

crematorium

a facility for burning the bodies of the dead

🙠 **Questions for discussion**

1. If you had lived in ancient times, what do you think you would have thought about an afterlife? Why?

2. What similarities do you see in people's attitudes, ideas, or practices regarding death and the afterlife today, and those of ancient peoples?

3. Do you tend to locate heaven or hell in a certain place or direction? Explain.

4. Do the injustices you see people getting away with ever lead you to think there must be consequences in the next life for those actions? Explain.

5. What images have you had from early childhood until now about what heaven and hell might be like? Where do you think these ideas came from?

6. How would you respond to someone who maintains that Jesus said in the Bible that God will send sinners to the eternal fires of hell?

A living hell

Read the following true account and respond to the questions.

Sister Emmanuelle was a French nun teaching college in Egypt when she was informed that she was getting too old to teach and it was time for her to retire. Sister Emmanuelle, however, prayed to God that she might be sent instead to serve in the most miserable place on earth. Her prayer was answered when she was sent to what people of the area referred to as "the city of garbage," the slum outside Cairo where the tens of thousands of people live who collect the city's garbage.

People have described the area as what hell must be like—hot, with choking smoke and intolerable smells. Those who have lived here during the last hundred years have been considered society's dregs. Because they live among the dirty trash their food and clothes come from the garbage others have discarded. The place has been considered so violent that not even the city's police will enter it.

But Sister Emmanuelle is loved by the people of the city of garbage, who run to greet and embrace her. With the money she has obtained from Catholic and other charities, she has had schools, medical facilities, homes, and places of worship built for the Muslims and the Christians who live there.

Sister Emmanuelle, who was raised in a wealthy family, now lives in the same type of rat-infested tin dwelling as the rest of the people here, with no running water or electricity. She considers it better than a palace.

Others see her as determined and strong spirited, but Sister Emmanuelle considers herself too impatient to be called a saint. She gives no free handouts, which she believes offend people's dignity. She requires that people work for what they receive. Gradually, through coaxing and education, she is helping to change the violent, abusive ways of the "garbage people."

Sister Emmanuelle's simple but valiant effort has helped to change others' behavior, too. The government is now preparing to build a far better place for the "garbage people."

Sister Emmanuelle's efforts have been based on her belief that, before one can help change people's environment of poverty and hopelessness, one must show them that they and their lives, as persons who are God's children, are valuable. To do this, one must live among them. One must share and understand the everyday experience of those whom others reject as outcasts.

What can one old woman do? Sister Emmanuelle, in her eighties, succeeded in bringing hope and love to a place of living hell.

Questions for discussion

1. What similarity does the "city of garbage" have to traditional images of hell?

2. In what ways was Sister Emmanuelle able to help the people of this city? Why do you think she was able to do this so successfully?

3. What belief were Sister Emmanuelle's efforts based on? How did she put this belief into practice?

4. How do you think Sister Emmanuelle probably views death and life after death? Why?

5. How is Sister Emmanuelle's approach different from one based on a "pie in the sky when you die" attitude?

6. What does her example shows about how one can live most fully? Explain.

Resurrection

"I believe in the resurrection of the body. . . ."

                Apostles' Creed

This phrase from the Creed expresses the Catholic belief in the transformation of our bodies at the end of time. The apostle Paul describes it this way:

Listen, I will tell you a mystery! We will not all die, but we will all be changed. . . . the dead will be raised imperishable, and we will be changed. For this perishable body must put on imperishability, and this mortal body must put on immortality.

        1 Corinthians 15:51–53

This doesn't mean, however, that you'll once again be reunited with all the same fat molecules you once consumed in those fast-food hamburgers and banana splits! As any student of forensic pathology will tell you, the human body inevitably decays after death.

Eventually the atoms which form our bodies will become part of earth's wondrous cycle of physical renewal and rebirth—part of the earth itself, then perhaps of plants, and even perhaps a part of someone else's body again. Even while we're alive, the physical elements which make up our bodies are periodically replaced by other ones which come from the food we eat. But belief in the resurrection of the body doesn't mean two people will end up in heaven sharing the same bones!

We're much more than dust and ashes. **Resurrection of the *body* would certainly include that which truly identifies each of us as a unique individual**—that which makes you **you** and not someone else. We won't lose our individual identities in the life we live beyond this one.

It's a basic principle of physics that energy and physical matter can never be completely annihilated, but only transformed to a new way of existing. How this change happens often remains a mystery, something scientists still don't

Respect for the dead flows from our belief in resurrection.

completely understand. To believe that our bodies will be resurrected at least means that **all that is unique and best about us will ultimately be transformed and glorified in a spiritual way,** but exactly how this will happen is a mystery.

In this earthly life, our spiritual self is intimately connected with our physical self. We can't do without either one! The spiritual aspect of yourself can learn and grow only by means of your bodily experiences. Without your ability to reason and love—the spiritual aspects of yourself—your body would just occupy space but without meaning or purpose. You **are** a physical-spiritual being. In this life, your body isn't merely something you have. It's essential to who you are.

For these reasons, Christians have always shown respect for the human body, even after death, and buried it with appropriate dignity. This is why the Church still recommends burial of the body, although cremation is allowed in certain circumstances.

> *When Christ who is your life is revealed, then you also will be revealed with him in glory.*
> *—Colossians 3:4*

1. How would you explain to a non-Catholic what the Catholic belief in the resurrection of the body means?

2. What basic physics principle parallels what will happen in a spiritual way with the resurrection of our bodies? Explain.

3. How would you explain to someone why the Catholic Church recommends that human bodies be buried rather than cremated?

4. What do you find most comforting about the Christian view of death? Why?

We'll meet again

Jesus' resurrection conquered death and changed its whole meaning. Now we know, when we grieve at the death of a loved one or face our own death, that **death isn't only the natural end of earthly life. It's also the beginning of everlasting life.** It's a passage, a transition from light to Light and from life to Life.

> *When this perishable body puts on imperishability, and this mortal body puts on immortality, then the saying that is written will be fulfilled:*
>
> *"Death has been swallowed up in victory."*
>
> *"Where, O death, is your victory? Where, O death, is your sting?"*
>
> *1 Corinthians 15:54–55*

Because of Christ, the Christian knows that death is **not** the final answer. Faith in Christ's victory over death enables us to remain close to those whom death has seemed to take from us. It gives us the hope that our loved ones now experience true peace and joy in God's love. It gives us the assurance that one day we'll meet again. Death just means goodbye for a time, not meaningless permanent loss. ▷▪

". . . he will wipe every tear from their eyes.
Death will be no more;
mourning and crying and pain will be no more,
for the first things have passed away." —Revelation 21:4

Life everlasting

I believe in life everlasting. . . .
Apostles' Creed

Heaven

Not all the Jews of Jesus' time believed in a life beyond death. Those who did thought of the afterlife as a place in the underworld called *sheol* (literally, "the grave"), but were unsure of what it was like. Jesus, however, was positive and definite about the afterlife. He preached that those who kept God's commandment to love would experience **eternal life.** But what did Jesus mean by this?

If you really think about it, it's hard to believe in the traditional concepts of life after death. You know that the world isn't flat. You realize that "up" and "down" are relative concepts—what is "up" for us is actually "down" for one who lives on the opposite side of the globe, and sideways for millions of people in between!

If heaven were a place in outer space, then where would hell be—in the earth's interior? Place-oriented concepts don't make much sense anymore. How, then, are we to think of life after death? What are the other alternatives?

You've already experienced the fact that your happiness or unhappiness doesn't depend upon what place you're in, but on what you think or feel regardless of where you are or what happens to you. When we call this a *state of mind,* we're really referring to a non-material, spiritual aspect of existence.

In this life, our happiness is generally affected by two things: how physically comfortable or uncomfortable we feel, and the nature of our relationships with others. In the life beyond this one, without being subject to physical pleasure or pain, our happiness will depend only on the nature of our relationships with God and others.

Life after death, then, is a state of being, a state of existence, rather than a place we can point to with a compass. **Heaven** is the ultimate and final state of total happiness. **The ultimate fulfillment of heaven is being completely loved and loving in communion with God and with all those who are united with God.**

> *Beloved, we are God's children now; what we will be has not yet been revealed. What we do know is this: when he is revealed, we will be like him, for we will see him as he is.*
>
> *1 John 3:2*

The Church's term for this blissfully happy experience of God is *beatific vision*. Those who die friends with God, in God's grace, and whose love is perfectly purified meet God "face to face." They experience eternal salvation. They are free forever from all evil and suffering, and from the loneliness of separation from God and others.

Heaven, then, is the perfection of life, the realization of our most profound human hopes and desires.

Imagining paradise

Where will we **be** in our lives after death? Possibly anywhere and everywhere we might actually conceive of being and wish to be. If you close your eyes and imagine that you're at your favorite place, you can almost **be** there mentally. In fact, in a sense, you **are** there. You're experiencing what it's like within your mind the same way you'd experience it if you were actually there physically.

For now, our physical body limits us to one place. But as works of science fiction show, it's possible to conceive of a life in which our spiritual self freely moves elsewhere at will while remaining present to this world and those we now know and love here. It's interesting, isn't it, how scientific fact and fiction today actually make the Christian ideals of the afterlife seem more rather than less possible.

There is no way, though, to fully imagine, describe, or understand what heaven is, as the sharing of God's life forever. **Like us, Scripture speaks of heaven in terms of ideal human images** such as complete peace and unity, or fullness of light.

And there will be no more night; they need no light of lamp or sun, for the Lord God will be their light, and they will reign forever and ever.

Revelation 22:5

Scripture also speaks of heaven as a joyful wedding celebration, as God's house with room enough and a special place for everybody, as paradise, as a heavenly city. Scripture even envisions heaven in terms of the finest wine! As long as we realize they're only symbols, such images are about the best we can do. It's not really possible to completely imagine the unimaginably wonderful.

". . . no eye has seen, nor ear heard, nor the human heart conceived, what God has prepared for those who love him."

1 Corinthians 2:9 ❧

> *For now we see in a mirror, dimly, but then we will see face to face. Now I know only in part; then I will know fully, even as I have been fully known.*
> *—1 Corinthians 13:12*

❧ Questions for discussion

1. Why don't up/down concepts about the afterlife make much sense anymore?

2. What most affects your happiness?

3. How would you describe to a small child what Catholic belief is about heaven? How would you describe this to a non-Catholic teenager who asked you about it?

4. What would you say to a child who asked you if he'd one day see his dead dog again in heaven?

5. What insights from science fiction have you seen or read that would be compatible with the Catholic belief about heaven? Explain.

6. What contemporary images would you choose to represent what you think heaven is like? Are any of these similar to the ones used in Scripture for this? Explain.

"The Lord God will be their light."

1. How would you explain to someone what Catholic belief is about purgatory, and why Catholics believe this?

2. According to Catholic teaching, who judges us when we die?

3. What is the difference between the particular judgment after death and the final judgment?

4. Those who say they've had near-death experiences sometimes report seeing the details of their whole life flash before them. If you were to grade your performance in life thus far after a similar experience, what grade (from A–F) would you probably give yourself? Why?

5. Why shouldn't the symbols used in the biblical book *Revelation* be interpreted as literally forecasting how the world will one day end?

6. What does the Bible say on worrying about when and how the world will end?

second coming

Jesus' coming again in glory at the end of time

particular judgment

the determining of each person's final destiny immediately after death

Final preparation

What about those who aren't either perfectly loving or completely unloving when they die? In this life at least, most people seem to fit into this in-between category.

Remember that, because of God's gift of human freedom, even God can't force anyone to experience heaven or hell. That would be one of the logical contradictions we talked about in chapter 5, because by its nature love must be a free choice. You can't be forced to love God completely now—or to reject God's love, and the same will be true when you die.

Catholic tradition has always held that **those who are good but imperfect in love when they die will eventually experience heavenly bliss.** First, though, their love must be purified until they are able to love and accept God's love fully. This temporary state of purification is known as *purgatory.* Catholics are encouraged to pray—especially in the Eucharist—for those who have died and may be undergoing this final preparation for experiencing the complete, lasting happiness which is heaven.

Final judgments

Unfortunately many Christians still think of God as a stone-hearted judge who, at the end, will tally up all our good and bad deeds in life and then reward or sentence us to punishment accordingly. So let's look at what Catholic belief is about this and why.

The Christian Scriptures actually talk about two kinds of final judgment. The last judgment, the one mainly referred to in Scripture, is the final meeting of all humanity with Christ when he returns in glory at his **second coming** at the end of time. Scripture also refers to the **particular judgment** by which each person's individual final destiny will be determined immediately after death according to the person's deeds and faith.

Some Christians talk about the second coming and last judgment as if this were going to happen tomorrow. Every once in awhile you'll hear people trying to predict the world's end. (People have been making such forecasts unsuccessfully for thousands of years!) Some Christians also speak of a "rapture" which is supposed to occur when those faithful to God are first plucked out of harm's way and taken to be with God.

At the end of our life, we shall be judged by love.
—St. John of the Cross

Christians who predict the world's end and await the rapture usually base this on a literal interpretation of the Bible's last book, *Revelation* (also called *The Apocalypse*). **Its original authors, however, used a highly symbolic writing style popular at their time to communicate hope to early Christians who were being persecuted for their faith.** They didn't intend the symbols in the book to be an accurate future forecast, and neither should we.

Certainly no one but God knows when or how humanity and our world as we know it will come to an end. But Scripture also makes it quite clear that, instead of wasting our time worrying about the world's end, we should get to work living better lives right here and right now! ❧

We are witnesses to all that he did. . . . God raised him on the third day and allowed him to appear . . . to us who were chosen by God as witnesses, and who ate and drank with him after he rose from the dead. —Acts 10:39–41

Final destiny

Who does determine our final destiny, and how? First of all, God does not sentence people to eternal punishment! Such an idea contradicts these two important Catholic beliefs: **God is absolute Goodness**, not an unmerciful monster who damns people to an eternal torture chamber! And **God gives each of us the freedom to choose between good and evil.**

To be united with God forever, we must freely choose to love God. When we refuse to love, we're the ones who punish ourselves. **Hell** is the state of excluding oneself forever from communion with God and those united with God. Rejecting God's love by sinning gravely cuts one off from human happiness and closeness to God. **If heaven is the experience of the fullness of God's love, then hell would be the opposite—eternal self-chosen separation from God.**

The Catholic Church does not believe in the type of **predestination** which holds that how we behave in this life doesn't really matter because God has already decided who will ultimately be saved. Belief in God's existence doesn't, by itself, guarantee being preordained for eternal bliss. Likewise, God doesn't "send" or predestine anyone to hell. God will never stop us from loving. We're the only ones who can choose to do that.

All who hate a brother or sister are murderers, and you know that murderers do not have eternal life abiding in them.

1 John 3:15

Love is, of its nature, a free choice. If we're free, we must therefore be capable of choosing to love or to not love. If we're to be able to choose eternal Love, we must also be able to choose hell (the complete absence of God's love).

That is why Catholic teaching holds that hell must be a possibility. But we can hope and pray that God's grace ultimately wins over every human heart, and that hell is a destiny no human being has ever chosen or will ever choose.

The Lord . . . is patient with you, not wanting any to perish, but all to come to repentance.

2 Peter 3:9

Jesus cautioned us, however, that we will separate ourselves from God if we don't help those in serious need, especially the poor and helpless.

"Truly I tell you, just as you did it to one of the least of these who are members of my family, you did it to me."

Matthew 25:40

Lest heaven seems too easy to attain, try to imagine this: What would loving fully really mean for you? How easy would you find it—or how hard—to truly love **everyone,** including those who seem most unlovable? How easy is it for you to forgive those who have deliberately hurt you? To completely experience God's love, this is what Jesus said we must learn to do.

I ponder "What is hell?" I maintain it is the suffering of not being able to love.
—Fyodor Dostoyevski

We are called to use our human freedom responsibly by helping and not harming others. We must help feed the hungry, befriend the lonely and lost, assist the poor, care for the sick and, yes, even for criminals in prison. Changing our selfish, uncaring ways is a process of **conversion** which will probably take most of us at least this lifetime!

Questions for discussion

1. According to Catholic belief, who determines our final destiny? Does God send anyone to hell? Explain.
2. Does the idea of hell raise any further religious questions for you? Explain.
3. Why must hell be a possibility if heaven is?
4. How did Jesus say we can separate ourselves from God? What did he say we must do to attain eternal life?
5. How would you describe to an older child what the Catholic belief is about hell? How would you describe this to a non-Catholic teenager who asked you about it?
6. What contemporary images would you choose to represent what you think hell is like? Are any of these similar to the traditional ones used of hell in the past? Explain.
7. What do you find the hardest about loving others as Jesus said we should do?

predestination
belief that God has chosen beforehand those who will ultimately be saved and that one's actions in this life therefore cannot change one's destiny

conversion
change of heart and mind, change of attitude and behavior

What will get you through the "pearly gates"?

The following are the responses various persons gave when asked by a newspaper reporter, "What will get you through the pearly gates of heaven?" Read them, and then respond to the questions.

Andy: *One guy got bit by a rattlesnake and I had to take out the poison. . . . I got a knife, sucked the blood and I took him to the hospital. I saved his life.*

Vickie: *The bravest thing I did was I got married and had children. It takes a lot to have a child. It takes patience and courage.*

Christine: *I've believed in God my whole life. That would get me in. I've been raised Catholic. I feel I would be welcome there. I know God as my personal friend. . . .*

Cathy: *I've saved every stray animal within a 100-mile radius of my home. I'm serious. I'm a kind person. I am. I think that must get me through.*

Carlton: *The one act that would get me through is [serving on the local school board]. I figure that deals with children and community service and that's the best way to get in.*

Steve: *I think I would be stuck there for a while. I can't think of anything.*

Kyle: *I've done some work with [mentally and physically disabled persons] at their homes. You just try to help them out and play games. I'm a caring person.*[3]

Questions for discussion

1. What does each person seem to think is a good enough reason to merit eternal life? Based on what Jesus taught, would you agree? Explain.
2. Rank the reasons given above in the order that you think they best exemplify ways to attain eternal life according to what Jesus said. (Note that some responses might contain more than one reason.)
3. What is your reaction to Steve's response? Do you think he might be overlooking something? Explain.

A new heaven and a new earth

Technology has now reached the point where even scientific researchers wonder if humans might perhaps someday be able to live forever in this life. Certainly people are living longer all the time. One day perhaps medicine will be able to completely conquer disease and aging, and regenerate body parts.

However, when asked whether they'd like to live forever if they could remain healthy and happy, many people say they'd choose not to, or that they're not sure. Perhaps they understand that extending our earthly life indefinitely will never completely satisfy the human heart.

Deep down, each of us desires a more magnificent and sublime existence, and one without the physical pain and the inescapable emotional suffering we sometimes experience here. We seek something far better than we can ever know or imagine in this life. Despite our fears of death, **we realize that God has called us to a higher destiny than our earthly existence can ever fulfill.**

Yet it's also true that in another sense, according to Jesus, we've been born never to die.

. . . Jesus . . . abolished death and brought life and immortality to light through the gospel.

> *2 Timothy 1:10*

The Christian is already risen with Christ. In a way, we're already living forever. What we need to do is to make our life so meaningful, by how we love God and others, that we will want the experience of this love to continue forever. That's what "eternal happiness" will include, and it's the kind of happiness we should begin to realize in this life.

At the end of time, God's reign will be fulfilled. According to the Scriptures, humanity and the universe will be transformed and made new. The unity of everyone on Earth that we all hope for, and God's desire for all things to become one in Christ will finally be realized. In this new realm, there will be no more suffering. We will learn the full meaning of our lives.

In fact, **this promised renewal of all things has already begun in Christ, and it continues in the good that is done by those who are the Church.** So rather than prompting us to become less concerned about humanity and our universe, we should take better care of our earthly environment. We should work even harder for peace and unity, so that all humanity will be prepared for God's reign. The fact that our earthly days are numbered tells us not to waste time on empty pursuits, or on feeling sorry for ourselves.

Time is precious. We have an unknown, but limited, span in which to fulfill the meaning of our life. So think about how you use the time you have every day. Make every day of your life meaningful in the ways that really matter. ❧

❧ Questions for discussion

1. Why will extending our earthly life indefinitely never completely satisfy us?

2. Had you ever thought before about the fact that you are already living forever? Does realizing this make any difference in your outlook on life? Explain.

3. What prompts you from time to time to think about the fact that your earthly days are limited? Does this realization affect your outlook or behavior? Explain.

When Christ appears [at his second coming] he will simply be manifesting a transformation that has been slowly accomplished under his influence in the heart of the mass of humanity.
—Pierre Teilhard de Chardin, adapted

Time is precious.

What would you want to last forever?

Read the following ideas about "heaven on earth." Then respond to the questions.

Earth is a place where we build our heaven.

God doesn't invite us to pass into the next world.

Rather, [God has come] into this world . . . redeemed it . . .

and, someday, . . . [will] crown [God's] work and ours

by making it eternal.

We're in this world forever. . . .

And it may well be that heavenly joy will consist,

not in having our human faculties suspended,

but in living our human life to the full.[4]

Questions for discussion

1. Describe the kind of world you think would be worth lasting forever.

2. What is your idea of the kind of life that, for you, would be worth lasting forever and ever and ever . . . ?

3. What one thing would you like to do to make every day of your life more meaningful in a way that really matters?

What about reincarnation?

One question often asked is "Can Catholics believe in reincarnation?" **Reincarnation** literally means "to be enfleshed again" and is a main belief of the Hindu religion. Reincarnation involves the belief that after death one comes back again to live another life in another body—that of a plant, animal, or human being. Most of those who believe in reincarnation also believe that who or what one is reincarnated as depends upon how good one has been in the previous life. Thus, the better one is in this life, the better off one will be when next reincarnated.

If you think it might be nice to be reincarnated, consider this: Most people in the world who do believe in reincarnation don't ever want to have to come back again! They consider reincarnation a result of not having become perfect enough to be united once and for all with God. In fact, part of Hindu religious practice is based on ways to avoid being reincarnated.

Catholics believe in the human spirit's immortality—that who we are as a unique individual will continue to exist forever. We might get temporary amnesia, but we won't forever lose our basic personal identity. **Practically speaking, belief in reincarnation means the loss of this unique personal identity.** That amounts to annihilation of the self, not immortality.

In this life, we could need plastic surgery which gives us a totally different outward appearance. We might be given organ transplants and assume parts of someone else's body. But we'll never become—or come back being—somebody **else**. We'll always remain **us.**

Have you ever walked into a room you've never been in, yet you feel like you've been there before? This common experience of *deja vu* also leads some individuals to believe in reincarnation.

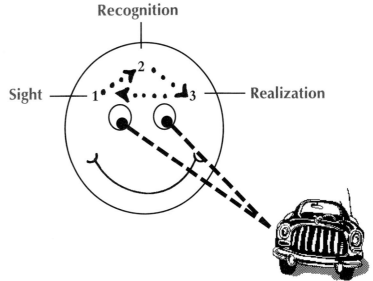

But the next time you have a *deja vu* experience, instead of jumping to the conclusion that you were once Cleopatra or Napoleon, remember the common-sense guideline: **Never presume a supernatural explanation for an unusual phenomenon where a natural explanation is just as possible.** In fact, there are many possible natural explanations for these *deja vu* experiences.

Some scientists think these perceptions probably result from a reordering of the brain's electrical connections involved in our thinking process. Normally, we see something first, then recognize what we see, and finally realize that **we** are doing the seeing and the recognizing. In *deja vu* experiences, these three steps may be switched around. This would account for the sensation of seeming to recognize as familiar a place you've actually never been before.

Another possible explanation for this phenomenon has to do with the connection between our genes and how we remember things. It appears that the things we know are kept within our brain cells in the form of nucleic acid patterns. Some scientific research suggests that perhaps some of this knowledge, along with the other genetic material, is passed on from one generation to another.

reincarnation

belief that one's spirit is reborn in another body

deja vu

the feeling that one is reliving an experience one has already had before

extrasensory perception

the ability to perceive things without the use of one's senses

🐚 Questions for discussion

1. Why don't most of those who believe in reincarnation want to be reincarnated?

2. What do Catholics believe about the human spirit's future? How would it be against this to believe in reincarnation?

3. What types of experiences lead many people to believe in reincarnation for nonreligious reasons? What natural scientific explanations might account instead for these experiences?

4. What would your advice or guideline be for people on how to live so they won't have to fear what lies beyond this life?

Could this account for what child prodigies seem to know instinctively, or for other such unusual occurrences? Are there whole libraries of knowledge in your brain that you haven't accessed yet? Might your children one day inherit everything you learn from studying for your math tests? Who knows? But this is another possible natural way of explaining the extraordinary—without resorting to belief in reincarnation.

Contrary to what popular "mind-readers" claim, no one has conclusively demonstrated scientifically yet that such a thing as ESP (**extrasensory perception**) actually does occur. Just because you and your friends occasionally finish each other's sentences accurately doesn't mean you're using ESP. It probably means you know each other fairly well, or share very similar thought patterns, ways of thinking. After all, one reason you're friends is probably that you think alike in certain ways!

The brain does send out electrical impulses when we think. Perhaps the ongoing scientific research into the human mind and its potential will one day show us conclusively that we can pick up thoughts transmitted from across the room or the world. Some scientists theorize that electrical impulses may continue to reverberate forever in space. If that ever does prove to be true, maybe we will someday be able to listen in on the words, events, or even thoughts of those who lived centuries ago.

In any event, there are possible (though not yet proven) natural scientific explanations for why some people experience the sensation of having lived before, or seem to recall details about a previous time or person. Actually, there are usually much simpler explanations—such as fraud!—for the claims to have lived before.

So don't jump to conclusions about having been reincarnated. Look for possible natural ways to explain seemingly bizarre occurrences. (You'll probably find these even more fascinating.)

Above all, remember that **what's important is what you do and are in this life.** Be a kind, loving person in this life and you won't have to fear what's beyond the grave. 🐚

Our senses are a major way by which we perceive things.

If you could live yesterday over

Read the following and respond to the questions.

In our society most people don't believe they've lived as someone else in a previous life, or that they'll be reincarnated in a future life as somebody else. Here's what some have said, though, about how they'd relive aspects of this life if they could.

If I had my life to live over again,
I'd "swim more rivers,
climb more mountains,
kiss more babies,
count more stars.
Go barefoot oftener,
eat more ice cream,
ride more merry-go-rounds,
watch more sunsets.
Life must be lived as we go along."[5]

I would tell my parents more often that I love them.
I'd spend more time getting to really know my brothers and my sisters before leaving home for college.
I wouldn't take my friends for granted.
I would stop worrying about what I look like, and about what others think about my appearance.
I'd look at things longer, and be a better listener.
I'd laugh a lot more, and not take myself so seriously.
I would keep things in better perspective,
and wouldn't make little problems seem like big disasters.
I would ask for help more when I need it.
I'd hug a lot more.
I'd tell God a lot more how grateful I am just to be alive.

Questions for discussion

1. Which of the items above are most similar to what you'd do if you had the opportunity to live the last several years over again?

2. Suppose you found out that your time was up today but that you could first relive last week before you died, with one stipulation—that you couldn't change any of the week's events, but only your responses to them.

   • How would you respond differently? Why?

   • Which of your responses would be the same? Why?

3. Think of a day in your life that you'd like to live over much differently if you could.

   • What would you change about the day? Why?

   • If you couldn't change the day's events the next time around, how would you like to change your responses to them? Why?

Chapter review

1. We will live forever

- What did Jesus teach and what is Catholic belief about the forgiveness of sins? How is it linked to Christian baptism? Is God's forgiveness available to non-Christians?

- On what is the Christian hope in an eternal life of everlasting happiness based? How should Christians' lives reflect their belief in resurrection? What kind of hope should it provide?

- What is Catholic teaching and practice regarding the act of suicide and those who take their own life?

- Who, according to Catholic teaching, chooses our eternal destiny?

- What did Jesus say about death, and about eternal life and how to attain it?

- What does the Catholic belief in immortality mean?

- Why shouldn't good persons fear death and what comes after it?

- Describe what the traditional images of heaven and hell are, and where they came from—in particular, the Christian images of these.

2. Resurrection

- What does the Catholic belief in the resurrection of the body mean and include?

- Why does the Church recommend burial of the human body after death?

- How did Jesus' resurrection change the meaning of death? How is this belief reassuring and comforting for Christians?

3. Life everlasting

- What is the Catholic belief about what heaven is? What is meant by the *beatific vision?*

- What images are used in Scripture to speak of heaven? Why can't anyone completely imagine what heaven is like?

- What does the Catholic belief in purgatory mean?

- What two kinds of final judgment are referred to in the Christian Scriptures? What does each involve?

- Why shouldn't the images in the Book of Revelation about the world's ending be understood as literal prophecy about the world's end? How should Christians view the world's end?

- Who determines our final destiny, and how? What is the Catholic belief about hell, and why it must at least be a possibility?

- What type of predestination does the Catholic Church not believe in, and why?

- How did Jesus say we can separate ourselves from God? What did he say we must learn to do in order to truly love God?

4. A new heaven and a new earth

- When will God's reign be completely fulfilled? What is meant by the Catholic belief in the renewal of all things in Christ?

- How should Christians live in order to help continue this renewal?

- What do Catholics believe about the human spirit's future? How would it be against this to believe in reincarnation?

Projects and assignments

1. Read Paul's advice in 2 Thessalonians 2:1–3 and 3:10–13 to Christians of his time who were expecting the world to end soon. Write your own letter to someone today who seems too worried about the world's ending.

2. Catholics today may help choose from several designated readings which Scripture passages they would like read at the Eucharist celebrated when a loved one dies. Write a one-page paper explaining which two Scripture readings you would choose and why. (Do not quote the passage, just refer to it by book, chapter, and verses.)

3. Write a one-page paper about how the traditional images of heaven and hell are reflected in today's advertisements, movies, and so on.

4. Research further and write a one-page paper on, or give a five-minute presentation to the class on one of the following topics. Add your comments in view of the teaching presented in the Christian Scriptures and in Catholic teaching about death and the afterlife.

   • The portrayal of the afterlife in art and/or music in the past or today

   • The practices surrounding death and burial in our society or in your cultural tradition

   • What modern Hindus believe about reincarnation, and how this belief affects the ways they live

   • The possible natural scientific explanations for such things as *deja vu* or "near-death experiences"

   • The reasons for suicide among teenagers, and the resources available to teenagers in your community for helping to overcome the types of problems which sometimes lead to suicide

   • What famous athletes or others who have conquered major obstacles say about never giving up and never losing hope

   • Ancient or previous-century Christian images of the afterlife

   • A social situation in your community which causes people to lose hope, and some possible solutions

5. Write a one-page paper on practical ways you and other teenagers can contribute to the continuing renewal of the world which is already begun in Christ.

6. Write a song or poem of at least twenty lines on making every day count, on living in hope, or on coping with the death of a loved one

Part Three

Prayer, and Celebrating the Christian Mysteries

Chapter 9

Folded hands are a universal symbol of prayer.

Overview questions

1. What is prayer?
2. What has God told us about praying?
3. Why pray—does it really do any good to pray?
4. What did Jesus teach us about how to pray?

Prayer

Our Father who art in heaven,

> Help me to believe this day that there is a power to lift me up
> which is stronger than all the things that hold me down.

hallowed be thy name.

> Help me to be sensitive to what is beautiful, and responsive to what is good,
> so that day by day I may grow more sure of the holiness of life in which I want to trust.

Thy kingdom come.

> Help me to be quick to see, and ready to encourage, whatever brings the better meaning of God
> into that which otherwise might be the common round of the uninspired day.

Thy will be done on earth, as it is in heaven.

> Help me to believe that the ideals of the spirit are not a far-off dream,
> but a power to command loyalty and direct my life here on our real earth.

Give us this day our daily bread,

> Open the way for me to earn an honest living without anxiety;
> but let me never forget the needs of others,
> and [let] me want only that benefit for myself which will also be their gain.

and forgive us our trespasses, as we forgive those who trespass against us,

> [Help me be] patient and sympathetic with the shortcomings of others,
> expecially of those I love;
> and keep me sternly watchful only of my own.
> Let me never grow hard with the unconscious cruelty of those
> who measure themselves by mean standards, and so think they have excelled.
> Keep my eyes lifted to the highest, so that I may be forgiving,
> because I know how much there is of which I need to be forgiven.

and lead us not into temptation, but deliver us from evil.

> Let me not go carelessly this day within the reach of any evil I cannot resist,
> but if in the path of duty I must go where temptation is,
> give me strength of spirit to meet it without fear.

For the kingdom, the power and the glory are yours,

now and forever. Amen!

> *Walter Russell Bowie*[1]

Private prayer is one form of communication with God.

What is prayer?

Recent surveys show that almost everyone in our society prays, and that most people pray every day and say prayer is very important to their lives. Even many of those who say they don't believe in God say they pray sometimes! In the United States, Congress has officially declared the first Thursday of every May as the National Day of Prayer. Even psychoanalysts are beginning to understand more that prayer isn't an immature, infantile response to feeling helpless or out of control—that instead, prayer anchors us in "something deeper, more profound and true."

Those who pray say that prayer enriches their lives and means a great deal to them. It's a moving sight to see the present and former leaders of the world—the most powerful human beings on Earth—standing side by side at the funeral of a nation's leader with their heads all bowed in prayer and responding "Amen" aloud together. But just what is prayer? Why do people believe in praying? Does God really listen to and answer prayer? In these next two chapters we'll discuss these and other common questions about prayer.

First of all, **prayer is communicating with God in some way.** One prays whenever, wherever, and however one seeks to draw closer in communion with the living, true God. As we've already seen, just by existing we already have a permanent relationship with God—we continue to depend upon God for our very existence. But God also invites us to a far more personal kind of relationship—one which is just as vital to what our lives really mean and to our ultimate happiness. **In the broader sense, prayer is all the various ways we strengthen our personal relationship with God.**

So we pray, then, for the same reasons we communicate with anyone. *Communication* literally means "to be together, united, or one with." Real communication brings us closer in relationship to others in some way—whether by love, compassion, or understanding.

It's hard sometimes to know how to start a conversation with people. With God that's never a problem, because it's always God who initiates the communication. That's why prayer is a gift from God, as well as our effort to communicate with God. It's God who lovingly calls us to have a relationship. It's God's Spirit who prompts us to pray.

prayer

communicating with God, focusing on God in a spiritually uplifting way; also, asking for God's blessings; in the broader sense, all the ways in which people try to be closer to God

"Come," my heart says, "seek God's face!" Your face, LORD, do I seek.
—*Adapted from Psalm 27:8*

Questions for discussion

1. In what ways do you think that prayer to God is the same as communicating with other human persons? How do you think that it is different? Explain.

2. Why do you think it requires faith to believe in prayer? Do you think if God appeared to you in human form that it would really be easier to carry on a conversation? Explain.

3. Do you find communicating with God in prayer to be easier or harder than conversing with other people? Why?

4. How would you describe what prayer is and means for the Christian?

So whenever you're drawn to pray, you're really responding to God's invitation to hear what's on your mind, to help you sort through a problem or make a decision, or to just spend some quiet time being together and drawing closer.

One of the problems is that people often ignore God's invitation to pray, yet they think that if God appeared to us in human form it'd be an awful lot easier to carry on a conversation! But we might not recognize or believe that it really was God. It requires faith to believe in God, and it also requires faith to believe in prayer. As Jesus said to the woman at the well,

"If you knew the gift of God, and who it is that is saying to you, 'Give me a drink,' you would have asked him, and he would have given you living water."

John 4:10

In Jesus, God's self **has** been revealed to us most fully in human terms. Through Jesus, we know far more about God and are brought into a much closer relationship with God. Thus **Christian prayer is a covenant relationship between God and human persons in union with Christ.**

Actually, communicating with God is much easier than communicating with people, because prayer is always Heart-to-heart. You've no doubt had the experience of trying to communicate one thing to somebody, but being completely misunderstood. God's the only one who knows your every thought and understands your every feeling. So you can pray with complete assurance that you're always fully understood.

Good communication between people is a two-way street. True communication always involves shared understanding—both expressing something and being understood. In human communication, this can be difficult when someone isn't really listening. But God is always willing to listen. For our part, we should also be willing to listen to God.

Prayer is . . .

Read each of the following, and see which is closest to or furthest from how you would describe prayer.

Juan: *Prayer is opening a package and finding something special.*

Shalandra: *Prayer is our lives and how we lead them out of love for God.*

Warren: *If faith is friendship with God, then prayer is a conversation with your Best Friend.*

A purely sociological view: *Prayer is "a coherent and complex form of socially established cooperative human activity through which goods internal to that form of activity are realized in the course of trying to achieve those standards of excellence which are appropriate to, and partially definitive of, that form of activity, with the result that human powers to achieve excellence, and human conceptions of the ends and goods involved, are systematically extended."[2]*

Questions for discussion

1. Briefly, what is the view of prayer in the last description of prayer above?

2. In what sense is this last statement about prayer true? In what sense might it not be completely true? What is missing in this description?

3. Which of the above descriptions of prayer is closest to your own idea of what prayer is? Why? Which is furthest from your idea of prayer? Why?

4. What do you believe about prayer? What does prayer mean to you personally? What part does it have in your life?

5. Where and how did you first learn to pray? How would you teach a young child of your own to pray? What approaches would you definitely not use in doing this? Explain.

What has God told us about prayer?

Prayer in the Hebrew Scriptures

Every religion witnesses to humanity's search for ways to draw closer to God. Within the human heart, our Creator has placed a capacity for and a call to have a relationship with God. In response to God's invitation, people have always sought in some way to relate more closely with God. Jews and Christians believe that, **in the Old Testament, God has shown us many things about how to get closer to God through prayer.**

Through the biblical story of Abraham, God has told us that prayer should involve listening to God and having the faith to follow God's will. Abraham did this by following his conscience and refusing to sacrifice his son Isaac, even though that was the expected practice at the time. His faith in God led him to do the just and right thing.

Moses' relationship with God told us that we can relate with God "face to face, as one speaks to a friend" (see Exodus 33:11). Through Moses' example, we're encouraged to pray for one another, as Moses prayed that his people would return to God's ways. From the time of ancient Israel's King David to Jesus' time, the Hebrew Scriptures have shown us even deeper and more meaningful ways to pray.

We also learn from the Hebrew prophets about what it means to pray sincerely and from the heart. We learn to pray by our actions—by what we do for others, especially in trying to right the wrongs in our society. We learn that a part of prayer is conversion of heart—changing our attitudes and becoming better persons, rather than just being hypocrites who mouth empty pious words.

The psalms are the Old Testament's book of prayers. The psalms continue to have such great meaning for both Jews and Christians because they're so real. They tell us that we don't need fancy, formal words to reach God. They capture all types of human experience in language that is moving and at times beautiful, yet also completely honest and to-the-point.

The psalms express the same joy, gratitude, and feelings of praise we all experience at times. They put into words our cries for help when we're troubled or feeling like everything's hopeless, and they lead us to renew our hope by relying on God for strength. This is why the psalms are used so often as prayers in the Christian liturgy, and whenever groups of people—even from different religions—want to pray together.

Like the sacred history described in the Old Testament, **modern history** also records how humanity responds or fails to respond to having a relationship with God and with one another as God's children. As all of human history shows, despite the significant lapses and exceptions, humanity as a whole has been inching closer to one another and to God.

Once Earth's peoples were isolated. Now we're just a phone call away. Once slavery, inequality, and abuse were accepted as normal throughout the world. Now they've been recognized as inherently wrong. Religious beliefs and values that once were revolutionary are now helping to shape and renew nations and the world's future.

As the wars and other wrongs of the world testify, we've still got a long way to go to achieve the completely harmonious future we all dream about. The Hebrew Scriptures tell how God acted through people's responses to God in the events of human history. This tells us, too, that our relationship with God can't just be reserved for one day a week in church. Our lives as well as our words must be a prayer, a way we grow closer to God daily through our relationships and decisions, in the things we do and how we respond to people and to what happens to us. ❧

. . . I unfold all my troubles. . . .
No one cares about me. . . .
Listen to my cries for help,
I can hardly be crushed lower.—Psalm 142:2, 4, 6 (New Jerusalem Bible)

❧ Questions for discussion

1. What do each of the following in the Hebrew Scriptures tell you or mean to you personally about prayer?
   - The story of Abraham
   - Moses' relationship with God
   - The Hebrew prophets' idea of prayer

2. Are you familiar with any of the Old Testament psalms? Explain.

3. If God asked you to help compile a book of prayers that would be meaningful to teenagers today, what would you include? Why?

4. What do you think modern history tells us about humanity's relationship with God? About your relationship with God? Explain.

Presidents on praying

Read the following insights of two former U.S. presidents about prayer. Then respond to the questions.

One former U.S. president described himself as not having been a very religious person before. But he said, after he was elected to the presidency, "I prayed every night on my knees."

Another former president explained how "Prayer has always been important and personal for me. . . ." Although others describe him as someone "who usually avoids appearances and situations that play on emotion," the former president has described a time when he prayed with great emotion: "As he awaited the start of a war in which he would send 'other peoples' [children] to war . . . 'I had the tears start down the cheek . . . and I . . . no longer worried how it looked to others who were watching.' What mattered about prayer, he said, 'was how it seemed to God,' not how it seemed to others."[3]

Questions for discussion

1. Why do you think the first man began to pray daily—and on his knees—after he became president?
2. What does prayer seem to mean to the second former president? Why was he embarrassed about how he was praying in one instance? What did he decide about this?
3. Why do you think some teenagers seem self-conscious or embarrassed about praying or about admitting that they pray? Have you ever felt this way? Explain.
4. What do you think should matter most when a person prays? Why?

Why pray?

Why do you take the time and make the effort to communicate with those you care about? First of all, you believe that the other person cares enough about you to want to listen. You hope that by communicating you will grow closer to each other in trust, love, or understanding.

You pray in your distress and in your need;
would that you might pray also in the fullness of your joy
and in your days of abundance. . . .
And if it is for your comfort to pour
your darkness into space,
it is also for your delight to pour forth
the dawning of your heart.
—Kahlil Gibran

And so you tell someone the qualities you appreciate in them and thank them for their gifts or for their kindness to you. You ask a favor. Or you tell someone you're really sorry and ask their forgiveness. You tell someone how much you love them, praising the qualities or accomplishments you admire in them. Sometimes you just want to share your thoughts, feelings, and experiences with someone—to just take pleasure and joy in being together.

Why do people pray? We pray to God for one or more of the following reasons, which are actually similar to why we communicate with other people we love:

Prayer of adoration and blessing: To acknowledge God's greatness and goodness, and that God is the source of our many blessings.

You're the absolute best. I know You're where everything good that blesses my life really comes from.

Prayer of petition: To acknowledge our dependence on God, ask God's forgiveness for the wrongs we do, and ask for what we think is good and will truly help us and others realize our ultimate destiny.

Help, God! I feel so confused. It's like I'm drowning in an ocean of trouble. I know I've messed up, and that some of what I'm going through now is my fault. I'm sorry and I really will try to do better next time. But please help me now. I feel like I'm being pulled every which way, and I don't know where else to turn. Please help me sort it all out and do the right things this time.

Prayer of intercession: To ask God's merciful help for others, including our enemies.

You're kind and merciful. Please guide my friend who is really hurting right now. And help the other kids who are spreading the false rumors to stop and realize how rotten and hurtful they're being.

Prayer of thanksgiving: To express our gratitude to God for everything, and for particular blessings in our life.

I know I often complain to You, and that I ask You favors a lot. But this time (surprise) I just want to say thanks so much for my life, and for all the beautiful things You've given us on Earth. Thanks especially for my

new niece (who's won our hearts already). We're all really grateful that she's healthy. P.S. I also appreciate the good grade I got on that test I studied so hard for!

Prayer of praise: To express our delight at who God is, and just because God is.

Wow, another knockout sunset! Nobody can make 'em like You can. God, I'm so glad you're God. You really are the greatest!

Some people seem to think that there is only one form of prayer—that in which we ask God for something. But as you can see, there are actually several forms of prayer, each of which corresponds to one of the reasons why people pray. These are also the main reasons for and forms of praying used when Catholics pray together in the Church's various religious celebrations. The Eucharist, the Church's main prayer, expresses all of these forms of prayer.

The purpose and point of all prayer is to lead us to the love and happiness which come from loving God and others. In simplest form, a variation of a Hindu prayer expresses it this way:

Lord, please help me love You. Help me to love those whom You love. ❧

intercession

asking or pleading on behalf of someone else, as interceding for someone in prayer

❧ Questions for discussion

1. For what reasons do you usually communicate with other people? With God?

2. Which of the prayer examples given in this section seems most like what you experience at times? Why?

3. For what reasons do you think that people pray most often? Which form of prayer describes the way you most often pray? Explain.

4. How would you describe the purpose and point of all prayer?

5. How should one pray for one's enemies in time of war with another country? When being harassed by a group from school?

This monk's life centers around prayer in all its forms.

What good does praying do?

Read the following and respond to the questions.

In a college class, the instructor asked his students what they would do if a friend of theirs was thinking about getting an abortion after having been raped on a date. He said he was hoping that they would discuss how they viewed the rightness or wrongness of their responses in the situation.

One student, however, said, "Well, I guess I'd pray." Someone laughed; [the instructor] smiled and said: "That's nice, but then what would you do?" So the . . . discussion started. Prayer was not mentioned again. [But the instructor] went home and had second thoughts.

*"Was the student's answer entirely beside the point? He is not so sure. . . . Does [discussing right-wrong dilemmas] have no room at all for **piety?** And was he not [politely treating her response as inferior] when he thought the student's piety would keep her from getting her hands dirty or thinking hard?"*

*The instructor now wishes he had **taken her seriously,** so he takes us on a tour of what seriousness would mean. . . .*

"She might have answered [in] her own ways" and talked about how "calling on God" might help her to keep from putting other priorities above God. The young women might have acknowledged her own weaknesses. She might have said that praying " 'might let me see my friend in a new and different way, as one whose ultimate good depends on God rather than on my own efforts to achieve it.' " So she might have been given a fresh insight into how to help her friend.

Or the young woman might have talked about prayer as a kind of magic—as if praying would automatically produce the right results and spare her from having to really address the practical realities of her friend's problem.

After some reflection, the instructor thought that he might possibly have discussed with the students how people's experiences of prayer really can help expand their ability to know the best way to respond to moral problems.

*But the instructor also wondered "What if he **had** let the [young woman] go on and she had gone on and on—the way **pietists** often tend to do—and it had been hard to get to [the topic of the day's class]? She would have been monopolizing the discussion. Picture this:"*

The instructor: " 'Uh, that's enough; thank you. Others have a right to speak.' "

But the instructor thinks he would have asked her this instead: " 'And for whom would you pray?' "

Student: " 'Why, for [everyone], of course.' "

Instructor: " 'For the poor?' "

Student: " 'Yes, that they may have a fair share.' "

Instructor: " 'And for the voiceless?' "

Student: " 'Of course, that they may be heard.' "

Instructor: " 'And how might that help you to discern what you ought to do?' "

Student: " 'Well, I don't know exactly; that is . . . I might shut up and let others speak.' " [4]

piety

devotion to religious matters or beliefs; sincere participation in religious practices

pietists

those who emphasize religious externals so much that the real meaning of religious devotion is overshadowed, ignored, or contradicted

Questions for discussion

1. Why do you think one of the students laughed when the young woman responded that she would pray about the situation? Have you ever heard kids making fun of praying? Explain.

2. What was the professor's initial response to the young woman's remark? Why do you think he responded that way? Why did he later have second thoughts about his response and wish he had taken her seriously?

3. How would you describe the difference between piety or being truly pious, and being pietistic? Why is this difference important?

4. On what occasions have you appreciated someone's saying he or she would pray for you? Have you ever encountered someone who had a pietistic approach to prayer that bothered you? Explain.

5. If the professor had taken the young woman's response more seriously, what valuable insights does he think might have resulted? Why? Explain what you think might have happened.

What Jesus taught us about praying

Christians have additional reasons for praying. We believe in what Jesus said and showed us about God and about prayer. But when and where and how did Jesus himself pray? What does his own example teach us about praying?

The Christian Scriptures tell us that **Jesus prayed before the decisive moments in his life**—for instance, before beginning his public life and choosing his apostles, and before his crucifixion. **He also prayed more formally** in the Temple along with other worshipers of his Jewish faith. He participated in the traditional Jewish religious rituals, such as Passover, which he celebrated with his Jewish disciples.

Jesus often prayed with and for others, and he prayed on the cross as he was dying. The Christian Scriptures tell us that many times Jesus went off into the hills to pray alone, as in a garden on the night before he died, and when he needed some peace and quiet after being with the noisy crowds all day.

But now more than ever the word about Jesus spread abroad; many crowds would gather to hear him and to be cured of their diseases. But he would withdraw to deserted places and pray.

Luke 5:15–16

The Prayer of Jesus

He was praying in a certain place, and after he had finished, one of his disciples said to him, "Lord, teach us to pray. . . ."

He said to them, "When you pray, say. . . ."

Luke 11:1–2

Thus the Bible records how **Jesus taught his followers to pray.** What he taught them about praying and about everything else is really summarized in what we call *The Prayer of Jesus, The Lord's Prayer*. Bible scholars tell us that this prayer probably developed in the early Church as a combination of some of Jesus' actual words and a summary of his teaching about prayer as the early Christians, inspired by God's Spirit, understood it. So we shouldn't assume that we must always pray using this prayer's exact words. It's a good prayer to pray at times, but it's also intended as an example of how we should ideally try to relate with God.

Questions for discussion

1. On what occasions do you usually pray or think about praying?

2. Which of these occasions are similar to the situations in which Jesus prayed?

3. What do you think Jesus showed by example about prayer? Explain.

... apart from me you can do nothing.—John 15:5

*You are God's child.
Call home.*

In saying this prayer, Christians unite ourselves with Christ in wanting to work for complete human harmony, happiness, and union with God in the fulfillment of God's reign. This is why the Prayer of Jesus is considered the basic Christian prayer.

As for what people should pray for, most religious believers would agree on those things contained in summary form in the Prayer of Jesus. This is why it's one of the prayers often used when Christians of different faith backgrounds join in praying together. Because the prayer is so identified as being an official Christian prayer, many non-Christians say they would feel uncomfortable praying it. But they do acknowledge that this prayer expresses what people usually want to pray for. So let's take a closer look at this prayer and what it means.

Let us boldly draw close

We dare to say,

"Our Father, who art in heaven. . . ."

Since we're not able to step outside the categories familiar to our human experience and imagination, how then should we address God? Perhaps, just to keep from stereotyping God, it's best to sometimes address and think of God in a variety of different ways (as has been done throughout Christian tradition). In fact, Jesus had some ways of addressing God in prayer that were boldly different for his time.

Since we are God's adopted children, Jesus revealed to us that we should relate to God as *our Father*—as to an **always-loving** parent. But addressing God as *Father* doesn't mean that we should think of God as being male. God's qualities include the fullness of all personhood. And Jesus himself also used feminine images to speak of God.

In this parish, members of the community join hands to pray The Lord's Prayer.

So in your personal prayer, if you want, it's okay to pray to God in terms that compare God to a mother. But those who say religious believers create God in their own image also make a point worth considering. Remember, God goes beyond all categories we creatures can imagine. So casting God in concrete as a "Him" or a "Her" makes a false idea or idol out of God.

Not all parents are good and loving. Some abandon their families. Some are emotionally cold, or even abusive. And all parents are imperfect, sometimes in a bad mood and shooing their children away or interrupting instead of always-welcoming and fully listening to their children's conversation and questions.

Instead, Jesus encouraged us to relate with God as a small child would the **ideal loving parent.** Perhaps most startling about this, though, was Jesus' calling God *Abba*—the word which is translated *Father* in our Bibles. If we more accurately interpreted what this word meant and implied in Jesus' time, we might call God *Daddy* or *Mommy*— or one of the other affectionate names a small child calls a loving parent, step-parent, or guardian.

When children become older, however, they begin to use more formal names for their parents instead—like *Mom* and *Dad*. This change is usually quite deliberate. It reflects the natural growth process of distancing ourselves somewhat from our early childhood relationship of total dependence on those who have raised us.

So when Jesus used the word *Abba* of God, he wasn't giving us God's official name or title. He was teaching us the kind of relationship we should have with God: We should feel as free to approach God as a child who feels completely safe, secure, trusting, and loved in a loving parent's arms. He was telling us to be totally open with God, and not to feel shy or fearful or self-conscious.

Thus Jesus taught us that the first thing to do when we pray is to completely and freely entrust ourselves to God. Draw near to God, he told us, with the complete freedom and confidence of a small child who exclaims "Mommy!" or "Daddy!" while running to be lifted into a loving parent's arms. And just as a small child aspires to be like a beloved parent, so we should want to be more like God.

Catholics pray this Prayer of Jesus together at the Eucharist and in other liturgical celebrations for another reason, too. The phrase *Our Father* expresses the communion we share with one another, and it's a prayer that we'll all grow closer and become more united. Notice that we don't address God as **the** Father, but as **our** Father!

The word *our* here doesn't mean that we own or have a monopoly on God. It actually implies two things: Individually we each have a personal relationship with God, and together we're all God's children—which makes us one another's brothers and sisters. So prayer is never a completely private matter— it always has a social dimension: We are Church praying. Someone has given a good example of really meaning this when we pray to *our God*:

> *While the Spanish civil war was raging, the chaplain of one of Franco's troops arranged a . . . mass for those fallen in battle. He was announcing the intention of the mass as "for our fallen" when one of the [soldiers] interrupted him: "Just a moment, Father. We want it 'for our fallen and for their fallen.'" Here was a man who had learned the meaning of the "our" in "Our Father." He was* **sane.** [5]

In living as we pray, we should also include rather than exclude others, as God's love includes us all. And we should rebel against all the ugly kinds of attitudes and divisions that keep us from being a harmonious human family.

🔖 Questions for discussion

1. Describe what the Prayer of Jesus is, where it came from, and what it means for Christians.

2. If you were asked to lead a prayer for a group including persons of other faiths, when would—and wouldn't—the Lord's Prayer be a good prayer to choose? Explain.

3. What do you think about the idea of addressing God in a variety of different ways? What are some examples of how the Church has done this throughout Christian tradition?

4. What name did you call your parent(s), stepparent(s), or guardian(s) when you were just a small child? What name(s) do you use now? What does this reflect about the development of your relationship?

5. What was so bold about Jesus' telling us we should relate to God as "our Father"? What did he mean—and not mean—by this? Explain.

6. What's wrong with thinking of God as **a** male or as **a** female?

7. In terms of what Jesus said, how might those who have known only abusive parents relate to God?

8. What does the "our" in *our Father* mean for Christians? Have you ever thought about this before? Explain.

9. What have you usually thought of when you hear or pray the phrase *who art in heaven*? What does it really mean and express?

Likewise, in praying *who art in heaven* as Jesus told us, we're referring not to God as in a place distant from us, but to God's majesty and God as present in our hearts. When we pray this, we're saying, in effect, that we believe God is **here,** among us—especially in the hearts of those who are good, kind, and just. So, in a sense, this statement reflects our faith in humanity, as well as, and because of, our belief in God. 🔖

You are holy

"Hallowed be thy name.
Thy kingdom come."

There are times we want to thank others for being so thoughtful, or for being good to us. We're grateful for their kindness to us, and we want to let them know that. Or maybe we want to praise someone for something, or compliment the person on something we like or admire about them.

Some people, however, relate to others mainly in a limited, functional, self-centered way. They don't let themselves get close to another person—unless they need a big favor. Perhaps most common, however, is taking people for granted. After a few years of marriage, couples who love each other very much often start to do this. They begin to talk only about practical things and neglect to speak about and show their feelings of affection for each other.

It probably shouldn't be surprising, then, that people often neglect their relationship with God, too. Some people communicate with God only when "necessary." They'll ask God for favors when things seem desperate—like around exam time, game time, or prom time! But they thank God only rarely, for the outstanding things.

Isn't it kind of sad that we all don't acknowledge more the Love who is the ultimate source of **all** goodness in the world and in our lives? We should express to God more often our gratitude and our praise. Yet how do we give adequate thanks for the air we breathe, the beauty we find in nature, our abil-

ity to reason, for the opportunities to experience love and happiness, for our life itself? The very least we can do is try.

In proclaiming the holiness of God's name, we praise God's goodness. We ask that people recognize God's holiness more and more in action—by leading better lives. Our prayer and our life can't be separated. Likewise a nation's destiny can't be separated from the goodness (or lack of it) of its people.

We have forgotten the gracious Hand which has preserved us in peace and multiplied and enriched and strengthened us, and have vainly imagined in the deceitfulness of our hearts that all these blessings were produced by some superior wisdom and virtue of our own.
—*Abraham Lincoln*

The fulfillment of God's reign isn't the same as improving culture and society, but it isn't separate from this either. God's reign is much more than creating an earthly utopia. When we pray that God's reign be fulfilled, we are expressing our faith in this future of justice, peace, and joy which God has promised to bring about—one far better than we humans could ever create alone. But we're also saying that we're willing to serve this cause by promoting peace and justice in the world here and now.

You know what's best

"Thy will be done on earth, as it is in heaven."

This is the part of the Prayer of Jesus that people often have the most trouble **really** meaning. After praying for a specific favor, we're afraid to let go of our ideas of what we want—or think we want—and leave it up to God to help bring about what is really best.

Figuring out God's will takes prayful thought and honest communication.

Perhaps part of our problem comes from having realized, certainly by the time we became teenagers, that even the most loving human parents don't **always** know what's best for their kids. But we need to remind ourselves that, unlike human parents, God's love for us is always complete and unconditional, and God is always perfectly wise. God wants our ultimate happiness, and the union of everyone in love, even more than we do! Because only God really knows what will help us achieve that, we're also asking for God's help here to do what is good and right.

God **always** wills your ultimate happiness, and God is not even capable of ever harming you. Remember, that would contradict God's own goodness. (We'll discuss this more in a later chapter.) When you pray that "God's will be done," you're really praying for your happiness and that of others. So, when you pray, always leave things in God's hands—no one will ever take better care of them, or of you.

Figuring out what God's will is, though, is another matter. Some people have a magical, superstitious idea about this—for instance, that if they open the Bible to a certain page, the passage they read will tell them what decision to make. But it's not that easy!

God has given us our human intelligence, our ability to reason logically to conclusions. When we pray, we should ask God to help us use these God-given abilities to discover what is truest and best and most right, and then act accordingly. That's the best way to really learn and follow God's will.

In God's will is our peace.
—Dante Alighieri

Questions for discussion

1. Do you think people compliment or thank each other enough? Do you do this often enough? Explain.

2. Why do you think that even people who say it's the most important thing in their life often neglect their relationship with God?

3. What does praying each of the following mean to you, and why?
   • Hallowed be thy name
   • Thy kingdom come
   • Thy will be done on earth, as it is in heaven

4. Do you have trouble really hoping that God's will be done in a situation about which you are praying? Why is this often hard for people to really mean when they pray?

5. What are you really praying for when you pray that God's will be done? Explain.

6. How does God intend for us to discover what God's will is?

Lincoln's reflections on God's will

Probably no one has been challenged with more difficult decisions than was Abraham Lincoln in deciding whether or not to plunge the country into war. It was clear that he wanted to do the right thing, to do God's will, but, in addition to praying about the matter, here's what he said about how he discovered what God's will is.

I am approached with the most opposite opinions and advice, and that by religious [persons], who are equally certain that they represent the divine will. I am sure that either the one or the other class is mistaken in that belief, and perhaps, in some respects, both.

I hope it will not be irreverent for me to say that, if it is probable that God would reveal [God's] will to others, on a point so connected with my duty, it might be supposed that [God] would reveal it directly to me; for, unless I am more deceived in myself than I often am, it is my earnest desire to know the will of Providence in this matter. And if I can learn what it is, I will do it.

These are not, however, the days of miracles, and I suppose it will be granted that I am not to expect a direct revelation. I must study the plain, physical facts of the case, ascertain what is possible, and learn what appears to be wise and right.[6]

Questions for discussion

1. What challenges did Abraham Lincoln face?
2. What did he say about those who offered him their advice and opinions as representing God's will? What was Lincoln's response?
3. How did Lincoln believe he could best discern God's will in a given situation?
4. What do you think of Lincoln's approach to learning God's will? How do you try to discover God's will in your own life?

Give us what we need today

"Give us this day our daily bread. . . ."

Certainly our relationship with God shouldn't just amount to "Gimme, gimme, gimme." But, after all, it is God who has made us "only human." And our Creator understands that we have very practical concerns—not just sometimes, but every day.

Bread in some form is a basic food in every society. Because it is usually less expensive and the ingredients are more widely available, it's often a main part of the diet of poor peoples and in poor countries. People soon begin to starve when they lack even bread to eat. So, as a staple of human existence, bread is also a symbol of human survival.

When we pray for "our daily bread," we are really praying for what we truly need to survive and grow—both materially and spiritually. Praying to God for our "daily bread" isn't completely self-centered either. It shows that we trust God, and that we believe God is the source of all life and good things.

Because we trust God, we shouldn't be so worried about obtaining what we need that we don't really enjoy what we have. In your own life it's a good idea to live as this prayer indicates—**taking things one day at a time**. Don't let yourself get so depressed and overwhelmed by tomorrow that you become spiritually paralyzed and give up trying today.

It's also true that **"God helps those who help themselves."** We shouldn't just sit around saying "God (or our families, or the government) will provide," instead of doing what we can to care for ourselves and those for whom we're responsible! Prayer shouldn't just amount to asking God for things instead of also working to achieve them ourselves.

I have lived to thank God that all my prayers have not been answered.
—Jean Ingelow

Notice that the Prayer of Jesus uses the word *us,* rather than just *me.* We're praying for everyone's needs—for those who are hungry, suffering, helpless, or without hope. We're also praying for those who are spiritually starved because they lack the values and the hope that God's word could bring for everyone **if** it were truly practiced.

There's never going to be peace and justice in the world if we don't all believe in and work for it. So our prayer to God must also be our commitment to God to try to help those for whom we pray.

Pray as if everything depended on God and work as if everything depended on you.
—Attributed to St. Ignatius Loyola

Forgive us—as we forgive

"And forgive us our trespasses, as we forgive those who trespass against us . . . ."

To trespass means to do wrong, to step past the limits of what is morally right. When we wrong, hurt, or realize that we've been taking for granted someone we love, we feel distant from the person. We want to express that we're sorry we've done something to separate us. Wanting to get back together again, we tell the person how we feel. We ask the person to forgive us and to continue our close relationship as before.

Sometimes we pray for the same reasons—to reconcile and get in touch again with God. In the Prayer of Jesus, we pray for the same forgiveness which we ourselves are willing to extend to others. But, if God is all-forgiving, why is forgiving others—including our enemies—a necessary condition for becoming reconciled with God?

There's an old saying that goes, "The friend of my friend is also my friend."

God's love includes everyone. So our hearts can accept God's merciful forgiveness only to the extent that we're willing to forgive others. We can be only partly but not fully reunited in friendship with God as long as we're closed to showing mercy to others.

Be with and help us always

"And lead us not into temptation, but deliver us from evil."

For the kingdom, the power and the glory are yours, now and forever. Amen!

God would never lead or tempt us to do wrong, but wants to free us from evil. The word *lead* here actually isn't an accurate translation, but it's still the one most widely used in our language. The meaning of the original Greek word, however, was that God not **let us give in** to temptation.

We need to be careful that our hearts don't lead us in the wrong direction. And, when we're tempted to do something we know we shouldn't, we should rely on the help God has promised us to resist it. Finally, we also pray here, as Jesus did the night before his death, that we and others be spared, if possible, from terrible suffering in our lives.

The *Final Doxology* concludes the Prayer of Jesus with the last statement in praise and adoration of God. The word *Amen* is a common way for Jews and Christians to end a prayer. It's the very last word in the Bible itself, and it ends the main Christian creeds. God has been called the Amen of perfect faithful love, and Jesus has been referred to as the Amen of our Father's love for us.

Amen means "Let it be so," and it comes from the same root as the word *believe.* So it's like saying "We believe and trust in God's faithful love and in the faith of our baptism, and we believe in living what we've just prayed." So in our minds, *Amen!* should also mean "Let's do it!" 🙠

🙠 Questions for discussion

1. What does "bread" represent in the Prayer of Jesus? What do you usually mean by praying for "our daily bread"?
2. What is your response to the idea that "God helps those who help themselves"? Explain.
3. Are there any things people pray for that seem superficial, selfish, phony, or even wrong to you? Explain.
4. Do you ever find it hard to forgive others as you want God to forgive you? Explain.
5. What is meant by saying that "the friend of my friend is also my friend"? Do you find this true in your own experience? How does it apply to asking God's forgiveness? Explain.
6. Does God ever actually "lead us into temptation"? Why do Christians pray to God *lead us not into temptation?*
7. What do you mean when you conclude a prayer with "Amen"? How would you like for your life to be a living Amen?

doxology

hymn of praise to God

Is this how to pray?

In many cities, Christians are holding "See You at the Pole" prayers. Student-run Bible clubs ask the student members to gather around the flagpole for prayer before or after class at the public school they attend. Their civil right to do this has been upheld, as long as the school lets any student group use the flagpole area for any other type of gathering.

When a popular star professional basketball player resigned from the game because he had become infected with the AIDS virus, the team's coach—also a good friend of the player—made the announcement from center court just before the evening's game. Then he called on both teams (who, like the fans, were stunned at the news) to gather around him for a prayer that "echoed through the sports arena." At a news conference, his voice cracking with emotion, he said that he was responding to the player's letter which had informed him of the news and that he was sending back his prayers. Of the player, he said "More than anything now, he needs our love and support."

Questions for discussion

1. What is your reaction to the idea of praying in each of the situations described above? Why?

2. Can you describe circumstances in which it would be a good idea for students to rally around the flagpole and pray? In which this would not be a good idea? Explain.

3. Outside of formal religious services, describe the most and least meaningful instances of praying together with others which you have experienced. Explain why each has and has not been meaningful to you.

Students gathered in prayer.

Chapter review

1. What is prayer?

- What is prayer in terms of one's personal relationship with God? What dimension is added to this in Christian prayer?
- To what is prayer a response?
- Why does it require faith to believe in prayer?
- What type of communication should prayer involve?

2. What has God told us about prayer?

- What has God revealed about prayer in the biblical accounts of Abraham, Moses, the Hebrew prophets, and in the psalms?
- What does modern history record about humanity's relationship with God?

3. Why pray?

- What are the five main reasons for and forms of praying? What does each express?
- What is the Catholic Church's main prayer, and what does it express?
- What is the purpose and point of all prayer?

4. What Jesus taught us about praying

- What added reasons do Christians have for praying?
- When, how, and why did Jesus pray? What does his example teach us about praying?
- What is the Lord's Prayer, where did it come from, and why is it considered the basic Christian prayer?
- What does each part of the Lord's Prayer really mean in Catholic belief?
- What should Catholics understand "God's will" to be, and how should we understand what God's will is in a particular situation?
- What does it mean to say that God helps those who help themselves?
- Why is forgiveness, including forgiveness of enemies, a necessary condition for reconciliation with God?
- What is the Final Doxology? What does the Amen which concludes prayers mean?

Projects and assignments

1. Read the prayer of the Hour of Jesus, including Jesus' prayer of unity in John 17:1–26. Then write a one-page paper explaining how Jesus' own personal prayer here compares with what he told us elsewhere—in the Prayer of Jesus (the Lord's Prayer)—about how we should pray.

2. Read the parable Jesus spoke in Luke 18:9–14 to some people who prided themselves on being virtuous and despised everyone else. Write a paper on the ways you think this type of religious hypocrisy is present in our society and what you think Jesus would say about it today.

3. A local newspaper's editorial says that "the best morality in the world grows out of the quiet hour one spends with God." Write a letter to the editor of the paper giving your comments on this statement—and on what you think about a newspaper's editorial column advocating personal prayer.

4. Write a two-page research paper about the various ways Hindus, Buddhists, Muslims, Jews, and other non-Christians pray, comparing these with what Jesus said about prayer, and giving your own responses.

5. Write a two-page research paper about the various ways non-Catholic Christians pray, comparing these with what Jesus said about prayer, and giving your own responses.

Chapter 10   The Path of Prayer

"Be still, and know that I am God!"

Psalm 46:10a

Prayer for bad times

Dear God:

Help me be a good sport in this game of life.

I don't ask for an easy place in the lineup.
Put me anywhere you need me.
I only ask that I can give you 100 percent of everything I have.

If all the hard drives seem to come my way,
I thank you for thinking I'm strong enough to face the tough ones.
Help me remember that you'll never let me have more trouble than I can handle.

And help me, Lord, to accept the bad breaks as part of the game.
May I always play fair,
no matter what the others do.
Help me study the Book so I'll know the rules.

Finally, God, if things go against me
and I'm justly benched by something I've done wrong,
or by something I can't control, like sickness or old age,
help me to accept that as part of the game, too.
Keep me from whimpering that I was framed or that I got a raw deal.

And when I finish the final play, I ask for no trophies, fame, or applause.
All I want is to believe in my heart that I played as well as I could
and that I didn't let you down.

Adapted from a prayer by Richard Cardinal Cushing

Overview questions

1. What's the best way for a person to pray?

2. Why does it seem hard to pray sometimes?

3. What good does it do to pray—does God really answer our prayer?

4. How can we tell what God is communicating to us in prayer?

Guides for praying

Does the complaint, "You spend too much time talking on the phone!" sound vaguely familiar to you? Like most teenagers, you probably spend a lot of time conversing with your friends. But, what do you say to each other for hours and hours? Much of the time you probably just enjoy passing the time together talking about things like movies, music, sports, school, or people.

These conversations are important ways you expand your knowledge and awareness, explore the world, and find out what other people are like. You're learning about yourself and building and enriching your relationships. Regularly communicating with people you care about keeps your relationships alive and growing, so they don't dull and die. For the same reason, we also need to regularly touch minds and hearts with God. ⸕

I believe that if we are to be hope-filled people, if we are to be rainbow callers, we need to fall deeply in love with God and treasure the promises we hear in the scriptures. We need to experience laughter, to delight in life's incongruities. We need to have a time each day to recall God's presence and believe again in the wonders and beauties around us. We also need to keep searching for people who believe and hope for what we hunger for in our hearts.
—*Joyce Rupp*

Pray sincerely

Doesn't it bother you when you're talking with somebody who seems to have a nose-in-the-air attitude of superiority? Or when someone is always reaching for a compliment? **The proper attitude for communicating sincerely with God and anybody else is humility.** This means not putting on a false front or attitude of either superiority or weakness. It means respecting both the other person and yourself, and being honest about each other and the relationship.

When domineering individuals demand that others show them "respect," they're really just being bullies. Respect means being **appropriately considerate** of each other. It doesn't mean being intimidated by or afraid of someone, or looking up to someone who doesn't deserve it.

Relating with people in a humble way means understanding that we're equal in dignity and worth. It also means respecting the type of relationship we have with each other. You don't relate the same way with your peers as you do with your principal, or with an acquaintance as with a close confidante. Not respecting the nature of the relationship is rude and disrespectful. It's not honest. It doesn't accept who each person really is. That's why you don't like being asked personal questions by somebody who doesn't know you well enough, or object to being talked to like a child when you're not.

Having a humble attitude when praying to God means respecting who God is and who we are. We should never be afraid of God, but we should recognize that God is infinitely good and wise, while we have lots of limitations and weaknesses. Humility means realizing that we depend on God for our very existence, that our human dignity comes from being God's child, and that God is the ultimate source of all the good things we experience in life.

⸕ **Questions for discussion**

1. What do you usually talk about with your friends? What have you learned about life, yourself, and other people through these conversations?

2. What do you usually talk with God about? Are there any things you don't talk to God about because you think God's probably not interested? Explain.

3. What role does communicating regularly play in your relationship with your friends? In your relationship with God? Explain.

🕮 Questions for discussion

1. How do you feel when someone seems to have a superior attitude, or always to be fishing for a compliment? Why do you feel this way?

2. Do you agree that the greatest conceit is thinking you're humble? What do you think being a truly humble person means—and should not mean?

3. What role do you think genuine humility should play in communicating with others? In communicating with God?

4. What do you think various teenagers mean by wanting others to "respect" them? Which are and are not examples of really respecting someone?

5. How do you feel about praying to God when you're angry? About feeling upset with God? How does praying help you deal with your anger?

If you approach God humbly, don't worry about your language or grammar. Just be honest. With God (and probably only with God!) you never have to worry about saying the wrong thing or being misunderstood. God won't be offended by what you say or shocked by how you say it. (God already knows how you feel anyway.)

So go ahead and tell God how angry you are about something, or even how upset you are with God. (The Bible tells us some of God's best friends have told God quite candidly at times how angry they were about things—or even how upset they were with God!) Then ask God to help calm and enlighten you so you can understand and resolve what's really causing your anger, or at least discover how to release it in positive, nondestructive ways. Besides, as Jesus told us, saying lots of holy words doesn't mean anything unless prayer is sincere. 🕮

Take time to pray

Even couples very much in love must schedule time for each other—to talk, to enjoy each other's company. In our fast-paced lives, this requires effort, planning, and determination! Couples also need to keep learning about how they can communicate better. This will happen over time **only if** they both work at it. Serious communication problems must be addressed right away, maybe with some outside guidance. When partners don't communicate well, their relationship suffers and sooner or later dies.

It's the same with our relationship with God, who is really our number one Best Friend. A former military pilot profoundly realized this when he was captured as a war prisoner. While being interrogated, he tried to keep up his spirits and not reveal any information despite being hit with a club and prodded with increasingly powerful electrical jolts. Whenever the brutal interrogators did manage to extract more information from him, he'd feel dejected—as if he had "sold out" his country and his companion pilots. But he said that "there was always time for prayer. 'When there's only you in that cell, God is your only friend.' "[1]

Realize how much God is always your Friend, too, and **make time for prayer a priority in your busy schedule.** Many people like to pray at certain times of the day—while getting ready in the morning, while going to and from work or school, before meals or classes or work, or at night before going to sleep. But also don't limit your heart—pray whenever something inspires you to be aware of God's presence and love.

Listen

In prayer, as in human communication, we shouldn't monopolize the conversation. **We should try to listen to as well as talk to God.** But God doesn't talk to us out loud or through mental neon signs. So how can we understand what and how God is communicating to us? This isn't always so easy to do accurately—without "putting words in God's mouth"!

When somebody says definitively, "This is what God told me. . . ," like Abraham Lincoln we have a right to be skeptical. How do we know—how does the other person know—that this is what God is really saying? Barring unlikely miracles, we have to mentally translate the person's words to mean, "This is what I **think** God **might** be telling me."

Through prayer, God can also guide us to seek the truth later, through studying facts, reasoning through ideas, and discussing the possibilities with others—including people who disagree with us. God may inspire us to come to the truth by vigorously debating with each other. One way of listening to God is to listen to the wisdom God communicates to us through others.

Like discerning God's will, listening to God in prayer shouldn't be viewed **superstitiously!** God may inspire us with a solution to a problem while we're praying. But not everything that pops into our heads while we're praying is a good idea. **We should always question the worthiness of these insights using our God-given intelligence and ability to reason to logical conclusions.** We need to weigh these against what our religion teaches—especially Jesus' teaching in the Gospels—and what our conscience tells us. Thus we will have a reliable way of listening to God in prayer.

Sometimes the best way to listen to God is to listen to ourselves—take a good, deep look at how we view life and why, and how our attitude affects our relationships. We can prayerfully probe why our faults cause us so many problems, or why we don't always realize or use the talents and abilities God has given us. Sometimes even prayerfully pondering our dreams can be a way of listening to God, but because they're part of us and our subconscious mind—not because God is sending us supernatural visions at night!

Often, though, God doesn't tell us anything new in prayer. Instead, God helps open our mind to what, in so many ways, God and others have been trying to tell us all along. We, in turn, must learn to open our hearts, and listen. 🍂

Find a prayerful place

A church is still considered the appropriate place for the parish community to gather for the more formal prayers of the Church liturgy. It can be a favorite place for personal prayer, too. But **personal prayer can be formal or informal.** You can also pray sitting on the beach, kneeling on your knees, or skiing down a mountain. In a busy household, some complain that the only place they can get the time alone for peace and quiet and prayerful reflection is in the bathroom!

This is why **it's important to find or even create a special place for prayer that calms your spirit and gives you the needed privacy.** This might be your bedroom with the door closed, the lights turned low, and soothing background music playing—or lying outside under the sky or a favorite tree. Nature's beauty and serenity often invite us to commune with God.

Recognizing this, one landscape architect recently built a beautiful, peaceful "prayer garden" next to his parish church. He originally created it as a place where those who are terminally ill might have their spirits uplifted and might find some comfort and quiet in praying. But many people now stop there to pray on their way home from work or school.

But whenever you pray, go into your room and shut the door and pray to your Father who is in secret; and your Father who sees in secret will reward you.
—Matthew 6:6

Jesus prayed alone in a variety of places—in the hills, in a garden. He encouraged us to find the solitude we need for prayer. But is it ever hard to find the time and privacy for prayer because others won't let you be alone, or think you must always be busy **doing** something? We all need some time **every day** free from other pressures and obligations to just **be**—time to relax and reflect, to refresh our spirits, to pray. That isn't being lazy or wasting time So if necessary, tell your family members why you'd like a little quiet time alone each day—and respect their need for this, too.

superstitiously

believing in a way which contradicts or is not consistent with reason or fact, attempting to control God by saying certain words or performing certain actions

🍂 **Questions for discussion**

1. Have you ever wished someone you care about would spend more time with you? Who in your life should you spend more time communicating with than you do? Explain.

2. Have you sometimes felt like God was your only Friend? Do you think you communicate often enough with your Best Friend, God?

3. How do you feel when somebody isn't really listening to what you're saying? When somebody tries to "put words in your mouth"? Explain.

4. How—and when—does God speak (and not speak) to us through prayer?

5. Give some examples of how listening to God in prayer can be viewed superstitiously. Give examples of more reliable ways of listening to God in prayer.

6. Surveys show that many people in our society pray for God's help and try to follow God's advice. What is your response to this? Why?

spirituality

the style or manner in which one relates to God

🖎 Questions for discussion

1. Outside of church, where is your favorite place to pray? Why?

2. If you were in charge of creating a place for prayer in your school, what would it be like, and why? Do you think something like this would be a good idea? Explain.

3. Do you usually find it easy or difficult to find the time and place you need for being alone? For prayer? Explain.

4. What advice would you give teenagers who are having trouble finding the time and place they need for personal and prayerful solitude?

Having a suitable place to pray in solitude is important, but it's also possible to pray in a noisy, crowded public place. As Hindu wisdom says, "Do not seek happiness and solitude merely by withdrawing from the busy world. You may find them even in a crowded place. True happiness and solitude are within you." 🖎

Expand your spirit

A former speechwriter for the president of the United States says that once a developing nation attains the bare necessities of life and figures out **how** to live, the next task for a country is a spiritual one—to figure out **why** to live. Once they have achieved basic standards of life and liberty, people are then able to—and need to—focus on what the "pursuit of happiness" really means.

Once they discover (often the hard way) that fame, money, power, and alcohol or other drugs don't bring true happiness, even the wealthiest and most famous look to religion for the meaning that their lives lack. Maybe this explains why our society is now so interested in **spirituality**. The media have finally discovered that people **are** interested in religion and in developing life's spiritual dimension. So we're seeing and hearing much more about this in newspapers, best-selling books, movies, and on television.

Prayer is sacramental. It is there to begin with. We do not work our way toward it from a distance, or master it as an achievement, like Spanish or cooking. Our task is not to manufacture it but to surrender to the prayer we already possess, to get out of its way.
—Miriam Pollard OCSO

Spirituality helps us focus on more than the basic necessities of life.

The problem is that prominent media personalities are promoted as spiritual experts without having much common sense or solid education about spiritual topics. Movies, news, and talk shows feature the unusual or controversial—the oddball deviation and the bizarre exception always draw a crowd. So religion is treated as a curiosity in order to attract larger audiences and advertising funds. Movie stars make lots of money publicizing nonsense like "psychic" connections or alleged "past life" experiences.

Real spiritual experts don't fraudulently, financially, emotionally, or psychologically rip people off, or advertise their own holiness. Like Mother Teresa, they willingly share their beliefs, but mainly by putting a solid spiritual life into action—by doing good hard, honest work for others. They give God due credit, but with a humility that is sincere and not pretended or showy (it seems fashionable to display one's "humility" these days). With unfaked love, proved not by pious words but by action, they reflect God's goodness rather than publicizing their own. ❧

Spiritual fads and superstitions

The Church encourages Catholics to actively develop our spiritual life in a sound, truly Christian way. Many trustworthy forms of **Christian spirituality,** or approaches to the spiritual life, have developed throughout Christian tradition. (Some of the main styles of praying we will discuss in the next section have resulted from these.) Christian spirituality has also adapted valuable insights and practices from other cultures and religions—such as Native American prayers and ceremonies, or Hindu and Buddhist forms of meditation. Today Catholics have many resources for individual help in improving their relationship with God—from parish prayer groups to well-trained and trustworthy spiritual directors.

But there are also greedy gurus who'll promise you certain spiritual re-

sults—for a price. Stores may sell "potions" such as "jinx or hex remover," "success glow," "confusion" (to confuse other people), "double cross," and "love lotion" as gag gifts. But serious practitioners of voodoo-like practices which claim to use God's power to cast so-called magic spells on people (as one country's military commander recently did) are not compatible with Christian belief. In reality, voodoo's only power is the fear instilled by powerful drugs which cause such severe mental damage that victims do become like zombies or living corpses. Other inhumane practices, like animal or human sacrifice, are also not compatible with being Catholic, nor is interpreting standard Catholic prayers and rituals in outlandish superstitious ways.

Catholic belief definitely needs to be further expressed in the unique ways people of different cultures naturally pray! But **inhumane practices, or superstitions which offer or promise specific supernatural results, contradict and deny basic Catholic beliefs.** The above examples illustrate rather clearly the nature and harm of superstition. The more common superstitious notions about God and prayer, however, are usually more subtle—like secretly fearing that God won't hear us unless we move our lips while we're praying. Our hearts may sometimes be too hard to hear what God is trying to tell us, but God is not hard of hearing!

Deep down in me I knowed it was a lie, and [God] knowed it. You can't pray a lie—I found that out.
—Mark Twain, **Huckleberry Finn.**

God guarantees to answer all sincere prayers for what is good. But we must never appeal to God in prayer to harm someone. Even in war, we must pray that evil will be overcome by good, and not that God will eternally damn the enemy. And we must never use means that try to force either God or us to

❧ Questions for discussion

1. What evidence do you see that our society is focusing more on spirituality and the real "pursuit of happiness"? Why do you think this is happening, or do you?
2. In what ways have famous persons you know of sought the happiness their lives and relationships have lacked? Which of these ways have turned out to be good for them? Which have been harmful?
3. What approaches to spiritual topics do you usually see portrayed or discussed in the media? What do you think about these? Why?
4. What is the problem with assuming that prominent media personalities are experts in any field other than their own? Why is viewing them as spirituality experts dangerous?
5. What public figures do you think are genuinely humble and sincere about their religious beliefs? Which ones seem to you to be showy or pretentious about them? Give reasons.

Christian spirituality

the styles or ways Christians relate with God because of their specifically Christian beliefs about God and Jesus

Questions for discussion

1. What is the difference between Catholic spirituality and those which contradict basic Catholic beliefs? Use examples to explain.

2. Why must we never appeal to God in prayer to harm someone?

3. How would you describe the religious environment you've grown up with and its influence on you?

4. Do you have a tendency to be superstitious? How can you avoid being a victim of "spiritual fadism" or fraud?

automatically act in certain ways in order to produce certain results. So remember three things:

1. God is all-good.
2. God can never harm.
3. God cannot be bought and will not be used.

Our first source of spiritual life is the religious environment we've grown up with in our families. In that cultural environment, you first formed your attitudes about God and prayer and how

to relate with God. Now it's time that you begin examining and continuing to develop your own spiritual style, to expand your spirit in a more adult way. As you do this, don't be swayed by "spiritual" fads or frauds—especially if you already know you're easily tempted to be superstitious. Remember the sound truths you've learned. Hold on tightly to what you know in your heart is **really** true, and pray for God's help to choose your spiritual path wisely.

Let love be genuine; hate what is evil, hold fast to what is good. . . .
—Romans 12:9

Channeling and chain prayers

There have always been so-called spiritual mediums who promise to connect people with the dead or with other spiritual beings in the life beyond. Some claim to be "channelers" through whom these spiritual beings allegedly speak. Catholics do believe that, living and dead, all who love God are a communion of saints—we can pray for and influence each other in positive ways. But this is far different from superstition which trivializes or tries to manipulate spiritual realities to suit our wishes and purposes.

Unfortunately, too many people are attracted to quick, clever gimmicks rather than insisting on only solid substance. Such religious gimmicks are usually superstitious. They insult us religious believers and give genuine religion a bad name. They also harm innocent, gullible people, by leading them on a spiritual path that falsely promises easy solutions to difficult problems. For most religious believers, faith is far more complex and meaningful.

Yet today major networks make superstitions seem believable by promoting and advertising them as factual and authentic. This distorts and trivializes true Christian spirituality. Maybe it's time for those of us who recognize the difference to speak out. Read the following true accounts, and then see what you think.

A major television network recently featured, as part of a news-related program, a woman who claims to help people enrich their spiritual life by getting in touch with their guardian angel. In the segment, she led a group to prayerfully reflect a few moments and told them to write their reflections down on paper. She then suggested that what they had written was really what their guardian angel was telling them to write. (Another talk-show facilitator said she's convinced that her guardian angel does all sorts of nice things for her daily, like helping to arrange her shoes where she'll readily find them.)

Recently, someone had a chain prayer published in the local newspaper's classified section. The prayer begins, "Holy Spirit who solves all problems," and includes a prayer of thanksgiving. Accompanying the prayer is this statement: "Say this prayer for 3 days. After 3 days request will be granted. This prayer to be published immediately after favor is granted."

Questions for discussion

1. What is the difference between praying for one another and trivializing or trying to manipulate spiritual realities to suit our wishes and purposes?

2. Why do quick, clever religious gimmicks attract people? Why are these harmful?

3. Why are the two examples described above forms of superstition rather than of genuine prayer?

4. What media examples have you seen that trivialize the spiritual or lend credibility to superstitions? Which do you find most objectionable, and why?

5. How do you think you and other viewers can and should help influence the media to portray prayer and religion in more authentic ways?

Styles of praying

Jesus told us to "pray always" (see Luke 18:1). Actually, you can pray, communicate and commune with God anytime and anyplace without using special "holy" words. Prayer always involves our mind and heart, but you can pray to God in the same ways you communicate with other persons—by talking, listening, reading, writing, or by your actions. You can also pray to God through your thoughts alone, and heart-to-Heart.

There are really as many styles of praying as there are people who pray. Next though, we'll discuss the main prayer styles throughout Christian tradition.

Pray without ceasing.
—1 Thessalonians 5:17

THE FAMILY CIRCUS®   By Bil Keane

"When we say silent prayers in school, does God hafta be a mind reader?"

1-14
©1994 Bil Keane, Inc.
Dist. by Cowles Synd., Inc.

"Reprinted with special permission of King Features Syndicate"

Conversational prayer

How do you start conversations with your friends? Probably with standard words or phrases like "Hi, what's happening?" Set conversation starters help us break the initial silence with an invitation to communicate, and they set the friendly tone for the conversation. Then we just talk naturally. The usual concluding phrases, like "Bye, see ya," confirm that our relationship is ongoing and that our communication is "to be continued."

Conversational prayer is mentally or vocally talking with God. You can use your own words, but standard formula prayers can also help you converse with God. In addition to the Prayer of Jesus, here are a few other standard prayers Catholics are encouraged to pray:

The Sign of the Cross is praying the words, "In the name of the Father, and of the Son, and of the Holy Spirit," often accompanied by touching one's forehead, chest, and each shoulder to form a cross on the body. This distinctly Christian prayer-action proclaims belief in our Creator who is Love, in our Redeemer who showed us how much God loves us all, and in God's Spirit who gives us the wisdom and ability to share this love with others.

At Jesus' time the cross represented criminal shame, punishment, suffering, despair, and death. Wearing a small cross around your neck in those days would have been like wearing a symbolic electric chair! Yet Jesus' resurrection has transformed the cross into the symbol of life, love, and hope. Thus Christians pray both to and through Christ.

Jesus is the shortest, simplest standard Christian prayer, but its meaning ("God saves") encompasses all of Christian belief.

Come, Holy Spirit is a good quick prayer when you need guidance or inspiration.

The Liturgy of the Hours is a daily prayer combining psalms and other Scripture readings arranged to suit times of the day and yearly religious seasons.

Questions for discussion

1. What do you think Jesus did—and didn't—mean by telling us to "pray always"? Realistically, how can we do this?

2. How is just "saying prayers" different from praying?

3. What are your standard ways to start and conclude a conversation with your friends? A conversation with God?

4. How would you explain to a non-Christian what each of the main Catholic standard or formula prayers means?

5. If you'll pardon the pun, one teenager says the Sign of the Cross is his way to "sign on" and "sign off" with God and that this expresses his identity--who he is because of what he believes in. What does it represent to you? Why?

6. What's your favorite formula prayer? Your favorite short prayer? Explain.

7. When do you usually choose to use a formula prayer in praying? When do you usually just talk with God spontaneously? Explain.

The Hail Mary (in Latin, *Ave Maria*) echoes the biblical words honoring the way Jesus' mother lived her life in God's service, and asks her to help us do the same. Praying the *rosary* (a series of Hail Marys and other prayers said while meditating on Gospel mysteries) actually developed in the Middle Ages as a substitute for the Liturgy of the Hours among those who couldn't read. But the idea of using a string of beads as a prayer counter, as in praying the rosary, is actually a more ancient practice borrowed from Eastern religions like Hinduism.

In personal prayer, formula prayers can be like the standard phrases used in ordinary human communication—a way to start, an invitation to communicate, or a way to wrap up our conversation while continuing our relationship with God. But prayer words should never just be mouthed in an empty, meaningless way. They should always lead us to what all prayer really is—heart-to-Heart communication.

It is better in prayer to have a heart without words than words without a heart.
—Mahatma Gandhi

This shrine to Mary is an invitation to prayer.

Calling God . . .

Have you ever thought about all the various names people have for the Ultimate Reality they worship? Whom we call **God,** others know as **Brahman, Vishnu, Lord Buddha, Allah, Yahweh, Dieu, Dio. . . .** But when it comes to referring to God in prayer, many peoples don't limit themselves as much as most in our society seem to do.

In Christian tradition and liturgy, there have actually been many titles for God (some of which we've already mentioned). Native Americans have likewise had many names for the **Great Spirit.**

There's so many different ways of saying the same thing. You can always say just what you mean . . . in English we say, God. But his Indian father, Cuyloga, told him there were more than twenty ways to say God in Delaware and each one means something different.[2]

One student has asked, "When I pray, I call God *Ralph*—is that okay? Somehow it's just hard for me to relate to somebody called *God,* at least in a personal way, like when I'm praying within myself.

"I honestly do respect God and all, but it's like *Ralph* is much easier for me to really talk to. Otherwise I feel God's just way beyond me and far away."

Questions for discussion

1. Do you feel as at ease in praying to God as you do in talking with your closest friend? Why or why not?

2. How would you feel about addressing God in prayer by another name such as "Ralph"? Why?

3. Which of the titles for God are most meaningful to you? Why?

4. Have you ever started calling any of your friends by a new name? What difference might this make in a relationship?

5. Do you ever call *God* something else, or have you ever considered the idea of referring to God by another name when you pray? What difference might this make in your relationship with God?

6. Why does the student refer to God as "Ralph" in prayer? Do you think the student is irreverent in doing so? When would this be irreverent, and why?

Reflective prayer

Reflective prayer (meditation) involves searching to understand the real, spiritual meaning of life in view of your belief in God. Reflecting or meditating is taking some time to think seriously within yourself about a personal problem, or a relationship, or a social issue.

Reflecting helps you to see things more clearly, from a better perspective, and focus on positive solutions, directions, or attitudes. Your reflections may result from something you experienced during the day, a conversation you've had, or from something you've read, discussed in class, or seen on TV. Personal or social crises or controversies spark serious reflection.

To really reflect deeply, you need a stretch of time. Just a few minutes isn't nearly enough. In fact, unnecessary interruptions may be somewhat irritating when you're in a reflective mood. Some privacy and peaceful surroundings can help you concentrate. Quiet music and relaxation exercises can help to calm your body, and to still, clear, and focus your mind and heart. Or maybe you prefer perfect silence.

But have you ever reflected on the same things over and over without gaining any new insights? Have you ever

Whenever you pray, if you pray sincerely, you will discover new feeling and meaning in it— something you didn't know before that will give you fresh courage; then you will understand that prayer is an education.
—Dostoyevski, **The Brothers Karamazov**

I can do all things through him who strengthens me —Philippians 4:13

mantra

repetition of a word or sound to relax, clear, and focus the mind; used by many as a preparation for prayer

🕭 Questions for discussion

1. When and how do you do most of your serious or prayerful reflection? How do you feel this helps your life?

2. What do you usually require for getting in a reflective mood?

3. Do you ever find as you reflect on something that you seem to be going in a mental and emotional circle? Why do you seem to be getting nowhere in that instance?

4. What is the difference between ordinary reflection, and religious meditation or prayerful reflection? Why is this difference important?

5. What added benefit can religious meditation offer? What does it involve?

6. Why do we need prayerful personal reflection time when we're the least likely to make time for it? How might you rearrange your schedule to make more time for this? Would you like to? Explain.

found yourself going in mental and emotional circles without growing or changing? Feeling this lack of guidance and sense of direction in life is leading more and more individuals to the practice of **prayerful** reflection which is known as religious **meditation.**

Religious meditation has a long, respected place in Christian tradition. Various saints and religious communities over the centuries have discovered and tested valuable practices which foster prayerful meditation. Religious meditation generally involves the same types of things you probably do whenever you do some serious thinking:

- Quiet your body and mind in God's presence.
- Read and think about what a Scripture passage or other spiritual reading means.
- Talk to God, and listen to God through your insights about how the reading's meaning relates to your life.

Lots of business persons get to work early to spend some time prayerfully reflecting before the day's activities begin. One marketing director says this helps him be a better person and do a better job. Others take time after work to reflect on how their day went, so they can set aside their work concerns and be more present for their family in the evening. Some find their best meditation time late at night when the day's obligations and interruptions are all over.

However and whenever is best for you, do regularly make time for serious and prayerful personal reflection. When you're most tempted not to make time is probably when you most need to reflect and pray—when you're busy, tense, and feeling pressured. You might be surprised at how regular prayerful reflection can help improve the quality of your personal relationships, your studies, and your other activities! So, here are some time-tested tips that can help you do this.

Prepare for reflection. Regularly set aside enough uninterrupted time and privacy. Find or create a reflective environment. Relax, quiet, and prepare your body and mind; seek an inner silence and stillness. You can't think clearly if you're physically uncomfortable and fidgeting! Find a comfortable position that also helps you stay alert.

Some Christians find the body and mind-stilling techniques of Hindu yoga and Buddhist meditation help in doing this. Some find that slow deep breathing or using a **mantra** helps clear the mind of distractions in preparing to reflect on deeper spiritual truths. A one-word prayer like *God* or *Jesus* can serve as a mantra. Or you might repeat a favorite formula prayer over and over—or just pray it slowly once, focusing on every word's meaning.

Use a reflection starter. Once you've prepared yourself for prayerful reflection, having a definite take-off point really helps, so here are some possible ways to begin: Ask God's Spirit for guidance and/or read a passage from the Bible (especially Jesus' life and teaching) or another spiritual book. Read a meaningful poem, or an insightful passage from a novel or article from the newspaper—or recall an especially moving or thought-provoking movie. Think about a work of beauty that especially stirs you—a form of art or an aspect of nature. Focus on each of your relationships, or the day's events.

Direct your reflection. Ask yourself questions that help you reflect on the deeper personal meanings, moral dimensions, and social implications of what you've read or focused on.

Reflect realistically. Don't just daydream about changing somebody else or saving the whole world. That may feel inspiring at first, but it quickly begins to seem overwhelming, unrealistic, impossible, and useless. The real, effective way to influence other people and change the world for the better is to focus instead on one simple, small, positive way to improve yourself.

Rely on God's help. Conclude your reflection in a positive way. For instance, give thanks for God's friendship and guidance, and ask God to help you put your insights into action. 🕭

Deep, or shallow?

Teenagers are sometimes accused—and accuse each other—of being superficial. Certainly many adults can fit this description as well. But what gives a person substance, character, depth? Why do some individuals seem more superficial than others? Your depth or superficiality isn't due to how intelligent or well-educated you are, or even to what you've experienced in life. It stems instead from how you **reflect** on what you learn and experience, and the kind of person you become as a result. Reflective prayer often plays a vital role in making the difference between someone who's shallow and someone of wisdom and substance.

Read the following teenagers' comments, and then discuss what you think about this in response to the questions.

Michael, age 17: *Why is it that some girls don't seem to have anything to talk about except surface stuff, like who did what to whom, who they saw at the concert last weekend, or who's wearing what? Or—and this really irritates me—they gossip a lot, usually about other girls I think they're jealous of. I mean, come on, can't they talk about anything else? These things are so superficial. Just once I'd like to feel like I'm having a real conversation with a real person about something deeper than soap opera level. Girls get so upset these days when they feel like they're not treated as equals. But then they talk and act dumb, like they don't have much upstairs to begin with. Sometimes I get the feeling that they're one beef pattie short of a hamburger—fluffy bread on the outside, and lots of sauce and frills, without any real meat on the inside.*

Kedra, age 16: *When I'm with my girlfriends, like, we'll talk about a lot of things that really matter to us. Sure, we talk about clothes and that kind of stuff. But we talk about lots of other things too, like politics and feelings and even God. That's what really bugs us about the guys we know. They just seem to want to talk about outside things—like how fast a certain car is, or sports. But, if you try to talk about what you really think or feel on the inside, they just sort of shrug and change the subject real fast. Can't they ever talk about something deep or personal? They say we're too serious about things, but they're so superficial. Some guys try to act so smart and macho, and come across looking so stupid. Sometimes I think most guys are about as deep as a puddle! And they think* ***we're*** *superficial![3]*

Questions for discussion

1. What idea do these teenagers seem to have about what makes a person shallow or superficial?

2. Do either of the teenagers give evidence of stereotyping persons of the other gender? Why is stereotyping others in itself a superficial response?

3. How would you describe a shallow or superficial type of person? A person who has substance, character, and depth?

4. Which of the teenagers' comments do you agree with? Why? Which ones do you think are shallow, and which contain some substance?

5. Why isn't your depth or superficiality due to how intelligent or well-educated you are, or on what you've experienced in life? Why does it depend on how you **reflect** on what you learn and experience and what kind of person you become as a result?

6. How can regular personal and prayerful reflection help make a difference between someone who's shallow and someone of wisdom and substance? What difference can **prayerful** reflection make here that ordinary reflection can't?

private prayer

individual prayer which focuses on our relationship with God and how it gives meaning and direction to our lives and other relationships

Prayer of presence

The prayer of presence (contemplation) is silent, wordless love of God. This involves simply, consciously, lovingly, being in God's presence. Words and thoughts aren't necessary, only the loving awareness of God's presence. It takes time, effort, and great trust to develop any relationship to the point where this more focused type of conscious loving presence can be sustained for a length of time without interruption or distraction.

The universe itself inhales and exhales the spirit of God. Humankind is no different. We too live in God's house, and [God's] house is a house of prayer.
—*Susan Annette Muto*

Most people experience brief moments of this type of communication with God. You've probably experienced such glimpses of a more intensely aware presence either with God or with someone else you're very close to. But when you do really connect and commune lovingly and wordlessly with someone—or Someone—aren't these moments extra special?

With your closest friends you can probably spend a length of time together without saying much or feeling awkward about the silence. Between good friends, this silent presence is comfortable. It reflects and fosters a personal trust that brings people closer. It's good to also communicate with God in this way—to get more deeply and trustingly in touch more often with the One who is the source of all that is, and of all that matters most.

Group prayer

In **private prayer** we pray individually. Most Christians pray formally in church. But, as Jesus told us, we can also pray anywhere together.

Some business persons pray together before negotiating important contracts. Some surgeons offer to pray with their patients before major surgery. The U.S. Congress has its own chaplain who leads the gathered representatives in prayer daily during each legislative session. Married couples often find that praying together enriches their marriage and helps keep their communication with each other open and their love alive. Families often pray together—some daily, as before meals or the children's bedtime.

Many Catholics participate in parish or school-sponsored prayer groups. Sometimes these are ecumenical prayer groups, which include persons of other faiths. Organized prayer group sessions often follow a format similar to that for reflective prayer—an opening prayer or song, a spiritual reading, reflection on and discussion of what the reading means and how it applies to everyday life, spontaneous prayers by those present, concluding prayer or song.

While watching some critical national or worldwide event unfold on TV, we often have a sense of being united in prayer with people across the country and around the world—even though physically we're thousands of miles apart. Praying with others in person, even outside weekly church services, can also help nourish the bonds of faith and human understanding that unite us more deeply in our personal relationships. 🐚

"Again, truly I tell you, if two of you agree on earth about anything you ask, it will be done for you by my Father in heaven. For where two or three are gathered in my name, I am there among them."
—*Matthew 18:19–20*

Many Native Americans believe that "Every move is a prayer."

Active prayer

Active prayer is a deed or a gesture which deliberately expresses one's love for God. This can take a more traditional or formal form, such as the various gestures used in the Christian sacraments, the sign of peace, the gesture of blessing, kneeling or genuflecting in worship, or gesture-prayer like the Sign of the Cross or religious dance.

It can also be more informal and spontaneous, like the young child doing somersaults for God! It can be acting in kind, just, honest, and right ways because you're aware of what your relationship with God means. It can mean courageously speaking out to defend what's right or to argue against what's wrong.

Native Americans have perceived that "Every move is a prayer." In fact, loving God by showing genuine concern for others—especially those who need your help—is one of the best ways to pray, to stay in touch with God. Jesus expressed this same idea about active prayer when he said that whatever we do—especially to the least, we do to him.

Active prayer can include word or thought prayers, or it may just be actions done in awareness of God's love and presence. But active prayer shouldn't be the only kind of prayer style we use. Couples often drift apart when they always do things for each other but don't frequently make enough time to sit and talk, think things through together, and just quietly enjoy each other's presence. Sooner or later their actions become habits, and the loving meaning behind them is forgotten. So it's important that we keep our relationship with God alive, too, by also praying in other ways.

Yet Jesus emphasized that prayer must always involve a commitment to put our love for God into action. Our other ways of praying should help us live so that we bring life and love to others. Otherwise all the other kinds of praying are empty and meaningless. Whenever you deliberately put your religious beliefs into practice by being kinder and more caring, you are praying—drawing closer in communion with God who is especially present among those who are less fortunate and in greater need of your time, attention, and goodness.

Prayer is heart-to-Heart communication.

🐾 Questions for discussion

1. How would you describe what active prayer means and includes? The difference between formal and informal active prayer? Give examples.

2. What is your favorite form of active prayer?

3. Why is active prayer so important? Why mustn't it be the only way we pray?

4. Have you ever felt shy or embarrassed about praying, even in private? Why do you think people sometimes feel this way?

5. Have you ever felt like maybe you weren't praying well enough because you weren't feeling very religious? Why isn't emotion necessary for real prayer?

6. What is necessary for prayer to be genuine? What sign is there that our prayer is genuine?

7. Do you feel you can be completely honest with God? Explain.

However you choose to pray, pray sincerely and wholeheartedly. Drop your pretenses and put everything you've got into it—your heart, mind, and even your emotions and imagination. Never feel shy, embarrassed, or inhibited with God. Likewise, don't make the mistake some people do who equate strong emotions or imaginative experiences with authentic religious or even supernatural experiences. It's not true that, unless you're feeling emotional about it, you're not really praying well or that God isn't listening to your prayer! Real faith and prayer can sometimes feel as dry as a desert, but they're no less real.

You go to pray: to become a bonfire, a living flame, giving heart and light.
—*Venerable José Escriva*

What will determine how genuine your prayer **really** is? As Jesus taught us, if your prayer is genuine, it will deepen your religious convictions and commitment. It will also prompt you to make positive changes in yourself and be more kind and helpful to others. And when you pray, **always know that the love you try to give to God is, at the same time, also God's gift to and God's way of loving you.**

So pray what's in your heart and on your mind—exactly as you feel and perceive it. You can **always** be completely honest with God. Jesus certainly was in Gethsemane the night before he was crucified, when he prayed that he not have to suffer and die! As long as you try to come closer to God, your prayers will be acceptable no matter what form of prayer you use, if it's honest and from your heart.

God is totally loving, and God loves you totally—no strings attached. You may cut yourself off from God, but you can never stop God from loving you—no matter what you do. God loves you as you are and accepts all of your sincere efforts to draw closer, no matter what place you choose or words you use to pray. As Eastern wisdom says,

No matter what road I travel,
I'm going home.

        Shinsho 🐾

"God is spirit, and those who worship must worship in spirit and truth." —*John 4:24 (New Jerusalem Bible)*

Personal praying styles

Someone has said, "There is no one right way to pray. . . . Nobody's way of prayer is like anyone else's. . . . if you are praying, you are already doing it right."[4] To an extent, this may be correct. But a growing number of situations raise serious questions about when group prayer is or is not a good idea in a particular situation. Read the following and respond to the questions.

One group of Christian employees have created a Bible study group at work. The company's president lets the group meet in a conference room during lunch. One participant says that when workers are under stress, reading and talking about a relevant Scripture passage helps them deal with their problems in a more Christian manner.

She says it strengthens employees to work better with others, and improves their work environment. Sometimes their boss joins the group prayer during coffee break. He says they pray for the workers' families or about work-related problems. He thinks "the workplace could use some prayer" but "people shouldn't be aggressive with it." He also says, "We don't try to hurt or offend anyone. We also owe our time to our job, so we don't take away from that. That is why we pray or study on breaks or before work."

Others say that, in a free society, management shouldn't actively promote a particular religion in the workplace. They say it can make workers of another or of no religion feel like second-class employees. They fear that hiring and promotion practices may, even if unintentionally, favor those of the same religion or Church.

Elsewhere, a non-Christian religious university's representatives are widely promoting a form of non-religious meditation in public schools. They use a humming sound mantra to calm and clear the mind. They claim that it releases creativity and intelligence and helps students be happier and behave better. Others protest that "it's just a way to introduce the group's own brand of religion by bringing it through the back door in a non-religious disguise."

Meanwhile, some fundamentalist Christians are actively lobbying local school boards to make teachers teach the details of the Bible's creation stories as literally true. Catholics and others object that this opposes **their** religious beliefs which do not interpret the Bible's every word literally.

In other places, there is growing concern that children in public schools are being made to feel ashamed of their religious beliefs. Recently, when a very young child drew a picture of God in school, the teacher tore it up, telling him that he can't draw religious pictures in school. In a high school, a teacher was instructed to remove the Bible from his desktop during school hours, even though he may keep on his desk other books on Buddhist and Native American religious beliefs.

In another city, a Catholic's co-workers in the county government voted him Employee of the Year. Those he has worked with know he is Catholic, that he thinks deeply and prayerfully about things, and that his religious faith means a great deal to him, because he is willing to talk about his religious beliefs when others bring up the topic. But, beyond promising to pray for someone who is having problems, the man neither apologizes for nor advertises his religious beliefs.

One of the persons who helped count the workers' ballots said that the comments on them were highly unusual this time— especially regarding a county government employee. Many remarked about how the man genuinely cares about people and always takes the time to listen and to help them with their work. They said he is always kind, works hard, and does a good job. Some remarked about his sincerity and humility. Some praised his wonderful sense of humor and positive way of focusing on problems and making their jobs much easier and more enjoyable. Others specifically mentioned that they admire him because he lives what it truly means to be a Christian. No one said a negative word about him.

It is such a joy when I awaken to salute God by singing.
—Blessed Teresa of the Andes

Questions for discussion

1. In what sense is the first statement in the article true, and not completely true?

2. One child jumps rope for God. A teenage girl reads to and prays to God about the contents of her diary. A teenage boy serenades God in the shower. What's your personal praying style?

3. How would you describe your personal spirituality, the way you usually relate with God?

4. What prayer style does each situation in the article describe? Which one impresses you most positively, and why?

5. What role do you think prayer should play in the workplace? Under what circumstances would you feel comfortable about praying at work? When would you find this objectionable? Explain.

6. What is your response to each of the situations described? What do you think is the best way in each case to respect and balance religious and other types of freedom? Explain.

7. How do you hope your relationship with God will affect your future job and work relationships? How does it affect your work and relationships with other students now?

Does God really respond?

Is praying just "throwing wishes in the air" or does God answer our prayer? Do you ever feel like God doesn't always hear your prayers? It's very interesting that we're apt to think this only when we don't get specific things we've asked for—not when we praise or thank God! Demanding results-or-else is just trying to use God to get what we want and get it our way.

We mustn't abuse prayer by relating to God as an almighty vending machine! We shouldn't pray superstitiously—expecting that if we pray in a certain way God will have to act in a certain way. (We don't like it when somebody tries to manipulate us that way!) We also shouldn't automatically conclude that our dreams or natural coincidences are God's voice or supernatural events. Prayer should never be just for show, to make someone look holy, or used to promote a political agenda.

Prayer is a mystery. Like communicating with others, prayer is based on belief. People might only pretend to listen to us while their thoughts are really far away. So we rely on others' responses to tell us when they've truly listened and understood us. But is there evidence God hears our prayer?

Grant us grace, Almighty [God], so to pray as to deserve to be heard.
—Jane Austen

Communicating with God takes faith and trust in God's goodness and love for us. Your own beliefs about prayer are based, for one thing, on what you believe about God's existence and what God is like. If you believe God exists and must be personal and loving in order to be God, then doesn't it necessarily follow that God is able and willing to listen and respond to you when you pray? Believing that prayer does no good really reflects not trusting enough in God's nearness and goodness.

So **the main reasons Christians believe God hears our prayer are God's own goodness and love for us, and Jesus' promise that God will listen and grant our prayer.**

Very truly, I tell you, if you ask anything of the Father in my name, he will give it to you. . . . Ask and you will receive, so that your joy may be complete.
—John 16:23–24

Prayer and God's goodness

Why believe that God always answers our prayer when we don't always seem to get what we're asking for? First let's look at what happens when we make requests of others who truly love us. Then let's examine why we **think** God hasn't answered us at times.

Even when we know someone has heard our request and truly has our best interests at heart, we still don't always get our way. Why not? Because (although we hate to admit it) what we **think** is best for us isn't always what is **really** in our best interests.

A good parent, friend, or doctor might correctly see, for instance, that answering our request our way would hurt us terribly rather than be good for us. So out of genuine concern for our well-being, they'll refuse to do or give us what we're asking for. (In fact, if we could see clearly that it wouldn't be good for us, we wouldn't want them to give us what we're asking for!) Someone who lovingly must refuse our request will help us live without what we

Questions for discussion

1. Describe the difference between praying and just throwing wishes in the air.

2. When you failed to receive something you prayed very hard for, how did you feel about having prayed—sorry you did, angry, or what?

3. Why do you think people tend to feel God is not listening when they ask for something in prayer, but not when they thank or praise God?

4. How can prayer be abused superstitiously? Describe a superstitious and a non-superstitious way to view dreams as a possible way God speaks to us.

5. Do you ever get the impression that politicians stage participation in public prayer just to promote their image or agenda? Explain.

6. Do you ask God for things in prayer? Do you always feel God hears and answers these prayers of yours? Explain.

thought we wanted, and try to help us be happier in other ways—perhaps giving us something even better.

Likewise, when praying to God, we should ask only for things we think will be good for us or make us or someone else happy. We don't—and shouldn't ever—ask that we or someone else be made miserable or harmed. We ask God for favors we perceive as good. But since we're not all-wise, we're bound to be mistaken at times about what is really for the best. We might not realize we're asking God for the wrong things. We can't know, as God does, that something else much better will make us happier in the long run.

Ask, and it will be given you. . . . For everyone who asks receives. . . . —Luke 11:9–10

God loves us totally and wants our ultimate happiness more than we do. So God **can't** answer us by responding in ways that won't be good and life-giving. That would logically contradict God's nature and goodness. But **in some way God will always answer our prayer by offering us the possibility for increased happiness and love.** In fact that is the first way God always does respond to our prayer.

Through prayer, God won't automatically solve all your problems for you. If God must answer "no" to your specific request (remember, *no* is a real answer!), God will still respond positively. God will grant what you're **really** always asking for—the possibility for even greater happiness for you and others. Pray, though, that God's Spirit enlighten you so you know what's truly for the best. After all, that's what God and you both really, ultimately want.

What Jesus said about asking God

We'll never really be able to prove scientifically that God truly answers prayer. But Christians believe this based on who we believe God is and on our belief in Jesus and his words.

Jesus encouraged his followers to pray, and to pray in his name. When individuals implored his assistance for themselves or for others, in response Jesus offered them both physical and spiritual help. As Jesus said, God knows what we want before we ask for it. Yet God respects our freedom and waits for us to ask. Many times Jesus assured us that, in one way or another, God will always give us what we ask for in prayer. What we're always really asking for is happiness.

Even if our prayer doesn't seem to be answered right away, Jesus told us not to give up and to keep on praying, because God really will respond. Jesus also reminded us that God is far better than we are. If even we who are imperfect fulfill the requests of those we love, how much more will God, who is all-perfect and all-loving, fulfill our prayer! As Christians we believe that not only should we pray in Jesus' name, but that Jesus also prays for and with us when we pray.

We Christians might also agree with some Buddhists that, in a way, prayer is its own answer. In the very act of praying, we already receive what we're above all praying for—greater openness to and union with ultimate Happiness and Love. So don't save praying just for church or special occasions. If you believe that God loves and is near you, then believe in prayer. No thought or feeling of yours is insignificant to God. You're always important. You always matter. You're always lovable. You're always loved. ❧

❧ Questions for discussion

1. What reasons seem best to you for believing God always answers prayer?

2. If a friend begged you for something you absolutely knew would be greatly harmful, would you give it to your friend? Why or why not?

3. Describe a time you were mistaken about what was actually in your best interests. How can we be mistaken about this when asking God for things?

4. Why is "no" a legitimate answer to a specific request in prayer? Explain **how** Catholics believe that God always answers prayers.

5. Why did Jesus encourage us to ask God for things in prayer?

6. If at first our prayer doesn't seem to be answered, why keep praying?

We have what we seek. It is there all the time, and if we give it time it will make itself known to us.
—Thomas Merton

Faith and healing

Many frauds claim to be "faith healers." Some are exposed by investigators who discover how they operate: The "faith healer" accurately pinpoints an audience member's medical problems while being fed this information through a hidden earphone by a colleague who has conversed with the audience member beforehand. But what about the increasing number of scientific studies which claim to show that prayer "works"? Read the following and respond to the questions.

> *Praying for sick patients can help them heal, even if they don't know they are being prayed for, suggests a [medical journal report]. [Over a two-year period, a doctor] studied about 400 patients in the coronary care unit at [a major medical center]. Although many studies have looked at the power of intercessory prayer by people who know the patient, this is the first study of praying by strangers for strangers.*

> *In the study, patients were divided into two "blind" groups. The prayers were offered by Christians [in the local area] who had no contact with the patients.*

> *Of those who were prayed for, 85 percent either improved or did not get worse. In the other group, 73 percent improved or did not worsen.*

> *[The doctor] says he expected that friends and families would be praying for all of the patients, no matter which group they were in. That blurred the distinctions between the two groups and "may have resulted in smaller differences observed between the two groups."*[5]

A cardiologist at a major medical center finds that praying can have physical and mental benefits. He "has found that prayer and meditation can lower blood pressure, alleviate pain and stress, and bring about peace of mind." It is becoming more understood that praying can have physical and mental as well as spiritual benefits. Prayer has been found to relieve stress and pain, lower blood pressure, and help achieve a peaceful state of mind.

Many doctors pray for and with their patients and believe praying sometimes makes a miraculous difference in the outcome of medical treatment. Other doctors are skeptical, saying there have always been unexpected medical recoveries. So, is it the medical treatment or the prayer which has made the "miraculous" difference?

Most doctors think that praying can't hurt and might help. Other doctors think that promoting prayer steps outside the bounds of scientific medicine. One has asked this: If reliable studies ever do show that prayer helps as definitively as medication, will or should doctors be sued for not praying with or for their patients? Some say viewing prayer as a scientific remedy can be extremely harmful—making people feel guilty that, if they aren't cured, then it's because they didn't pray hard enough.

Questions for discussion

1. What alleged faith healings have you heard about? Which do you consider frauds? Do you still wonder about the validity of any? Explain.

2. Do you pray for those you care about who are sick or undergoing major surgery? How would you feel before life-threatening surgery if you knew many people were praying for a successful outcome for you? Explain.

3. Did the doctor in this study seem aware that his patients were being prayed for? What do you think is the importance that a scientific study be "blind" so patients not know they are being prayed for? Be "double-blind" so neither patient nor doctor is aware of this?

4. Why did the doctor say the distinction between the two groups of patients was blurred? What did he say may have happened as a result?

5. What might account for prayer's physical and mental benefits? For unexpected medical recoveries?

6. What do you think about trying to demonstrate prayer's effectiveness scientifically? What harm might this cause? What might Jesus say about this? Explain.

7. Why isn't it true that not recovering from an illness is due to someone's not praying hard enough? Why is this idea opposed to Catholic belief?

8. How did Jesus respond to ill persons? Why do you think he mainly spent his time teaching, instead of physically healing everybody in the world? What do his words and examples tell us about faith and healing?

When it's hard to pray

If you sometimes find it hard to pray, don't feel like taking the time to pray, or just don't feel anything when you pray, then you're not alone. **Prayer, like all good communication, requires the effort and perseverance to keep trying.** When two people give up on trying to communicate with each other, their relationship is doomed. Prayer is also essential to our relationship with God.

If you usually find it hard to pray, you might reexamine what you mean by prayer. Some people approach prayer as only a mental or psychological exercise. Popularly advertised meditation techniques are often merely relaxation exercises—ways to empty the mind of worries and distractions. Some find an afternoon nap is equally good for this!

Relaxing from the day's tensions can prepare us to relate better with our family members, but it's no substitute for direct communication and spending time with them. Likewise, some mental relaxation techniques are an excellent way of preparing to pray. But, unless they also involve communicating or communing with God, they're different from prayer in the Christian sense.

"What good is prayer?" some ask. "I don't have time to pray," say others. Well, that's sort of like saying breathing won't make you rich, or you're too busy to breathe! Breathing might not put money in your pocket, but if you stopped breathing, your body would die without the oxygen needed to keep your organs alive, renewed, and properly functioning.

Prayer is what your spirit needs to breathe. It can help you sort through the problems that weigh you down, give your life far greater meaning, and keep you on the right track. Otherwise you can just go through the motions in life, wondering why it all seems so pointless.

So prayer isn't an escape from or interruption of life's important realities; rather, prayer can help you really live as fully as possible. God, who keeps you in existence, is your life's most important Reality. Your time and your life are in God's hands anyway. Prayer is as necessary as breathing. Even in the middle of life's greatest turmoils, we always do have the time and ability to pray.

Does God seem far away? Guess who moved.
—Anonymous

Prayer is possible at any time.

Don't get discouraged

Some people get discouraged after awhile when they realize that praying hasn't made them perfect! That's as unrealistic as married couples who become disillusioned in a few years by small imperfections in their relationship. The closer in love they become, the more aware they're naturally going to be of faults and differences. But this can be a positive sign that the relationship is growing, not an indication that it's on the rocks.

. . . God, who searches the heart, knows what is the mind of the Spirit, because the Spirit intercedes for the saints according to the will of God.
—Romans 8:27

1. Do you ever find it hard to pray? Have you ever wanted to pray but felt, for some reason, that you couldn't? Explain.

2. What is the difference between mental relaxation and prayer in the Christian sense? How can these relaxation techniques help us pray?

3. In what sense is prayer like breathing? Not an escape from or interruption of life?

4. How can discouragement about faults after praying be a positive sign?

5. Have you ever been comforted or strengthened by knowing that someone else was praying for you? Explain.

6. Why do Catholics believe someone else is always praying with and for us?

7. What things typically distract you during prayer or private reflection? When might these distractions be telling you something you should listen to? When is it better to ignore them?

In prayer, such discouragement can be a positive sign that we're becoming more aware of what our relationships with God and others could be. So we may become dissatisfied that we don't experience that more fully. Then we need to make some adjustments and sail on, not abandon ship! Jesus urged us to keep praying, and not to lose heart (Luke 18:1).

In your own life, you know that you're not always a perfect friend. Maybe you've lost friends because of stupid things you've said or done. Maybe you've been hurt by friends who let you down. But God is your one Friend who will never ever let you down, no matter how imperfect you are. So never let your lack of perfection discourage you from talking things over with your always-faithful Friend.

Meditation is meant to affect us, to change and transform our heart. It challenges our current assumptions, opinions, prejudices.
—*Susan Annette Muto*

Remember also that **prayer always has a social dimension.** Although we may pray privately, the rest of **the Church also prays with and for us.** So at times when you feel too alone and discouraged, take comfort and support from knowing that others are praying for you.

Have you ever tried to pray or think about one thing when your mind kept wandering aimlessly, or to problems or things you had to do? Mentally wandering instead of really paying attention is a common problem people have in communicating with each other and with God.

Some distractions, though, can be enlightening. They might be the Holy Spirit's way of redirecting you to what you should really be talking and reflect-

ing with God about but are maybe ignoring. Otherwise, it's good discipline to deliberately refocus our heart on God, just as we often need to pay better attention when communicating with other people.

Never worry that you can't find the words to pray. Simply let your confusion, your joy and gratitude, or your heartache and tears be your prayer. God is your Friend who **always** understands. Remember,

. . . the Spirit helps us in our weakness; for we do not know how to pray as we ought, but that very Spirit intercedes with sighs too deep for words.
Romans 8:26 ☙

The possibilities of prayer

Are your ideas and style of praying too narrow and confining? Do you connect prayer with those life experiences which mean the most to you? Do you communicate with God as you'd like to communicate with someone you love deeply and trust completely?

Once you overcome the stereotype of prayer as just saying "holy" words, **the possibilities for communicating with God are endless.** Listening to your favorite music can be a way to pray. So can dancing, exercise, or other physical activities. Just focus your heart on God. Prayer doesn't have to involve certain sacred words.

Whenever you're aware of being in touch with Someone whose goodness, truth, beauty, love, or meaning is infinitely beyond what you're experiencing, that's a form of prayer or at least an invitation to commune with God. Prayer is recognizing all the awesome dimensions of Ultimate Meaning in your life. All meaningful experiences are special openings to prayer. In fact, when prayer is understood this way, you may be praying far more often than you realized.

So you can live a very prayerful life without spending most of it on your knees! You don't have to address God by name in order to pray. Simply be aware of God's presence in the middle of everyday realities, like jogging or riding a bike. When, because of your belief in God, you do what is good and loving, that's active prayer. We can all learn from the Native Americans' attitude about praying:

> *Whenever, in the course of the daily hunt the red hunter comes upon a scene that is strikingly beautiful or sublime—a black thundercloud with the rainbow's glowing arch above the mountain, a white waterfall in the heart of a green gorge; a vast prairie tinged with the blood-red of sunset—he pauses for an instant in the attitude of worship. . . since to him all days are God's.*
>
> —*Ohiyesa, Santee Dakota physician and author speaking in 1911 about the manner in which his people worship.*[6]

If I consistently refuse to take time for reflection, I run the risk of a dull, uninspiring existence, a kind of death in life.
—Susan Annette Muto

Questions for discussion

1. At what times in your life have you felt closest to God in prayer? Why? The furthest away from God in prayer? Why?

2. How do you pray, when you can't find the words?

3. Being honest, what stereotypes have you had in the past about prayer and praying? How can these stereotypes be overcome?

4. What is the best way to live a prayerful life? What living person most exemplifies what this means to you? Why?

Is prayer a miracle drug?

Read the following article and respond to the questions.

All those learned men and women of medicine said basically the same thing to me once I had emerged from wherever God puts your mind while people are trying to save your life in a hospital.

They said it was a miracle I had lived from what were the most complicated of complications that arose during what was supposed to have been a fairly routine heart valve replacement surgery [several] weeks ago.

To a man and woman, those doctors and nurses said to me after the critical time had passed, "We exhausted all medical possibilities. We did everything we knew to do for you, and it probably wouldn't have been enough. What saved you was prayer."

Can you believe that? Great men and women of science saying such a thing [in this day and age]?

Prayer?

Surely not. It had to be some new miracle drug developed by researchers. . . . It had to be one of those cardiac pumps they said they attached to my heart when it just up and decided not to beat anymore.

No, they said. It was prayer.

A friend said, "Everybody I saw said they were praying for you. A man said his church held a special prayer service for you. You had a lot of people asking God to spare you."

What [I did] to deserve any of that I don't know, but I do know I had spent a lot of time in my life doubting. At one time or the other, I doubted it all: spirituality, love, the basic good of humankind.

But this flirtation with the end of me has removed a lot of that doubt. If the medical experts say prayer brought me back from certain death, who am I to doubt them?

And prayer only works if there is someone or something to grant the favor asked. My faith and belief in that someone or something not only has been restored but it has been forevermore cast in my soul as the great truth beyond all others.

But now comes the hard part. I owe a lot of thank yous. I must thank those who are responsible for the fact I'm still amongst the quick. The . . . doctors and nurses know how I feel about them. They are the best of the best.

But what do I do about the prayerful? Say simply, "Hey, everybody who prayed for me, Thanks"?

It's got to be more profound than that. I snatched away a new life. I have been to the other side of the veil and came back from behind it.

Here is what I would like to do: I would like to gather all who lifted a voice when I stood in need of it so badly and, one by one, I would like to hug them around the neck and say, "I love you and I thank you for my life."

For the record, even if you didn't pray for me, it's nice to be with you again, too.

To be honest, it's just nice to be.[7]

Within the year, further medical complications developed and the author died. In the meantime, he married the woman to whom he had been engaged for a year.

Questions for discussion

1. Have you experienced or heard of "miraculous" results of prayer? Explain.

2. Why do you think the man seemed astonished that the medical personnel felt he was saved by prayer? Why do you think he seemed to take their word for it, when he hadn't had much faith in prayer before?

3. What did the prayers of others mean for this man? Why?

4. What is the only reason the man feels prayer could possibly work? What do you think is the real reason his faith in God was restored?

5. Obviously, the man wanted to live. Do you think his and others' prayers were answered even though he died within the year? Explain.

Chapter review

1. Guides for praying

- Why is regular communication an important part of human relationships and of one's relationship with God?

- What is the proper attitude for communicating sincerely with God and others? What does this mean with regard to prayer?

- Why is it important to make time to pray?

- Why is it also important to listen to God in prayer? How can one do this without being superstitious about it?

- What is an appropriate place for personal prayer? Why is finding a suitable place for this important?

- What is meant by one's spirituality? How can Catholics develop a personal spirituality in a way that is sound and truly Christian, rather than superficial or superstitious?

2. Styles of praying

- What did Jesus really mean by telling us to pray always?

- Explain each of the following styles of praying—conversational prayer (meditation), reflective prayer, prayer of presence (contemplation), group prayer, and active prayer.

- What should conversational prayer include?

- What types of standard or formula prayers are there, and what is the meaning and significance of each of these: the Sign of the Cross; the name Jesus; Come, Holy Spirit; The Liturgy of the Hours; and the Hail Mary?

- What are the steps of reflective prayer? Why is each important?

- What is the importance of seeking inner stillness and silence in prayer?

- Other than in normal worship services, what is the value of group prayer?

- What types of active prayer are there? Why is praying in this way necessary for Christians? Why should Christians also pray in other ways?

3. Does God really respond?

- How is prayer a mystery, and what does this require of us? How is this different from viewing prayer superstitiously?

- What are the main reasons why Christians believe God hears and responds to our prayers? More specifically, what did Jesus say about this?

- How does God respond to prayers in which we ask for things? Why don't people always seem to get what they request?

- What does Jesus' example show us about praying to God?

- Why bother to ask God for things, when God knows beforehand what we want?

- Why is it important to keep praying, even when God doesn't grant our specific request soon or at all?

4. When it's hard to pray

- Why is it important to pray even when it's hard or we don't feel like it?

- What are some good ways of overcoming discouragement, distractions, lack of feeling, stereotypes, and other difficulties of praying?

- How can one live a prayerful life without escaping from or continually interrupting life's other important realities?

Projects and assignments

1. Read Luke 1:39–56, and then write a one-page paper commenting on why Mary has been called the "perfect pray-er."

2. Read the account in Exodus 5:19–6:13 about a few occasions on which Moses ("God's friend") got upset with God. Then write a one-page paper explaining the insights this passage gives you about talking and relating with God.

3. Attend a group prayer meeting in your parish. Then write a one-page paper commenting on your response to participating in the group prayer session.

4. Write a two-page paper on the role you think prayer should and should not play in a free society.

5. Write your own reflections on the Way of the Cross, or illustrate these in a collage or other creative way which shows how each station relates to today's problems.

Chapter 11 Religious Celebrations

Do you have eyes, and fail to see?
Do you have ears, and fail to hear?
And do you not remember?

> *Mark 8:18*

We give you praise and thanks . . .
that you are God. . . .
You know us and so we live.
You love us and so we are your people.

Blessed are you . . .
that you have given us this day and this hour.

Blessed are you . . .
in all the things you have made:
in plants and in animals
and in people, the wonders of your hand.

Blessed are you . . .
for the food we eat;
for bread and for wine
and for laughter in your presence.

Blessed are you. . .
that you have given us eyes to see your goodness
in the things you have made
ears to hear your word,
hands that we may touch and bless and understand.[1]

> *John L'Heureux*

Overview questions

1. What role do ritual and ceremony play in human life and in communication with God?
2. What is the Catholic liturgy? How is it celebrated?
3. What are signs and symbols? What role do they play in sacramental celebrations?
4. What is the importance of sacred times and places in religious celebrations?

Celebrating religious beliefs

Like most people, when you believe in something very strongly, you probably don't just think or talk about it. Most likely, you also celebrate it by some action, gesture, or ritual. Throughout history people have celebrated important convictions with actions like songs, ceremonies, dances, parades, and even fireworks. Celebrations connected with religious beliefs have always been among the most important ones. This chapter will discuss both why people celebrate at all, and why Catholics celebrate the Christian mysteries of the seven sacraments.

We need to be in touch

When we love someone, we want to keep in touch with the person. When someone close to us goes away, we hope the person will write, call, or send a picture. We're not very good at keeping very deep feelings or special occasions to ourselves. We want to share them. So, we hug or kiss someone, or throw a party, or cheer together when our team has scored. Sometimes we laugh with someone, sometimes we cry together. We often find that life's experiences are too meaningful not to share. And so, we **celebrate** them—**together.**

We need these visible signs of communication in order to really celebrate. Sometimes we do need to be alone with our sorrow or our happiness. Every special experience always has a uniquely personal aspect which we can't fully share with anyone. Much of the time, though, we like and need to share what we can—to celebrate things together. Experiencing life's most meaningful moments all by ourselves would be frustrating and lonely.

Many of our celebrations are spontaneous. We don't use formal phrases or planned actions. But we do rely on words, gestures, or actions which have a common meaning: handshakes celebrate making a new acquaintance or reaching an agreement, "high fives" celebrate a triumph, kisses celebrate affection, and so on. These spontaneous celebrations are an important part of life. ❧

Rituals

Some occasions call for a more formal, planned celebration. Usually, these involve some kind of ritual, or a **ceremony** containing several rituals—ways of repeating things which others have done before us to celebrate the occasion. Although we like to live informally in general, we also like to celebrate more formally at times with ritual and ceremony.

Ceremonies celebrate something in a certain set way. This makes the celebration seem more special—particularly when we use the words or gestures only on these special occasions. It's because we don't share a solemn promise every day to confirm our ordinary friendships that it's so special in a wedding ceremony. **Tradition also increases meaning.** Repeating the same words and gestures others have used multiplies their significance for us. They carry the weight and meaning of all who have spoken or done them before us—of the tradition behind them.

Sharing in the same words and actions is what enables us to celebrate together. If we had no communal ways of celebrating, we sure would miss a lot! There would be no rallies, no dances, no weddings, no funerals, and probably no hugs or kisses. We could express our beliefs and feelings only in completely unique and individualized ways, and by ourselves—but not with other persons. We're social beings, though, and **we need to celebrate our shared experiences together.**

❧ Questions for discussion

1. What do you mean by a "celebration"? Why do you think people like to celebrate? Why do you?

2. What are your three most favorite occasions for celebrating, and why? What do you like to do to celebrate these occasions with others?

3. What words, gestures, or actions do teenagers commonly rely on in celebrating spontaneously? What meaning does each seem to have?

ceremony

combination of two or more ritual gestures

ritual

action or actions repeated in a particular manner on similar occasions by a person or group

🕮 Questions for discussion

1. In an age of freedom and spontaneity, why do people still like to celebrate certain things in traditional ways? Why do you?

2. What are your favorite traditional rituals, ceremonies, or celebrations? Why?

3. How does each of these involve the three elements of ritual or ceremony?

Rites and ceremonies use the ordinary and earthy elements of our existence and, by encircling them, render them holy.
—*Gertrud Mueller Nelson*

Celebrating with others in traditional, familiar ways is also comfortable. Because we already know what's expected, we don't feel awkward—like we have to figure out how to respond at each point. So if there weren't any rituals, we'd invent some! We'd eventually think of welcoming home a heroine or hero with a parade, and of setting aside special time and procedures to celebrate graduations, marriages, and for sharing loss and grief. Where no such ceremonies existed, people have created them to celebrate special occasions together.

Ritual celebrations or ceremonies usually involve three things:

1. An occasion special to more than one person

2. The desire to celebrate this occasion together

3. The use of signs and symbols to outwardly express this community experience

Rituals, then, consist of words and actions we repeat together on similar occasions to celebrate what something means to us. 🕮

Rites

Read the following story about a young prince who comes to earth from another planet and discovers a fox who wishes to be his friend. Then respond to the questions.

The fox gazed at the little prince, for a long time. "Please—tame me!" he said.

"I want to, very much," the little prince replied. "But I have not much time. I have friends to discover, and a great many things to understand."

"One only understands the things that one tames," said the fox. "[People] have no more time to understand anything. They buy things all ready made at the shops. But there is no shop anywhere where one can buy friendship, and so [people] have no friends any more. If you want a friend, tame me. . . ."

"What must I do, to tame you?" asked the little prince.

"You must be very patient," replied the fox. "First you will sit down at a little distance from me—like that—in the grass. I shall look at you out of the corner of my eye, and you will say nothing. Words are the source of misunderstandings. But you will sit a little closer to me, every day. . . ."

The next day the little prince came back. "It would have been better to come back at the same hour," said the fox. "If, for example, you come at four o'clock in the afternoon, then at three o'clock I shall begin to be happy. I shall feel happier and happier as the hour advances. At four o'clock, I shall already be worrying and jumping about. I shall show you how happy I am! But if you come at just any time, I shall never know at what hour my heart is to be ready to greet you. . . . One must observe the proper rites. . . ."

"What is a rite?" asked the little prince.

"Those also are actions too often neglected," said the fox. "They are what make one day different from other days, one hour from other hours. There is a rite, for example, among my hunters. Every Thursday they dance with the village girls. So Thursday is a wonderful day for me! I can take a walk as far as the vineyards. But if the hunters danced at just any time, every day would be like every other day, and I should never have any vacation at all."

So the little prince tamed the fox.

And when it came time for the little prince to depart, the fox made him a present of a secret:

"Goodbye," said the fox. "And now here is my secret, a very simple secret: It is only with the heart that one can see rightly; what is essential is invisible to the eye."²

Questions for discussion

1. What did the fox mean by being "tamed"?
2. What was the little prince's excuse at first for not wanting to tame the fox? What was the fox's reply?
3. What did the fox say the little prince must do to tame him?
4. What did the fox explain that a rite is and means? Why did he say rites are so important in "taming" someone?
5. What was the fox's parting secret to the little prince? What insight does the fox's secret provide into human relationships, and the role rites (rituals) play in these?

In touch with God

People have always needed and desired to communicate with the divine in the same physical ways we still celebrate with one another today—by using signs and symbols in rituals. Anthropologists tell us that, from the dawn of human civilization, people worshiped their gods with ceremonial **rites.** In fact, the origins of art, music, and dance are traced to this desire to celebrate religious beliefs in visible, physical ways. Thus, early humans

1. communicated together as a group with their gods

2. in a physical way, rather than only by thoughts or words

The gods early peoples worshiped were closely related to daily survival needs. They realized more than we sometimes do how all of life has a religious dimension. Sometimes they ritu-ally asked their gods for favors. At other times, their rituals expressed their gratitude to the gods.

Religious rituals certainly surrounded life's peak moments—birth, assuming adult responsibilities, eating meals of celebration and communion, reconciling with those who had violated tribal codes, illness and death, human fertility (the successful bearing of offspring), and appointing new tribal leadership. It is very interesting how well these parallel the religious occasions Catholics celebrate ritually today in our sacred **liturgical rites** and sacraments. ❧

Christian, recognize your dignity.
—St. Leo the Great

---

rite

a way of acting solemnly in a set manner, as in a ceremony or formal service

liturgical rites

formal church ceremonies

❧ Questions for discussion

1. Why do you think people seem to need and want
   - to connect with God by using ritual signs and symbols?
   - to celebrate life's important events with God as well as with one another?

2. Happy or sad, what are the five most important occasions in a person's life that call for some sort of ritual or celebration? Why is ritual an important part of these occasions?

What is the liturgy?

liturgy

structured formal worship; the Church's official prayer, including the Eucharist and other sacraments

Do you ever have days when you feel like you're losing the struggle to cope with all your problems? A famous coach and sportscaster was often asked by young athletes for his expert advice. His team had won the national basketball tournament against all odds. But what he always told the athletes was that the most important game they'd ever play was life itself. The advice he gave them about how to win—and proclaimed even more strongly in the final months when he knew he was losing his own battle against cancer—was, "Never give up. Never give up! NEVER give up!" This belief, as a community of faith, is what Catholics celebrate in our **liturgy.**

When the odds seem against you in life, why not give up? Why can we hope to finally win—to rise above suffering in this life, and to rise from death to experience eternal glory? Because, in Christ, God has redeemed us once and for all. But unlike other events that happen and then are over, this one continues to remain present for all time. Now God's power, God's Spirit, is our strength.

> *For as often as you eat this bread and drink the cup, you proclaim the Lord's death until he comes . . . so that God may be all in all.*
> *—1 Corinthians 11:26 and 15:28*

For our sake Jesus suffered and died, and then God raised him from suffering and death to eternal glory. So we've been saved and continue to be saved by God from a fate worse than death—from a final dead end of non-existence, or the everlasting pain of unhappiness and loss of all hope. This means that no matter how much evil, pain, and suffering we have in this life, in the end these things won't beat us. Not even death will defeat us. Our goal is life—life in which God is "everything to everybody." We're the ones who, by God's power, will win.

In Christ's victory over death, God has already triumphed as the clear winner and shown us how we can too. This victory, this passing over from death and despair to life and hope in union with Jesus and by God's power, is the paschal mystery. It's this paschal victory which Catholics mainly recall, proclaim, and celebrate in our liturgy and try to live in the way we face each day's possibilities and problems.

The word *liturgy* originally referred to a public work or service for the people. But, for Christians, it means joining in God's work. It means that with God's strength to support us, and

In the liturgy, Christians join in God's work.

united as Church, we can overcome hate with our love. We can beat despair with hope. We can triumph over dishonesty with truth. We can defeat wrongs and intolerant actions with justice and cooperation.

Like the ideal coach, Christ has played the game of life before us—and completed it perfectly and victoriously. His words and example tell us how to do this. They also tell us that, to do so effectively, we've got to prepare ourselves well and work together as one body. What we celebrate in the liturgy together, we've also got to work for together every day in order to realize our common dreams. It's got to be a team effort. 🕊

Celebrating the liturgy

As Church, all of us are the *sacrament of unity.* It's the whole community, as the Body of Christ, who share in Christ's priesthood and celebrate the liturgy in union with Christ. So the sacraments are meant to be public, not private individual celebrations.

The liturgy's visible signs proclaim to us what life means and show us how we're to live it together. Through the liturgy, God's Spirit especially empowers us to do this. This is why the liturgy is considered the source of Christian life. But we need to prepare our hearts so that we're open to God's active presence, both in the liturgy and in our lives. God can help us only to the extent that we cooperate!

Our **liturgy must also be our action**—our conscious response to what God proposes to help us do in life. We must let it help transform us from isolated individuals trying to live a good life alone into a single, unified body— the Body of Christ—working together to improve our society and world. Our active participation in the celebration and our team effort to live as Christians is essential.

We can't do everything or be nearly as effective alone. Our unity as the assembled Church, as one Body, must go beyond racial, social, gender, or other human divisions. Together, as Church, we're to be the visible sign which shows other people how much God loves **all** people.

In the liturgy (especially in the Eucharist) Christ remains especially present in many ways—in the sacraments and their ministers, in God's word in Scripture, and in us and our prayers and songs as we prayerfully gather together. The liturgy is God's lifegiving blessing upon us as we go forth to bring God's love to others. It's also our response in faith and love to the many great blessings God has already given us in life and in the universe around us.

Because the Bible is God's word to us, **Sacred Scripture plays an especially important part in Catholic liturgy.** But have you ever wondered why Christian liturgical celebrations contain so many readings and prayers (mostly psalms) from the Old Testament, and not just from the Christian Scriptures? Remember that the whole Bible—Hebrew and Christian Scriptures—contains God's revelation to us. In addition, our Christian liturgy's structure and content has roots in Jewish prayer and liturgy.

How do Catholics participate in the liturgy? Liturgy is an action and so it involves a more active style of praying. Instead of just sitting passively in the pew, Catholics take an active part as a community in the liturgy's action. We pray, sing, and respond to God's word together. We also participate in other liturgical actions. For example, we extend to one another the sign of peace, bring the gifts to the altar, and come forward to partake of Communion at the Eucharist. Catholics may also participate in other ways: presiding, reading the Scriptures, being a commentator, leading prayers, acting as a server or a formal witness at a wedding, being a godparent or Eucharistic minister, or

🕊 Questions for discussion

1. At what times are you tempted to "give up"? What keeps you from doing so?

2. What reason do Christians especially have for not giving up on ourselves or on life's positive possibilities? How does the Catholic liturgy celebrate this?

3. In what ways should Catholics live the liturgy we celebrate?

☙ Questions for discussion

1. What is meant by saying that, as Church, we are the sacrament of unity?

2. Why can God help us only to the extent that we cooperate? How does this apply to our participation in the liturgy?

3. What positive things do you think Christians can accomplish together as Church that individual Christians can't do alone?

4. Of the ways Christ is present in the liturgy, which are you usually the most and the least aware of? Explain.

5. If you attended a Catholic liturgy in Africa, or one in a Catholic church here that is not of the Roman Rite, what would you expect to find the same as in your local parish? What do you think—or hope—might be different? Explain.

belonging to the choir. Teenagers can volunteer to serve in most of these ministries.

Are Catholic liturgical celebrations the same in other countries? Yes and no. Catholics all over the world celebrate the same beliefs in different but unified ways which remain faithful to the apostles' tradition. The liturgy always has the same essential meaning and main parts, but it may be adapted in various ways to the local language and culture. That way people can participate more meaningfully.

Certain other *liturgical traditions* or *Catholic rites* have a much longer, well-established history in the Church. The most widely celebrated liturgical tradition in our part of the world is the Roman (or Latin) Rite. But there are many other Rites, such as the Byzantine (Eastern countries), Armenian, Maronite (Lebanon), or Ethiopian (Africa) Rites which are equally important. These Catholic Rites or liturgical traditions are fundamentally the same, but each expresses Catholic beliefs in a different traditional style.

The liturgies all Catholics celebrate together on earth, however, are just a taste of what we'll experience when we all share God's glory together with all good persons we love who have gone before us. That will be the real celebration! ☙

Orthodox Patriarchs officiate at services in the Church of the Holy Sepulchre in Jerusalem.

What good are rituals?

Read the following and respond to the questions.

From a narrowly rational or [practical] point of view, ritual is nonsense, a waste any way you look at it. All the money lavished on candles, cathedrals, prayer books, and incense; all the time spent in worship and sacrament;
all the energy that goes into rising up and sitting down, kneeling and prostration, circumambulation and singing—to what end? . . .

To [some Native Alaskans] rubbing noses is a friendship ritual. To us it's simply funny. . . .

Yet . . . ritual plays a part in life which nothing else can fill,
a part which is by no means confined to religion.
For one thing, ritual eases us through tense situations and times of anxiety. . . .
Ritual . . . channels our actions and feelings at a time when solitude would be unbearable. . . .
Ritual also rouses courage. . . .

From the triviality of an introduction to the trauma of death,
ritual smoothes life's transition as perhaps nothing else can.
But it also serves another function. In times of happiness it can intensify experience and raise joy to celebration. . . .
The opposite of dead weight, [ritual] consecrates a daily pleasure.[3]

Questions for discussion

1. What reasons does the author give for saying that ritual seems to be wasteful nonsense?

2. Do you consider rubbing noses a ritual? Why is it a ritual for some Alaskans? What rituals in our society take the place of rubbing noses? Explain.

3. What roles in life does the author say rituals play that nothing else can fill?

4. What rituals—whether formal religious ones or not—can you think of that

   • Help ease us over awkward or tense situations

   • Help us direct and share our feelings until we're able to handle them on our own

   • Help us face tragedy with courage

   • Give us a more intense appreciation of something or someone

   • Help us celebrate our joy in life and life's goodness

circumambulation

walking around

> ### ⚜ Questions for discussion
>
> 1. Why do you rely on visible signs and symbols as well as on words to express your beliefs and feelings?
> 2. Why can symbols be more meaningful than signs as ways of expressing feelings for someone? Give three examples of this other than those discussed in the text.

Signs and symbols

To communicate with each other, we use signs and symbols—words or gestures which represent our feelings and what we mean. If others didn't understand these outward signs and symbols in much the same ways we do, we couldn't share our inner thoughts and feelings. Without a common physical or verbal way to express things, we wouldn't be understood by anyone. We wouldn't even have a way to tell people hello or that we love them.

In the Southern part of the United States, people who know and like each other have traditionally used "hey" instead of "hi" or "hello" as a greeting. In other parts of the country, however, calling out "hey" is considered rude or understood as an attempt to get someone's attention instead of as a greeting. Likewise, different forms of hand greetings have become common in our society, so that it's sometimes awkward to know which one to use when greeting someone. Can you see why common forms of expression come in handy? They enable us to communicate with one another and to be mutually understood.

Words or gestures with a common meaning are therefore the signs and symbols by which we communicate ourselves to one another. We use some words and gestures quite often and save others for special occasions. We tell many people "hi" and wave to them in friendly greeting. But wedding bands are exchanged with only one.

A sign points to or explains something else. A symbol is a fuller, more meaningful sign because it also contains a quality it points to or explains.

It's nice when someone we care a lot about gives us a physical token as a sign of our relationship. But it's even more meaningful if the gift in some way symbolizes the other person, or the nature of our relationship. Hearing "I love you" can sure mean a lot. To also receive a ring whose unending circle (not its cost) represents a lasting bond of love is even more meaningful. So there's an important difference between a **sign** and a **symbol,** and this difference affects the meaning and importance of what is communicated.

We may like to think we're much more advanced than our early human ancestors, but we are still human. A side of us still needs and seeks to express our relationship with God through physical, sensory signs and symbols. Like early humans, at times we want to do this as a community—along with others who share our religious convictions. It is through the signs and symbols of sacred ritual celebrations that we are able to "touch" together the God in whom we believe. ⚜

Sacramental signs and symbols

The universe itself and the physical signs of creation all point to God as their ultimate Creator. They are also symbols whose own qualities reflect how great God is and yet how close. As symbols, they express the ways God acts in our lives—as the sun does to enlighten us, as the stars do to guide people, as water does to nourish and cleanse us. . . .

In teaching and healing others, Jesus used many physical signs which also served as symbols to tell us about and bring God's presence to us. Physical signs like water, fire, oil, and the laying on of hands are similarly used as symbols in religious celebrations like the Catholic liturgy.

In the Church's sacramental celebrations, signs and symbols communicate God's own life to us. The liturgy's ritual words and actions form the language through which God initiates the communication and we, in turn, respond. In the **liturgy of the word,** we listen and respond to God's word in the Bible. This makes present to us in reality what the Bible's words describe—God's saving love. This is also why the Bible is treated with signs of reverence in the liturgy, as by placing it in a special location.

Singing and music have always been important in Christian liturgy. To emphasize this, St. Augustine once wrote that "One who sings prays twice." In the liturgy as elsewhere, song and music help us express what is in our hearts in ways that words alone can't. Appropriate religious song and music—especially that drawn from Scripture—also help us participate more fully and help make the liturgy more meaningful to us.

> *Then he touched their eyes and said,*
> *"According to your faith let it be done to you."*
> *—Matthew 9:29*

For Catholics, **sacred images**—such as religious art, sculpture, or architecture—also reflect our belief in Christ and move us to communicate with God in prayer. Like a photograph or other personal symbol of someone we love, religious images help make present the One whose beauty and goodness they call to our minds. Rather than being like a bad photograph of someone or a tacky imitation which belittles the real thing, religious images should faithfully reflect who Catholics believe God is. They shouldn't contradict, distort, or cheapen what we believe about God.

In addition to the seven sacraments, Catholics also make use of sacred signs called **sacramentals.** The Church approves of certain things—for instance, crosses, medals, rosaries, or religious dance—to help us make holy our other life experiences, and prepare us to participate more fully in the sacraments themselves. **Blessings** of persons, meals, things, or places are especially meaningful sacramentals. Although many official Church blessings are reserved to ordained **clergy,** every baptized Christian may bless. In fact, we ourselves are to be a blessing for others.

But sacramentals don't give someone or something magic powers! If you drink and then drive, or if you drive carelessly, the blessed medal around your neck or on the dashboard sure isn't going to save your life. Relying on sacramentals in that way, or believing that they contain powers in themselves is superstitious. Blessings and other sacramentals praise God and are the Church's prayer that God will help us make good use of the gifts and abilities God has given us! If one doesn't truly believe and try to live what the medal or cross around one's neck signifies, then wearing it insults rather than represents and proclaims the Christian faith.

Catholics often also have other unofficial religious expressions of faith which are unique to their particular culture. These are encouraged as long as they are in keeping with the true spirit and priorities of the gospel and the Catholic faith. Thus, these forms of popular piety must truly enrich the Christian's life and not lead people to false or superstitious religious views, beliefs, or practices.

Questions for discussion

1. What types of signs and symbols are used in Catholic liturgy? How do these communicate God's life to us?
2. Why do readings from the Bible, and singing and music play an especially important role in Catholic liturgy? What role do sacred images play?
3. What role do sacramentals play in the Catholic faith? What false ideas do people sometimes have about sacramentals? Give examples.
4. What forms of popular piety are most common in your family or cultural background? Which ones are important to you? Explain.
5. How can a person tell the difference between an authentic or a superstitious form of or approach to popular piety?

Life symbols

Think about what each of the following symbolic drawings represents to you. Then respond to the questions.

Questions for discussion

1. If you think of each of the circles above as a symbol, what does each one represent to you? Why?
2. How is each of these a symbol, rather than just a sign?
3. What title, or sign, would you give each of the circles that would indicate the meaning it has for you? Explain.
4. How does each circle relate to your ordinary life events or experiences? To nature? To God and your beliefs?
5. Which carries the more powerful meaning in each instance: the symbolic drawing, or the title/sign? Explain.
6. Why do symbolic pictures mean different things to different people?
7. Why is the meaning of a sign more limited than that of a symbol?
8. What "signs" have you seen that use a symbolic drawing rather than, or along with, words to communicate something? Why is the symbol more effective than words by themselves?

Sacred times and places

Sacred time

As with us, every day is "today" with God. But there is also a cycle to our year and even to life itself, which gives us meaningful memories to look back on and dreams and experiences to look forward to. These cycles help make the past and the future present to us in ways which further enrich our lives here and now.

In fact, our memories and anticipations can be more meaningful than the actual experiences they recall or look forward to. We can view past experiences more objectively now and understand them better than we could at the time. Our plans and hopes for the future may be more ideal than events turn out to be. So you might find, for instance, that you enjoyed preparing for a certain holiday more than you did actually celebrating it.

To *commemorate* means to "remember with." Among our fondest memories of past experiences are those we share and relive together when reminiscing with our family or long-time friends. Those are the experiences which helped bond us into the close-knit relationships we have today. **The liturgy is a sacred commemoration** in which Catholics recall together the historical events which have formed and shaped us as God's people, and which bond us together as Church today—as it will generations of Catholics to come.

We think back on our ordinary memories in the context of the year and its seasons. Catholics' religious commemoration also takes place within a yearly cycle that is composed of seasons of **sacred time. Throughout the liturgical seasons of the Church year, we recall together the mysteries of our redemption.** Just as our birthdays, anniversaries, and other special occasions occur within the seasons of our ordinary year, the Church's **cycle of feasts** occurs within the seasons of the Church year.

Unlike our calendar year, however, **the liturgical year always centers around Easter because it is the greatest Christian feast.** Since the apostles' time, Sunday (the "Lord's day") has been celebrated as the first day of the liturgical week. It represents the first day of creation and was the day of Jesus' resurrection. The Liturgy of the Hours, as mentioned in the last chapter, is arranged to suit the times of day and the liturgical seasons. ❧

---

liturgical seasons

portions of the year which commemorate the main Christian mysteries of redemption

Church year

liturgical year, the annual commemoration and celebration of the main Christian mysteries

cycle of feasts

the annual religious observance of certain days in honor of Christ, and his mother Mary and other saints for their role in Christ's work

---

❧ Questions for discussion

1. How would you describe the cycle of life? Of the year? How do you relate your past memories and future hopes to the various parts of these cycles?

2. What annual celebration do you most look forward to and enjoy preparing for, and why? Do you find actually celebrating the occasion as enjoyable? Explain.

3. What things do you enjoy reminiscing about with your family or friends? Do you sometimes enjoy your memories more than you did the events at the time? Explain.

4. What do Catholics recall in the liturgy, and how does this affect us as Church today and for the future?

5. What are the seasons of the liturgical year? What does each one anticipate or celebrate? Which is your favorite liturgical season, and why?

Seasons of the liturgical year

Easter (in springtime [Nothern Hemisphere]—from Easter Sunday to Pentecost)
- celebrates Jesus' resurrection and our redemption and glorious destiny

Ordinary Time (in summer and autumn—between Pentecost and Advent)
- focuses on Jesus' life and teaching

Advent (from the fourth Sunday before Christmas to Christmas)
- looks back to how God prepared the world for Christ's historical coming, and prepares us for Christ's rebirth in our lives

Christmas (from Christmas to the feast of Epiphany in January)
- celebrates Jesus' incarnation and his continuing presence among us

Ordinary Time (between the Christmas season and Lent)
- focuses further on Jesus' life and teaching

Lent (from Ash Wednesday, forty days before Easter, to Easter)
- reflects on Jesus' temptations, trials, suffering, and death, and helps us overcome our sinfulness to prepare us for experiencing Easter glory

Sacred places

Catholics believe that every place on earth is sacred, and that God has entrusted the earth into our care. Most of all, **the place of Christian worship is the gathering of Christians** ourselves. We are to come to God as "living stones . . . precious in God's sight" (1 Peter 2:4). We are the living bricks of which the Church is built. We are "God's house." Catholic church buildings are therefore more than just places to gather for worship—they represent and highlight the living Church.

Catholic churches are a place of prayer and worship for the local Catholic community—and especially the place where the Eucharist is celebrated around the altar and reserved in the tabernacle. Our churches are also where the sacred oil of chrism is kept for celebrating the sacraments. The lectern is a focal point from which God's word is proclaimed.

Each Catholic church has a **baptistry,** containing a main font or basin, where the Sacrament of Baptism is celebrated. Many Catholics also use the blessed (holy) water from one or more (usually smaller) fonts to bless ourselves with the Sign of the Cross. This recalls the promises of our baptism and our continuing commitment to living what being Christian means.

The church building represents the living Church who journey together toward a future when we will all gather with God forever in everlasting happiness. Catholic teaching emphasizes that the church is God's house in which **all** God's children—without exception—are always warmly welcome. 🍂

Remembrance is a form of meeting. —Kahlil Gibran

> *. . .like living stones, let yourselves be built into a spiritual house. . . .*
> —*1 Peter 2:5*

🍂 **Questions for discussion**

1. What is the most important place of Christian worship, and why? Do you think Christians usually realize this? Explain.

2. What do Catholic churches contain? What do these buildings represent and what role do they play in Catholic worship?

3. What are your favorite and least favorite types of church buildings? Why?

A church is built as a sacred space.

Chapter review

1. Religious celebrations
- Why do we use visible signs and symbols in our ordinary celebrations?
- What is a ritual? What is a ceremony? Why are rituals and ceremonies an important part of life?
- What do rituals and ceremonies involve, and why does this increase their meaning?
- How have people always used rituals and ceremonies to communicate with the divine? What role did religious rituals play for early humans? How do these parallel the occasions for which the seven sacraments are celebrated?

2. What is the liturgy?
- As a sign, what does a sacrament commemorate, demonstrate, and look to in the future?
- What does *liturgy* mean and involve for Christians who celebrate it together?
- Who is the main priest of the liturgy? Why and how must the liturgy also be the action of those who participate?
- Why must the liturgy be a community celebration?
- In what sense is the liturgy God's blessing?
- In what ways is Christ present in the liturgy? Why is each important?
- How may Catholics participate in the sacred liturgy?
- Are Catholic liturgical celebrations always the same throughout the world?

3. Signs and symbols
- Why are signs and symbols important in human communication? In communicating with God?
- What is the difference between a sign and a symbol? Why is this difference important?
- How did Jesus use physical signs and symbols? What role do they play in the Church's sacramental celebrations? What role do singing, music, and sacred images play in the Catholic liturgy, and why?
- What are sacramentals, and what is their relationship to the seven sacraments? What role should popular piety play—and not play—in Christian life?

4. Sacred times and places
- In what sense is the liturgy a sacred commemoration?
- Explain each of the following: sacred time, liturgical seasons, the cycle of feasts, the liturgical year.
- Explain what Catholics consider the most important places of Christian worship.
- What do Catholic church buildings contain and represent?

Projects and assignments

1. Research and write a two-page paper about one of these topics:
   - The role of ritual for teenagers in our society
   - The importance of signs and symbols (in general and in religious worship)
   - How the design of church buildings influences the way people participate in religious services there
   - The difference between good and poor-quality religious art and images
   - The religious rituals of early humans
   - Non-Christian worship rituals

2. Read the passages surrounding each of the following places in the Christian Scriptures where Jesus is described as touching someone to heal them: Matthew 8:3, 9:29; Mark 1:41, 6:56, 7:33; Luke 5:13, 7:14, and 22:51. Write a one-page paper on why you think Jesus responded in the physical ways he did.

3. Research and write a two-page paper on the history of one of the following religious celebrations: Easter, Pentecost, Passover, Advent, Christmas, Lent.

Chapter 12 The Sacraments

Overview questions

1. What seven sacraments does the Catholic Church celebrate?

2. What does each sacrament mean for Catholics?

3. What main liturgical signs are used in celebrating each sacrament? What do these signs represent?

4. How do we live the sacraments?

"Do this in remembrance of me."
                    Luke 22:19

Light of our world,
Thank you for your example of love and goodness.
Lead us to walk in your way.
Help us make every day a new beginning.
Fix what is broken in us.
Be our strength when we are weak.
Link us together, heart to heart,
as we share the gifts you have given us
and join hands to forgive and heal and help each other.
Help us keep our promises and commitments.
Search for us when we're lost.
Show us the way home.

The Eucharist is the central sacrament of the Catholic Church.

The Seven Sacraments

The Sacraments of Initiation

Baptism
Confirmation
Eucharist

The Sacraments of Healing

Reconciliation
Anointing the Sick

The Sacraments at the Service of Communion

Holy Orders
Marriage

The seven sacraments

The seven sacraments are the main sacred ritual celebrations of the Catholic faith. In general, the sacraments are physical expressions (involving actions and words), given us through Jesus. They effectively give us the power and presence of God's Spirit **(sacramental grace)** in the special ways that each sacrament's symbolic actions and words represent. **The sacraments are signs and actions of God's living presence and power among us that enable us to participate in God's own divine life.** The sacraments express our faith and make it stronger.

So there are two things at the heart of celebrating each sacrament:

- **Recalling,** by sacred words and symbolic actions, God's saving actions in human history
- **Asking** that God's Spirit make these saving actions present in our own words and actions today, so we become more united in love with God and with one another

As God's actions, the sacraments don't depend on how holy or unholy the minister or the participant is. But **the good that the sacraments do does depend on our being open to receiving the power of God's loving presence,** and on the visible ways we respond to God's action in our lives. We do this first of all by believing that Jesus' words are true—that God does want to be our strength in certain special ways.

But, if we're not careful, we can become just like the religious hypocrites whose behavior we criticize as unchristian. Instead, we need to realize how meaningful our important religious celebrations really are. We've got to live as well as celebrate our faith. Otherwise liturgical celebrations can seem like just dull, empty routines.

Religious observances should express what we find truest and most meaningful about God, ourselves, other people, and the world. So next we'll discuss the seven sacraments Catholics celebrate, and how they really should enrich our lives. Each of these sacraments actually deserves further discussion, but that is an entire course by itself.

Questions for discussion

1. What seven sacraments does the Catholic Church celebrate? How are they signs and actions?

2. Is the sacrament itself just as genuine and effective if the minister of the sacrament is not a good person? If the participant is not? Explain.

3. What do you think is the best way to keep religious services from just becoming dull, empty routines? To avoid becoming a religious hypocrite?

4. What religious celebrations are the most meaningful to you? The least meaningful? Explain both.

sacramental grace

the power by which God's Spirit heals and transforms in a special way through each sacrament

Sacraments of Christian Initiation

becoming a member of a group by means of a special process or ceremonial rituals

As a young child, you may have become a member of a neighborhood club by going through a certain "initiation" process or ceremony. **One becomes a Catholic through a process of Christian initiation which occurs in several stages.** This process is accomplished by these three sacraments:

The Sacraments of Christian Initiation

Baptism begins our new life as a Christian.

Confirmation completes baptism by strengthening us to truly live as Christians.

Eucharist nourishes us so we become more like Christ, and completes the Christian initiation process. 🐚

🐚 Questions for discussion

1. What kinds of initiation rites or processes do you recall from childhood? Did you ever participate in any of these? Explain.
2. How would you explain to a non-Catholic friend the process by which one becomes a Catholic?

. . . so we too might walk in newness of life.
—Romans 6:4

Birth, beginnings, belonging

"We acknowledge one baptism for the forgiveness of sins."

Nicene Creed

Baptism celebrates God's and the community's invitation to join with others in living a life of Christian love. It also celebrates the newly baptized Christian's acceptance of this invitation. Baptism begins a new and lasting relationship with God and the Church community which all Christians share in some sense. This is why baptism is considered essential for Christians. It's important to remember, though, that **all persons who sincerely seek God and try to do God's will—even though they haven't been baptized—can be saved, and can experience eternal life.**

Baptism permanently consecrates the person to share in Christ's priesthood and participate fully in Christian life and worship. So baptism can be celebrated only once for anyone, and a duly baptized Christian is not baptized again when becoming a Catholic. Thus, Christian baptism celebrates belonging—being joined with all Christians in a common effort to pray for and achieve love and unity among all people. Baptized Christians who belong to the Catholic community not only have certain responsibilities to fulfill as Catholics, but we are also guaranteed certain rights within our Church.

Liturgical signs of the Sacrament of Baptism:

- baptizing by immersing the person in water or pouring water on the person's head
- while saying "I baptize you in the name of the Father, and of the Son, and of the Holy Spirit."

Thus, the signs of baptism which celebrate birth, beginning, and belonging are words and water. Christians are baptized in the name of the Holy Trinity—of our God who is personal, caring, and ever-present and empowering. In baptism, God's loving welcome and the person's acceptance of God are so complete that all the person's sins are completely forgiven. So baptism really is a brand new beginning.

. . . serve one another with whatever gift each of you has received. —1 Peter 4:10

Water is an ancient religious symbol of life, cleansing, health, and growth. In Christian baptism water stands for the life of love we are to live. It also represents the constant cleansing we all must do to rid ourselves of what keeps us from loving. Finally, water stands for the health, strength, and growth we need to live a life of Christian love.

Could you baptize someone? The priest (or bishop) is the usual minister of the Sacrament of Baptism. However, anyone (yes, even a non-Christian) may baptize in case of necessity—as long as the person does so with the same gestures and words the Church uses and has the intention of doing what the Church does in baptizing someone.

Why are babies baptized? In the very earliest days of the Church, only adults were baptized as they came to believe in and wished to follow the way of life Jesus had preached. But these adults also wanted their children to be able to share in this meaningful way of life. So early on the practice began of baptizing infants, and infant baptism still is and will remain the more frequent practice. It should be emphasized, though, that adult baptism represents the full implications of baptism, because it involves both the gift the baptized person receives and the baptized person's commitment to conversion.

'When an infant is baptized, we celebrate the birth of a new human being and the beginning of a divine life of loving that is meant to last forever.' We extend to this child God's gift of Christian faith, the freedom of sharing and growing for a lifetime in Christian love, and our support as a Christian community in helping the child to do this.

Baptism also represents an invitation which can be refused or rejected. No one should ever be forced into being

Song for an infant's baptism

We give thanks for you, God's precious gift to us.
We're glad that you are here!
We celebrate your birth, and welcome you.
You come into our world so innocent and helpless.
We want to help you grow in faith and hope and love.
Please join us in the human adventure
as we journey to our God together,
and build lasting bonds of love.

baptized. In the case of infants who are baptized, they need to ratify by subsequent acts of faith promises made for them by their parents and godparents. Jesus never forced anyone to follow him, and, as we've already discussed, God can't make people "believe" against their will. Baptism welcomes us to the real freedom of God's children—to the Christian way of life and union with God and others. Baptism isn't, however, just a one-time ceremony. It's a lifelong sacrament which we must constantly renew by how we pray, worship together, and live.

Questions for discussion

1. How is baptism like an invitation?

2. Why is baptism essential for Christians? Can those who aren't baptized be saved? Explain.

3. What do the liturgical signs of baptism express about the meaning of this sacrament?

4. Could you ever baptize someone? Explain fully.

5. How did the practice of baptizing infants originate? Why does adult baptism represent the full implications of baptism?

6. What would having your children baptized as infants mean to you, and why? What would you respond to those who claim that this takes away a person's religious freedom?

Baptism is a lifelong sacrament.

Questions for discussion

1. What are you looking forward to about reaching the age of legal adulthood, and why? What new rights and responsibilities will this involve for you?

2. What parallels do you see between confirmation and reaching adulthood in our society?

3. At what age are individuals confirmed in your diocese? At what age do you think a person can fully appreciate what it really means to be confirmed in one's religious faith?

4. What do each of the liturgical signs of confirmation represent?

5. What does being confirmed in your faith mean to you? Explain.

confirmation sponsor

one who formally represents the Christian community's continuing support of the person being confirmed

godparent

person who formally assumes the responsibility of helping the baptized Christian grow in faith

chrism

oil blessed on Holy Thursday and used during the Rite of Confirmation

Christian commitment

One of life's big birthdays is that which marks our assuming adult rights and responsibilities in our society. Likewise, **confirmation celebrates the perfecting and deepening of the relationship with God and the Church which is celebrated in baptism.** In confirmation, we assume in a more mature way the responsibility of living as Christians in the Church and in the world. This gift of God helps us live and witness to our Christian faith more fully. As with baptism, it is also permanent so that confirmation can be celebrated for an individual only once.

In the Roman (or Latin) Catholic Rite, the bishop is the usual minister of confirmation. The baptized person may be confirmed when old enough to understand and profess the Christian faith and to assume the responsibilities of being a Christian. The person being confirmed is sponsored by an adult (**confirmation sponsor**)—preferably a baptismal **godparent**—who represents the continuing support of the other dedicated Christians in the Church community. In the Eastern Catholic Rites, even for infants, confirmation and participation in the Eucharist are celebrated immediately after baptism.

Then Peter and John laid their hands on them, and they received the Holy Spirit.
—*Acts 8:17*

Essential liturgical signs of the Sacrament of Confirmation:

• the anointing with the special oil of sacred **chrism** (the forehead is anointed in the Roman Rite)

• the laying of the minister's hand on the person's head

• along with the words, "Be sealed with the gift of the Holy Spirit."

The anointing with sacred chrism symbolizes being especially strengthened and empowered to better live and share the Christian way of living. Without being pushy about it, you may help someone a lot just by appropriately sharing your religious convictions. Many adults and teenagers are searching desperately for meaning in their lives. There are also so many distorted, superstitious notions of religion out there that you can do others a great service by showing them a genuinely positive and life-affirming approach to religious faith and religious freedom. So as the sign of this sacrament indicates, don't be shy or embarrassed about witnessing to your religious beliefs.

Unity in Christ

As Christians we dare to believe that God is closer to us than the food we eat. As Jesus prayed at the Last Supper, all humanity is meant to be fully united with God—and with one another. That is the meaning and purpose of the Eucharist. **The Eucharist is called the heart and summit of Church life.** It celebrates all the love we experience and wish to experience in our lives.

It is Christ who, through the ministry of the priest, both offers the Eucharistic sacrifice and is the gift offered. **In the Eucharist, Christ is truly present among us in several ways:**

• In the essential signs of the sacred bread and wine (the height of Christ's Eucharistic presence, which is consecrated to become Christ's body and blood at the Eucharist by the priest's invoking the Holy Spirit's blessing and saying the words Jesus spoke at the Last Supper—"This is my body. . . . This is the cup of my blood. . .")

• In the liturgical ministers and all the gathered people

• In God's word proclaimed in the Scriptures

The Eucharist is the redemptive sacrifice and memorial of Jesus' death and resurrection. To understand what this really means, think about what these words mean:

- **Sacrifice** means "to make holy." The Eucharist celebrates that in Jesus' once-and-for-all sacrifice of praise and thanksgiving, we, our world, and everything good we do have been "made holy." The Eucharist is our offering of thanks and praise for all things good and beautiful.

- A **memorial** is something which helps us remember, so we won't forget. As a living memorial, the Eucharist tells us not to forget how much Jesus' life, death, and resurrection has shown that God loves us all.

- **Redeem** means "save from," or "buy back"—as in being ransomed from a kidnapper. The Eucharist makes present the actions of our salvation in Christ, of our being saved—redeemed—from being captive to sin and evil, despair, and selfishness. The Eucharist celebrates the many gifts, or graces, of our salvation—our being given a reason for living and loving here and now, and for hope in an everlasting happy future. It is also our prayer that God will continue to bless us.

As are the other sacraments, the Eucharist is our community celebration. It's not just another opportunity for praying privately (which we can do any time and any place). In the Eucharist we celebrate with God and with others who believe as we do our common convictions about what we are to mean to one another. The most important parts of the Eucharist, which must always be included, are:

The Liturgy of the Word: proclaiming God's word in Sacred Scripture

The Liturgy of the Eucharist: which includes

- Thanking God for all our blessings— especially for the gift of God's Son, Jesus

- The consecration of bread and wine
- Communion: the receiving of the body and blood of Christ (by those who have not completely alienated themselves from God by serious sin)

"I am the living bread. . . . Whoever eats of this bread will live forever. . . ."
—John 6:51

The Christian Scriptures tell us that we **are** "the body of Christ." We're also told to **receive,** in communion, the "Body of Christ." There is a vital connection here. When we receive Christ's body in the Eucharist, we're also receiving all other persons. This includes those we love—and those we find hardest to love.

Participating in communion brings us closer to God and strengthens the bonds we share with people we already like and love. It's also our prayer together to come a little closer to those we don't! God forgives us our less serious faults and failings and gives us strength to avoid harming others and separating ourselves from God in serious ways. This is why we should partake of communion every time we participate in the celebration of the Eucharist—and why Church law says Catholics must do so at least once a year.

The Eucharist celebrates, in Christ, what we are meant to mean to one another.

Teenagers sometimes complain that the Eucharist (Mass) as celebrated in their parish is "boring." They usually explain that they're referring to homilies which seem irrelevant to their spiritual needs, to a lack of good music (or being expected to sing in a key that's too high or low), and to feeling like they're just sitting there but not really participating. It's true that there are often ways liturgical celebrations could be improved to better reflect the cultural di-

❧ Questions for discussion

1. Why is the Eucharist the heart and summit of Catholic life?

2. Why is each of the ways Christ is present in the Eucharist important? Which of these are you usually the least aware of? Explain.

3. If you were kidnapped and held for ransom, what price (if they could afford any amount) would you expect your loved ones to pay to buy you back? How would you feel about it if someone gave their life to get you back safely? Explain.

4. What does it mean to say that the Eucharist is a sacrifice and a memorial? That it makes present Christ's actions by which we have been redeemed?

5. Why is the Eucharist a community celebration and not a form of private prayer? What does this mean in terms of how Catholics should participate in it?

6. Why is each main part of the Eucharist so important? What does each main part mean?

7. Why do you think that, according to surveys, the vast majority of adults and teenagers in our society who attend weekly worship services do so because they want to, and not because a person or law requires them to do this? How do you feel about this personally? Why?

8. What do you find most meaningful about the Eucharistic celebrations you've participated in?

9. What do you think would help religious celebrations become more meaningful to you? Why?

versity and needs of those who participate. Catholic teaching emphasizes, in fact, that the faithful should be able to participate fully in the liturgy!

Preventing boredom, though, can also depend on the interest we bring to a celebration. Just because we're dissatisfied with a few things (even if justifiably so), we shouldn't miss the real meaning of an important celebration—whether it's a graduation, a wedding, or the sacred liturgy. This is certainly true regarding the Eucharist. Realistically, one style of celebrating will never please everyone. People's needs and preferences vary too widely. But there are often ways of accommodating different groups better.

So if you find that the liturgy doesn't seem meaningful to you, first examine your own attitude and what you honestly try to bring to the celebration. Then approach your local pastor about it. But don't just mention what you don't like—also offer your positive comments and recommendations, and your practical help. Many priests would gladly listen to positive suggestions if they knew people would support them. ❧

"Those who eat my flesh and drink my blood have eternal life, and I will raise them up on the last day. . . ."
—John 6:54

The Sacraments of Healing

Forgiveness and reunion

Do you ever feel guilty or bad because of something you said or did? Have you ever tried to make things right with someone when your rudeness or unkindness had messed up the relationship? Do you want to be a better person than you sometimes are? These common experiences are part of what the Sacrament of Reconciliation means.

When we wrong someone, we know we need to be forgiven. We want to know we're still okay and that everything will be all right. Sometimes we'll apologize in order to reconcile with someone. But sometimes we can't, or even an apology doesn't seem enough—especially when we realize we've wronged God and wounded our own personal dignity. It's often harder to forgive ourselves for the careless or deliberate harm we've caused others than it is to forgive others for having hurt us.

> *. . . God . . . has given us the ministry of reconciliation. . . .*
> *—2 Corinthians 5:18*

Because it's a **deliberate** offense to divine goodness, and to all God has created as good—including ourselves, sin is the worst type of evil there is. It has the worst consequences in terms of damaging our relationships with God and others and debasing what it means to be human. Even our legal system reserves the harshest punishments for crimes which are intentional and premeditated.

When we do what we know is wrong, we also hurt all humanity—and all Christians in particular. We assault what it means to be a human being. We give others an untrue example of what being Christian means—in others' eyes, we become the type of hypocritical Christian we criticize.

> *Do not imitate those who deceive themselves by saying: "I will sin and then go to confession." . . . Is it not madness to wound oneself . . . [so] that a doctor will . . . heal the wound?*
> *—St. John Bosco*

Through Jesus, God has entrusted to the Church the special ministry of reconciling us sinners with God. **In the Sacrament of Reconciliation, we express our guilt and sorrow in a visible, concrete way for sins committed after baptism, and we celebrate God's reassurance that we're once again a good and worthwhile person.** We certainly can be sorry just in our own minds and hearts. But it feels much better when someone else tells us that "it's okay," and we're okay—that we're forgiven and everything will be all right. **God alone—not the priest—forgives sin.** Sacramental reconciliation celebrates the belief that God is all-forgiving and understanding and will always accept our sincere sorrow and our efforts to try again.

Reconciling with God is a process which involves sorrow and change. First we ask for God's merciful help and forgiveness. We think about the past and express our genuine sorrow for the wrongs we've done. Hoping in God's mercy, we look to the future and are determined not to sin again.

The signs of sacramental reconciliation are four actions which reflect this process of repentance and conversion:

- **Repenting:** We carefully examine our conscience in view of our belief in God—we think about what deliberate wrongs we've done since our last formal reconciliation with God, and we're truly sorry for them. Our repentance is perfect if we're sorry because we love God.

> *Bear with one another and, if anyone has a complaint against another, forgive each other; just as the Lord has forgiven you, so you also must forgive.*
> *—Colossians 3:13*

❧ Questions for discussion

1. Without forgiveness and reconciliation, what would happen to your relationships? Explain.

2. What do you find it hard to forgive others for? To forgive yourself for? Which is usually harder—forgiving someone else or forgiving yourself for doing the same type of thing? Explain.

3. Why is sin the worst evil?

4. What is the difference between
   - Being sorry for having done wrong, and being forgiven
   - Being forgiven, and feeling forgiven?

5. Why does it help to have someone else **tell** or **show** you that you're really forgiven?

6. Why isn't it correct to say that the priest forgives Catholics their sins in confession? What is the priest's role in sacramental reconciliation?

7. What process does reconciling with someone you've wronged usually involve on a personal level? How does this compare with the process involved in sacramental reconciliation?

8. What different ways of celebrating sacramental reconciliation are there? Which way is preferred? What is your preference, and why?

9. What do you personally find most meaningful about the Sacrament of Reconciliation? Most difficult? Explain.

But even if we're imperfectly sorry, for other reasons, God still willingly forgives us.

- **Confessing:** We tell the priest all the major wrongs (the grave sins) we remember that we haven't confessed in reconciliation before.

- **Making reparation:** We intend to try to repair the damage our wrongs have caused, and we actively try to do this. Doing the acts of reparation proposed by the priest can help us break our bad habits and begin acting more like the Christian we say we are.

Between the bridge and the river, he repented and was forgiven.
—St. John Vianney

- **Being absolved:** God is always willing to forgive us. We receive God's forgiveness from the moment that we're truly sorry for our sins. God's forgiveness and our reconciliation with God in Christ's name are formally proclaimed and celebrated in the priest's absolution (the sign of the cross made over us together with the words of God's forgiveness).

Some non-Catholics find it hard to understand how Catholics can tell their sins to anyone, much less a priest. Some Catholics do find this difficult. Catholics also realize, though, that priests are human beings who at times are also guilty and need forgiving. In fact, after listening to so many human failings, priests probably understand better than anyone about failure and forgiveness. They realize that we all do wrong, but no matter what we've done, we're worthy in God's eyes of being forgiven.

Sacramental reconciliation isn't just unloading faults and guilt. It reconciles us with God and the rest of humanity, especially those who, as the Christian Church, have been given a bad name by our sinfulness. Participation in this reconciliation means that serious sin no longer separates us from the love of God and others. In this sacrament, God opens our hearts to love, and gives us the opportunity and help to become a better person as we do something positive to help overcome our faults.

Catholics may celebrate reconciliation privately and individually with the priest. The preferred way of celebrating this sacrament, however, is with a **communal reconciliation service** that also includes individual confession and absolution. The opportunity for individual confession helps us grow spiritually in personal ways. We have the option of talking over the faults which trouble us face-to-face with the priest, or anonymously from behind a screen.

Celebrating reconciliation together as a community reminds us that we're not the only ones who fail from time to time, and that we must learn to forgive and help one another. It also reminds us that sin isn't just a private matter—that our deliberate wrongdoing affects others as well as ourselves.

As Jesus told us, God considers our being forgiven and reconciled to be a sacred, joyful experience. The Sacrament of Reconciliation celebrates this beautiful gift God has given us. If you avoid sacramental reconciliation because it doesn't seem meaningful or necessary for you, then perhaps try talking your problems over with a priest who really seems to understand you well, and the problems you're coping with and trying to overcome.

But at least know this: Whenever you need someplace to turn, there is somewhere you can go to receive the assurance of another human being—and of the whole Catholic Church—that **God will always care about, forgive, and joyfully welcome you.** ❧

Strength, healing, and hope

Have you noticed that whenever you're sick you tend to get discouraged and down on yourself, others, and life? But if someone lovingly soothes your forehead and reassures you, don't you feel a bit better? It probably helps make your illness more bearable and your attitude more positive so that you look forward to recovering. In fact, medical science finds that our inner attitude and strength actually play an important part in our physical recoveries.

The Christian Scriptures tell us that Jesus laid his hands on people and healed them, offering them renewed spiritual strength as well. **Catholics continue Jesus' healing ministry through many works of charity, and especially in celebrating the Sacrament of Anointing the Sick.** In this sacrament, the priest and those gathered around the sick person, celebrate God's special concern for those who are suffering and who need reassurance and hope.

. . . he touched her hand, and the fever left her, and she got up and began to serve him.
—Matthew 8:15

The sacramental anointing of the sick is a source of spiritual strength (grace), peace, and hope—and possibly a source of physical strength as well—for those who are seriously ill and for those coping with the difficulties of old age. **Viaticum**—the final reception of communion—is actually the last sacrament for the dying person. In fact, the main reason the Eucharistic bread is kept in Catholic churches is so it remains available for those who are seriously ill or dying.

Any Catholic in danger of dying because of aging or illness should ask for this special anointing, and may do so again each time the person becomes seriously ill, or if the illness gets worse. The anointing of the sick is God's reassuring touch for those who, due to illness or serious surgery, especially need comfort and courage.

The liturgical signs of the Sacrament of Anointing the Sick:

- the priest's anointing of the person on the forehead and hands (in the Roman Rite)
- with the sacred oil of strength and health
- along with the priest's asking God, on behalf of the whole Church, for the special help (grace) of this sacrament

This anointing is usually in the form of the cross which stands for courage and hope in the midst of suffering. As a result of this sacrament, individuals draw the strength, courage, and peace from being united with Christ's suffering to endure their own suffering in a Christian way. This sacrament also extends God's forgiveness to those unable to celebrate sacramental reconciliation. It brings healing if that is for the person's ultimate welfare and otherwise helps the person prepare for crossing over to eternal life.

In the **Christian funeral rites,** Catholics acknowledge our grief and loss, but we also celebrate the joy of passing, as Jesus did, from death to new and everlasting risen life. Preferably in the context of the Eucharist, we celebrate the communion of saints whereby those living and dead who remain close to God also continue to be closely linked and present to us.

Many Churches now hold community celebrations of the anointing of the sick, encouraging all those with life-threatening physical illnesses to receive this holy anointing. Many Catholic parishes expand this healing ministry by holding other related prayer services designed to help those who need emotional and psychological strength and healing. Praying together can give us the inner strength and community support we need to rise above our problems.

Questions for discussion

1. How does being sick with a bad cold or the flu affect your thoughts and attitude?

2. Have you ever been very seriously ill or close to dying—or known someone who has? What does a person think about, and what meaning do you think one's religious convictions have at such times? Explain.

3. How would you describe the Sacrament of Anointing the Sick? What do you think it would mean to you as a Catholic who was seriously ill or dying?

4. Why shouldn't this sacrament be thought of as the "last rites"? What do each of the liturgical signs of this sacrament mean? What is the last sacrament for Catholics?

5. Have you ever been to a Catholic funeral? To a non-Catholic funeral service? What stands out in your mind about the meaning of such funeral services, and why?

6. Have you ever participated in this Sacrament of Anointing the Sick, or in a related type of prayer service? Why do you think those who are depressed or emotionally troubled often find such community prayer services helpful?

Viaticum

"nourishment or support for the journey," Sacrament of the Eucharist for a dying person

Baptized at the beach?

Read the following actual news account and respond to the questions.

You've heard of [the expression] baptism by fire. How about baptism by accident?

That's what happened Sunday when an 8-year-old boy wandered into a church group at [the local beach], was mistaken for a church member and dunked in the Gulf of Mexico.

The boy told his mother . . . that people had submerged him against his will at 4:15 p.m. She complained to the lifeguards, who summoned police.

Before the officers arrived, though, the leader of the . . . church . . . apologized to [the mother]. Her son wasn't hurt.

"[The church's leader] stated the child had wandered into their group," a police report said. "[The church leader] thought the child was a member of the church."

A woman who answered the phone Monday at the . . . church said [the church's leader] didn't want to comment.

[The mother] said Monday that she would "like them to pick a quieter time and to be more careful—that they know who they are baptizing."

[A lifeguard] said baptismal services are held at the beach about six times a year, and there had never been any complaints about them before.

"It was definitely strange," [the lifeguard] said of the mistaken dousing.[1]

Questions for discussion

1. What does the expression "baptism by fire" mean? Why is water rather than fire the symbol used in baptism? Why do you think the symbol of fire has sometimes been connected with the meaning of confirmation?

2. How did the boy's mother, the lifeguard, and the police each respond to the "accidental baptism" incident? What do you think of how they responded?

3. How would you have responded had you been the boy's parent? The lifeguard? The police who came to the scene? Explain.

4. Presume that the mother was not a Christian. Suppose that she was suing the Church leader for "wrongful baptism," sincerely believing that her son had actually been "made" a baptized Christian by mistake. Based on what Catholics mean by the Sacrament of Baptism (including infant baptism), and believe about religious freedom:

   • How would you argue the case if you were the attorney defending this non-Catholic Church's leader?

   • How would you argue the case if you were the attorney representing the boy and his mother?

   • If you were the judge in the case, would you agree to hear the case or dismiss it as having no merit? Explain.

   • If you did decide the case as judge, how would you rule if you became convinced that

      — The "baptism" had been unintentional?

      — The church leader had known that the boy was not a member of the Church but had deliberately "baptized" him anyway?

5. In the situation that actually did occur, if you were the boy's parent and both you and your son were baptized Catholics, how would what your faith means to you apply here regarding:

   • What a sacrament is in general, and what the Sacrament of Baptism means?

   • How baptism is to be celebrated?

   • How the Sacraments of Baptism and Confirmation should be lived in regard to religious freedom and Christian charity?

   • What sacramental reconciliation means, and Catholic efforts regarding ecumenism and interreligious dialogue?

   • How you really would choose to respond to the situation? (Explain.)

Water is one of the objects used in sacramental celebrations.

The Sacraments at the Service of Communion

The call to guide and serve

In picking the twelve apostles, Jesus chose the Church's first leaders. Their mission, he said, was to preach his word to others and minister to their spiritual needs. As he blessed and shared his personal presence with them in bread and wine, so they were to share this presence with others. As he washed their feet, so they were to guide Christians in being Christ's continuing presence for others.

The apostles were given God's Spirit to continue Jesus' work of being living signs of God's presence for others. Through the Sacrament of Holy Orders, they appointed successors who would continue to guide the Church in celebrating and living the Christian liturgy.

The apostles' successors in the early Church were chosen because they seemed to possess a special gift for preaching, guiding the community in living out their beliefs, and ministering to the needs of others. These leaders also represented Jesus' promise to always remain with and guide those who chose to follow him. Since that time the Catholic Church has continued to celebrate the ordination of these new leaders to the ministerial priesthood.

By our baptism, all faithful Christians participate in Christ's priesthood. We are called to share God's word and love with others as Jesus did. As Church, we are a priestly people—in a real sense, we are priests who share in the *common priesthood of the faithful*. **The Sacrament of Holy Orders celebrates ordained priests' special ministry to share in Jesus' mission by serving in Christ's name and person in the middle of our Christian community.**

This *ministerial priesthood* is essentially different from the common priesthood because it includes the gift of God's special strength for being of service to the Christian community in teaching,

> *Of this gospel I have become a servant according to the gift of God's grace that was given me by the working of his power.*
> *—Ephesians 3:7*

celibate

promising to remain single (to not marry) for religious reasons

For centuries the Church has

deaconesses

women who assisted the apostles and, later, the early Church in certain service and liturgical ministries

🔖 Questions for discussion

1. What does it mean to you that all Christians are considered priests by baptism? What is the difference between this common priesthood and the ordained, or ministerial, priesthood?

2. How would you explain to a non-Catholic the role and ministry of bishops, the pope, priests, and deacons in the Catholic Church?

3. What do each of the liturgical signs of the Sacrament of Holy Orders represent and celebrate?

4. Are all Catholic priests required not to marry? Explain.

5. What role did deaconesses play in the early Church community?

6. What valuable services do you think priests provide in today's Church? In what ways might priests do this more effectively? Explain.

divine worship, and pastoral leadership. Since the apostles' time, three degrees of ordained Christian ministry have been essential to the Church's structure: that of **bishops,** of **presbyters (priests),** and of **deacons.** Each is ordained for particular ministries that help guide and serve all Christians in fulfilling our mission.

The **bishop** receives the fullness of ordination to this role of leadership in guiding and serving. The bishop is a member of the episcopal college, and the visible leader of the local Church community. (The pope, as St. Peter's successor, is a bishop chosen to guide the entire Church.) **Priests** are the bishops' co-workers in the local Church community. **Deacons** are not ordained priests, but are ordained for special functions which, under the bishop's authority, involve teaching, divine worship, pastoral guidance, and being of charitable service.

Do not neglect the gift that is in you. . . .
—1 Timothy 4:14

The liturgical signs of the Sacrament of Holy Orders:

• the bishop's laying hands on the one to be ordained, and

• the solemn prayer of consecration which asks that God give the ordained person the special strength and help of the Holy Spirit to fulfill the responsibilities of the ordained ministry

It was through the laying on of hands that the Christian Scriptures say Jesus often cured the sick. A loving touch can be a source of strength and healing, of renewed confidence and courage. The laying on of hands in ordination also represents the clergy's ministry of touching the lives of others in special ways with God's love. Ordination celebrates the special nature of a lifelong calling

and commitment. Once ordained, one is ordained a bishop, priest, or deacon for life and can never be re-ordained.

In the Roman Rite, candidates for ordination must willingly promise to remain **celibate** (to not marry) for life. (Candidates who are already married may be ordained as deacons, however.) Since remaining single is not essential to priestly ordination, however, sometimes Protestant clergy who are already married when they become Catholics are permitted to be ordained as Catholic priests.

. . . rekindle the gift of God that is within you through the laying on of my hands. . . .
—2 Timothy 1:6

authorized that only baptized men who are suitably qualified may be ordained. The Christian Scriptures tell us, however, that in the early Church many women served as **deaconesses.** They assisted the apostles and the early Church in offering spiritual guidance and in certain liturgical ministries and sacramental celebrations. In recent times, Church officials have been studying the nature and role of deaconesses' ministry in the early Church to see if this form of ministry should be revived as a valuable service in today's Church community.

As Catholics, we all need to understand that the primary meaning and purpose of the ordained ministry isn't to construct and repair church buildings, but to preach about love of God and others and to guide and serve—just as the meaning and purpose of our vocation in life isn't accumulating material wealth, but living lives of Christian love. Clergy and laity must help each other remember and live our proper priorities, so that neither of us becomes preoccupied with nonessentials and distracted from what is really most important in our way of life. 🔖

Faithful, life-giving love

The Hebrew Scriptures tell what our Creator has revealed to us about the sacredness of marriage. They also compare God's intimacy with us to that of a groom and his bride—God is said to want to be this close to us, and to love us this much. So Christians have always viewed marriage between a woman and a man as a special celebration of love and union.

Marriage is an intimate communion of life and love by which a couple freely consent and desire to give themselves to each other in a lasting and faithful sacred covenant of life-giving unity and love. By its nature, marriage is designed to be for the good of the marriage partners, and their having and properly raising children. Catholic teaching considers unity, unbreakability, and openness to having children as essential to marriage.

Catholic teaching also views the divorce or remarriage of baptized persons as separating "what God has joined together." But this does not separate these persons from the Church or prevent them from living Christian lives and raising their children as Catholics. In the Catholic **annulment process,** the Church also realizes that sometimes couples hadn't intended to enter from the beginning, or were incapable of entering, into the same kind of union that the Church means by marriage. It may therefore grant such a couple a *declaration of nullity* which acknowledges that, so that they may each marry someone else in the future with the Church's full blessing.

Catholics view marriage between baptized Christians as a bond which Jesus raised to the dignity of a sacrament. In this sacrament, the couple's mutual promise of lifelong intimacy and faithfulness symbolizes the unity Christ and all Christians share, as well as how much we should love God and others. The Sacrament of Marriage signifies and celebrates divine and human love and fidelity.

Marriage is a public institution vital to the social good—to all of us—because marriage is the beginning of family life. Current social research confirms that in our society the best environment for children to be born and raised in is the home of a loving married couple. The Christian home is the "house church." It's where children first learn to love God and others, and acquire the values and personal skills they need to participate in and make a positive contribution to society and the Church community.

Catholics therefore celebrate marriage in a public liturgical wedding ceremony before a priest or Church-authorized witness, and other witnesses, family members, and friends. It is the couple who marry each other and who confer upon each other the Sacrament of Marriage. The priest witnesses the couple's intention that their marriage means what Catholics mean by marriage and blesses their union on behalf of God and the Church community.

The liturgical sign of the Sacrament of Marriage:

- the couple's mutual promise to love each other faithfully for the rest of their earthly lives

All the spouses do and are for each other from then on—from their sexual lovemaking to really listening to each other, to doing the dishes—is a way of living this sacrament. Throughout their lifetime together, each time they engage in sexual union or an ordinary action which is truly love-making, the married couple renews the sacramental bond between them. Thus, marriage is the sacrament which proclaims and celebrates the significance and sacredness of human loving. &

Questions for discussion

1. Describe each of the following.
   - What marriage means to you
   - What marriage as a sacrament, and the liturgical sign of this sacrament, proclaim
   - Catholic teaching about divorce, remarriage, and the annulment process
   - Why marriage is a public and social institution
   - The importance of the family in the Church and society
2. Who really marries a couple? Explain.
3. What does being married in a religious ceremony mean to you? Explain.
4. Surveys have found that women in our society who take their religious convictions seriously also have a more satisfying sexual relationship with their husbands.
   - What might account for this?
   - What might this show about the religious meaning of marriage?

Space colony

You were chosen, along with 100 other persons, to start a space colony. You all know that you must live in the colony for the rest of your lives and repopulate it from among yourselves. As you begin life together on your new space colony home, it is clear that you need to make certain decisions as a group.

Unfortunately, there is no religious leader in the space colony. But the group feels that certain occasions should be set aside for everyone to celebrate in a special way. The things everyone has agreed they'd like to celebrate are given below. You've been charged with determining how each occasion is to be celebrated. To do this, you must respond to the questions below.

1. The birth of a new space colony member

2. Making an adult commitment to fulfill one's obligations in the colony

3. A way of showing **penitence** and a ceremony for being reconciled when someone has wronged the others in the colony

4. A ceremony for celebrating unity and harmony among those on board

5. A marriage ceremony

6. A ritual for those who are seriously ill or dying

7. A ceremony for installing a new leader

Questions for discussion

1. What words and actions would be most meaningful in a ritual for this occasion? How would you combine these into a ceremony?

2. At what time and place should each be celebrated?

3. Who would preside at each of these ceremonies? How would you meaningfully involve all of the children, teenagers, and adults in each ceremony?

4. How do these rituals parallel those celebrated in the seven sacraments?

penitence

guilt, sorrow, regret, remorse

Human beings have a need to celebrate.

Chapter review

1. The seven sacraments

- What is a sacrament?
- What seven sacraments does the Catholic Church celebrate?
- What are the sacraments a sign of, and what do they express?
- What two things are at the heart of celebrating each sacrament?
- What does the good that the sacraments do depend—and not depend—upon?
- Why must the sacraments be lived as well as celebrated?

2. Sacraments of Christian Initiation

- What is the process of Christian initiation?
- What does this process include? What sacraments does it involve?
- What is the meaning of each of the sacraments of Christian initiation?
- What are the main liturgical signs for each of these sacraments?

3. The Sacraments of Healing

- What are the sacraments of healing as celebrated by the Catholic Church?
- What harm does sin cause, and why is it the worst type of evil?
- What does the Sacrament of Reconciliation express and accomplish?
- Who actually forgives sin?
- What does the process of reconciling with God involve?
- What are the signs of sacramental reconciliation?
- What is the preferred way of celebrating this sacrament? Why?
- How do Catholics continue Jesus' healing ministry?
- What does the sacramental anointing of the sick mean and celebrate?
- What is Viaticum?
- When may and should Catholics ask for the anointing of the sick?
- What are the liturgical signs of this sacrament?
- What do the Christian funeral rites celebrate for Catholics?

4. Sacraments at the Service of Communion

- What does the Sacrament of Holy Orders mean and celebrate?
- What is the common priesthood of the faithful? How is it related to the ministerial (ordained) priesthood?
- What are the degrees of ordained ministry in the Catholic Church? What role does each play in the Church community?
- What are the liturgical signs of the Sacrament of Holy Orders?
- Are Catholic priests married?
- What role did deaconesses play in the early Church community?
- What is marriage? Why is it sacred?
- What is essential to marriage as a sacred covenant?
- How does Catholic teaching view divorce and remarriage?
- What is the Catholic annulment process?
- When and why is marriage considered a sacrament in the Catholic Church?
- What is the liturgical sign of the Sacrament of Marriage? What does this sacrament proclaim?
- What role do marriage and family life play in the Church and in society?
- Who marries the couple?

Projects and assignments

1. Write a prayer or song of at least fifteen lines for celebrating one of the following occasions: the Eucharist, the baptism of a child or adult, confirmation, a wedding ceremony, a communal celebration of anointing the sick, a priest's or deacon's ordination, a communal celebration of the Sacrament of Reconciliation.

2. Read the following Christian Scripture passages about forgiveness and reconciliation: Luke 6:37, 15:7, and 17:4; and Matthew 5:7 and 23–24. Write a one-page paper describing the insights you have about forgiveness as a result of reading these passages.

Part Four

Living as a Christian

Chapter 13 Christian Morality

Christians attempt to live according to the Law of Love.

I pray that you may have the power
to comprehend, with all the saints,
what is the breadth and length and height and depth,
and to know the love of Christ
that surpasses knowledge,
so that you may be filled
with all the fullness of God.
                    Ephesians 3:18–19

Creator God,

Your love and goodness are beyond all that we humans can imagine.
Thank You for creating us with the intelligence to understand the wonders of our world,
and for the freedom to love You and one another.
Help us every day to really appreciate how good it is to be alive.
Keep us free in spirit, so material things don't weigh us down.
Help us to be gentle and kind—especially to the weakest and the lost among us.
Help us to console and comfort one another,
and to find confidence and comfort in our belief in You.
Give us the courage to live our convictions,
to be strong defenders of what is right and true.
Soften our hearts to show compassion and forgiveness—
especially when we stubbornly resist.
Guide us to focus on the goodness that exists in others,
and on the good that we can do.
Help us be peacemakers instead of troublemakers,
but help us to follow our conscience whatever it costs.
We rely on You, and know that You'll keep Your promises to never let us down.

Overview questions

1. What does it really mean to be alive and to be human?

2. What does it mean to live fully as human persons?

3. What are the Beatitudes? What do they tell us about human happiness and fulfillment?

4. What is human freedom? What role does it play in human life and happiness?

5. What is conscience, and should we follow our conscience?

6. How can we make sure our conscience is correct?

7. What moral principles has God given us to help us form and follow our conscience?

Human dignity

What's so important about people? Why do we matter in the whole scheme of things? Are people more important than animals? What makes us different from computers? The answers to these questions are becoming more important than ever. As a society, we will have to make many major decisions as humanity continues exploring such things as robots, virtual reality, and artificial life forms. So you'd better understand and be prepared to explain to others just what it is that makes you human, and different from machines and dolphins.

So God created humankind in his image,
in the image of God he created them;
male and female he created them.

Genesis 1:27

This Bible passage sums up why three major world religions—Judaism, Christianity, and Islam—believe we human beings are of such special value: because God has told us that God has made us like God. This does not mean (as some religions other than these three believe) that we are now gods or a piece of god ourselves.

As the Bible also makes very clear, however, only God is God. You aren't and never will become your biological parents. You are a unique, distinct individual person. But, in a few ways at least, you have been created in their image. More than just sharing certain physical and genetic characteristics, you participate in their human nature—in what makes them human persons. **Being created in God's image means that the essential qualities that make us human also enable us to share, in a limited way, in God's nature**—in what makes God God.

A child is called to share in more than just a common human nature with the parents. The child is also called to grow in a special loving relationship with parents and other siblings as part of a family community. In a similar way, we humans are all God's children. God has created us to share in God's divine nature and to live in relationship with God and with one another as God's family.

So we get our dignity as human persons from our Creator. This means that, although we or others may violate it, no one—not individuals or governments—can ever really take away our fundamental human dignity because God has made it an essential part of who we are.

Being alive

The Bible tells us that **life is a gift from God.** But what does it means to live, to be alive? To understand your nature and dignity as a human person, you must first answer that question.

On seeing a long thin black object wiggling on the floor, you might presume it's alive and run the other way! But not everything that moves is alive. On the other hand, **inanimate** objects seem motionless, but we know from science that they're not completely inactive. Among the trillions of non-living things that exist, even the smallest rock contains millions of atoms and molecules moving around inside. Yet we don't consider such objects—or their moving molecules and atoms—to be **living** things.

Biologists used to define **living organisms** as those which take in nourishment and obtain energy from it, grow, make an effort to adapt to their various surroundings, and can reproduce themselves. For human beings, the spaghetti and meatballs we eat provide the nourishment and energy to run and grow taller. We adjust to icy weather by putting on a coat when it snows. We can beget children. On a purely physical level, such things qualify us as living organisms. But, even so, the general definition of a living thing can describe a daisy or a virus as well as you and me. ❧

❧ Questions for discussion

1. Why do you believe we human persons are creatures of special value?

2. What does it mean to you to say that we're all "children of God"?

3. Have you ever mistaken an inanimate object for something alive? How would you describe the difference between the two?

4. Why isn't motion alone enough to indicate that something is alive?

---

inanimate

not living or alive, without life

---

living organisms

those which take in nourishment and are capable of reproducing

What makes us uniquely human?

life principle

the essence of life, soul, that which enables something or someone to be a living being rather than an inanimate object, that which enables one to move under one's own initiative

rationality

the ability to arrive at correct connections between and conclusions about causes and their effects, ability to reason

free will

the ability to make independent choices of one's own without being controlled by something or someone else, the ability to decide freely

moral freedom

the ability to freely choose between good and evil

moral choice

ability to choose between good and evil

Being human

What does it mean, then, not just to be alive, but to be human?

Biologists make a further distinction between animal and plant life: Animals, including human beings, have some sort of **life principle** enabling them to move about under their own initiative. A plant must be moved a distance by something or someone else, but a child can walk on his or her own. But a dog or even a single living cell such as an amoeba can also move about under its own power. So how are we, as living beings, different from Fido and flu viruses?

Some would say that human life differs from plant and other animal life because we can communicate, think, and experience emotions. Yet researchers are discovering that some animals, such as dolphins and whales, not only communicate with each other but

might also be able to fulfill some definitions of what it means to think. If so, are they human? Some artificial life researchers speculate that robots may one day be able, by some definitions, to think and even to reason—maybe even better than many of us humans. Will that make a robot more human than you are? Some animals even appear to express emotions. Does that make them human, too? What does make you uniquely human?

Christians believe God has gifted us with three essentials which make us human:

- We are rational.
- We are free.
- Our spiritual dimension is immortal.

Rationality is our ability to reason, to come to logical conclusions, to understand. Freedom, or **free will,** is our ability to decide, to make free choices. **Moral freedom** is our ability to make free **moral choices**—free choices between good and evil. Non-human animals may be able to "think" according to their instincts or training. Robots may one day be able to "reason," by some definitions. But robotic thought processes, like the instincts and emotions of non-human animals, will always be limited to and completely depend upon the results of built-in, preprogrammed tendencies.

As human persons, we are more than just products of our physical heredity and social environment. We're not only rational; we're also free. Robots and non-human life forms will never be able to make free, moral decisions—not unless God one day gifts them, too, with "humanity." If there are already such beings in outer space, then they, too, share our humanity—and are meant to share as we are in God's love and God's promises.

Ironically, it's our ability to freely choose to be imperfect that makes us "perfectly human"! We would just be robots if God had preprogrammed us to think, do, say, feel, and choose only what is good. Yet, imperfectly as we sometimes use it, our rational freedom also enables us to become more perfect by freely choosing good over evil, and love over unkindness and hatred.

So our ability to eat French fries, gain weight, play tennis, open an umbrella when it rains, and beget babies may describe our characteristics as living organisms. But they're not what make us **human.** Our free will and our ability to use it rationally help make us human. How we use our rational freedom in choosing our immortal destiny is what determines what kind of human persons we become.

Being truly alive as human persons involves far more than the purely material, biological functions of absorbing and obtaining energy from food, physical growth, adapting to one's surroundings, and reproduction. It involves spiritual nourishment, energy, growth, change, and fulfillment. Catholicism proposes that human persons are the only creatures on our planet whom God has created for our own sake, rather than for the good or use of another creature. God has destined each of us for eternal happiness. Unlike other non-human life forms, **each human person's life-principle (soul) is spiritual, rational, free, and immortal.**

Being fully human

Biologists will agree, from a purely scientific viewpoint, that human persons have a **human** life principle, a human soul, unique to our species. Christians and many others believe in addition that **our human life principle is spiritual, rather than material, and it is immortal**—everlasting. Our human spirit's individuality is God's gift to us and shares God's own life. Individually, we're created in God's image, and we can find our ultimate personal fulfillment only in sharing in God's love now and forever.

> *". . . your way of life should at all times reflect the goodness of Christ."*
> —*Rite of Confirmation*

Our free will and ability to reason also make us uniquely human because they enable us to make moral choices. **God calls us to use our reason and freedom to seek out and love what is good and true in order to realize our fullest human potentials.** Indeed, we ultimately determine our everlasting happiness by how we exercise our rationality and freedom in relationship with God. Christians look to Jesus as our ideal of how to do this. He has shown us that to be truly happy and **live fully** as human persons, we must love God by loving others generously and unselfishly.

Questions for discussion

1. In view of what was discussed in this section, describe the fundamental differences between
   • A pencil and a dandelion
   • A watch, a tree, a tiger, and you
   • You and a reasoning robot

2. In your own words, explain why
   • Your abilities to eat French fries, gain weight, play tennis, open an umbrella when it rains, and beget babies aren't enough to make you human
   • Your ability to freely choose to be imperfect is one of the things that makes you "perfectly human"
   • Your rational freedom enables you to become a more perfect human person

3. What would the essential differences be between you and an android (a science-fiction machine designed and electronically programmed to resemble a human being)?

4. If we one day discover living beings elsewhere in our solar system, how will we be able to determine whether or not they are human, like us earthlings?

live fully

to use our distinctively human abilities, the gifts God has given us, to love God and others

✺ Questions for discussion

1. In your own words, describe and explain what it means to be "fully human":
   - In purely scientific terms
   - In religious terms
   - According to what you truly desire in life

2. What does Catholic belief say about each of the following, and which of these beliefs do Catholics share in common with other Christians and non-Christians?
   - God's relationship with us
   - What determines our ultimate happiness
   - How we can best respond to and return God's love
   - Living fully as human persons

3. Why won't material things ever be enough to make you fully happy as a human person?

So while we may live humanly because of reason and freedom, we only live fully depending on how we use these abilities, these gifts God has given us. Dogs can pile up bundles of bones, but no quantity of these can ever make them happy in human terms. Nor will accumulating lots of possessions and money ever make us humanly happy either.

True human happiness is linked to what makes us human in the first place! It's directly related to how we exercise our God-given human rationality and freedom. We become happy and fully human to the extent that we use our distinctively human abilities for good rather than for harm, for love rather than for hate, generously rather than selfishly—to turn toward rather than away from God and others. ✺

You shall be holy, for I the LORD your God am holy.
—Leviticus 19:2

Generosity is a sign of true humanness.

Interview with an alien—part 1

Read the following two paragraphs. Then complete the remainder of this activity by following your teacher's instructions.

The National Aeronautics and Space Administration of the United States has formally begun the $100 million project of searching for extraterrestrial intelligence in the universe. Recent evidence suggests that there may indeed be many planets out there on which some form of life could exist. Through this project scientists will attempt to discover whether we're the only creatures who look at the sky and wonder if there's any other intelligent life out there.

The alleged "encounters with aliens" frequently described in the various sensationalistic media are generally no tribute to humanity's intelligence! But for the sake of this activity, let's assume that there is intelligent life out there. Let's also assume that you do encounter an alien from a distant planet.

You interview Elethea

A vehicle crash lands on Earth from outer space. Military and scientific authorities hold the only surviving occupant in "protective custody" to determine whether or not it poses a threat to humanity.

It is your assigned task to interview the alien in order to determine three things:

- The nature of the alien—whether it is an android or possesses genuinely human characteristics
- Whether the alien is a good or evil being
- Whether the alien's intentions toward humanity are good or evil

The alien is able to understand you and to communicate with you in the English language. It tells you that its name is Elethea.

Questions for discussion

1. What questions would you ask the alien in order to determine
   - Whether or not Elethea is human as we earthlings are
   - Whether Elethea is a good or an evil being
   - How fully human Elethea is
   - What Elethea's mission is and whether Elethea's intentions toward humanity are good or evil ones
2. What would you especially look for to convince you of Elethea's humanity and good intentions? Why?

Interview with an alien—part 2

Elethea interviews you

This time the tables are turned. While on a peaceful exploratory space mission, your ship crashes on an unknown planet.

You, the sole survivor, are taken into "protective custody" by what apparently are the authorities of the beings which inhabit this planet. One of their representatives, Elethea, now interviews you in order to determine what kind of a creature you are and whether or not you pose a threat to them and their planet.

Presume that you are convinced the inhabitants of this planet, including Elethea, are essentially human and are peaceful and good rather than warlike and evil. Elethea is able to understand and communicate with you in English.

Questions for discussion

1. In response to Elethea's questions, how would you explain:
   - What it means to you to be human?
   - Your ultimate purpose in living as a human person?
2. How would you go about trying to convince Elethea that:
   - You are a good rather than an evil being?
   - Your mission is truly a peaceful one, and that you have no intentions of harming the inhabitants of Elethea's planet?
3. If intelligent extraterrestrial creatures are ever discovered, what would that mean in terms of Catholic beliefs about being human?

Which would you really rather be?

Record your response choice for each of the following eight questions. Then respond to the discussion questions below.

If you could be only one or the other in each instance, but not both, would you choose:

1. To be extremely rich — or to be happy?
2. To be the most powerful and influential person in whatever field of work you choose — or to be happy?
3. To experience maximum physical pleasure and never suffer physical pain or discomfort — or to be happy?
4. To never have any difficult experiences in life — or to be happy?
5. To never have anyone wrong you or deeply hurt you emotionally — or to be happy?
6. To be a famous sports figure or other kind of celebrity — or to be happy?
7. To always get your way, and, if you wish, to marry the person of your dreams — or to be happy?
8. To be so popular that no one ever dislikes, criticizes, or avoids you — or to be happy?

Questions for discussion

1. Did you choose any of the alternatives over happiness? Why or why not?
2. If you could have both, which of the alternatives above would you choose in addition to also being happy? Do any of them seem incompatible with true happiness? Explain.
3. Why does each of the alternatives not necessarily include or bring happiness?
4. Why do you think people who pursue one or more of the appealing alternatives so often end up being unhappy? Do you think it's because they meant to choose these things over happiness? Explain.
5. What would you be willing to give up in life in order to be really, truly happy forever and ever? What would you be willing to do in life in order to achieve this?

Living happily forever

The be *attitudes*

"Living happily ever after" isn't just one of the standard endings for daydreams and fairy tales. If given the chance, we'd all like to live happily forever. In fact, that's probably the only thing everybody in human history will ever agree on! The question, though, is: What is true happiness, and what is the real way to achieve it?

As you've just demonstrated in the previous activity, genuine happiness is not a matter of achieving fame, power, or material wealth. (Isn't it a shame, though, that this isn't always so obvious?) Instead, happiness is a matter of the heart.

How do we find real, lasting happiness? Politics, athletics, economics, mathematics, literature, science and technology, and even psychology can't provide a full enough answer. Only religion directly addresses our human quest for true and everlasting happiness. For, as you discussed in the beginning of this course, we have an inner longing which only God's love can satisfy. By themselves, however, even religious observances aren't enough. Those Christians who equate religion only with fasting or with long faces completely misunderstand Jesus' message and mission:

"Woe to you . . . hypocrites!
For you [make religious offerings]
and have neglected the weightier
matters of the law:
justice and mercy and faith.
It is these you ought to have practiced
without neglecting the others.

Matthew 23:23

Thus religion also provides a framework of guidelines to help us keep our priorities straight in discovering the truth about what is right and wrong. It tells and shows us how to be as happy as we can possibly be both in this life and beyond:

I have come so that they may have life
and have it to the full.

John 10:10

Ultimately, happiness is God's beautiful gift of loving us, and our acceptance of God's love. Happiness is therefore partly a subjective experience. It doesn't depend on what happens to us, but on how we perceive it—whether positively or negatively. It's our **attitude** in life that makes the difference.

If we have a positive attitude, we can cope with life's misfortunes and still be happy—but only if our positive attitude is founded on something solid. A superficial positive attitude, on the other hand, is just a smiling mask. It hides (perhaps even from ourselves) our inner emptiness, dissatisfaction with life, and unhappiness.

What, then, is the best kind of positive attitude to have? Even many non-Christians agree that, in the values he preached and how he lived them, Jesus gave us the means to reach real happi-

ness. Listening to and heeding his words can save us from depressing lives of evil, meaninglessness, and despair. The **Beatitudes** of Jesus give us a summary list of these values.

Beatitude means "happiness." The Beatitudes tell us the kind of persons we need to **be** and the kind of **attitudes** we need to have in order to be truly happy in life. They give us a standard we can use for figuring out how to relate with people and how to use material things. In essence, this is what these "be attitudes" tell us (see Matthew 5:3–11):

Be free in spirit. Don't weigh yourself down by focusing your mind and heart on material things and pleasures. These are only temporary and of limited value in themselves. Instead, seek things of everlasting importance—like love and mercy and justice—that can never wear out or be stolen: "For where your treasure is, there your heart will be also" (Luke 12:34).

Be gentle and kind in how you view and treat others. Those who may seem the least worthy of it will often be the ones who need your gentle kindness the most.

Be comforted and confident when you suffer, for one day you will never have to suffer any more. Instead, your suffering will be replaced with a boundless joy that will never end.

Believe in and never give up working for what you know is right. Have the courage to live your convictions. Your happiness can lie only in being true to yourself: What will you get out of it in the end if you gain the whole world, but ruin or lose yourself? (See Luke 9:35.)

Be compassionate and forgiving, in your heart as well as in your behavior. Remember, nobody's perfect—"but for the grace of God, that could be me."

. . . in seeking you, my
God,
I seek a happy life. . . .
—St. Augustine

The Eight Beatitudes

*"How happy are the poor in spirit;
theirs is the kingdom of heaven.*

*Happy the gentle;
they shall have the earth for their heritage.*

*Happy those who mourn;
they shall be comforted.*

*Happy those who hunger and thirst for what is right:
they shall be satisfied.*

*Happy the merciful:
they shall have mercy shown them.*

*Happy the pure in heart:
they shall see God.*

*Happy the peacemakers:
for they will be called children of God.*

*Happy those who are persecuted in the cause of right:
theirs is the kingdom of heaven."*

—Matthew 5:3–10 (New Jerusalem Version)

Questions for discussion

1. In your own words, describe what "true happiness" and "living happily ever after" really mean to you.

2. Why aren't religious observances alone enough to lead to human happiness and fulfillment? What is the role of religion in this, according to what Jesus taught?

3. In your own words, describe each of the following attitudes, and give at least one realistic example of each:
   - An attitude which seems positive but is superficial
   - An attitude which is both positive and solidly founded
   - The best kind of positive attitudes to have, according to Jesus
   - An attitude which somewhat damages love and relationships
   - An attitude which destroys love and relationships

4. Which of Jesus' Beatitudes do you find easiest to live by, and why? Which seems the hardest for you to live by, and why?

Be a good person and look for goodness in others and in life. Free your mind from evil. In doing so, you will experience God whose very nature is goodness. The goodness or evil your heart intends is what you give to others—and to yourself. (See Luke 6:45.)

Be a peacemaker. Be the kind of person who brings people together, not someone who creates divisions.

Be willing to put up with whatever it costs to follow your conscience, your innermost convictions about the truth. If you're made fun of or punished for it, then you're in excellent company with all the courageous persons who have ever stood up for what they believe in. Remember, too, that God has promised to richly reward you for your troubles.

Freedom

God has left us free to make our own decisions in life. **Human freedom—the ability to act or to not act—is a precious gift.** Freedom is our ability to decide, to make voluntary choices between good and evil. Our freedom is also a permanent gift from God.

If our human freedom came from anywhere else but God, then whoever gave it to us—whatever ruler or government—would have the right to take it away. In fact, that was pretty much how things operated in the historical past, when a single ruler had absolute control over subjects. It's still how tyrannical leaders try to operate today—whether in running a country or a local street gang.

Likewise if human freedom were seen, not as God-given, but as just another possibility for the human species, then one might argue that it's really not a necessary and fundamental right. It's precisely because human liberty is recognized as coming from God that it is an **inalienable right**—one which can never be taken away from us. Therefore, protecting all human persons' gift and right of human freedom throughout the world is an important and a sacred task.

Let love be genuine;
hate what is evil,
hold fast to what is good.
—Romans 12:9

There is, however, no such thing as total freedom from everything. Having freedom doesn't give us the right to say or do anything we please. The very meaning of freedom implies either a freedom **from** something or a freedom **for** something. So it's not being attached to something that holds us down, it's not being attached to something against our will—or being attached to the wrong things.

Our freedom allows us the choice to decide what we will become or remain attached to. And, as we've seen, it's only if we choose what is good that we can find what is really good for us and others. Your own fear of being a victim of gang violence or date rape is paying the price for the wrongful ways in which so many others today abuse their freedom.

Our choices determine what results, what happens to us and others. When we exercise our freedom to make a choice, we can't blame somebody else for the outcome. Our free acts are ours, not somebody else's. **We're responsible for the choices we make voluntarily.**

You know from watching trial procedures on television that one's responsibility for an action can be lessened or completely absent without a conscious awareness of what one is doing, or if one is unable to control one's behavior. You're not responsible for what you do while you're sleepwalking—unless you know ahead of time that you're inclined to shoplift in your sleep and don't take reasonable measures to prevent it. Pressure, force, fear, or other mental, emotional, and social factors can play a role in diminishing the extent of personal responsibility for an action.

Conscience

It's not military forces or missiles or bombs that will determine the world's future, but what people decide is right or wrong to do with them. Some people say they determine what is right and wrong according to how they **feel.** But heaven help us all if nuclear decisions and the world's fate are ever decided only on the basis of emotions!

Your emotions and hunches can play an important role in pointing out to you what may be right or wrong before you stop to really think about it. And ideally, your feelings will motivate you to do what you recognize is right—you'll do it because you feel like doing it, rather than just because you think it's what you should do.

Questions for discussion

1. In what sense and why is human freedom a precious and permanent gift? What does this imply for governments and their citizens?

2. Does freedom mean you have the right to do anything you want? What would happen if everyone exercised total freedom without considering the consequences? Explain.

3. What choices are you responsible for in life? Why?

4. Have you ever made a choice that, because of circumstances, wasn't a completely free one? Explain.

5. What factors can diminish a person's responsibility for an action? Does this mean that the person isn't responsible enough to be punished if the action is a crime? Explain.

☙ Questions for discussion

1. Do you ever determine what is right or wrong based on how you "feel" about the situation? What do you mean by doing this?

2. How would you prefer others to live and decide in ways that affect you—according to their conscience and innermost convictions, or simply by doing what they feel like doing at any given moment? Why?

3. Do your feelings ever confuse you when you're trying to figure out the right thing to do in a situation? Do they ever guide you correctly? Explain.

4. How would you describe the differences between your feelings and your conscience?

5. How do you usually handle hateful or destructive feelings toward others? Is it wrong to get such feelings? What is the best way to handle them? Explain and give examples.

6. Why is fully informing your conscience so important before making a moral decision?

7. When should you follow your conscience? Can your conscience ever be wrong—and, if so, would following it be wrong also? Explain.

---

fully informing one's conscience

doing what is necessary to discern what is morally correct according to objective standards of right and wrong

Similarly, your feelings should also make you feel like not doing what is wrong. But, as you also know, it doesn't always happen this way. By itself, how you feel about something isn't always an accurate way to tell whether it's right or wrong. Have you ever done the right thing, for instance, and still felt guilty about it because it ended up hurting somebody's feelings?

There are important differences between feelings and conscience! In themselves, feelings like love, desire, joy, hate, fear, sadness, and anger are neither good nor bad. It's only when we use our ability to reason and to choose in connection with these feelings that they become good or bad.

Feeling anger, or even hatred, toward someone who wrongs us is a natural response to being wronged. But encouraging these negative feelings to remain and grow in ourselves is wrong. First of all, it lessens our human dignity. It also increases the likelihood that we will act out our negative feelings by harming the other person.

Most often God speaks to us through our ability to reason to what is morally good and evil—through our conscience. **Conscience is our ability to reason to a conclusion about the morality—the goodness or evil nature—of an action.** When we do what is wrong anyway, it's our conscience that keeps nudging us to be sorry and make amends for it.

To make correct moral decisions, our conscience must be well-formed and well-informed. When making a moral decision, we must think about what is good for everybody who's involved and not just about what's good for ourselves. **Fully informing one's conscience** involves recognizing that there are objective standards for determining right and wrong, and taking the necessary steps to discover which course of action is the morally correct one.

Conscience can be formed incorrectly, for instance, when children become so accustomed to doing wrong that they learn to view it as acceptable. Or when they are so strongly and con-

tinually influenced by social factors like peer or media pressure that they can't tell right from wrong. Many children, in fact, are being brought up to have no conscience. When they commit a violent crime, they feel no remorse for their action and no sorrow for the harm they caused the victim. If they're sorry about anything, it's only that they got caught and will be punished.

People can also fail to take enough time to consider all the factors involved in making a moral decision. Therefore they can judge the situation wrongly. Like any wise judge or jury, to find the truth we've got to consider all the necessary facts we can before we conclude what is right or wrong.

People must always follow the judgment of their conscience when they are certain that it's the correct one. This is true even if the evidence shows later that we were mistaken—after all, we can only do the best we can! Our conscience makes a correct judgment when it reasons to what is true and in keeping with God's law.

Our conscience, too, can be incorrect at times. For example, we might be ignorant of something we need to know in order to make an accurate judgment. Or maybe we do have all the information, but make a mistake in our reasoning process that leads us to draw the wrong conclusion. We're guilty of such ignorance or mistakes only to the extent that we were careless about trying to discover what the right choice really is. ☙

Forming a correct conscience

How can we make sure that our conscience is accurate? First we should examine what our conscience seems to be telling us through our feelings, by thinking things over thoroughly, and by praying for God's guidance. Then we should compare our initial judgment with what our religious beliefs tell us about God's moral law. For Christians, this means that our conscience should always agree with and never be opposed to Jesus' teaching. Catholics should also take into account what the Church's official teaching tells us about moral matters.

> *. . . test everything;*
> *hold fast to what is good;*
> *abstain from every form of evil.*
> —*1 Thessalonians 5:20–22*

The things some people claim God "tells" them in prayer certainly aren't ideas we'd agree with when it comes to right and wrong! In fact, many of these so-called "messages" from God offend everything Catholics believe God is and Jesus taught. People sometimes try to justify evils like cult brainwashing, child abuse, slavery, racism, violence, or promising salvation in exchange for money by claiming that "this is what God told me." Or they superstitiously (and mistakenly) equate dreams or unusual coincidences with "God's voice."

How, then, does God speak to us? How can you distinguish what God is telling you from your own thoughts and feelings? Catholicism proposes that God speaks to us through our correctly formed—and sufficiently informed—**conscience** which tells us what good is and how to choose it, and what evil is and how to avoid it. This is the **natural moral law** which we follow above all by loving God and our neighbor, and by living the kind of life that witnesses to the human dignity this natural law expresses.

This natural law has remained the same and unchangeable throughout human history because it is God's loving guide to human happiness. People sometimes joke that, along with a birth certificate, we should have been given an owner's manual telling us how to succeed in life, and what pitfalls and problems to avoid. Well, the natural law is kind of like a built-in owner's manual of life which lets us share in our Creator's wisdom, goodness, and purpose in creating us.

This natural moral law tells us what our basic rights, responsibilities, and duties are as human beings—what to do and what to avoid in order to be happy both now and forever. This is why all other types of human-made laws must be based on the principles of this natural law. We discover the natural law through our conscience—by using our ability to reason to correct conclusions about what is morally good and bad, right and wrong. ৯

Questions for discussion

1. How can people tell whether their conscience is accurate or not?

2. If your job involved working with young children who have become criminals because they have been raised without developing a conscience, how would you help them to develop a correct conscience? Explain.

3. When people claim that God is telling them to do something, what might they mean by this? If their claims differ from what you believe your conscience is telling you, how can you tell which is really "God's voice"?

4. How does God speak to people regarding matters of right and wrong?

5. What things do you think a person can know are right or wrong without being told or taught? Explain.

Our conscience helps us choose what is good and right.

Freedom of conscience

Read the following statements on what the Catholic teaching says about religious freedom. Then respond to the questions below.

1. *Hence everyone has the duty, and therefore the right, to seek the truth in matters religious, in order that each person may with prudence form for himself or herself right and true judgments of conscience, with the use of all suitable means.*

2. *Truth, however, is to be sought after in a manner proper to the dignity of the human person and our social nature.*

3. *The inquiry is to be free, carried on with the aid of teaching or instruction, communication and dialogue.*

4. *In the course of these, people explain to one another the truth they have discovered or think they have discovered, in order thus to assist one another in the quest for truth.*

5. *Moreover, as the truth is discovered, it is by a personal assent that individuals are to adhere to it. . . .*

6. *For, of its very nature, the exercise of religion consists before all else in those internal, voluntary, and free acts whereby a person sets the course of her or his life directly toward God.*

    "Declaration on Religious Freedom," Documents of Vatican II, *adapted for inclusive language.*

Questions for discussion

1. What duty and right does Catholic teaching say every person has regarding religious matters?

2. How is a person to form right and true judgments of conscience?

3. What helps should a person use in the search for religious truth? Why must this inquiry be free?

4. Why must individuals' response to truth be by "personal assent"?

5. What does the exercise of religion first of all consist of?

God's Law of Love

In addition to the natural law, God has also revealed to us the Law of Moses (summed up in the Ten Commandments), and the Law of Christ (expressed most of all in Jesus' Sermon on the Mount—see Matthew 5–7). Some of the truths contained in the Law of Moses are the same as those our hearts, our conscience, can discern in the natural law. But God revealed them to us more clearly because, as we will see, we don't always read or heed our hearts correctly!

The Ten Commandments have since become the moral basis for legal codes and civil laws throughout the world. They provide moral principles by which all persons should live. In addition, Christians view the Law of Moses as a preparation for Jesus' moral teaching in the Gospels.

Never undertake anything for which you wouldn't have the courage to ask the blessings of heaven.
—Georg Christian Lichtenberg

Jesus supported the Law of Moses and completed it by explaining even further what it should mean and by showing us how, by giving us God's special help (as in the sacraments), to live our faith in God more lovingly in practical ways. This Law of Christ is a gift from God and a guide to love and human freedom. The Beatitudes and Golden Rule are powerful enough alone to change the world, because they are guides to changing the human heart, which is where all human behavior comes from.

This is why the Christian should always use Jesus' example as the standard by which to measure how authentically good an idea or course of action is. In fact, the two main commandments of Christ's Law include the Ten Commandments of Moses' Law and the moral concerns they address:

. . . "love the Lord your God with all your heart, and with all your soul, and with all your mind."
Matthew 22:37

- *I am the LORD your God . . . you shall have no other god before me.*
- *You shall not make wrongful use of the name of the LORD your God. . . .*
- *Observe the sabbath day and keep it holy. . . .*
Deuteronomy 5:6–7, 11, and 12

. . . "love your neighbor as yourself."
Matthew 22:39

- *Honor your father and your mother. . . .*
- *You shall not murder.*
- *Neither shall you commit adultery.*
- *Neither shall you steal.*
- *Neither shall you bear false witness against your neighbor.*
- *Neither shall you covet your neighbor's wife.*
- *Neither shall you desire . . . anything that belongs to your neighbor.*
Deuteronomy 5:16–21

In forming our conscience, then, we should draw on our religious faith and on God's word in the Bible, and ask God's help to enlighten us. But how can we do this and yet avoid "putting words in God's mouth" or claiming that God is telling us things that, in reality, are actually opposed to God's laws of love and justice? How do we figure out the right thing to do in a moral dilemma when the answer isn't clear? Here are some questions to ask yourself:

- Based on what I know of Jesus' **entire** life and message (not just one isolated Bible passage), what would he say or do in this situation?

- What did Jesus say or do or advise others in similar situations?

- What does my religious tradition teach that would apply here?

ethics

the study of the moral dimension of values, principles, judgments, and standards by which to measure what is morally right or wrong

Questions for discussion

1. Why wasn't our conscience enough—why did God also reveal parts of the natural law more clearly? What do you think might have happened if God hadn't done this? Explain.

2. List at least ten civil laws which are based on the moral principles contained in the Ten Commandments.

3. How do Jesus' commands to love relate to the Ten Commandments?

4. In addition to the Commandments, why should Christians always use Jesus' example as our standard for measuring what's right and wrong?

5. How would you advise Christians to figure out—without "putting words in God's mouth"—what is the right thing to do in a difficult moral dilemma?

6. Which of the questions suggested do you usually ask yourself when trying to make a difficult moral decision? What do you think of the one recommended to college students in business ethics courses? Explain.

"Let your heart hold fast my words;
keep my commandments, and live."
—Proverbs 4:4

You can also think about somebody whose goodness and integrity you admire, and ask yourself these questions:

- How would this person probably view this?
- What would she or he do here?

Likewise, you might find helpful this question, which college students in many business and legal **ethics** courses are being taught to ask themselves before making a moral decision:

- Would I be able to defend this action as morally right if everybody I knew found out about it and it made news headlines?

For the whole law is summed up in a single commandment, "You shall love your neighbor as yourself."
—Galatians 5:14

Loving one's neighbor has many dimensions.

Explanation or excuse?

Read the following summaries, which are similar to several actual high-profile legal cases. Then, presuming that you are on the jury hearing each case, and based only on the limited information given, respond to the questions below.

Two young men who are brothers are charged with first-degree murder for killing their parents. The brothers admit that they shot their mother and father as their parents were watching television one evening at home. They also admit that, on seeing their mother still alive, one of them went outside to reload the gun, and then returned and fired the fatal shots that killed her. The brothers claim that they had been subjected to years of sexual and emotional abuse by their father, and killed their parents out of fear that their parents were planning to have the brothers killed for threatening to expose the parents. There seems to be little or no concrete evidence to substantiate the brothers' sexual abuse claims.

A wife was accused of seriously mutilating her husband one night with a kitchen knife. She says that shortly after he came home drunk and raped her, he fell asleep. She then went into the kitchen to compose herself and get a glass of water. She says that, when she saw the kitchen knife, she began to think about the abuse she had endured from her husband, and, with those images filling her mind, she grabbed the knife and went back to the bedroom where she mutilated him as he slept.

There appears to be ample evidence that the husband had, in fact, physically abused his wife on several occasions. A few of these times, the wife had left him and went to stay with friends. Once she moved to another city, and the husband left her alone when the couple lived apart. Friends and family members had encouraged her to leave him permanently because he clearly posed a serious danger to her and was unwilling to get the counseling help even his employer told him he needed.

But each time, the wife had voluntarily returned to reconcile with her husband. She said that one reason she kept returning to him was that her Catholic religion believes that marriage is a lasting and sacred commitment. In other testimony she also said that she had been attending services at a non-Catholic church.

Each time the wife returned to her husband, his abuse of her continued. Shortly before the night of the incident for which she was arrested, the wife had obtained some pamphlets from a center for battered women. But, she says, she hadn't read them yet.

Sharon had sex with her boyfriend Ramon, even though she knew beforehand that she carries the HIV virus which leads to AIDS, Acquired Immune Deficiency Syndrome. AIDS is deadly because it weakens the person's immune system so that one who contracts AIDS eventually dies. Since then Ramon has tested positive for HIV and is now charging Sharon with infecting him with the deadly virus.

Questions for discussion

1. Based only on what you know about each situation as presented above, to what extent do you think that the individuals who committed the violent act in each case probably were or were not morally responsible for their harmful actions? Why do you think this in each instance?

2. If you were on the jury in each case, would you find each of the accused individuals:

    • Fully guilty of deliberately harming someone

    • Partly guilty of this because the circumstances lessened their ability to understand right from wrong in the situation

    • Partly guilty because, even though they probably realized at the time that what they were about to do was wrong, the circumstances lessened their ability to control their behavior in the situation

    • Not guilty because the circumstances completely destroyed their ability to make any kind of a rational decision in the situation

    • Other (explain)

3. If you were on a jury, when would you be inclined to accept having been abused as an excuse for the person's criminal behavior? When would you be inclined not to accept such abuse as an excuse, but only as an explanation for the crime? Explain.

Chapter review

1. Human dignity

- Where do we get our dignity from as human persons, and why is this important?
- What does it mean—and not mean—to say that we humans are created in God's image?
- Why is life a gift? What is essential to being a living being?
- What essential gifts from God make us human—and different from non-human living beings?
- What is the difference between our life principle as a human person, and that of other living non-human beings?
- How are we called to realize our fullest human potential?

2. Living happily forever

- How can human persons find complete and lasting happiness?
- Why can't we find this in material things, or even in religious observances by themselves?
- What role does religion play in helping us find human happiness?
- In what sense is happiness a gift? A subjective experience?
- What is meant by having a solidly based rather than superficial positive attitude in life?
- What are the Beatitudes of Jesus, and what do they tell us about the kind of persons we need to be and the kind of attitudes we need to have in order to be truly happy?

3. Freedom

- What does human freedom mean and involve?
- Why is it important to recognize that our human freedom comes from God, and why is it important to protect this sacred gift?
- Why isn't our right to freedom absolute?
- What kinds of choices are we responsible for?
- What kinds of factors may help diminish the extent of personal responsibility for an action?

4. Conscience

- What role do feelings play in conscience?
- What important differences are there between our feelings and our conscience?
- What is conscience, and how can we make correct moral decisions according to our conscience?
- When do we have an obligation to follow our conscience?
- How can we help make sure that our conscience is correct and that we correctly identify what God is telling us through our conscience?
- What is the natural moral law, and what role does it play in human conduct and in developing human-made laws?
- What does Catholic teaching say about freedom of conscience?

5. God's Law of Love

- Why did God reveal certain moral truths to us?
- What are the Law of Moses and the Law of Christ? How are they related? What main moral guidelines does each include?
- Why should Christians always use Jesus' example as their standard of moral conduct?
- List the Ten Commandments.
- What things is it helpful to consider in informing one's conscience before making a major moral decision?

Projects and assignments

1. Write a one-page paper, or a song or poem of at least twenty lines on what it means to you to be alive and to be fully human.

2. Interview five adults and five teenagers, asking each this question: What does it mean to you to be human, as distinct from being a human-like robot? Record or videotape the responses and play a five-minute segment of these for the class. Write a paragraph, or videotape a segment adding your own responses in view of what you've discussed in this chapter.

3. Read the Beatitudes of Jesus in Matthew 5:3–10. Then write a two-page paper rephrasing these "be attitudes" in your own words, and telling why you think each is an important guide for living.

4. Read chapter 5, 6, or 7 of Jesus' Sermon on the Mount in Matthew's Gospel. Based on what you read, write your own eight guidelines for living and having a positive attitude about life.

5. Write a two-page paper on one of the following topics:

   • The importance of human freedom, and what you think are some of the main potential threats to human freedom in our society today

   • The importance of religious freedom, and what you think are some of the main threats to religious freedom in our society today

   • A common ethical situation teenagers experience, and how teenagers can best form and follow their conscience in facing this dilemma

   • Specific ways you would try to raise a child of your own to form and follow a correct conscience

   • Some of the ways people in our society fail to assume personal responsibility for their behavior—and then try to blame the results on other causes

Chapter 14

Good and Evil, Suffering and Hope

Overview questions

1. What is evil, and what questions does it raise with regard to faith in God?

2. What types of evil are there? What is the difference between hurt and harm?

3. Where did evil originally come from? Why are we so tempted to do what is evil at times?

4. What is virtue, and why is the power of goodness stronger than that of evil?

5. What is meant by personal and social responsibility?

6. Why does God allow pain and suffering?

Do not look forward to the changes and chances of this life in fear;
rather look to them with full hope that, as they arise,
God, whose you are, will deliver you out of them.
God is your keeper.
God has kept you safe thus far.
Hold on tightly to God's hand,
and God will lead you safely through all things;
and, when you cannot stand,
God will bear you in His arms.
Do not look forward fearfully to what may happen tomorrow.
God will either shield you from suffering,
or will give you strength to bear it.

St. Francis de Sales

Lord, help us face our future with hope.
Keep us out of trouble and safe from harm.
When our suffering seems more than we can stand,
help us rely on your love and strength to see us through.

Hope can help us surmount difficulties of all kinds.

The problem of evil

Genocide! . . . AUSCHWITZ!

Auschwitz with its three million dead!

Auschwitz with its warehouses crammed with eyeglasses.

Auschwitz with its warehouses crammed with boots and clothing and pitiful rag dolls.

Auschwitz with its warehouse of human hair for the manufacture of mattresses! . . .

Auschwitz, where the bones of the cremated were broken with sledge hammers

and pulverized so that there would never be a trace of death.[1]

Perhaps nothing in modern history so represents the utmost in **deliberate** evil as the genocide by Hitler's Nazis which intended and attempted to exterminate the entire Jewish people. We cannot comprehend such a massive, malicious assault on human life and dignity, and we ask, "Why, God, why?" We see a relative or friend suffering and dying from AIDS and we look at all the other human misery in today's world and question, "Why?" We attend a loved one's funeral and we anguish, "Why?"

The existence of human evil, pain, and suffering is probably the main thing that tempts people to doubt God's existence or question God's goodness. Nothing else gets to the heart of belief in God as does our experience of human suffering. Some conclude that, because people suffer, there can't be a God—or, if there is, that God cannot be good.

. . . There must be

Thousands! . . .

Millions and millions of humanity

Burned, crushed, broken, mutilated,

Slaughtered, and for what? For thinking!

For walking round the world in the wrong

Skin, the wrong-shaped noses, eyelids:

Sleeping the wrong night wrong city—

London, Dresden, Hiroshima.

There never could have been so many

Suffered more for less. . . .

I heard upon his dry dung heap

That [one] cry out who cannot sleep:

"If God is God[, God] is not good,

If God is good[, God] is not God . . . ."[2]

This chapter will look at the problem of reconciling the existence of a good and loving God with that of evil, pain, and suffering in the world. But while discussing these things in the classroom, don't forget the very real suffering of others, or your own painful experiences. Let's not speak too easily about these matters whose seriousness is beyond mere words and human comprehension. 🍂

What is "evil"?

People commonly speak of "social evils" and "moral evils." But what **is** *evil?* There are many beliefs about why evils happen. Here are some of the main theories about the nature of evil:

Evil as reality. In this view, evil is a spiritual or material reality which has a separate existence of its own just as we do. Some believe this evil is embodied in a material reality or being—the kind of creature typically seen in science fiction horror movies. Others believe evil is a spiritual reality—an evil god or a devil—which exercises destructive force or **demonic** power in the world or in human lives.

Evil as the absence of good. In this theory, evil isn't a reality in itself, a thing or being, but a description of the absence of good from people or things. Thus, "evil" describes what occurs when health, happiness, success, or love

Questions for discussion

1. What is the greatest pain, suffering, or evil you've experienced? That you could ever imagine happening?

2. Does the problem of pain, suffering, and evil ever cause you to question God's existence or God's goodness? Why or why not?

3. What instances of pain, suffering, and evil in the world today bother you the most, and why? The least, and why?

deliberate

intentional, something one both knows and wills

demonic

evil or cruel, like an evil spirit or devil

❧ Questions for discussion

1. Have you mainly viewed evil as a separate material or spiritual reality, as the absence of the good, and/or as a deliberate choice for harm—or as combination of these? Or have you generally viewed it in some other way? Explain.

2. What questions do you have about the nature of evil?

are missing. Or evil is perceived as that which goes against something's essential nature and purpose. Thus, murder is evil because it is contrary to human life, dignity, and goodness.

Evil as deliberate choice. This theory sees evil as something for which human beings alone are responsible. According to this view, we're the only source of evil, and only the harm people deliberately intend is truly evil. Thus, evil is a deliberate choice, intent, or wish to harm. This theory defines harm as that which is opposite something's basic nature and purpose. So in this view, pain and suffering aren't always either harmful or evil. ❧

Our choices affect other people.

Catholic belief about the nature of evil

Catholic belief confirms our personal experience—that evil is a real part of human life, as it has been throughout human history. Out of respect for human freedom, God permits moral evil to occur. But God who is all-good can never cause what is evil. Moral evil can be caused only by rational creatures who abuse the God-given gifts of freedom. All rational creatures God has created have this moral freedom to accept or reject the good.

Scripture and Church Tradition do speak of the existence of pure spirits, some of whom, like humans, have abused the gifts of reason and freedom and may tempt human persons to do the same. The New Testament book of Revelation, which is written using highly symbolic images, contains this description:

And war broke out in heaven; Michael and his angels fought against the dragon. The dragon and his angels fought back, but they were defeated, and there was no longer any place for them in heaven. The great dragon was thrown down, that ancient serpent, who is called the Devil and Satan, the deceiver of the whole world—he was thrown down to the earth, and his angels were thrown down with him.

Revelation 12:7–9

This very poetic language shows us what happens with the abuse of freedom. Whatever else this passage means (and we don't know exactly what else it means), it makes it clear that good ultimately triumphs over all evil.

True evil itself is not a material or a spiritual creature. **Evil is the free and deliberate wrongful choice made by those of God's creatures who have the gift of free will.** Evil is abuse of the gifts God gives us. We have the freedom God has given us to accept or reject goodness. Thus evil can have no real existence of its own apart from the deliberate wrongful choices of God's creatures.

We know that Jesus often used concrete images to illustrate the good and evil tendencies within the human heart. When we examine moral and social evils like the Holocaust, we have to wonder whether evil of such magnitude could have been caused purely by humanity. Such evils at least raise the question of whether there is some dimension of evil beyond what we're acquainted with.

The Bible seems to assume that there are good and bad pure spirits who are somehow able to influence us. Scholars tell us that the biblical passages in which Jesus refers to an "Evil One" may have been referring to a spiritual being. Or in some instances this may have been an expression Jesus (or those who later wrote down his teaching) used in referring to the source and experience of wrongdoing in the world.

Cartoonists' depictions of devils wearing red suits, having a long tail, and wielding a pitchfork, however, trace back to the imaginative dramatizations of biblical passages and events that were once performed in medieval mystery plays. Such graphic images of Satan are based not on reality, but on the natural human tendency to anthropomorphize—to give human characteristics to spiritual realities. Nonsense about evil ghosts and goblins is purely the product of human imagination.

Whatever is out there, God has created for good. Practices like **satanism,** however, whereby people seriously try to contact evil spiritual beings, are opposed to human dignity and to God because they are directed toward an evil rather than a good end.

We know that human beings can freely and deliberately make choices which are morally evil. To believe otherwise is to deny our own free will—and therefore to deny that we're human. In this sense evil can also be described as an absence of good in us. It goes against our essential nature and purpose as human persons, which is to reflect and return God's love and goodness. ❧

Types of evil

In general, there are three types of evil.

Natural or physical evils are those which result in physical harm to human persons from the workings of nature and the operation of natural laws and forces. Earthquakes, for example, result from pressures built up within the earth. Cancers result from changes that take place in a body's cells. Some natural evils, such as hurricanes and earthquakes, are (at least for now) beyond the scope and control of human beings. Others, like certain illnesses and diseases, can be alleviated or eliminated by human intervention. These types of physically harmful natural phenomena are called evils by us because of the pain and destruction they so often cause to us and our environment. In themselves, it would be more accurate to refer to them as imperfections in nature rather than evils as such.

Moral evils are those people cause and for which human individuals are responsible. These evils are not due merely to the forces or functioning of natural laws and processes. Personal intentions or actions which are deliberately harmful are morally evil, morally wrong, even though there may be no laws prohibiting such thought or behavior. Moral evil, religiously speaking, is known as *sin*. For the Christian, moral evil consists in going against one's conscience to violate the natural law, or the law of love God has revealed in the Ten Commandments and in the teachings of Jesus. It is the abuse of the gift of freedom God has given us so we can love God and one another.

Sin is any deliberate word, action, or desire that goes against God's moral law which is designed to ensure our basic happiness and well-being as human persons. Sin is actually unreasonable—it goes against our basic human desire (which is also God's desire for us) to be loving and loved, to be completely happy. As we've already pointed out, sin is the worst kind

❧ Questions for discussion

1. Who causes moral evil? Why can God only permit, but never cause evil?

2. What does the poetic language of the Book of Revelation say about good and evil?

3. What is true evil? Why can evil have no real existence of its own?

4. What might Jesus' references to "the Evil One" have been intended to mean?

5. What were you taught to believe about the existence of evil beings such as Satan? Has this caused any questions or problems for you regarding belief in God? Explain.

6. As human persons, why must we be able to make morally evil as well as morally good choices?

Questions for discussion

1. In your own words, explain the differences between physical evils and moral evil, and between moral evil and social evil.

2. Why aren't physical evils really evil in the truest sense?

3. What is sin? What is moral evil for the Christian?

4. What does the seriousness or degree of a moral wrong depend upon?

5. What are some major social evils you see in the world today? As individuals, how do we contribute to these social evils—or to preventing and eliminating them?

of evil there is because it deliberately offends God's goodness and everything God has created good. It damages or severs our relationships with God and others, and damages who we are as human persons.

A moral wrong may be slight (venial sin) to most serious (mortal sin), depending on whether it damages or completely destroys in us the love of God and others which is essential for human happiness both here and in the life beyond. Sin doesn't hurt God, because God cannot be harmed. But, as you experience when somebody gossips hurtfully about you, sin sure does harm us!

Social evils are the wrongful behaviors of people as a group—whether a small social group, or a bloc of nations. Social evil (social sin) results from the repeated piling up of many personal wrongs. It stems from individuals' causing evil directly, or supporting evil by not avoiding or limiting it out of laziness, indifference, fear, deliberately turning the other way, or silent assistance. Social evil is made even worse by taking advantage of others' evil actions for one's own gain, or by just giving up on trying to stop it and offering lame excuses like "it's impossible to change the world."[3]

These protesters are questioning the morality of war.

The difference between hurt and harm

People often confuse what is truly **harmful** with what they find to be **hurtful.** Unpleasantness or pain can be hurtful and yet not be harmful. For example, receiving a shot of an antibiotic to cure an illness can hurt but is usually beneficial. Victims of floods, tornados, and other natural disasters generally manage somehow to bring love and goodness out of these difficult experiences.

However, moral and social evils are by definition essentially harmful. They somehow thwart (or intend to thwart) the realization of our dignity and potential as human beings. They prevent our essential happiness and violate our physical or spiritual integrity and goodness. Under certain circumstances, one might break a social law without committing a moral wrong. But violating our conscience by deliberately intending or doing what is truly harmful is always morally wrong. Social evils multiply the harm of individual moral evil even further.

To be morally evil an act must:

1. Be opposed to one's reasonably well-informed conscience.
2. Involve knowingly and freely intending what one knows is harmful to oneself or others.

Moral and social evils are based on our sound and reasonable perceptions of what is harmful, and our intention to wish or cause this harm. Firing a gun at someone with the intent to kill would not be murder legally speaking if the gun contains no bullets and physically injures no one. But it would be murderous morally speaking. The resulting harm would be the deterioration and corruption of one's own goodness as a human being to the same extent as if, in pulling the trigger, one had killed someone.

Punishing legitimately or acting in self-defense is not evil—provided that one's motive is to do good rather than to get even. Revenge does further harm for its own sake. Morally legitimate punishment, on the other hand, protectively removes the criminal from society to prevent further harm, hopefully rehabilitates the person, and serves as an example to deter others from committing crimes.

Moral evil presumes that we recognize the potential for evil in an act or thought, **and** that we intend for that evil to happen. So moral evil is quite different from an unintended harmful side effect which happens indirectly while one is directly trying to accomplish something good.

The pull of evil

You know all too well that moral evil, sin, exists in this world. You've suffered harm from others, and you've probably wronged them, too. As we all know from experience, it's sometimes a struggle to do the right thing. Our movies often depict how this struggle divides us inside, pulling us between good and evil on personal and social levels.

But why are people sometimes cruel and mean? Why do **we** sometimes do things we know aren't right? Where did this tendency in all of us come from?

As the Bible explains, the temptation to lean toward evil has been present from humanity's very beginning. When the very first human persons gave in to the temptation to knowingly do something wrong, that first abuse of human freedom, that **original sin,** ultimately affected all of us. Goodness was no longer the only thing people experienced. That first introduction of moral evil profoundly affected human nature from then on. As a result, human history has traced the record of human selfishness, violence, greed, and corruption down through the centuries. And it's all too obvious that these moral struggles and evils still plague us today.

Questions for discussion

1. Why is something which is hurtful not always harmful—or vice versa? When might it be both? Explain and give examples.
2. Why are moral and social evils essentially harmful by definition?
3. What does a morally evil act presume and require? Why?
4. Why is intention so important in determining the subjective morality of one's action?

Questions for discussion

1. In your own words, explain where the human tendency to do wrong originally came from.
2. What types of things most influence you to do good, and why? To do what is wrong, and why?
3. Why do individual moral evils so often lead to social evils? How has this happened at your school?
4. Why is no moral wrong unimportant?
5. As a teenager, what types of moral evil are you afraid might affect you?

To the extent that we've been influenced by others' goodness, we're more inclined to do good ourselves. But to the extent that we've been influenced by others' lies, coldness, and selfishness, we've also been pulled in those directions. If a smile is contagious, so is back-biting. Listening to the daily news shows how the results of sin multiply.

Eventually, individual moral evils lead to social evils on a much greater scale. One person does wrong, so another person does wrong, which influences more people to do wrong. Finally, things seem to get out of control—in the school parking lot, or the sports stadium or concert arena, or the neighborhood, or the legislature, or the country, or major parts of the world.

No moral wrong is unimportant. For unless we fight our tendencies to do wrong in small ways, bit by bit we become more complacent about it and tempted to do wrong in more serious ways. We can see, for example, how this affects our society's legal system. A mere warning by law enforcement personnel, or a slap on the wrist by the courts, sends the message that spousal or child abuse or drunken driving isn't so bad. So people are more tempted to continue these types of behavior until they end up fatally harming someone.

Teenagers in our society have the most reason to fear some of the cruelest results of sin. As a group, you are the most frequent victims of murder, rape, and violent crimes in general in our society. Students carry knives and guns to school in order to feel safe. Mothers tell their children to lie on the floor while watching TV in case a stray bullet comes through the window. Lots of kids are scared. But evils like these don't happen by themselves. Sin by sin and individual by individual—people cause moral and social evil to happen and let it continue.

The inner struggle

St. Paul wrote about the problem of struggling with evil tendencies within ourselves. Read what he had to say, and then respond to the questions.

I do not understand my own actions.
For I do not do what I want, but I do the very thing I hate.
Now if I do what I do not want, I agree that the law is good.
But in fact it is no longer I that do it, but sin that dwells within me.
For I know that nothing good dwells within me, that is, in my flesh.
I can will what is right, but I cannot do it.
For I do not do the good I want, but the evil I do not want is what I do.
Now if I do what I do not want,
it is no longer I that do it,
but sin that dwells within me.
        Romans 7:15–20

Questions for discussion

1. In your own words, what is Paul saying in the above passage?
2. When do you most often feel like this yourself, and why?
3. Does Paul really mean that he's not the one doing the sinning when he does wrong? Explain.
4. How do you think evil initially entered the world? Presuming that the biblical story about eating forbidden fruit is symbolic, what do you think the original sin probably really was? Explain.
5. When did you first become aware of the existence of evil in your own life? Explain.

The power of goodness

As strong a hold as evil gets in someone's personal life or in the world, the power of good is far greater and can overcome it. For goodness is God's power, and Jesus' resurrection makes clear that good will always triumph in the end. Christians call this power of goodness God's **grace.** Jesus' redeeming life and death have made us worthy of this gift of the power of goodness, and shown us how to use it to bring us closer to God and others.

As Jesus told and showed us, loving kindness—and only loving kindness—can ultimately overcome all the evil in the world. Evil is cast out by good! God gives us the gift, the grace and power of goodness, in many special ways. But we must also ask God for it, and earn it by the loving ways we try to use this power of goodness as perfectly as we can. To the extent that we truly live our baptism and beliefs as Christians, we can overcome the tendencies left behind by original sin which influence us to do wrong instead of what we know is right.

Being a force for good is a main concern of society as well as of religion! In many parts of the United States, a teenager who steals your wallet can be arrested and fined or jailed. But, in a public school, it may be that the teenager isn't allowed to be formally taught to respect your property rights or that stealing is wrong! Many children receive no moral education at home, while their peers are constantly encouraging them to ignore their conscience.

These children may eventually come to have no idea—or a twisted notion—of what is right and wrong. Many also suffer neglect and abuse which further buries their conscience. Their views about what is and is not acceptable human behavior become even more severely distorted. Finally, threats of punishment can't even convince them that there's anything wrong with murdering you, much less with stealing your wallet.

It's no wonder everybody's afraid to walk alone on a public street at night, or even during the daytime in many cases. As a result, we're being forced to realize as a society that morality isn't just a matter for the Churches. It's important to teach about basic, commonly held moral values at home and at school as well.

So then, each of us will be accountable to God. Let us therefore no longer pass judgment on one another, but resolve instead never to put a stumbling block or hindrance in the way of another. —Romans 14:12–13

Catholics should play an active role in supporting basic moral education in society. But when you voice your opinion in a letter to the editor or at the local school board meeting, also remember that our faith tells us this: We have an equally serious responsibility to see that moral education in a public context respects, rather than violates, individuals' religious freedom!

Yet politicians and sociologists are now agreeing that nothing the political or legal system could possibly do can eliminate the severe crime problems which now plague our society. Only religion, they are saying, has the means to do this adequately, because only religion addresses the real source of crime—the struggle between evil and goodness within the human heart. Since we are perhaps the largest organized group of any kind, some have said that the Catholic Church has the potential to be the greatest force for good in the world. In any event, as Catholics we do have an enormous responsibility to help change the world for the better.

What our Judeo-Christian tradition tells us is that human and religious **virtues** are needed to effectively counter the vices of personal sin and social crime. **Three theological virtues— faith** (our belief in God), **hope** (our desire for God), and **charity** (our love of God, and therefore of others as ourselves)—help keep our relationship with God strong. They also help guide and give meaning to all other human virtues.

grace

the gift of God's healing and guiding help, presence, strength, life, and loving friendship; God's loving favor toward people

virtue

a regular attitude of being determined to do what is good and right

theological

of God, having to do with God or things related to God; literally, words about God

As God's chosen ones, holy and beloved, clothe yourselves with compassion, kindness, humility, meekness, and patience. . . . Above all, clothe yourselves with love, which binds everything together in perfect harmony.
—*Colossians 3:12 and 14*

☙ Questions for discussion

1. Why do Christians believe that the power of good is always stronger than and will always ultimately triumph over the power of evil?

2. What is the greatest power for good, and why?

3. In what ways do you consider yourself a force for good in your school? In your family? In your community?

4. If you were responsible for teaching older children to understand right from wrong—to develop a conscience—how would you go about doing this?

5. Why is morality a social and family, as well as a religious, matter?

6. What type of moral education would you support in public schools, and why? What type would you not support, and why?

7. Why can only religion address the real source of crime in our society?

8. What are virtues? What are the theological and cardinal virtues, and why do you think these are important?

9. In your own words, explain each of the four main moral human powers or virtues, and why you think each is important for a person to live.

The four main human powers God has given human persons are called moral virtues or **cardinal virtues.** The more we use and value them, the more these powers can help guide our intelligence, freedom, feelings, and actions in the right direction:

The four main moral human powers

- **Prudence** helps us act wisely rather than rashly, so we make sound judgments about what is right and how to achieve it.

- **Justice** gives us the constant determination to see that all persons (and God, too) get what is fairly due them.

- **Fortitude** gives us the strength and courage to face difficulties without giving up, and to not stop seeking what is good.

- **Temperance** helps us keep our priorities properly balanced in life, so that we don't emphasize physical pleasure and material goods more—or less—than we should. ☙

Social responsibility

Every society considers certain actions wrong. Some behaviors, such as riots, disrupt the common order. Others, like murder, attack a fundamental principle on which society itself rests. Civil laws generally reflect a society's moral convictions. **Some things which are illegal, however, may not be immoral in themselves**—jaywalking, for example. **Other things which are immoral might not always be illegal in society**—lying to your parents or friends, for instance.

It's obvious that **morality isn't strictly a private, individual matter.** God has created us to live among others in society in order to develop our own human nature. But **the human person must always be society's first and most important concern.** To ensure this, we all need to see that we uphold the same virtues and values as a society that we think are important for all of us to live by as individuals.

As a matter of **social justice,** we should see that our society respects the equal dignity and rights of every person as we would like for it to respect our dignity and our rights. **We're all equal in dignity,** but we're also obviously different and not all equal in human circumstances. God has created us to need and help each other and to share with one another our spiritual gifts and material goods—especially with those who are less fortunate.

We should therefore see to it that society's values and priorities are just, and apply equally and fairly to all persons. Otherwise, you may feel safe among your friends and families, but you'll have great reason to fear that government or law enforcement agencies or businesses can treat you or anybody else unfairly as an individual. Not everybody will always have as much money and opportunity as everyone else. That's the luck of life. But those of us who do have more than others also have a greater responsibility to look out for others' needs, and to be generous with what we have. And when the economic and social differences between people become too great, so that they're clearly unfair and wrong, we all must especially work hard to eliminate such unjust inequalities so that everybody has a fair chance in life.

All legitimate authority comes from God. While every human community needs some type of authority in order to survive and progress, **all human authority is based on the moral order God has placed within human nature.** Whether parents, babysitters, student bodies, or national or international governments, any kind of authority can be legitimate only if it uses morally acceptable means and is dedicated to defending and promoting the common good it oversees. This **common good** must include three goals: promoting and respecting basic personal rights and freedom, spiritual and economic prosperity, and both social and personal peace and security.

. . . return to your God, hold fast to love and justice, and wait continually for your God.
—Hosea 12:6

We should participate in and support groups and organizations which promote the common good and try to improve the human condition. We have a moral obligation to do a good job in the areas over which we have personal responsibility—whether in our family, at school, or at work. But no government or other type of social institution should ever replace or take away individuals' moral rights and responsibilities. In fact, **the purpose of any larger social institution should be to protect and promote the rights and responsibilities of smaller groups and individuals.** Viewing things in the opposite way, with the larger groups as most important, leads to tyrannical structures in which only one person or group has complete control.

Where evil does get out of control in an aspect of society—such as with a major drug problem or high crime rate, stricter law enforcement alone will never be enough to stop it. Only a change of heart by individuals, and just reforms which address the real underlying causes of the problems, can really solve and prevent serious social problems. For Christians, this involves praying for God's help and caring enough about others to find ways to help change both individuals' hearts, and unjust or unwise social policies. Somewhere in

what Jesus taught are the keys to solving every social problem—if only we're wise enough to properly use them.

Personal responsibility

It's easy to be "horrified" by the senseless drug-related killings announced every other day in the news, and to say "they should all be locked up behind bars." It's harder to have to admit to oneself that casually using illegal drugs, or laughing it off when friends do so, is actually participating in and promoting the same brutal network. It's easy to think "how terrible" that a blind paraplegic person is beaten and robbed. It's harder to face the fact that cutting someone down with words at school can be equally demeaning and cruel.

"And will not God grant justice to his chosen ones who cry to him day and night? Will he delay long in helping them? I tell you, he will quickly grant justice to them."
—Luke 18:7–8

It's simple to say how "absurd" it is that nations settle disputes with missiles, bombs, and bloodshed. It's more difficult to avoid getting into physical or verbal fights over personal disagreements. It's easy to be "shocked" when someone is mowed down by a drunken driver, but not so easy to protest the idea of getting drunk when among one's peers. As citizens, we get understandably angry when we're lied to or defrauded by dishonest politicians. It's harder to realize that the same thing is wrong with copying homework assignments, cheating on tests, or copying the computer programs and tapes of friends rather than buying them oneself.

Questions for discussion

1. Why isn't morality strictly a private, individual matter?
2. Why can some things be illegal but not immoral in themselves, and vice versa?
3. What should society's first and most important concern be? Why?
4. What is social justice? What rights and responsibilities does it involve?
5. How does human authority relate to God? When can it not be morally legitimate, and why?
6. What must looking out for the common good include? Why?
7. In what sense are smaller social groups actually more important than larger ones?
8. How would you describe your role as an individual in addressing the larger problems of society and social justice?

❧ Questions for discussion

1. In what ways do you find that your personal behavior contradicts what you say you believe about social wrongs?

2. Why is it generally harder for us to admit and correct our individual wrongful behaviors than to criticize criminals, politicians, or celebrities for their behavior?

3. How would you describe what assuming personal responsibility for your actions means and involves?

It's easy to say "that's awful" when beaches are closed because of contaminated garbage washing ashore. Apparently it's not so easy to recycle bottles and cans and not to litter. It's easy to feel sorry for the hungry and homeless in the world. It's not so easy to refrain from being attracted to or judging others by the cars they drive or the clothes they wear.

For centuries, "God fearing Christians" tried to use their religious faith to justify racism, sexism, and slavery. They looked to the Bible for arguments to support their claims, rather than for the truth which might challenge them. That's why we need to keep going back to the Gospels to let Jesus' message challenge as well as console us. We have to admit that we're sinners, and recognize our sins and the harm they do us and others. Instead of saying, "Poor me, I couldn't help it" and making excuses like "Everybody else does it," we need to stop rationalizing and stand for something.

We need to understand that sin is a social reality, and not just a personal matter. Our individual moral failures either affect others directly, or they do so by affecting us directly and therefore the ways we relate to others. And we need to admit to others and ask their forgiveness when we've wronged them. ❧

Random acts of senseless kindness

Read the following and respond to the questions.

A class of college students had been discussing the various reasons for and causes of the random acts of senseless violence which occur in our society. While watching a segment on TV about another such violent act, the professor wondered what might happen if people became "victims" of **gratuitous** *kindness instead of senseless violence.*

So for homework he challenged his students to help make the world a kinder, better place by doing one kind deed. He assigned his students to each commit one unexpected "random act of senseless kindness" and then to write about what happened.

Since then, the idea has caught fire throughout the world. Businesses and individuals have started displaying signs and bumper stickers encouraging everybody to commit one "RASK" a day. Organizations have even sprung up to promote the idea among members and others.

One three-decade experiment at a major university has confirmed that kindness has a "ripple effect." It has confirmed that those who receive or witness a kindness are more likely to do something kind themselves for someone else. It has also been found that people often remember and still appreciate these small kindnesses years later.

Questions for discussion

1. What "random acts of kindness" have you received from others? How did these make you feel, and why?

2. What do you think would happen in our society if most people committed at least one RASK a day? Explain.

3. What is meant by the ripple effect of kind deeds? Have you experienced this effect in your own life? Explain.

4. What RASKs have you committed lately? How did it make you feel—especially when only you and God knew that it was you who had done it?

5. List at least five good ways you can think of to commit a RASK at school, and at least five good ways to commit a RASK at home.

gratuitous

free, having no strings or obligations attached

Pain and suffering

There is an important difference between pain and suffering, and what is meant by **evil.** Good ends can be achieved as a direct result of pain or suffering, but not as a direct result of evil. Suffering is also different from pain. **Suffering** is our emotional, psychological, or spiritual distress at experiencing pain, injury, or loss. Although we describe suffering as "painful," **pain** is actually a physical sensation. It usually produces suffering, but not always.

A pearl is a temple built by pain around a grain of sand.
—Kahlil Gibran

People can sometimes control, lessen, or remove the sensation or perception of pain as suffering through hypnosis or other mind-control techniques. Due to a mental or physiological disorder, some people actually experience as pleasurable things which are painful and produce suffering for the rest of us. **Sadism,** for example, is the disorder whereby a person experiences pleasure in mistreating or inflicting pain on others. **Masochism** is the disorder whereby a person experiences pleasure in mistreating or inflicting pain on oneself.

How shall my heart be unsealed unless it be broken?
—Kahlil Gibran

There are people who suffer from a disease which renders them unable to experience physical pain. They can be mortally ill or injured but, without any symptoms other than pain (which they do not experience), they have no way of discovering this in time to seek successful treatment. Thus, physical pain is not evil in itself. It is simply the way our bodies tell us something is wrong.

Likewise, suffering isn't necessarily an evil in itself. To understand why this is true, take a look at what life would be like without the human ability to suffer. Suffering enables us to feel distressed at pain, injury, or loss. Without the human experience of suffering, there would be no compassion or courage, and probably little appreciation of goodness or love. We would lose the very opportunities which give rise to the most noble and beautiful of human traits and experiences.

Your pain is the breaking of the shell that encloses your understanding.
—Kahlil Gibran

Sometimes, though, mass human suffering overwhelms us. We should indeed abhor the social evils which result in war, poverty, starvation, homelessness, disease, crime, brutality, and despair. But it is also true that a million people cannot suffer any more than one individual is capable of suffering:

> We must never make the problem of pain worse than it is by vague talk about the "unimaginable sum of human misery." . . . There is no such thing as a sum of suffering, for no one suffers it. When we have reached the maximum that a single person can suffer, we have, no doubt, reached something very horrible, but we have reached all the suffering there ever can be in the universe. The addition of a million [companion]-sufferers adds no more pain.[4]

The experience of human suffering is just as real and painful for a single person as for a thousand. We should always stand in awe of any human person's suffering, and do what good we can to alleviate and prevent it.

Questions for discussion

1. In your own words, describe the differences between pain, suffering, and evil.
2. Why isn't pain always experienced as suffering? Why isn't suffering necessarily evil? Can pain or suffering ever be evil? Explain.
3. What good does pain accomplish? What good can suffering accomplish?
4. What do you think people and the world would be like without any pain? Without suffering? Would you really want a world where no one would ever have known pain or suffering at all? Explain.
5. In what sense is the suffering of one person as important as the suffering of thousands?
6. What responsibility do we have to help alleviate human suffering? In what practical ways can you help do this?

Faith crisis

Read the following true account. Then respond to the questions.

It should have been routine surgery. His wife should have been out of the hospital and home within a few days. But one unforeseen complication after another kept occurring. As soon as doctors would treat one successfully, another one would arise.

Finally, late one night the man was told that his wife may have developed pneumonia. In her already weakened condition, the doctor said that, if she had, her chances of pulling through would only be about 50–50. "Go home and get a good night's rest," the doctor had insisted. "She'll be fine until morning, and we won't know the test results until then."

An active Catholic all his life, the man had prayed for his wife before the surgery, asked God's help as each of the other complications had arisen, and thanked God as each one was resolved. But now as he made the drive home, his heart seemed torn apart at the thought of possibly losing her.

When he got home, in a state of exhaustion and panic, he tried to pray. But he found himself just feeling angrier and angrier at God. "How could you let this happen to her? She's such a wonderful person and I love her so much!"

Questions for discussion

1. Why did the man get angry at God? Do you think God minded his being angry?
2. What was the man experiencing about the problem of suffering in relation to faith in God?
3. Have you ever witnessed or suffered something which caused you to get angry at God? To doubt your faith in God? Explain.
4. When you meet God face to face, what one question would you like to ask God about the problem of pain, suffering, and evil? Why is this question so important to you?

Why does God allow suffering and evil?

. . . even there your hand shall lead me, and your right hand shall hold me fast.
—Psalm 139:10

Someone tells us that God loves us as a father loves his children. We are reassured. But then we see a child dying of inoperable cancer of the throat. His earthly father is driven frantic in his efforts to help, but his Heavenly Father reveals no obvious sign of concern.[5]

Why does God allow pain, suffering, and evil? Is God responsible for these? How can a good God even allow these?

Christians believe that it doesn't make logical sense to conceive of God as a partly evil cause of evil. For that denies God's essence as total Love and Goodness, which is what enables God to offer us an ultimate future of unending happiness without pain, suffering, or evil.

To believe in no God is to eliminate the only real possibility for completely making sense of and ultimately drawing good and hope from all the pain, suffering, and evil in the world. Without God, some people would never know life or a future without overwhelming pain and suffering. It would be totally senseless and purposeless.

Tiger

"Reprinted with special permission of King Features Syndicate"

God permits moral evil out of respect for our human freedom. Being all-good, God could allow pain, suffering, and evil only for a greater good, much like a loving parent allows a child the freedom to fail and fall for the child's own growth. But as Christians we also believe that:

You can trust God not to let you be tried beyond your strength,

and with any trial he will give you a way out of it and the strength to bear it.

1 Corinthians 10:13
(New Jerusalem Bible)

This is very different from saying that God directly wills, intends, or sends pain, suffering, or evils to torment or test us. God does **not** "send" us trials such as cancers or AIDS or abusive relationships to punish us or to "test" our love or endurance! God is the one who gives us strength to grow as persons in spite of and because of our suffering. God helps us to draw good from pain, suffering, and evil by becoming more loving and giving as a result of it. God helps us prevent what is hurtful from also becoming harmful to ourselves or others, and helps us make something good of it instead.

We've already seen what kind of a world it would be if God had prevented us from experiencing pain and suffering. But what about evil? If God had not given us the ability to choose evil, we wouldn't be capable of choosing the good either. We'd be mindless robots programmed to "be nice" and "do good" and say "I love you." But these words and actions would be meaningless. We wouldn't, in fact, be human.

Human love and goodness, by definition, must be freely chosen. And the ability to choose implies free will—and therefore the freedom to choose evil, the opposite of what is good. Pain, suffering, and evil must therefore exist if we're to be human at all. 🙒

Why so much pain, suffering, and evil?

We've discussed some reasons why God might allow pain, suffering, and evil to happen. But wouldn't there have been a better and less unpleasant way to accomplish the same good things than by pain and suffering? God deliberately didn't program the world and people to be entirely perfect, but has

🙒 Questions for discussion

1. Why can an all-good God logically not be the cause of evil?

2. Why does it make more sense to Christians to face the problem of pain, suffering, and evil with increased faith in God than it does to respond to these by denying one's faith in God? Does this make sense to you? Explain.

3. What does St. Paul say we can count on from God when we suffer? Why is this different from believing that God sends us suffering or difficulties to test us?

4. Why does God permit moral evil? What do you think the world would be like without the possibility for moral and social evil? Would you really want to live in such a world? Explain.

5. How have your personal experiences of pain, suffering, and evil affected your beliefs about God, and why?

6. Which approach to coping with the problem of pain, suffering, and evil do you think is easier?
   - Denying God's existence
   - Believing that God is both good and evil
   - Believing in a good God who allows these for some greater good

7. Do you ever think in terms of God as "sending" you difficulties or suffering to test you or to make you a better person?

8. Have you ever heard others say things like, "God never sends us more suffering than we can bear"? What do such remarks imply about God?

🔊 Questions for discussion

1. What do you mean by pain, suffering, or evil that is "excessive"? Can you think of any reason which would justify allowing these to occur? Explain.

2. Have you ever been through an experience that was very difficult for you at the time, but which you now see was worthwhile? Explain.

3. What do Jesus' suffering and death show us about coping with our own pain and suffering?

4. How would you respond to someone who says that hoping and believing in a future that makes up for all of life's difficulties is just a flimsy attempt to explain the unexplainable? Explain.

5. What does Jesus show us our responsibility is in relation to the suffering of others?

6. In what sense do pain, suffering, and evil remain a mystery for us in this life? What do you think is the best way to respond to this mystery in our own lives, and why?

given us the opportunity to participate in God's design of building a new and more perfect creation.

It's foolish and unreasonable, though, to pretend we can solve what essentially must remain a mystery. Some degree of pain may be necessary to warn us to seek help. But why excruciating pain, especially for those for whom no help is available? We can understand how our response to suffering can help us become more good and loving persons. But why do unloving persons sometimes seem to suffer little while deeply good persons suffer a great deal? Why do the innocent suffer—those who have never done anything wrong? For the Christian, the answer to these questions lies in answering another one: Why did Jesus suffer as he did—he who was most good, loving, and innocent of all?

Jesus' suffering and death redeemed us. By triumphing over pain, suffering, and evil, Jesus brought us back from having to remain captives of evil and despair forever. His resurrection in glory responds to the mystery of evil and excessive suffering by giving us hope—

the hope "that what we suffer in this life can never be compared to the glory, as yet unrevealed, which is waiting for us" (Romans 8:18).

Ultimately, this hope is the only thing that can make sense of and give meaning to what would otherwise be utterly senseless and futile. This hope gives dignity to those who suffer human misery in the promise of a future that will make all we've endured seem worthwhile. In the meantime, we're encouraged to pray, "deliver us from evil," and to ask, as Jesus did in Gethsemane, that, if it be for the best, the cup of suffering pass from us.

We're also urged to help relieve the suffering of others, and to work to replace the moral evil in the world with loving kindness. Yet sometimes we must stand helpless, as did Jesus' mother at the foot of his cross. We pray that God will draw good from what appears to be senseless human suffering. And we say with Job: "I have been holding forth on matters I cannot understand . . ." (Job 42:3). 🔊

Why?

Given your own convictions about the meaning of human pain, suffering, and evil, how would you respond to each of the following persons if they asked you why this had to happen?

1. A friend permanently disabled in an accident caused by a drunken driver. . . .

2. A friend whose ten-year-old brother has just died after a battle with cancer. . . .

3. The younger sister of a close friend of yours killed in a motorcycle accident. . . .

4. A friend whose mother dies and who has three young brothers and a sister. . . .

5. A girlfriend of yours who is raped. . . .

6. A boy whose girlfriend breaks up with him. . . .

Questions for discussion

1. How would you respond to each of these persons if they asked you how God can be good and allow such a thing to happen? Explain.

2. How would you respond, and why, if each person asked you, "Why did God cause this to happen?"

Chapter review

1. The problem of evil
- What questions or problems do pain, suffering, and evil raise regarding faith in God?
- What is evil? Describe the three theories about the nature of evil that were discussed in this chapter.
- Why does God permit moral evil to occur?
- What do Scripture and Church Tradition say about evil?
- Describe the three types of evil discussed in this chapter.
- What is the difference between hurt and harm? Why are moral and social evils essentially harmful in themselves?
- For an act to be morally evil, what is required?

2. The pull of evil
- Where did the human tendency to do evil initially come from?
- How and why does moral evil lead to social evils?
- Why is no moral wrong unimportant?
- How are teenagers in particular affected by moral and social evils?
- What does St. Paul say about our inner struggles against evil?

3. The power of goodness
- What power for good do Christians believe is greater than the power of evil?
- Where does this power for good come from, and how are we to use it?
- Why is the power of moral goodness a main concern of society as well as of religion today?
- What role should Catholics play regarding moral education in our society?
- Why does religion play an especially important role in combatting moral evil with moral good in our society and world?
- List and describe the three theological virtues and the four main (cardinal) moral virtues.
- How can each of these virtues help guide our intelligence, freedom, feelings, and actions in the right direction?
- Why isn't morality strictly a private, individual matter?
- What is social justice, and how can we promote it in our society?
- What is legitimate human authority, where does it come from, and what is it based on?
- Why can only a change of heart really address the underlying causes of major social problems?
- What personal responsibility do we have as individuals for the social evils which occur, and how can we help eliminate these?

4. Pain and suffering
- Explain the differences between pain, suffering, and evil. Why are pain and suffering not necessarily evils?
- What good can pain and suffering result in?
- Why does God allow suffering? Why does God permit evil?
- What is wrong with saying that God "sends" us suffering or trials to "test" us or to make us better?
- Why are pain, suffering, and evil a mystery?
- What does the Christian faith tell us about good and evil, suffering and hope?

Projects and Assignments

1. Research some of the ways in which good and evil—their nature, causes, and origins—have been depicted and personified throughout history (for example, Greek and ancient mythology, Native American lore). Write a two-page paper reporting your findings and giving your reactions based on the ideas contained in this chapter.

2. Find at least five newspaper articles describing some type of evil in the world. Explain what type of evil each describes. Also explain how these evils might be accounted for without blaming God for them.

3. Conduct one of the following interviews. Record or videotape the responses and play a five-minute segment of these for the class. Write a paragraph, or videotape a segment adding your own responses in view of what Catholic teaching says about this.

    - Five very young children about their ideas and examples of the worst "bad" and the best "good" they can think of

    - Five adults or teenagers about their ideas of the worst evils and the most noble "goods"

Chapter 15 Believing

But as for you, continue in what you have learned and firmly believed, knowing from whom you learned it.

2 Timothy 3:14

The Nicene Creed

We believe in one God,
  the Father, the Almighty,
  maker of heaven and earth,
  of all that is, seen and unseen.

We believe in one Lord, Jesus Christ,
  the only Son of God
  eternally begotten of the Father,
  God from God, Light from Light,
  true God from true God,
  begotten, not made, one in Being
  with the Father.
Through him all things were made.
For us and for our salvation
  he came down from heaven:
by the power of the Holy Spirit
  he was born of the Virgin Mary,
  and became man.

For our sake he was crucified under
  Pontius Pilate;
  he suffered, died, and was buried.

On the third day he rose again in
  fulfillment of the Scriptures;

he ascended into heaven
  and is seated at the right hand of the
  Father.
He will come again in glory
  to judge the living and the dead,
  and his kingdom will have no end.

We believe in the Holy Spirit,
  the Lord, the giver of life,
  who proceeds from the Father and the
  Son.
With the Father and the Son he is
  worshiped and glorified.
  He has spoken through the Prophets.
We believe in one holy catholic and
  apostolic Church.
  We acknowledge one baptism for the
  forgiveness of sins.
  We look for the resurrection of the
  dead,
  and the life of the world to come.
  Amen.

What if . . .

Answer each question as honestly and as specifically as you can. In doing so, imagine actual situations. . . . What would the world be like . . .

1. If everyone loved only for the sake of getting something in return?
2. If justice were not important?
3. If no one believed that all people are equal?
4. If no one valued conscience but did only what they felt like doing?
5. If no one believed in unity and companionship among people as an ideal?
6. If there were no mercy or forgiveness or reconciliation among people?
7. If goodness were not considered an ideal?
8. If peace among people(s) were not an ideal?
9. If no one were honest?
10. If no one were ever humble?
11. If gentleness were not considered a virtue?
12. If those who suffered had no hope? If no one tried to help those who suffer?
13. If no one were generous?
14. If everyone always sought revenge?
15. If no one were compassionate?
16. If everyone always judged every action of others?
17. If everyone valued **only** material things?

Questions for discussion

1. In what specific ways to you think that religious beliefs have affected human history? Do you think these influences have been good or bad?
2. Do you agree that people's misunderstanding and misinterpretations of their own religions have often been to blame for the selfish, brutal, or inhuman conduct which has sometimes occurred in the name of religion? Why or why not? Can you give any examples to support your opinion?
3. Do you think that religious beliefs still do influence the lives of people very much—even of those who are not "religious believers"? Explain.
4. What do you think this world would be like now if there had been no religions or religious teachings? Explain.
5. What do you think the world be like now and in the future if everyone believed only in material rather than spiritual values? Explain.

Religion and humanity's future

A few people still think religion is irrelevant to life—that it's just another nice idea. People often don't realize the incredible impact for good that religious beliefs have had upon the course of human history and have in our world today. In fact, religion very much affects how people live. For religion **is** life—life lived and based on certain beliefs about God which influence our conduct and decisions.

There was a time when the values advanced by religion were something new and radical. We tend to forget this, because we take so much for granted what we've been taught since childhood. But it's only by prayerfully examining, being truly convinced of, and really living our religious beliefs that they can enrich our lives and better our world.

Today, as never before, humanity must either work together in harmony or face self-annihilation. Either with bombs or with environmental pollution, we can now destroy our planet. Or we can build together a much more ideal world of harmony and peace, happiness and love. We can either believe in the religiously based values which will save us all, or we can believe they're of no use or meaning. Humanity's future depends upon which of these we choose.

If you're tempted to doubt that your religious convictions can make a difference, then consider for a moment all those who have ever influenced your life for the good. (It's amazing how much impact very small kindnesses can have.) Most of these persons are probably unaware of how, or how much, they have influenced you. But it's likely that how they influenced you was at least partly based on the ways they believe in living their religious convictions. You, too, are probably unaware of some of the positive ways your beliefs about God and about religion have led you to influence others.

Humanity is made up of individuals like us. So changing the world for the better depends on each of us. In doing and being good for others, you drop a pebble into the pond where ripples continue to spread beyond any limit you can imagine. **Believe that you can make a difference in this world, because you can.**

Sometimes people confuse real religion with warm and cozy feelings about God. Others are turned off to religion by excessive emotionalism and sentimentalism. Genuine faith, however, is based on devotion and belief that are far deeper and stronger than feelings. Someone can be emotionally moved by a beautiful homily on God's love and "feel" very close to God, yet remain basically unchanged in the way he or she treats others. Such religious emotionalism is shallow and usually tainted with some degree of hypocrisy—one of the things Jesus preached against most often and strongly.

The best way to live our faith as Christians and to love God is to love others. But in trying to do so, remember that "Love is not how you feel about someone, but the way you treat them no matter how you feel." ❧

❧ Questions for discussion

1. In what sense do you think one's religion should be one's "way of life"?

2. If an objective observer were to describe the way you try to live, which of your religious convictions would probably be the most obvious? Explain.

3. How do you feel your religious beliefs have influenced your life and happiness thus far? Explain.

4. What is the difference between emotion and emotionalism, and between sentiment and sentimentality?

5. What impact do you believe your life can have on humanity's future? Explain.

I give you a new commandment,
that you love one another.
Just as I have loved you,
you also should love one another.
—John 13:34

What I believe

As you develop your own practical creed to live by, consider the religious beliefs summarized in the Apostles' Creed which have been discussed in this text. Also consider Abraham Lincoln's personal creed—and how the way he lived it affected a nation's future.

The Apostles' Creed

I believe in God,
the Father almighty,
creator of heaven and earth.

I believe in Jesus Christ, his only Son, our Lord.

He was conceived by the power of the
Holy Spirit
and born of the Virgin Mary.

He suffered under Pontius Pilate,
was crucified, died, and was
buried.
He descended into hell.

On the third day he rose again.

He ascended into heaven
and is seated at the right hand of the
Father.
He will come again to judge the
living and the dead.

I believe in the Holy Spirit,
the holy catholic Church,
the communion of saints,
the forgiveness of sins,
the resurrection of the body,
and the life everlasting.
Amen.

Abraham Lincoln's Creed

I believe in God, the Almighty Ruler of nations,
our great and good and merciful Maker,
our Father in heaven,
who notes the fall of a sparrow
and numbers the hairs on our heads.

I recognize the sublime truth announced in the Holy Scriptures
and proved by all history
that those nations are blessed
whose God is the Lord.

I believe that the will of God prevails.
Without him, all human reliance is vain.
With that assistance I cannot fail.

I have a solemn vow registered in heaven
to finish the work I am in,
in full view of my responsibility to my God,
with malice toward none;
with charity for all;
with firmness in the right,
as God gives me to see the right.

May your Creed be like a mirror for you.
Look at yourself in it,
to see if you believe everything you say you believe.
And every day, be glad about what you believe.
—St. Augustine

Questions for discussion

1. Based on his personal creed and his historical actions, what would you say Abraham Lincoln believed about each of the following?

   • God and his relationship with God

   • Faith

   • Good and evil

   • The future

   • Prayer

   • God's will

   • Human dignity and equality

   • Human freedom

2. From what you know of history, how do you think Lincoln tried to live by his creed? Do you think he succeeded? Explain.

3. How did the ways Lincoln tried to live his religious beliefs affect the course of a nation? What influence do you think it had on the world of today? Why?

4. How did Lincoln's personal creed reflect some of the content and meaning of the Apostles' Creed?

Faith is a beacon of light in life.

Your journey of faith

Adults sometimes wrestle for years with the problems created by their religious education and upbringing. Those who grew up in a rigid religious environment where no honest questioning was tolerated may later rebel against religion and belief in God. Equating religious belief with the ways they were raised, they may avoid religion.

Such individuals are actually rebelling not against religion or God but against ideas and attitudes **about** believing which they've found unacceptable, and perhaps rightly so. Those who feel that religious beliefs were imposed on them as children by fear or pressure may harbor resentment for all things religious. Or they may reject the unreasonable guilt and fear which their religious upbringing encouraged. Others simply resent having had to observe religious practices which have never had any personal meaning for them.

What such persons often do then is to "throw out the baby with the bathwater." Instead of distinguishing between the real nature of religion, and the perhaps unfortunate ways they were taught to believe in it, they dump everything overboard. They discard what could otherwise be the most meaningful part of their lives.

Teenagers commonly question the idea of automatically being expected to behave and believe in certain ways. This is generally a healthy sign of beginning to achieve one's necessary independence and sense of personal integrity. So if you feel somewhat resentful or rebellious about religion, realize that this is not unusual. Also try, though, not to confuse the real meaning of the religious beliefs you've been taught with what you disagree with or resent about the ways you were taught them. Don't let what someone has done to you in the past cause you to discard the meaning with the mistakes.

"You, O worthy one, are perhaps indeed a seeker, for in striving towards your goal, you do not see many things that are under your nose."
—Hermann Hesse, **Siddhartha.**

Believing in God, like believing in people, is a lifelong process of learning to grow in trust, love, and acceptance of mystery. This isn't always a simple thing to do. But don't be dismayed that you don't already have all the answers to your questions. As you search to deepen your religious convictions, you might remember this advice:

Be patient toward all that is unsolved within your heart,

and try to love the questions themselves.

Do not seek the answers which cannot now be given you

because you would not be able to live them,

and the point is—to live everything.

So, live the questions now.

And perhaps you will gradually, without noticing it,

live along some distant day, into the answer.

> *Rilke*

In the meantime, never apologize for your religions beliefs. Hold fast to what you find to be true. For what you believe in will be what you value. What you value will determine how you live and act. Your choices and decisions will, in turn, determine what your life means to you, and what you are able to give to and share with others. All of this will determine your life's happiness . . . .

For now we see in a mirror, dimly, but then we will see face to face. Now I know only in part; then I will know fully, even as I have been fully known. And now faith, hope, and love abide, these three; and the greatest of these is love.
—1 Corinthians 13:12–13

List of Key Words and Concepts

anti-semitism
prejudice or discrimination against Jews

attitude
one's mental and emotional outlook on living and on life's circumstances and experiences

B.C.E. ("Before the Common Era") and C.E. ("Common Era')
use of these abbreviations respects the fact that much of today's world does not believe in Jesus as their Messiah, Savior, or as God's Son.

canon of Sacred Scripture
the list of books officially accepted as part of the Bible for Catholics

canon
a rule or measure, an official list of rules, laws, or guidelines

catechesis
sharing instruction in the beliefs of faith

celibate
promising to remain single (to not marry) for religious reasons

ceremony
combination of two or more ritual gestures

charisma
personal magnetism, an appealing personality or style that others are drawn to follow

charismatic
having an especially appealing gift of leadership

chrism
oil blessed on Holy Thursday and used during the Rite of Confirmation

Christ
title for Jesus; from the Greek word for *Messiah,* meaning "anointed one"

Christian Scriptures
God's Revelation in Jesus, as taught by his apostles and written down under divine inspiration

Christian spirituality
the styles or ways Christians relate with God because of their specifically Christian beliefs about God and Jesus

Church council
formal gathering of bishops to address issues of faith, and of Church teaching and practice; an ecumenical council is one to which all bishops are invited

Church year
liturgical year, the annual commemoration and celebration of the main Christian mysteries

Church
originally from the Greek word *ekklesia,* meaning a gathering together of those who have full rights as citizens

clergy
those ordained to the priestly ministry

collegiality, college of bishops
all Catholic bishops united in teaching and leading the Catholic Church

communion of saints
the spiritual union in God which links together all good persons, living and dead

community
a group of people who share certain things in common

compassion
literally, "feeling strongly with"; expressing sensitivity to and understanding of others' thoughts, feelings, and difficulties

confirmation sponsor
one who formally represents the Christian community's continuing support of the person being confirmed

conscience
the ability of persons to determine right from wrong

conversion
change of heart and mind; in the Christian sense, an inner change of attitude leading to a total change of one's life to love of God and neighbor

covenant
the agreement whereby God has promised humanity lasting support and faithfulness, and whereby we are to follow God's ways

cult
an exclusive, extremist religious group which seeks to control or exploit members' thoughts and behavior

cycle of feasts
the annual religious observance of certain days in honor of Christ, and his mother Mary and other saints for their role in Christ's work

deaconesses
women who assisted the apostles and, later, the early Church in certain service and liturgical ministries

deliberate
intentional, something one both knows and wills

demonic
evil or cruel, like an evil spirit or devil

diocese
territory over which a bishop has jurisdiction (an archbishop is a bishop who usually oversees a larger territory called an *archdiocese*)

Divine Providence
the loving care with which God created and sustains the universe, and the purpose God has designed for it

Divine Revelation
the process of God's self-communication, and God's gift of making known to us truths about God which relate to us, our life's meaning, and our ultimate destiny

doxology
hymn of praise to God

ecumenical
worldwide, including representatives of peoples throughout the world

ecumenism
effort to achieve inter-Church understanding, reconciliation, and cooperation between Christian Churches

episcopal
pertaining to a bishop

episcopal conference
a nation's group of bishops

ethics
the study of the moral dimension of values, principles, judgments, and standards by which to measure what is morally right or wrong

fallibility
ability to make mistakes or to be wrong

finite
having definite limits or boundaries

free will
the ability to make independent choices of one's own without being controlled by something or someone else, the ability to decide freely

fully informing one's conscience
doing what is necessary to discern what is morally correct according to objective standards of right and wrong

generosity
willingness to share or give of oneself or one's goods to others

gentiles
persons who are not Jews

gentle
tender, responsive, kind, gracious, not rough or pushy

God's reign
the final, everlasting unity of persons with God and, in God, with one another

godparent
person who formally assumes the responsibility of helping the baptized Christian grow in faith

Golden Rule
Jesus' command to always treat others as we would want them to treat us

Gospels
the "good news" of Jesus' teachings as received from the early Christians and written in the Christian Scripture books of Matthew, Mark, Luke, and John

grace
the gift of God's healing and guiding help, presence, strength, life, and loving friendship; God's loving favor toward people

gratuitous
free, having no strings or obligations attached

hallmarks
signs of genuineness, authenticity, and quality

hell
the state of final self-exclusion from communion with God and those united with God

hierarchy
a progression of leadership or authority

holocaust
sacrificial offering among the ancient Hebrews in which the victim offered to God was completely destroyed

Holocaust
the Nazi attempt to exterminate all Jews during World War II

hypocrisy
knowingly acting the opposite of what one says one believes or represents

immortal
everlasting, living forever, never dying

inanimate
not living or alive, without life

infinite
without end or limitation

initiation
becoming a member of a group by means of a special process or ceremonial rituals

intercession
asking or pleading on behalf of someone else, as interceding for someone in prayer

interreligious dialogue
effort to achieve greater understanding and cooperation between, for example, Catholics and those of nonchristian religions

judgment
criticism, condemnation, ruling on the worth of

just
fair, right or accurate, having sufficiently good reason

laity, laypersons
Church members who are not ordained ministers

law
rule of behavior or conduct established by a group's authorities

lay
persons who are not members of a certain profession, or who are not ordained clergy

life principle
the essence of life, soul, that which enables something or someone to be a living being rather than an inanimate object, that which enables one to move under one's own initiative

literalist
one whose understanding of words is limited to their strict, exact sense

liturgical rites
formal church ceremonies

liturgical seasons
portions of the year which commemorate the main Christian mysteries of redemption

liturgy
structured formal worship; the Church's official prayer, including the Eucharist and other sacraments

liturgy of the word
portion of sacramental celebrations which includes a Scripture reading and the people's response to it

live fully
to use our distinctively human abilities, the gifts God has given us, to love God and others

living organisms
those which take in nourishment and are capable of reproducing

logical contradiction
a statement containing two ideas, each of which cancels the other out or contradicts the other

magisterium
the Catholic Church's highest teaching authorities

meditation
Prayerful reflection on God or religious beliefs

mercy
forgiveness or kindness—especially as shown to one's enemies or to the guilty

messiah
Savior and spiritual guide who Christians believe is Jesus

ministry
the ways one regularly reaches out to help and serve others

monotheism
the belief that only one God exists

moral choice
ability to choose between good and evil

moral freedom
the ability to freely choose between good and evil

omnipotent
unlimited in power

omniscient
all-knowing

oral tradition
the passing on of beliefs, laws, customs, and ideas through the spoken word

paraclete
one who is at your side to help, as the Holy Spirit

particular judgment
the determining of each person's final destiny immediately after death

paschal
passing over, as from death to life

pastoral
like a shepherd, looking out for the welfare of those in one's care; as Jesus was the Good Shepherd

penitence
guilt, sorrow, regret, remorse

Pentecost
commemorates God's Sinai covenant with the Jewish people, and the apostles' experience of the Holy Spirit which marks the birth of the Christian Church

pietists
those who emphasize religious externals so much that the real meaning of religious devotion is overshadowed, ignored, or contradicted

piety
devotion to religious matters or beliefs; sincere participation in religious practices

polytheists
those who believe more than one god exists

prayer
communicating with God, focusing on God in a spiritually uplifting way; also, asking for God's blessings; in the broader sense, all the ways in which people try to be closer to God

predestination
belief that God has chosen beforehand those who will ultimately be saved and that one's actions in this life therefore cannot change one's destiny

private prayer
individual prayer which focuses on our relationship with God and how it gives meaning and direction to our lives and other relationships

prophet
one who sees and tells the truth about the good and evil influences of certain human behaviors and their consequences

rationality
the ability to arrive at correct connections between and conclusions about causes and their effects, ability to reason

reconcile
bring together; resolve differences

redemption
act of buying back, as from slavery or sin

religious sect
organized religious group or denomination

repentance
true sorrow for wrongdoing, verified by trying not to do wrong again and by trying to undo the damage one has caused

righteous
standing right with God

rite
a way of acting solemnly in a set manner, as in a ceremony or formal service

ritual
action or actions repeated in a particular manner on similar occasions by a person or group

sacramental grace
the power by which God's Spirit heals and transforms in a special way through each sacrament

Sacred Scripture
the writings God inspired which contain the fundamental truths of God's Revelation for all peoples and all time

Sacred Scripture and Church Tradition
complementary ways God's truth is channeled to us, with Scripture being the touchstone by which Church Tradition develops

Sacred Tradition
the process by which God inspired certain individuals and groups to pass on basic truths of Revelation from generation to generation

sacrifice
literally, "act of making sacred or holy"

second coming
Jesus' coming again in glory at the end of time

self-revelation
making known personal aspects of oneself, as God's self-revelation in Sacred Tradition

sign
that which points to or explains something else

spiritual
of the spirit or soul, a non-material reality

spirituality
the style or manner in which one relates to God

superstitiously
believing in a way which contradicts or is not consistent with reason or fact, attempting to control God by saying certain words or performing certain actions

symbol
that which contains a quality it points to or explains

theological
of God, having to do with God or things related to God; literally, words about God

tradition
the handing down of beliefs, customs, and so on, from generation to generation

Viaticum
"nourishment or support for the journey," Sacrament of the Eucharist for a dying person

virtue
a regular attitude of being determined to do what is good and right

vow of chastity
sacred promise taken by religious to not marry

vow of obedience
sacred promise to do God's will in service to others

vow of poverty
sacred promise to live simply, unattached to material things

vows
sacred promises

written tradition
the passing on in writing of beliefs, laws, customs, and ideas

Photo Credits

Billy Barnes—28, 48, 72, 230, 236

Nancy Dawe—1, 21, 51, 93, 196, 215

Editorial Development—16, 75, 190

Stan Lapa—62, 68, 98, 129, 136, 143, 168, 173, 181, 212, 250,

Robert Roethig—238

James L. Shaffer—2, 9, 11, 13, 19, 32, 34, 38, 42, 45, 53, 55, 64, 77, 84, 91, 101, 105, 110, 117, 131, 145, 149, 152, 158, 164, 184, 188, 198, 201, 204, 209, 218, 220, 228, 234, 254

Steven and Mary Beran Skjold—82, 89, 135, 138, 155, 160, 179, 216, 227

Paul Swartzel—120

Cover Photo—Nancy Dawe

Endnotes

Chapter One

1. Thomas Chastain, © 1989 *Discover Magazine*, Reprinted with permission.

2. Excerpted from *Man Does Not Stand Alone* by A. Cressy Morrison. Copyright © 1944 by Fleming H. Revell Company. Renewed 1972. Used by permission.

3. From *Black Holes and Baby Universes* by Stephen Hawking (Bantam Books), as quoted in "Hawking Gets Personal," *Time* (27 September 1993): 80.

4. Reprinted with permission of *The Sarasota Herald Tribune*.

5. "Talk of God, Hamburgers Inspires Drifting Pilots," The Associated Press.

Chapter Two

1. This is stated in the "Dogmatic Constitution on the Church," *The Documents of Vatican II*, number 25.

2. This is emphasized in the papal encyclical, *Humanae Vitae*, number 4.

Chapter Three

1. "i thank You God for most this amazing" is reprinted from *COMPLETE POEMS, 1904–1962*, by E.E. Cummings, Edited by George J. Firmage, by permission of Liveright Publishing Corporation. Copyright © 1950, 1978, 1991 by the Trustees for the E.E. Cummings Trust. Copyright © 1979 by George James Firmage.

2. Quotes from Paul Davies, *The Mind of God: The Scientific Basis for a Rational World*, Simon & Schuster, 1992.

3. Slightly adapted from "Two Who Died in Snowbound Car Remained Calm 'in God's Hand,' " The Associated Press.

4. "Street Talk: Do You Believe in God? Why?" *The Sarasota Herald Tribune* (26 January 1988): 2.

Chapter Four

1. Information and quotation from "Carter Links Religion, Decisive Events," *The Sarasota Herald Tribune* (28 July 1990): 4E.

2. The questions and information in this questionnaire are based on *The Connecticut Mutual Life Report on American Values in the '80s: The Impact of Belief*, Connecticut Mutual Life Insurance Company: Hartford, Connecticut, 1981.

3. Adapted from "Declaration on Religious Freedom," number 10, *The Documents of Vatican II*.

Chapter Five

1. "Olympic Stories the Heartbeat of Prime Time," by Tim Leone in *The Sarasota Herald Tribune* (7 August 1992): 1C.

2. Kahlil Gibran, *The Prophet*, New York: Alfred A. Knopf, Inc., 1951, 78–79.

3. "Researchers Toying with Single Molecules," The Associated Press.

4. "Physicists Study Atomic Particle" by Vincent Kiernan, in *Tri-Valley Herald* (3 June 1988): 1.

5. "People, etc." in *California Today Magazine*, supplement in *The San Jose Mercury News* (24 October 1982): 4.

6. "Chinese Researcher Wows Local Doctors" by Mike Myslinski, in *Tri-Valley Herald* (26 November 1987): 20.

7. "Tide Lines: If We Damage Planet, How Long for Repairs?" by Mina Walther, in *The Sarasota Herald Tribune* (5 April 1992): 6F.

8. From another "Tide Lines" column by Mina Walther, in *The Sarasota Herald Tribune*.

9. "Tide Lines: The Heart: Body's Miracle Machine" by Mina Walter, in *The Sarasota Herald Tribune* (26 July 1992): 6F.

10. "How Do You See? Study Reveals" by Vincent Kiernan, *The Sunday Herald* (8 May 1988): 17.

11. "Discovery Challenges Theories of Universe," NY Times News Service.

12. Dr. Marian Diamond, source unknown.

13. Excerpted from "The Day I Played God," by Philip Elmer-Dewitt. Copyright 1990 TIME INC. Reprinted by permission.

Chapter Six

1. Excerpt from *The World's Religions* by Huston Smith (page 324). Copyright 1991 by Huston Smith. Reprinted by permission of HarperCollins Publishers, Inc.

Chapter Seven

1. "A Call to Prayer," as quoted in *A Sourcebook for the Community of Religions,* Joel Beversluis, project editor, Chicago, The Council for a Parliament of the World's Religions, 1993, 155.

Chapter Eight

1. Stacey McWhinnie, "Stacey's Play: Scene 10," in *The Sarasota Herald Tribune* (18 November 1991): 7A.

2. Permission granted by Ann Landers and Creators Syndicate.

3. *Tri-Valley Herald,* Pleasanton, CA.

4. Reprinted from *That Man Is You* by Louis Evely, translated by Edmond Bonin. © 1964 by The Missionary Society of St. Paul the Apostle in the State of New York.

5. Reprinted by permission from *The Station and Other Gems of Joy,* Robert J. Hastings.

Chapter Nine

1. "A Meditation on the Lord's Prayer" by Henry Sloane Coffin in *Joy in Believing,* edited by Walter Russell Bowie, Scribner.

2. Alasdair MacIntyre, as quoted in *Context: A Commentary on the Interaction of Religion and Culture,* Volume 21, Number 17, by Martin E. Marty (1 October 1989): 1.

3. Quotations of former U.S. President George Bush and information from "A Stiff Upper Lip Trembles as Bush Recalls War Prayer" by Ann Devroy, *The Washington Post* (7 June 1991).

4. Quotations from Allen Verhey, as quoted in *Context:* 1 and 2.

5. Simcox, Carroll E., comp., *A Treasury of Quotations on Christian Themes,* New York, A Crossroad Book; The Seabury Press, 1975, 141. Used by permission of Carroll E. Simcox.

6. Simcox 14.

Chapter Ten

1. Information and quotes from "Beatings and Prayer Marked Time for Former U.S. POW" by John King, The Associated Press.

2. Conrad Richter, *The Light in the Forest,* New York: Alfred A. Knopf, Inc.

3. Compiled from teenagers' discussions about how prayer can affect their relationships.

4. Quoted material is by Roberta Bondi, in "Religion—News in Brief: 'There's No One Way to Pray,' " from Wire Reports, in *The Sarasota Herald Tribune* (12 September 1992): 4E.

5. "Capsule: A Quick Look at Health News—Power of Prayer," compiled from staff and wire reports by Joette Dignan Weir, in *Tri-Valley Herald* (14 February 1989): 33.

6. Quotation and description of the author are from *Touch the Earth: A Self-Portrait of Indian Existence,* compiled by T.C. McLuhan, A Touchstone Book, Simon & Schuster, 1971, 36.

7. "A Miracle Drug Called 'Prayer' " by Lewis Grizzard.

Chapter Eleven

1. Adapted from "Canon of a Christian People" by John L'Heureux, copyright 1967 by John L'Heureux.

2. Excerpt from *The Little Prince* by Antoine de Saint-Exupery, copyright 1943 and renewed 1971 by Harcourt Brace & Company, reprinted by permission of the publisher.

3. Excerpt from *The World's Religions* by Huston Smith (pages 300–301). Copyright 1991 by Huston Smith. Reprinted by permission of HarperCollins Publishers, Inc.

Chapter Twelve

1. Reprinted with permission of *Sarasota Herald Tribune.*

Chapter Fourteen

1. *Exodus* by Leon Uris © 1958 by Leon M. Uris.

2. From *J.B.* Copyright © 1956, 1957, 1958 by Archibald MacLeish. Copyright © renewed 1986 by William H. MacLeish and Mary H. Grimm. Reprinted by permission of Houghton Mifflin Company.

3. See Pope John Paul II, "Reconciliation and Penance," Post-synodal Apostolic Exhortation (2 December 1984), number 16.

4. C.S. Lewis, *The Problem of Pain,* New York: Macmillan Publishing Co., Inc., and London, England: Collins Publishers, 1943, 116.

5. A. Flew in *Who Am I?* ed. Lowell D. Streiker, © 1970 Andrews and McMeel.

Index of Key Concepts